MACROMEDIA® FLASH® 8

REVEALED
DELUXE EDUCATION EDITION

MACROMEDIA® FLASH® 8

REVEALED
DELUXE EDUCATION EDITION

Jim Shuman

THOMSON

™

COURSE TECHNOLOGY

Macromedia® Flash® 8—Revealed, Deluxe Education Edition

Jim Shuman

Managing Editor:
Marjorie Hunt

Product Manager:
Jane Hosie-Bounar

Associate Product Manager:
Shana Rosenthal

Editorial Assistant:
Janine Tangney

Production Editor:
Kelly Robinson

Developmental Editor:
Rachel Biheller Bunin

Marketing Manager:
Joy Stark

QA Manuscript Reviewers:
Jeff Schwartz, Ashlee Welz,
Danielle Shaw

Composition House:
Integra—Pondicherry, India

Text Designer:
Ann Small

Illustrator:
Philip Brooker

Cover Design:
Steve Deschene

Revealed Series Vision

The Revealed Series is your guide to today's hottest multimedia applications. These comprehensive books teach the skills behind the application, showing you how to apply smart design principles to multimedia products such as dynamic graphics, animation, Web sites, software authoring tools, and digital video.

A team of design professionals including multimedia instructors, students, authors, and editors worked together to create this series. We recognized the unique needs of the multimedia market and created a series that gives you comprehensive step-by-step instructions and offers an in-depth explanation of the "why" behind a skill, all in a clear, visually-based layout.

It was our goal to create a book that speaks directly to the multimedia and design community—one of the most rapidly growing computer fields today. We feel that *Macromedia Flash 8— Revealed, Deluxe Education Edition* does just that—with sophisticated content and an instructive book design.

—The Revealed Series

Author Vision

Writing a textbook on a Web application and animation program is quite challenging. How do you take such a feature-rich program like Macromedia Flash 8 and put it in a context that helps users learn? My goal is to provide a comprehensive, yet manageable, introduction to Macromedia Flash 8— just enough conceptual information to provide the needed context—and then move right into working with the application. My thought is that you'll get so caught up in the hands-on activities and compelling projects that you'll be pleasantly surprised at the level of Macromedia Flash 8 skills and knowledge you've acquired at the end of each chapter.

What a joy it has been to be a part of such a creative and energetic publishing team. The new Revealed Series is a great format for teaching and learning Macromedia Flash 8, and the Revealed Series team took the ball and ran with it. I would like to thank Nicole Pinard, who provided the vision for the project, Marjorie Hunt and Jane Hosie-Bounar for their management expertise, and everyone at Course Technology for their professional guidance. A special thanks to Rachel Bunin for her hard work, editorial expertise, and constant encouragement. I also want to give a heartfelt thanks to my wife, Barbara, for her patience and support.

—Jim Shuman

SERIES & AUTHOR VISION

v

Introduction to Macromedia Flash 8

Welcome to *Macromedia Flash 8—Revealed, Deluxe Education Edition*. This book offers creative projects, concise instructions, and complete coverage of basic to advanced Macromedia Flash 8 skills, helping you to create and publish Flash animation. Use this book both while you learn and as your own reference guide. This text is organized into 12 chapters. In these chapters, you will learn many skills to create interesting graphics-rich movies that include sound, animation, and interactivity. In addition, you will learn how to publish your own Flash movies.

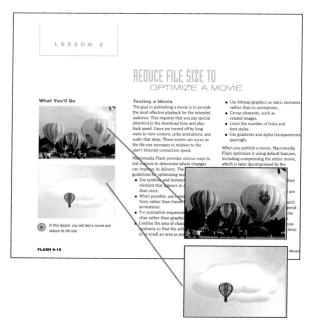

What You'll Do

A What You'll Do figure begins every lesson. This figure gives you an at-a-glance look at what you'll do in the chapter, either by showing you a page or pages from the current project or a tool you'll be using.

Comprehensive Conceptual Lessons

Before jumping into instructions, in-depth conceptual information tells you "why" skills are applied. This book provides the "how" and "why" through the use of professional examples. Also included in the text are tips and sidebars to help you work more efficiently and creatively, or to teach you a bit about the history or design philosophy behind the skill you are using.

Step-by-Step Instructions

This book combines in-depth conceptual information with concise steps to help you learn Flash 8. Each set of steps guides you through a lesson where you will create, modify, or enhance a Flash file. Step references to large colorful images and quick step summaries round out the lessons.

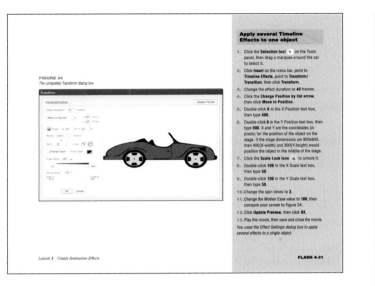

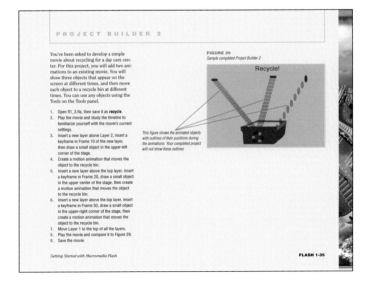

Projects

This book contains a variety of end-of-chapter materials for additional practice and reinforcement. The Skills Review contains hands-on practice exercises that mirror the progressive nature of the lesson material. Each chapter concludes with four projects: two Project Builders, one Design Project, and one Portfolio Project. The Project Builders and the Design Project require you to apply the skills you've learned in the chapter. Portfolio Projects encourage you to solve challenges based on the content explored in the chapter and to create a file for use in your portfolio.

CHAPTER 1   GETTING STARTED WITH MACROMEDIA FLASH

CHAPTER 3 **WORKING WITH SYMBOLS AND INTERACTIVITY**

CONTENTS

CONTENTS

CHAPTER 7 — IMPORTING AND MODIFYING GRAPHICS

CHAPTER 8   BUILDING COMPLEX ANIMATIONS

CHAPTER 9   USING ACTIONSCRIPT

CHAPTER 12 WORKING WITH BEHAVIORS AND COMPONENTS

Intended Audience

This book is designed for the beginner or intermediate user who wants to learn how to use Macromedia Flash 8. The book is designed to provide basic and in-depth material that not only educates, but encourages you to explore the nuances of this exciting program.

Flash Basic versus Flash Professional

Macromedia Flash 8 is available in two versions, Flash Basic 8 and Flash Professional 8. The underlying program is the same for both versions. However, several features in Professional are not available in Basic. These include custom easing controls, filters, blend modes, bitmap smoothing, some components and data binding, and several video features. In addition to screen-based visual development environment features, Flash Professional 8 provides tools for managing data interactively and for fostering team productivity. This book was developed using Flash Professional 8. If there are any steps that won't work in Flash Basic 8, we have provided alternate steps or instructions in the Student Online Companion for the book. To access the Online Companion, please go to *www.course.com/revealed/flash8dee*.

Approach

The book allows you to work at your own pace through step-by-step tutorials. A concept is presented and the process is explained, followed by the actual steps. To learn the most from the use of the text, you should adopt the following habits:

- Proceed slowly: Accuracy and comprehension are more important than speed.
- Understand what is happening with each step before you continue to the next step.
- After finishing a process, ask yourself: Can I do the process on my own? If the answer is no, review the steps.

Icons, Buttons, and Pointers

Symbols for icons, buttons, and pointers are shown each time they are used.

Fonts

Data Files contain a variety of commonly used fonts, but there is no guarantee that these fonts will be available on your computer. Each font is identified in cases where fonts other than Arial or Times New Roman are used. If any of the fonts in use are not available on your computer, you can

make a substitution, realizing that the results may vary from those in the book.

Windows and Macintosh

Macromedia Flash 8 works virtually the same on Windows and Macintosh operating systems. In those cases where there is a difference, the abbreviations (Win) and (Mac) are used.

Windows System Requirements

Macromedia Flash 8 runs under Windows 2000 and Windows XP, and requires an Intel 800 MHz Pentium III (or equivalent) or later processor, 256 MB of RAM (1 GB recommended to run more than one Studio 8 product simultaneously), 1024 x 768, 16-bit display (32-bit recommended), and 710 MB of disk space.

Macintosh System Requirements

Macromedia Flash 8 requires Mac OS X version 10.2.6 or above, a 600 MHz PowerPC G3 processor or later, 256 MB of RAM (1 GB recommended to run more than one Studio 8 product simultaneously), 1024 x 768, thousands of colors display (millions of colors recommended), and 360 MB of disk space.

Data Files

To complete the lessons in this book, you need the Data Files on the CD located on the inside back cover. Your instructor will tell you where to store the files as you work, such as to your hard drive, a network server, or a USB storage device. When referring to the Data Files for this book, the instructions in the lessons will mention the "the drive and folder where your Data Files are stored."

Projects

Several projects are presented at the end of each chapter that allow students to apply the skills they have learned in the unit. Two projects, Ultimate Tours and the Portfolio, build from chapter to chapter. You will need to contact your instructor if you plan to work on these without having completed the previous chapter's project.

Creating a Portfolio

The Portfolio Project and Project Builders allow students to use their creativity to come up with original Flash animations and screen designs. You might suggest that students create a portfolio in which they can store their original work.

1

GETTING STARTED WITH
MACROMEDIA FLASH

1. Understand the Macromedia Flash workspace.

2. Open a document and play a movie.

3. Create and save a movie.

4. Work with the timeline.

5. Plan a Web site.

6. Distribute a Macromedia Flash movie.

chapter 1

GETTING STARTED WITH
MACROMEDIA FLASH

Introduction

Macromedia Flash is a development tool that allows you to create compelling interactive experiences, often by using animation. While it is known as a tool for creating complex animations for the Web, Macromedia Flash also has excellent drawing tools and tools for creating interactive controls, such as navigation buttons and menus. In addition, Macromedia Flash provides the ability to incorporate sounds and video into an application. You can also use its publishing capabilities to create Web sites and Web-based applications, such as games.

In only a few short years, Macromedia Flash has become the standard for both professional and casual Web developers. The reason that Macromedia Flash has become so popular is that the program is optimized for the Web. Web developers need to provide high-impact experiences for the user, to make sites come alive and turn them from static text and pictures to dynamic, interactive experiences. The problem has been that incorporating high-quality graphics and motion into a Web site can dramatically increase the download time and frustrate viewers as they wait for an image to appear or for an animation to play. Macromedia Flash directly addresses this problem by allowing developers to use vector images, which reduce the size of graphic files. Vector images appeal to designers for two reasons. First, they are scalable, which means they can be resized and reshaped without distortion. For example, you could easily have an object, such as an airplane, become smaller as it moves across the screen without having to create the plane in different sizes. Second, Macromedia Flash provides for streaming content over the Internet. Instead of waiting for the entire contents of a Web page to load, the viewer sees a continuous display of images. For example, if your Web site has a Macromedia Flash movie that is played when the viewer first visits your Web site, the viewer does not have to wait for the entire movie to be downloaded before it starts. Streaming allows the movie to start playing when the Web site is opened, and it continues as frames of the movie are delivered to the viewer's computer.

Tools You'll Use

Properties | Parameters | Filters

Document
Untitled-2

Size: 550 x 400 pixels | Background: | Frame rate: 12 fps
Publish: Settings... | Player: 8 | ActionScript: 2 | Profile: Default
Device: Settings...

Document Properties

Title:

Description:

Dimensions: 550 px (width) x 400 px (height)

Match: ○ Printer ○ Contents ● Default

Background color:

Frame rate: 12 fps

Ruler units: Pixels

Make Default | OK | Cancel

Window Help

Duplicate Window | Ctrl+Alt+K

Toolbars ▶
✓ Timeline | Ctrl+Alt+T
✓ Tools | Ctrl+F2
Properties ▶
✓ Library | Ctrl+L
Common Libraries ▶

Actions | F9
Behaviors | Shift+F3
Debugger | Shift+F4
Movie Explorer | Alt+F3
Output | F2
Project | Shift+F8

Align | Ctrl+K
Color Mixer | Shift+F9
Color Swatches | Ctrl+F9
Info | Ctrl+I
Transform | Ctrl+T

Components | Ctrl+F7
Component Inspector | Alt+F7
Other Panels ▶

Workspace Layout ▶
Hide Panels | F4

Cascade
Tile

✓ 1 Untitled-1

Tools

View

Colors

Options

Untitled-1

Timeline | Scene 1 | 100%

Layer 1

1 5 10 15 20 25 30 35 40 45 50 55 60 65

1 | 12.0 fps | 0.0s

pasteboard —
store items
in library

drawings

UNDERSTAND THE
MACROMEDIA FLASH
ENVIRONMENT

What You'll Do

▶ In this lesson, you will learn about the development environment in Macromedia Flash and how to change Macromedia Flash settings to customize your workspace.

Organizing the Macromedia Flash Workspace

As a designer, one of the most important things to do is to organize your workspace—that is, to decide what to have displayed on the screen and how to arrange the various tools and windows. Because **Macromedia Flash** is such a powerful program with many tools, your workspace may become cluttered. Fortunately, it is easy to customize the workspace to display only the tools needed at any particular time.

The development environment in Macromedia Flash operates according to a movie metaphor: you create scenes on a stage; these scenes run in frames on a timeline. As you work in Macromedia Flash, you create a movie by arranging objects (such as graphics and text) on the stage, and animate the objects using the timeline. You can play the movie on the stage, as you are working on it, by using the movie controls (start, stop, rewind, and so on). In addition, you can test the movie in a browser. When the movie is ready for distribution, you can export it as a Macromedia Flash Player movie, which viewers can access using a Macromedia Flash Player. A **Macromedia Flash Player** is a program that is installed on the viewer's computer to allow Macromedia Flash movies to be played in Web browsers or as stand-alone applications. Virtually all computers that are connected to the Internet have the Macromedia Flash Player installed (a free download from the Macromedia Web site), allowing users to view and interact with Macromedia Flash movies and Web applications. Macromedia Flash movies can also be saved as executable files, called projectors, which can be viewed without the need for the Macromedia Flash Player.

When you start Macromedia Flash, three basic parts of the development environment (or workspace) are displayed: a main toolbar with menus and commands, a stage where objects are placed, and a timeline used to organize and control the objects on the stage. In addition, one or more panels may be displayed. Panels are used when working with objects and features of the movie.

Stage

The **stage** contains all of the objects (such as drawings) that are part of the movie that will be seen by your viewers. It shows how the objects behave within the movie and how they interact with each other. You can resize the stage and change the background color applied to it. You can draw objects directly on the stage or drag them from the Library panel to the stage. You can also import objects developed by another program directly to the stage. You can specify the size of the stage, which will be the size of the area within your browser window that displays the movie. The gray area surrounding the stage is the Pasteboard. You can place objects on the Pasteboard as you are creating a movie. However, neither the Pasteboard nor the objects on it will appear when the movie is played in a browser or the Flash Player.

Timeline

The **timeline** is used to organize and control the movie's contents by specifying when each object appears on the stage. The timeline is critical to the creation of movies, because a movie is merely a series of still images that appear over time. The images are contained within **frames**, which are segments of the timeline. Frames in a Macromedia Flash movie are similar to frames in a motion picture. When a Macromedia Flash movie is played, a playhead moves from frame to frame in the timeline, causing the contents of each frame to appear on the stage in a linear sequence.

The timeline indicates where you are at any time within the movie and allows you to insert, delete, select, and move frames. It shows the animation in your movie and the layers that contain objects. Layers help to organize the objects on the stage. You can draw and edit objects on one layer without affecting objects on other layers. Layers are a way to stack objects so they can overlap and give a 3-D appearance on the stage.

Panels

Panels are used to view, organize, and modify objects and features in a movie. The most commonly used panels are the Tools panel (also called the toolbox), the Properties panel (also called the Property inspector), and the Library panel. For example, the Property inspector is used to change the properties of an object, such as the fill color of a circle. The Property inspector is context sensitive so that if you are working with text it displays the appropriate options, such as font and font size.

You can control which panels are displayed individually or you can choose to display panel sets. Panel sets are groups of the most commonly used panels. In addition, you can control how a panel is displayed. That is, you can expand a panel to show all of its features or collapse it to show only the title bar.

Tools panel

The **Tools panel** contains a set of tools used to draw and edit graphics and text. It is divided into four sections.

Tools—Includes draw, paint, text, and selection tools, which are used to create lines, shapes, illustrations, and text. The selection tools are used to select objects so that they can be modified in a number of ways.

View—Includes the Zoom tool and the Hand tool, which are used to zoom in on and out of parts of the stage and to pan the stage window, respectively.

Colors—Includes tools and icons used to change the stroke (border of an object) and fill (area inside an object) colors.

Options—Includes options for selected tools, such as allowing you to choose the size of the brush when using the Brush tool.

Although several panels are available, you may choose to display them only when they are needed. This keeps your workspace from becoming too cluttered. Panels are floating windows, meaning that you can move them around the workspace. This allows you to dock (link) panels together as a way of organizing them in the workspace. You can also make room in the workspace by collapsing panels so only their title bars are displayed. You use the Window menu on the menu bar to display and hide panels.

Regardless of how you decide to customize your development environment, the stage and the menu bar are always displayed. Usually, you display the timeline, Tools panel, Library panel, Property inspector, and one or more other panels. Figure 1 shows the Macromedia Flash development environment with the stage, timeline, Tools panel, Library panel, and Property inspector displayed.

When you start a new Macromedia Flash document (movie), you can set the document properties, such as the size of the window (stage) the movie will play in, the background color, and the speed of the movie in frames per second. You can change these settings using the Document Properties dialog box, which can be displayed using the Document command on the Modify menu or by double-clicking the Frame Rate icon on the Timeline. You can also change the settings using the Property inspector. To increase the size of the stage so that the objects on the stage can be more easily edited, you can change the magnification setting using commands on the View menu.

FIGURE 1
Macromedia Flash default development environment

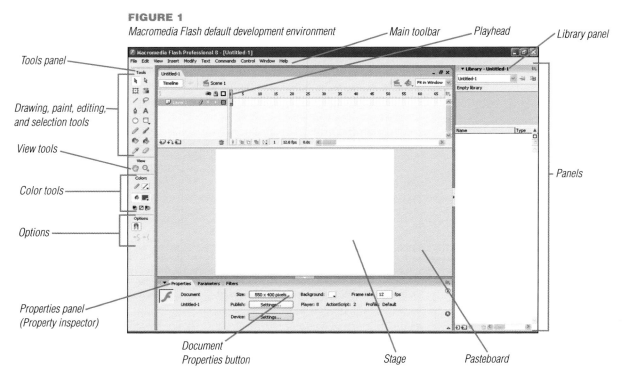

Tools panel

Drawing, paint, editing, and selection tools

View tools

Color tools

Options

Main toolbar   Playhead   Library panel

Panels

Properties panel (Property inspector)

Document Properties button   Stage   Pasteboard

FIGURE 2

The Open/Create screen

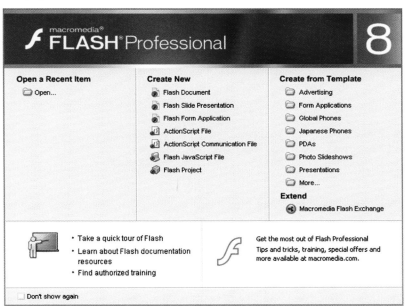

1. Click the **Start button** on the taskbar, point to **All Programs** or **Programs**, point to the **Macromedia** folder, then click the **Macromedia Flash 8 program icon** (Win).

   > TIP If you are starting Macromedia Flash 8 on a Macintosh, open the Finder, double-click the Applications folder, double-click the Macromedia Flash 8 folder, then double-click the Macromedia Flash 8 program icon.

   The Macromedia Flash Open/Create screen appears, as shown in Figure 2. This screen allows you to open a recent document or create a new Flash file. The File menu in the menu bar also allows you to open new or previously saved documents.

2. Click **File** on the menu bar, then click **New**.

3. Verify **Flash Document** is selected in the New Document dialog box, then click **OK**.

4. Click **Window** on the menu bar, then click **Hide Panels**.

5. Click **Window** on the menu bar, then click **Tools**.

6. Click **Window** on the menu bar, then click **Library**.

7. Click **Window** on the menu bar, point to **Properties**, then click **Properties**.

8. Click **File** on the menu bar, then click **Save**.

9. Navigate to the drive and folder where your data files are stored, type **workspace** for the file name, then click **OK**.

   The current workspace is typical of the development environment that you may want to start with when working with Macromedia Flash 8.

You started Flash, configured the workspace by opening and closing selected panels, and saved the document.

Working with Panels

1. Click the **Properties panel down arrow** in the title bar, as shown in Figure 3, to collapse the panel.

2. Click the **Properties panel arrow** in the title bar to expand the panel.

3. Right-click or **control-click** (Mac) the **Properties tab**, then click **Close panel group** to close the panel.

4. Click **Window** on the menu bar, point to **Properties**, then click **Properties**.

You opened and closed panels.

FIGURE 3

Property inspector panel

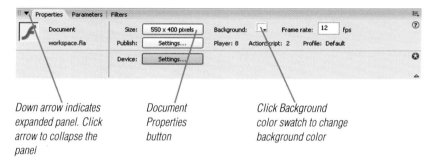

Down arrow indicates expanded panel. Click arrow to collapse the panel

Document Properties button

Click Background color swatch to change background color

FIGURE 4
Document Properties dialog box

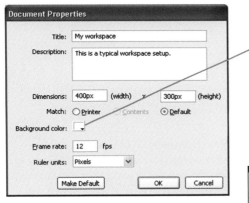

*Click Background
color swatch to change
the background color*

FIGURE 5
Completed changes to document

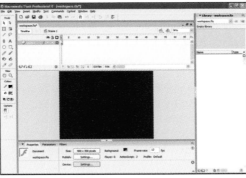

Change the Document Properties

1. Click the **Document properties button**
   [550 x 400 pixels] in the Property inspector to
   display the Document Properties dialog box.

2. Click inside the **Title text box**, then type **My workspace**.

3. Click inside the **Description text box**, then
   type **This is a typical workspace setup**.

   > TIP Text entered into the Title and Description
   > fields can be used by Web-based search
   > engines to display files developed using Flash.

4. Double-click the number in the **width text box**, type **400**, double-click the number in
   the **height text box**, then type **300**.

5. Click the **Background color swatch**, shown
   in Figure 4, then click the **blue color swatch**
   on the left column of the color palette.

6. Accept the remaining default values, then click
   OK to close the Document Properties dialog box.

7. Drag the scroll bars at the bottom and the
   right of the screen to center the stage.

8. Click **View** on the menu bar, point to
   Magnification, then click **Fit in Window**.
   Your screen should resemble Figure 5.

9. Click **File** on the menu bar, then click **Close**.

10. Click **Yes** (Win) or **Save** (Mac) to save the movie
    (if necessary).

*You set the document properties including the size
of the stage and background color, then set the
magnification.*

Understanding your workspace

Organizing the Macromedia Flash development environment is like organizing your
desktop. You may work more efficiently if you have many of the most commonly used
items in view and ready to use. Alternately, you may work better if your workspace is
relatively uncluttered, giving you more free "desk space." Fortunately, Macromedia
Flash makes it easy for you to decide which items to display and how they are arranged
while you work. For example, to toggle the Main toolbar, click Window on the menu
bar, point to Toolbars, then click Main. You should become familiar with quickly opening, collapsing, expanding, and closing the various windows, toolbars, and panels in
Macromedia Flash, and experimenting with different layouts and screen resolutions to
find the environment that works best for you.

OPEN A DOCUMENT
AND PLAY A MOVIE

What You'll Do

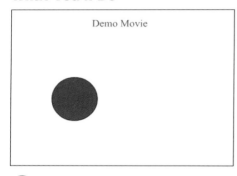

Demo Movie

▶ In this lesson, you will open a Macromedia Flash document (movie) and then preview, test, and save the movie.

Opening a Movie in Macromedia Flash

Macromedia Flash files are called documents and have a .fla file extension. If you have created a movie and saved it with the name mymovie, the file name will be mymovie.fla. Files with the .fla file extension can only be opened using Macromedia Flash. After they are opened, you can edit and resave them. Another file format for Macromedia Flash movies is the Macromedia Flash Player (.swf) format. These files are created from Macromedia Flash movies using the Publish command, which allows them to be played in a browser without the Macromedia Flash program. However, the viewer would need to have the Macromedia Flash Player installed on his or her computer. Because .swf files cannot be edited in the Macromedia Flash program, you should preview them on the stage and test them before you publish them. Be sure to keep the original .fla file so that you can make changes at a later date.

Previewing a Movie

After opening a Macromedia Flash movie, you can preview it within the development environment in several ways. When you preview a movie, you play the frames by directing the playhead to move through the timeline, and you watch the movement on the stage.

Control menu commands (and keyboard shortcuts)

Figure 6 shows the Control menu commands, which resemble common VCR-type options:

■ Play ([Enter] (Win) or [return] (Mac)) begins playing the movie, frame by frame, from the location of the playhead and continuing until the end of the movie. For example, if the playhead is on Frame 5 and the last frame is Frame 40, choosing the Play command will play Frames 5–40 of the movie.

When a movie starts, the Play command changes to a Stop command. You can also stop the movie by pressing [Enter] (Win) or [return] (Mac).

- Rewind ([Ctrl][Alt] [R] (Win)) or [option] [⌘] [R] (Mac) moves the playhead to Frame 1.
- Step Forward (.) moves the playhead forward one frame at a time.
- Step Backward (,) moves the playhead backward one frame at a time.

You can turn on the Loop Playback setting to allow the movie to continue playing repeatedly. A check mark next to the Loop Playback command on the Control menu indicates that the feature is turned on. To turn off this feature, click the Loop Playback command.

Controller

You can also preview a movie using the Controller. To display the Controller, click the Controller option on the Toolbar command of the Window menu.

The decision of which controls to use (the Control menu, keyboard shortcuts, or the Controller) is a matter of personal preference.

Testing a Movie

When you preview a movie, some interactive functions, such as buttons, that are used to jump from one part of the movie to another, do not work unless the movie is played using a Macromedia Flash Player. You can use the Test Movie command on the Control menu to test the movie using the Macromedia Flash Player.

You can drag the Playhead in the timeline to play the frames and display their contents on the stage. This process, called "scrubbing," provides a quick way to view parts of the movie.

FIGURE 6
Control menu commands

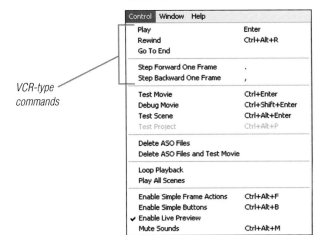

VCR-type commands

Open and play a movie using the Control menu and the Controller

1. Open fl1_1.fla from the drive and folder where your Data Files are stored, then save it as **demomovie.fla**.

2. Click **View** on the menu bar, point to **Magnification**, then click **Fit in Window**.

3. Click **Control** on the menu bar, click **Play**. Notice how the playhead moves across the timeline as the blue circle moves from the left to the right, as shown in Figure 7.

4. Click **Control** on the menu bar, then click **Rewind**.

5. Press [**Enter**] (Win) or [**return**] (Mac) to play the movie, then press [**Enter**] (Win) or [**return**] (Mac) again to stop the movie before it ends.

6. Click **Window** on the menu bar, point to **Toolbars**, then click **Controller**.

7. Use all the buttons on the Controller to preview the movie, then close the Controller.

8. Point to the **Playhead** in the timeline, then click and drag the **Playhead** back and forth to view the contents of the frames and view the movie.

You opened a Macromedia Flash movie and previewed it, using various controls.

FIGURE 7
Playhead moving across timeline

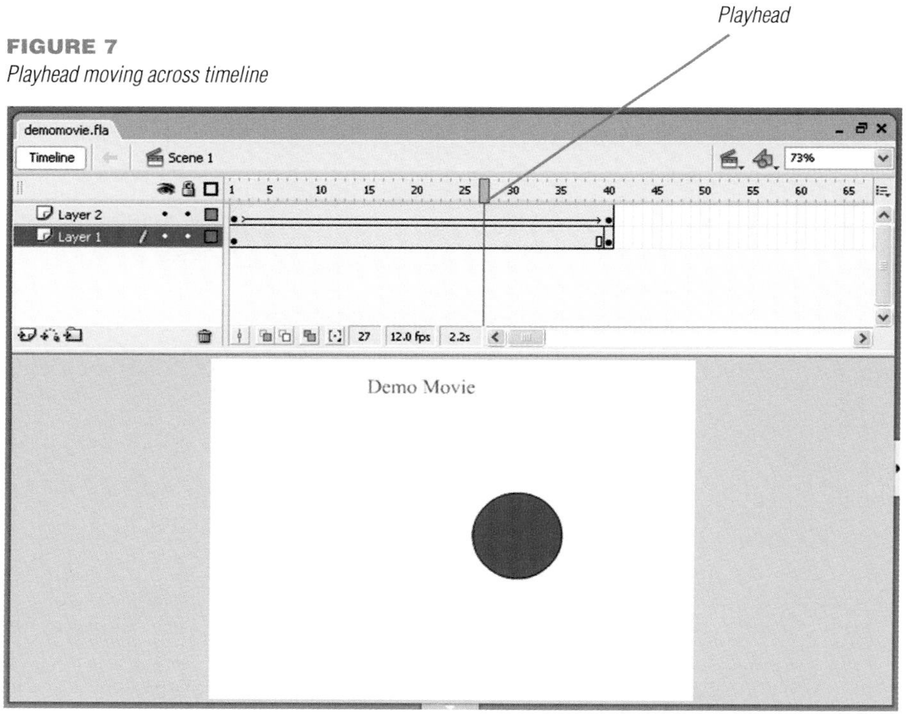

FIGURE 8
Macromedia Flash Player window

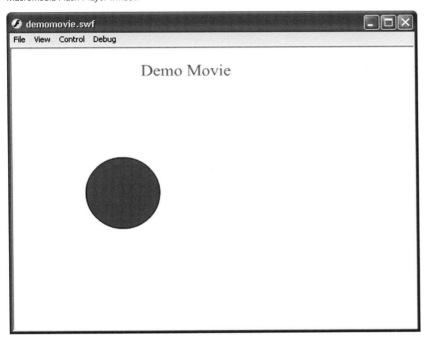

Test a movie

1. Click **Control** on the menu bar, then click **Test Movie** to view the movie in the Macromedia Flash Player window, as shown in Figure 8.

2. Click **Control** on the menu bar and review the available commands.

3. Click **File** on the menu bar, then click **Close** to close the Macromedia Flash Player window.

4. Navigate to the drive and folder where you saved the movie and notice the demomovie.swf file that has been created.

   TIP When you test a movie, Macromedia Flash automatically runs the movie in Macromedia Flash Player, which creates a file that has a .swf extension in the folder where your movie is stored.

5. Close demomovie.fla, saving changes if prompted.

You tested a movie in the Macromedia Flash Player window.

Using the Macromedia Flash Player

In order to view a Macromedia Flash movie on the Web, your computer needs to have the Macromedia Flash Player installed. An important feature of multimedia players, such as Macromedia Flash Player, is that they can decompress a file that has been compressed to give it a small file size that can be more quickly delivered over the Internet. In addition to Macromedia, companies such as Apple, Microsoft, and RealNetworks create players that allow applications, developed with their and other company's products, to be viewed on the Web. The multimedia players are distributed free and can be downloaded from the company's Web site. The Macromedia Flash Player is created by Macromedia and is available at *www.macromedia.com/downloads*.

CREATE AND SAVE
A MOVIE

What You'll Do

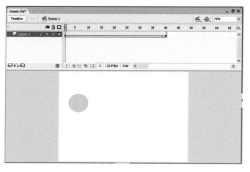

In this lesson, you will create a Macromedia Flash movie that will include a simple animation, then save the movie.

Creating a Macromedia Flash Movie

Macromedia Flash movies are created by placing objects (graphics, text, sounds, photos, and so on) on the stage, editing these objects (for example, changing their brightness), animating the objects, and adding interactivity with buttons and menus. You can create graphic objects in Macromedia Flash using the drawing tools, or you can develop them in another program, such as Macromedia Fireworks or Adobe Photoshop, and then import them into a Macromedia Flash movie. In addition, you can acquire clip art and stock photographs and import them into a movie. When objects are placed on the stage, they are automatically placed in a layer and in the currently selected frame of the timeline.

Figure 9 shows a movie that has an oval object created in Macromedia Flash. Notice that the playhead is on Frame 1 of the movie. The object placed on the stage appears in Frame 1 and appears on the stage when the playback head is on Frame

1. The dot in Frame 1 on the timeline indicates that this frame is a keyframe. The concept of keyframes is critical to understanding how Macromedia Flash works. A keyframe indicates that there is a change in the movie, such as the start or end of an animation, or the playing of a sound. A keyframe is automatically designated in frame 1 of every layer. In addition, you can designate any frame to be a keyframe.

The oval object in Figure 9 was created using the Oval tool. To create an oval or a rectangle, you select the desired tool and then drag the pointer over an area on the stage. If you want to draw a perfect circle or square, press and hold [Shift] when the tool is selected, and then drag the shape. If you make a mistake, you can click Edit on the menu bar, and then click Undo. In order to edit an object, you must first select it. You can use the Selection tool to select an entire object or group of objects. You drag the Selection tool pointer around the entire object to make a marquee selection. An object that has been selected displays a dot pattern or a blue border.

Creating an Animation

Figure 10 shows another movie that has 40 frames, as specified in the timeline. The arrow in the timeline indicates a motion animation. In this case, the object will move from left to right across the stage. The movement of the object is caused by having the object in different places on the stage in different frames of the movie. A basic motion animation requires two keyframes. The first keyframe sets the starting position of the object, and the second keyframe sets the ending position of the object. The number of frames between the two keyframes determines the length of the animation. For example, if the starting keyframe is Frame 1 and the ending keyframe is Frame 40, the object will be animated for 40 frames. Once the two keyframes are set, Macromedia Flash automatically fills in the frames between them, with a process called **motion tweening**.

Adding an Effect to an Object

In addition to animating the location of an object (or objects), you can also animate an object's appearance; for example, its shape, color, brightness, or transparency. The color of the circle on the left of the stage in Figure 10 has been lightened using the Brightness effect on the Property inspector. When the movie is played, the color of the circle will start out light and then become darker as it moves to the right.

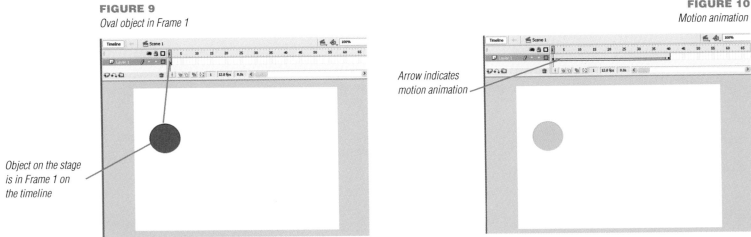

FIGURE 9
Oval object in Frame 1

Object on the stage is in Frame 1 on the timeline

FIGURE 10
Motion animation

Arrow indicates motion animation

Create objects using drawing tools

1. Click **File** on the menu bar, then click **New**.
2. Click **OK** in the New Document window to choose Flash Document as the new document to create, then save the movie as **tween**.
3. Click the **Oval tool** ○ on the Tools panel, then verify that the **Object Drawing option** in the Options panel is deselected, as shown in Figure 11.
4. Click the **Fill Color tool** on the Tools panel, then, if necessary, click the **red color swatch** in the left column of the color palette.
5. Press and hold **[Shift]**, then drag the **Oval tool** on the stage to draw the circle, as shown in Figure 12.

   Pressing and holding [Shift] creates a perfect circle. After releasing the mouse, the circle fills in red.
6. Click the **Selection tool** ▶ on the Tools panel, then drag a marquee selection around the object to select it, as shown in Figure 13.

   The object appears covered with a dot pattern.

You created an object using the Oval tool and then selected the object using the Selection tool.

Create basic animation

1. Click **Insert** on the menu bar, point to **Timeline**, then click **Create Motion Tween**.

   A blue border surrounds the object.
2. Click **Frame 40** on Layer 1 of the timeline.
3. Click **Insert** on the menu bar, point to **Timeline**, then click **Keyframe**.

(continued)

FIGURE 11
Object Drawing option

Object Drawing option
is not selected

FIGURE 12
Drawing a circle

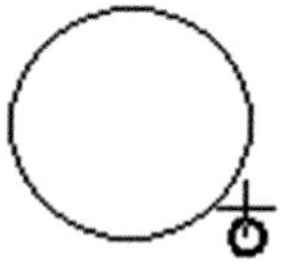

FIGURE 13
Creating a marquee selection

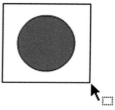

FIGURE 14
The circle on the right side of the stage

A second keyframe is defined in Frame 40, and Frames 1–40 appear shaded.

4. Drag the circle to the right side of the stage, as shown in Figure 14.

   The movement of the circle on the stage corresponds to the new location of the circle as defined in the keyframe in Frame 40.

5. Press **[Enter]** to play the movie.

   The playhead moves through the timeline in Frames 1–40, and the circle moves across the stage.

You created a basic motion tween animation by inserting a keyframe and changing the location of an object.

Change the brightness of an object

1. Click **Window** on the menu bar, point to **properties,** then verify that Properties is checked.

2. Click **Frame 1** on Layer 1, then click the **circle**.

3. Click the **Color Styles list arrow** in the Property inspector, then click **Brightness**.

4. Click the **Brightness Amount list arrow**, then drag the slider up to 70%.

   TIP You can also double-click the Brightness Amount box and type a percentage.

5. Click anywhere on a blank area of the Property inspector to close the slider.

6. Play the movie, then save your work.

   The circle becomes brighter as it moves across the stage.

You used the Property inspector to change the brightness of the object in one of the keyframes.

Using options and shortcuts

There is often more than one way to complete a particular function when using Macromedia Flash. For example, if you want to change the font for text you have typed, you can use Text menu options or the Property inspector. In addition, Macromedia Flash provides context menus that are relevant to the current selection. For example, if you point to a graphic and right-click (Win) or [control] click (Mac), a menu appears with graphic-related commands, such as distort and smooth. Shortcut keys are also available for many of the most common commands, such as [Ctrl] [Z] (Win) or ⌘ [Z] (Mac) for Undo.

WORK WITH THE TIMELINE

What You'll Do

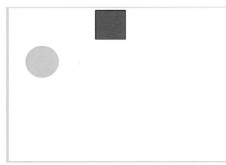

▶ *In this lesson, you will add another layer, allowing you to create an additional animation, and you will use the timeline to help organize your movie.*

Understanding the Timeline

The timeline organizes and controls a movie's contents over time. By learning how to read the information provided in the timeline, you can determine and change what will be happening in a movie, frame by frame. You can determine which objects are animated, what types of animations are being used, when the various objects will appear in a movie, which objects will appear on top of others, and how fast the movie will play. Features of the timeline are shown in Figure 15 and explained in this lesson.

Using Layers

Each new Macromedia Flash movie contains one layer, named Layer 1. **Layers** are like transparent sheets of acetate that are stacked on top of each other, as shown in Figure 16. Each layer can contain one or more objects. You can add layers using the Layer command on the Insert menu or by clicking the Insert Layer icon on the timeline. When you add a new layer, Macromedia Flash stacks it on top of the

other layer(s) in the timeline. The stacking order of the layers in the timeline is important because objects on the stage will appear in the same stacking order. For example, if you had two overlapping objects, and the top layer had a drawing of a tree and the bottom layer had a drawing of a house, the tree would appear as though it were in front of the house. You can change the stacking order of layers simply by dragging them up or down in the list of layers. You can name layers, hide them so their contents do not appear on the stage, and lock them so that they cannot be edited.

Using Frames

The timeline is made up of individual segments called **frames**. The content of each layer is displayed in frames as the playhead moves over them while the movie plays. Frames are numbered in increments of five for easy reference, while colors and symbols are used to indicate the type of frame (for example, keyframe or motion animation). The upper-right corner of the timeline contains a Frame View icon. Clicking on this icon displays a menu that provides different views of the timeline, showing more frames or showing thumbnails of the objects on a layer, for example. The status bar at the bottom of the timeline indicates the current frame (the frame that the play-head is currently on), the frame rate (frames per second), and the elapsed time from Frame 1 to the current frame.

Using the Playhead

The **playhead** indicates which frame is playing. You can manually move the play-head by dragging it left or right. This makes it easier to locate a frame that you may want to edit. Dragging the playhead also allows you to do a quick check of the movie without having to play it.

Understanding Scenes

When you create a movie, Scene 1 appears in the timeline. You can add scenes to a movie at any time. Scenes are a way to organize long movies. For example, a movie created for a Web site could be divided into anumber of scenes: an introduction, a home page, and content pages. Without them, scrolling through the timeline to work on different parts of the movie could become a very frustrating and inefficient way to work. Scenes have their own timeline. You can insert new scenes by using the Insert menu. Scenes can be given descriptive names, which will help you find them easily if you need to edit a particular scene. The number of scenes is limited only by the computer's memory.

FIGURE 15
Elements of the timeline

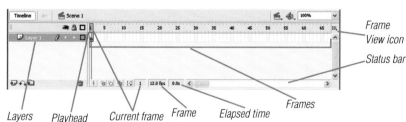

Frame View icon

Status bar

Frames

Layers Playhead Current frame Frame rate Elapsed time

FIGURE 16
The concept of layers

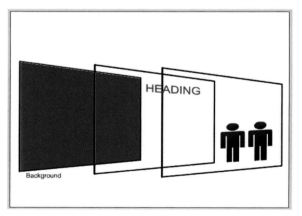

HEADING

Background

Working with the Timeline

Figure 17 shows the timeline of a movie created in Lesson 2 with a second object, a square at the top of the stage. By studying the timeline, you can learn several things about this movie. First, the second object is placed on its own layer, Layer 2. Second, the layer has a motion animation (indicated by the arrow and blue background in the frames). Third, the animation runs from Frame 1 to Frame 40. Fourth, if the objects intersect during the animation, the square will be on top of the circle, because the layer it is placed on is above the layer that the circle is placed on. Fifth, the frame rate is set to 12, which means that the movie will play 12 frames per second. Sixth, the playhead is at Frame 1, which causes the contents for both layers of Frame 1 to be displayed on the stage.

QUICKTIP

You can adjust the height of the timeline by positioning the mouse over the bottom edge, then dragging the border up or down.

FIGURE 17
The timeline of a movie with a second object

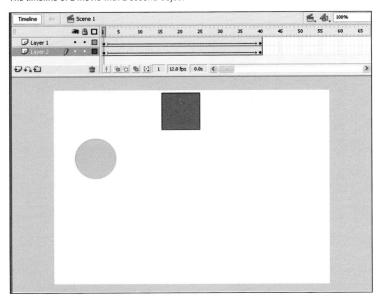

FIGURE 18
Drawing a square

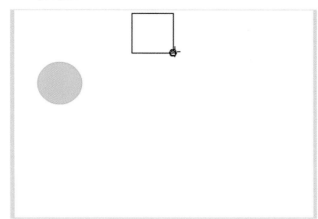

FIGURE 19
Positioning the square at the bottom of the stage

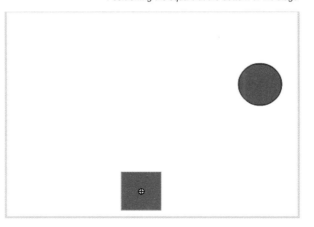

Add a layer

1. Save tween.fla as **layers.fla**.

2. Click **Frame 1** on Layer 1.

3. Click **View** on the menu bar, point to **Magnification**, then click **Fit in Window**.

4. Click **Insert** on the menu bar, point to **Timeline**, then click **Layer**.

   A new layer—Layer 2—appears at the top of the timeline.

You added a layer to the timeline.

Create a second animation

1. Click **Frame 1** of Layer 2 on the timeline.

2. Click the **Rectangle tool** 🔲 on the Tools panel, press and hold [**Shift**], then draw a square resembling the dimensions, as shown in Figure 18.

3. Click the **Selection tool** 🔧 on the Tools panel, then drag a marquee around the square.

4. Click **Insert** on the menu bar, point to **Timeline**, then click **Create Motion Tween**.

5. Click **Frame 40** on Layer 2, click **Insert** on the menu bar, point to **Timeline**, then click **Keyframe**.

6. Drag the square to the bottom of the stage, as shown in Figure 19, then play the movie.

   The square appears on top when the two objects intersect.

You drew an object and used it to create a second animation.

Work with layers and view features in the timeline

1. Click **Layer 2** on the timeline, then drag it below Layer 1.

   Layer 2 is now the bottom layer.

2. Play the movie and notice how the square appears beneath the circle when they intersect.

3. Click the **Frame View icon** 🖺 on the end of the timeline to display the menu, as shown in Figure 20.

4. Click **Tiny** to display more frames.

5. Click the **Frame View icon** 🖺 , click **Preview**, then note the object thumbnails that appear on the timeline.

6. Click the **Frame View icon** 🖺 , then click **Normal**.

You changed the order of the layers and changed the display of frames on the timeline.

FIGURE 20
Changing the view of the timeline

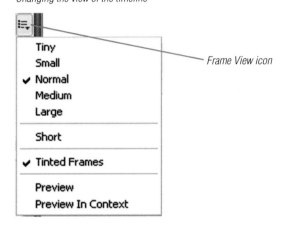

Frame View icon

FIGURE 21
Changing the frame rate

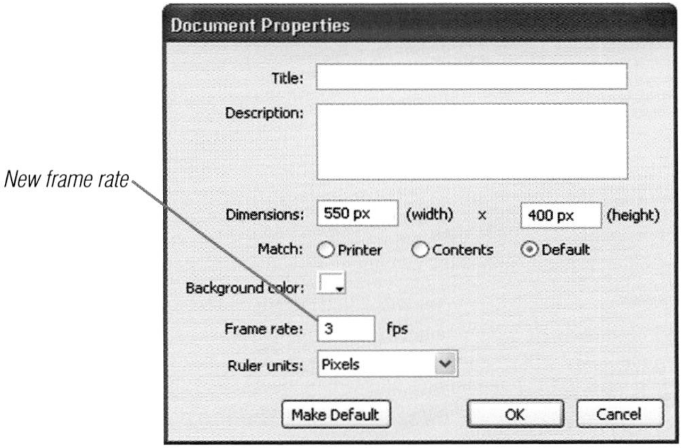

New frame rate

Modify the frame rate

1. Double-click the **Frame Rate icon** 12.0 fps on the bottom of the timeline to open the Document Properties dialog box.

2. Double-click **12**, type **3** in the Frame rate text box, then compare your Document Properties dialog box to Figure 21.

3. Click **OK**.

4. Play the movie and notice that the speed of the movie changes.

   TIP fps stands for frames per second. Frames per second is the unit of measurement for movies.

5. Repeat Steps 1 through 4, but change the frame rate to 18 and then to 12.

6. Click **Frame 1** on the timeline.

7. Drag the **playhead** left and right to display specific frames.

8. Save your work, then close layers.fla.

You changed the frame rate of the movie and used the playhead to display the contents of frames.

Getting Help
Macromedia Flash provides a comprehensive Help feature that can be very useful when first learning the program. You can access Help by clicking commands on the Help menu. The Help feature includes the Macromedia Flash manual, which is organized by topic and can be accessed through the index or by using a keyword search. In addition, the Help menu contains samples and tutorials that cover basic Macromedia Flash features.

PLAN A
WEB SITE

What You'll Do

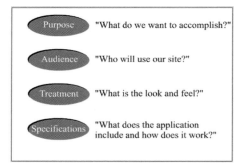

Purpose — "What do we want to accomplish?"

Audience — "Who will use our site?"

Treatment — "What is the look and feel?"

Specifications — "What does the application include and how does it work?"

▶ *In this lesson, you will learn how to plan a Macromedia Flash application. You will also learn about the guidelines for screen design and the interactive design of Web pages.*

Planning an Application

Macromedia Flash can be used to develop animations (movies) that are part of a product, such as a game or educational tutorial, delivered on CD-ROM or DVD. You can use Macromedia Flash to create enhancements to Web pages, such as animated logos and interactive navigation buttons. You can also use Macromedia Flash to create entire Web sites. No matter what the application, the first step is planning. Often, the temptation is to jump right into the program and start developing movies. The problem is that this invariably results in a more time-consuming process at best; and wasted effort, resources, and money at worst. The larger in scope and the more complex the project is, the more critical the planning process becomes. Planning an entire Web site should involve the following steps:

Step 1: Stating the Purpose (Goals). "What, specifically, do we want to accomplish?"

Determining the goals of a site is a critical step in planning, because goals guide the development process, keep the team members on track, and provide a way to evaluate the site both during and after its development.

Step 2: Identifying the Target Audience. "Who will use the Web site?"

Understanding the potential viewers helps in developing a site that can address their needs. For example, children respond to exploration and surprise, so having a dog wag its tail when the mouse pointer rolls over it might appeal to this audience.

Step 3: Determining the Treatment. "What is the look and feel?"

The treatment is how the Web site will be presented to the user, including the tone, approach, and emphasis.

Tone. Will the site be humorous, serious, light, heavy, formal, or informal? The tone of a site can often be used to make a statement projecting a progressive, high-tech, well-funded corporate image, for instance.

Approach. How much direction will be provided to the user? An interactive game site might focus on exploration, while an informational site might provide lots of direction, such as menus.

Emphasis. How much emphasis will be placed on the various multimedia elements? For example, a company may want to develop an informational site that shows the features of their new product line, including animated demonstrations of how each product works. The budget might not allow for the expense of creating the animations, so the emphasis would shift to still pictures with text descriptions.

Step 4: Developing the Specifications and Storyboard. "What precisely does the application include and how does it work?"

The specifications state what will be included in each screen, including the arrangement of each element and the functionality of each object (for example, what happens when you click the button

labeled Skip Intro). Specifications should include the following:

Playback System. The choice of what configuration to target for playback is critical, especially Internet connection speed, browser versions, screen resolution, and plug-ins.

Elements to Include. The specifications should include details about the various elements that are to be included in the site. What are the dimensions for the animations, and what is the frame rate? What are the sizes of the various objects such as photos, buttons, and so on? What fonts, font sizes, and type styles will be used?

Functionality. The specifications should include the way the program reacts to an action by the user, such as a mouse click. For example, clicking on a door (object) might cause the door to open

Rich Media Content and Accessibility

Macromedia Flash provides the tools that allow you to create compelling Web sites by incorporating rich media content, such as animations, sound, and video. Generally, incorporating rich media enhances the user's experience. However, accessibility becomes an issue for those that are visually, hearing, or mobility impaired, or have a cognitive disability. Designers need to utilize techniques that help ensure accessibility, such as providing consistency throughout the Web site in navigation and layout, labeling graphics, captioning audio content, and providing keyboard access.

(an animation), a doorbell to ring (sound), an "exit the program" message to appear (text), or an entirely new screen to be displayed.

User Interface. The user interface involves designing the appearance of objects (how each object is arranged on the screen) and the interactivity (how the user navigates through the site).

A flowchart is a visual representation of how the contents in an application or Web site are organized and how various screens are linked. It provides a guide for the developer and helps to identify problems with the

navigation scheme before work begins. Figure 22 shows a simple flowchart illustrating the site organization and links. A storyboard shows the layout of the various screens. It describes the contents and illustrates how text, graphics, animation, and other screen elements will be positioned. It also indicates the navigation process, such as menus and buttons. Figure 23 shows a storyboard. The exact content (such as a specific photo) does not have to be decided upon, but it is important to show where text, graphics, photos, buttons, and other elements, will be placed. Thus, the storyboard includes placeholders for the various elements.

Using Screen Design Guidelines

The following screen design guidelines are used by Web developers. The implementation of these guidelines is affected by the goals of the site, the intended audience, and the content.

Balance—Balance in screen design refers to the distribution of optical weight in the layout. Optical weight is the ability of an object to attract the viewer's eye, as determined by the object's size, shape, color, and so on. In general, a balanced design is more appealing to a viewer.

FIGURE 22
Sample Flowchart

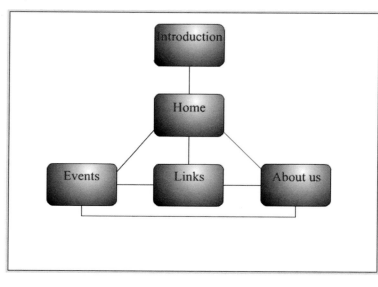

FIGURE 23
Sample Storyboard

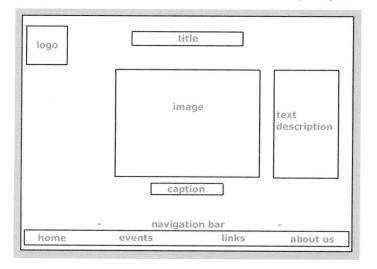

Unity—Intra-screen unity has to do with how the various screen objects relate and how they all fit in. Unity helps them reinforce each other. Inter-screen unity refers to the design that viewers encounter as they navigate from one screen to another, and it provides consistency throughout the site.

Movement—Movement refers to the way the viewer's eye moves through the objects on the screen. Techniques in an animation, such as movement, can be used to draw the viewer to a location on the screen.

Using Interactive Design Guidelines

In addition to screen design guidelines, interactive guidelines determine the interactivity of the site. The following guidelines are not absolute rules but are affected by the goals of the site, the intended audience, and the content:

- Make it simple, easy to understand, and easy to use. Make the site intuitive so that viewers do not have to spend time learning what the site is all about and what they need to do.
- Build in consistency in the navigation scheme. Help the users know where they are in the site and help them avoid getting lost.
- Provide feedback. Users need to know when an action, such as clicking a button, has been completed. Changing its color or shape, or adding a sound can indicate this.
- Give the user control. Allow the user to skip long introductions; provide controls for starting, stopping, and rewinding animations, video, and audio; and provide controls for adjusting audio.

Project Management

Developing Web sites or any extensive application, such as a game, involves project management. A project plan needs to be developed that provides the project scope and identifies the milestones including analyzing, designing, building, testing, and launching. Personnel and resource needs are identified, budgets built, tasks assigned, and schedules developed. Successful projects are a team effort relying on the close collaboration of designers, developers, project managers, graphic artists, programmers, testers, and others.

DISTRIBUTE A MACROMEDIA
FLASH MOVIE

What You'll Do

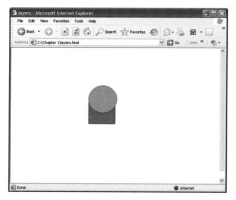

 In this lesson you will prepare a movie for distribution in various formats.

Distributing Movies

When you develop Macromedia Flash movies, the application saves them in a file format (.fla) that only users who have the Macromedia Flash program installed on their computers can view. Usually, Macromedia Flash movies are viewed on the Web as part of a Web site or directly from a viewer's computer using the Macromedia Flash Player. In order to view your Macromedia Flash movies on the Web, you must change the movie to a Macromedia Flash Player (.swf) file format and generate the HTML code that references the Macromedia Flash Player file. You can accomplish both of these tasks by using the publish feature of Macromedia Flash.

The process for publishing a Macromedia Flash movie is to create and save a movie and then click the Publish command on the File menu. You can also specify various settings such as dimensions for the window that the movie plays within in the browser, before publishing the movie. Publishing a movie creates two files: an HTML file and a Macromedia Flash file. Both of these files retain the same name as the Flash movie file, but with different file extensions:

- .html—the HTML document
- .swf—the Macromedia Flash Player file

For example, publishing a movie named layers.fla would generate layers.html and layers.swf. The HTML document contains the code that the browser interprets to display the movie on the Web. The code also specifies the Macromedia Flash Player movie that the browser will play. Sample HTML code referencing a Macromedia Flash Player movie is shown in Figure 24.

Macromedia Flash provides several other ways to distribute your movies that may or may not involve delivery on the Web. You can create a stand-alone movie called a **projector**. Projector files, such as Windows .exe files, maintain the movie's interactivity. Alternately, you can create self-running movies, such as QuickTime .mov files, that are not interactive.

You can play projector and non-interactive files directly from a computer, or you can incorporate them into an application, such as a game, that is downloaded or delivered on a CD or DVD.

FIGURE 24
Sample HTML code

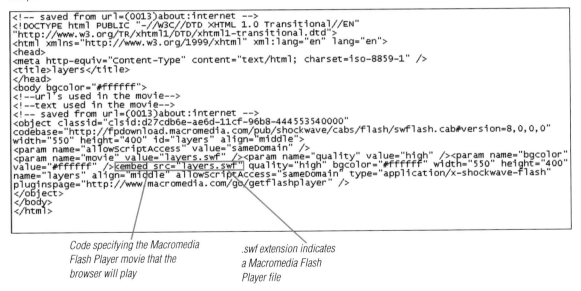

```
<!-- saved from url=(0013)about:internet -->
<!DOCTYPE html PUBLIC "-//W3C//DTD XHTML 1.0 Transitional//EN"
"http://www.w3.org/TR/xhtml1/DTD/xhtml1-transitional.dtd">
<html xmlns="http://www.w3.org/1999/xhtml" xml:lang="en" lang="en">
<head>
<meta http-equiv="Content-Type" content="text/html; charset=iso-8859-1" />
<title>layers</title>
</head>
<body bgcolor="#ffffff">
<!--url's used in the movie-->
<!--text used in the movie-->
<!-- saved from url=(0013)about:internet -->
<object classid="clsid:d27cdb6e-ae6d-11cf-96b8-444553540000"
codebase="http://fpdownload.macromedia.com/pub/shockwave/cabs/flash/swflash.cab#version=8,0,0,0"
width="550" height="400" id="layers" align="middle">
<param name="allowScriptAccess" value="sameDomain" />
<param name="movie" value="layers.swf" /><param name="quality" value="high" /><param name="bgcolor"
value="#ffffff" /><embed src="layers.swf" quality="high" bgcolor="#ffffff" width="550" height="400"
name="layers" align="middle" allowScriptAccess="sameDomain" type="application/x-shockwave-flash"
pluginspage="http://www.macromedia.com/go/getflashplayer" />
</object>
</body>
</html>
```

Code specifying the Macromedia Flash Player movie that the browser will play

.swf extension indicates a Macromedia Flash Player file

Publish a movie for distribution on the Web

1. Open layers.fla.

2. Click **File** on the menu bar, then click **Publish**.

3. Navigate to the drive and folder where you save your work.

4. Notice the three files that begin with "layers", as shown in Figure 25.

   Layers.fla, the Flash movie; layers.swf, the Macromedia Flash Player file; and layers.htm, the HTML document, appear in the window.

5. Double-click **layers.html**, then notice that the movie plays in the browser.

6. Close the browser.

You used the Publish command to create an HTML document and a Macromedia Flash Player file, then displayed the HTML document in a Web browser.

FIGURE 25
The three layers files after publishing the movie

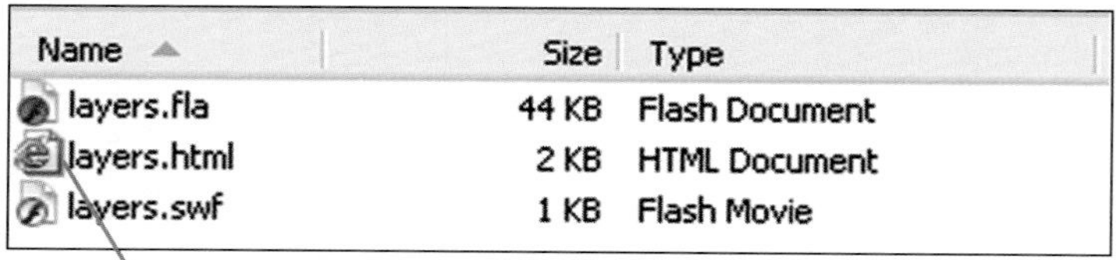

Name ▲	Size	Type
layers.fla	44 KB	Flash Document
layers.html	2 KB	HTML Document
layers.swf	1 KB	Flash Movie

Your browser icon may be different

FIGURE 26

The Flash Player window playing the Macromedia Flash Player movie

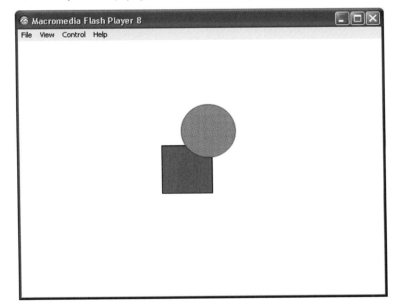

1. Return to Flash, click **File** on the menu bar, then click **Publish Settings** to open the Publish Settings dialog box.

2. Click the **Windows Projector (.exe)** (Win) or **Macintosh Projector** (Mac) **check box**, then deselect other file formats (if necessary).

3. Click **Publish**, then click **OK**.

4. Navigate to the drive and folder where you save your work.

5. Double-click **layers.exe** (Win), or **layers Projector** (Mac), then notice that the application plays in the Macromedia Flash Player window, as shown in Figure 26.

6. Close the Macromedia Flash Player window.

7. Close layers.fla in Macromedia Flash, saving your changes if prompted.

8. Exit the Macromedia Flash program.

You created and displayed a stand-alone projector file.

Start Macromedia Flash, open a movie, and set the movie properties and magnification.

1. Start Macromedia Flash, open fl1_2.fla, and then save it as **skillsdemo1**.
2. Display the Document Properties dialog box, add a title, **Animated Objects**, then add a description, **A review of skills learned in Chapter 1**.
3. Change the movie window dimensions to width: 550 px and height: 450 px.
4. Change the background color to blue. (*Hint*: Select the blue color swatch in the left column of the color palette.)
5. Close the Document Properties dialog box.
6. Change the magnification to 50% using the View menu.
7. Change the magnification to Fit in Window.

Display, close, and collapse panels.

1. Hide all panels.
2. Display the Tools panel, Property inspector, and the Library panel.
3. Collapse the Property inspector and Library panels.

4. Close the Library panel to remove it from the screen.
5. Expand the Property inspector.

Play and test a movie.

1. Drag the playhead to view the contents of each frame. Use the commands in the Control menu to play and rewind the movie.
2. Press [Enter] (Win) or [return] (Mac) to play and stop the movie.
3. Use the Controller to rewind, play, stop, and start the movie.
4. Test the movie in the Macromedia Flash Player window, then close the test movie window.

Create an object, create a basic animation, and apply an effect.

1. Insert a new layer above layer 2, then select Frame 1 of the new layer.
2. Draw a red circle in the lower-left corner of the stage, approximately the same size as the green ball. (*Hint*: Use the scroll bar on the timeline to view the new layer.)

3. Select the circle, then create a Motion Tween to animate the circle so that it moves across the screen from left to right, beginning in Frame 1 and ending in Frame 60. (*Hint*: Add a keyframe in the ending frame.)
4. Use the Selection Tool to select the circle (if necessary), then change the brightness from 0% to -100%, in the last frame of the animation.
5. Play the movie, then rewind it.

Add a layer, change the frame rate, and change the view of the timeline.

1. Add a new layer above layer 3, select Frame 1, then create a second circle in the lower-right corner of the stage that's approximately the same size as the circle you created in the lower-left corner of the stage.
2. Animate the circle so that it moves across the screen from right to left beginning in Frame 1 and ending in Frame 60.
3. Use the Selection Tool to select the circle, then change the brightness from 0% to 100%.
4. Play the movie.
5. Change the frame rate to 8 frames per second.

6. Change the view of the timeline to display more frames.
7. Change the view of the timeline to display a preview of the object thumbnails.
8. Change the view of the timeline to display the Normal view.
9. Use the playhead to display each frame, then compare your screens to Figure 27.
10. Save the movie.

Publish a movie.

1. Click File on the menu bar, then click Publish.
2. Open your browser, then open skillsdemo1.html.
3. View the movie, then close your browser.

Create a projector file.

1. Display the Publish Settings dialog box.
2. Select the appropriate projector setting for your operating systems and remove all of the other settings.
3. Publish the movie.
4. Navigate to the drive and folder where you save your work, then open skillsdemo1 projector file.
5. View the movie, then close the Macromedia Flash Player window.
6. Save and close the Macromedia Flash document.
7. Exit Flash.

FIGURE 27
Completed Skills Review

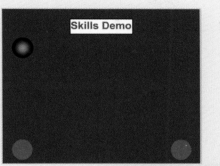

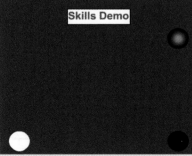

A friend cannot decide whether to sign up for a class in Macromedia Flash or Macromedia Dreamweaver. You help her decide by showing her what you already know about Macromedia Flash. Since you think she'd love a class in Macromedia Flash, you decide to show her how easy it is to create a simple animation involving two objects that move diagonally across the screen.

1. Open a Flash document, then save it as **demonstration**.
2. Use the tools on the Tools panel to create a simple shape or design, and place it off the left side of the stage, halfway down the stage.
3. Select the object and insert a motion tween.
4. Insert a keyframe in Frame 20, then move the object to the middle of the stage.
5. Insert a new layer, then select Frame 1 of the layer.
6. Create another object that covers the first object, then insert a motion tween for the object.
7. Insert a keyframe in Frame 40, then move the object to the right side off the stage.
8. Insert a new layer, then select Frame 1 of the layer.
9. Draw an object off the top of the stage, about midway across the stage.
10. Animate the object to move straight down and off the bottom of the stage for 40 frames.
11. Change the brightness of the object to 80% in Frame 40.

12. Add a background color.
13. Preview the movie and test it.
14. Save the movie, then compare it to the example shown in Figure 28.

FIGURE 28
Sample completed Project Builder 1

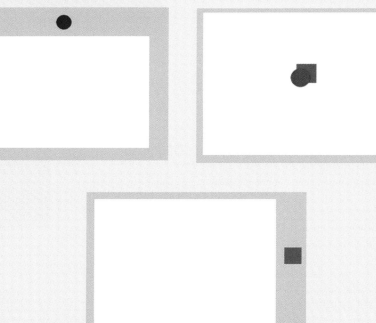

You've been asked to develop a simple movie about recycling for a day care center. For this project, you will add two animations to an existing movie. You will show three objects that appear on the screen at different times, and then move each object to a recycle bin at different times. You can use any objects using the Tools on the Tools panel.

1. Open fl1_3.fla, then save it as **recycle**.
2. Play the movie and study the timeline to familiarize yourself with the movie's current settings.
3. Insert a new layer above Layer 2, insert a keyframe in Frame 10 of the new layer, then draw a small object in the upper-left corner of the stage.
4. Create a motion animation that moves the object to the recycle bin.
5. Insert a new layer above the top layer, insert a keyframe in Frame 20, draw a small object in the upper center of the stage, then create a motion animation that moves the object to the recycle bin.
6. Insert a new layer above the top layer, insert a keyframe in Frame 30, draw a small object in the upper-right corner of the stage, then create a motion animation that moves the object to the recycle bin.
7. Move Layer 1 to the top of all the layers.
8. Play the movie and compare it to Figure 29.
9. Save the movie.

FIGURE 29
Sample completed Project Builder 2

This figure shows the animated objects with outlines of their positions during the animations. Your completed project will not show these outlines

Figure 30 shows the home page of a Web site. Study the figure and answer the following questions. For each question, indicate how you determined your answer.

1. Connect to the Internet, go to *www.course. com*, navigate to the page for this book, click the Online Companion link, then click the link for this chapter.
2. Open a document in a word processor or open a new Macromedia Flash document, save the file as **dpc1**, then answer the following questions. (*Hint*: Use the Text tool in Macromedia Flash.)
   - Whose Web site is this?
   - What is the goal(s) of the site?
   - Who is the target audience?
   - What treatment (look and feel) is used?
   - What are the design layout guidelines being used (balance, movement, etc.)?
   - How can animation enhance this page?
   - Do you think this is an effective design for the company, its products, and its target audience? Why, or why not?
   - What suggestions would you make to improve on the design, and why?

FIGURE 30
Design Project

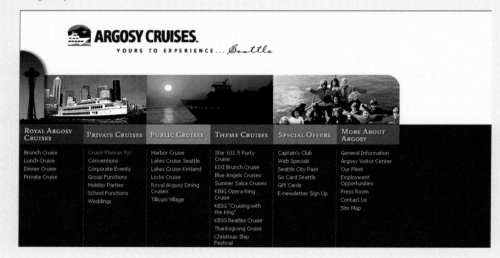

There are numerous companies in the business of developing Web sites for others. Many of these companies use Macromedia Flash as one of their primary development tools. These companies promote themselves through their own Web sites and usually provide online portfolios with samples of their work. Log onto the Internet, then use your favorite search engine (use keywords such as Macromedia Flash developers and Macromedia Flash animators) to locate three of these companies, and generate the following information for each one. A sample is shown in Figure 31.

1. Company name:
2. Contact information (address, phone, and so on):
3. Web site URL:
4. Company mission:
5. Services provided:
6. Sample list of clients:
7. Describe three ways they seem to have used Macromedia Flash in their own sites. Were these effective? Why, or why not?
8. Describe three applications of Macromedia Flash that they include in their portfolios (or showcases or samples). Were these effective? Why, or why not?
9. Would you want to work for this company? Why, or why not?
10. Would you recommend this company to another company that was looking to enhance its Web site? Why, or why not?

FIGURE 31
Portfolio Project

2

DRAWING OBJECTS IN
MACROMEDIA FLASH

1. Use the Macromedia Flash drawing tools.

2. Select Objects and Apply Colors.

3. Work with objects.

4. Work with text and text objects.

5. Work with layers and objects.

Introduction

One of the most compelling features of Macromedia Flash is the ability to create and manipulate vector graphics. Computers can display graphics in either a bitmap or a vector format. The difference between these formats is in how they describe an image. Bitmap graphics represent the image as an array of dots, called **pixels**, which are arranged within a grid. Each pixel in an image has an exact position on the screen and a precise color. To make a change in a bitmap, you modify the pixels. When you enlarge a bitmap graphic, the number of pixels remains the same, resulting in jagged edges that decrease the quality of the image. Vector graphics represent the image using lines and curves, which you can resize without losing image quality. Also, because vector images are generally smaller than bitmap images, they are particularly useful for a Web site. However, vector graphics are not as effective as bitmap graphics for representing photo-realistic images.

Images (objects) created using Macromedia Flash drawing tools have a stroke, a fill, or both. In addition, the stroke of an object can be segmented into smaller lines. You can modify the size, shape, rotation, and color of each stroke, fill, and segment.

Macromedia Flash provides two drawing modes, called models. In the Merge Drawing Model, when you draw two shapes and one overlaps the other, a change in the top object may affect the object beneath it. For example, if you draw a circle on top of a rectangle and then move the circle off the rectangle, the portion of the rectangle overlapped by the circle is removed. The Object Drawing Model allows you to overlap shapes which are then kept separate, so that changes in one object do not affect another object. Another way to avoid having changes in one object affect another is to place them on separate layers in the timeline.

Tools You'll Use

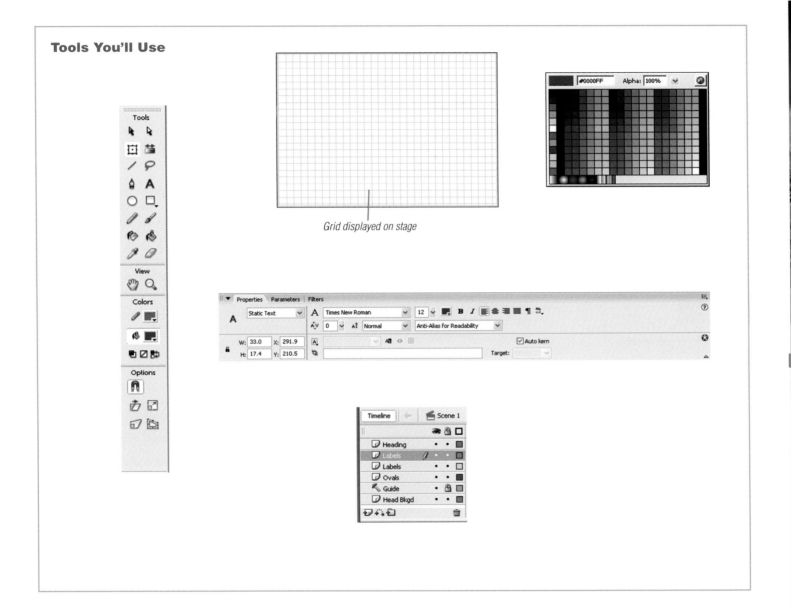

Grid displayed on stage

USE THE MACROMEDIA
FLASH DRAWING TOOLS

What You'll Do

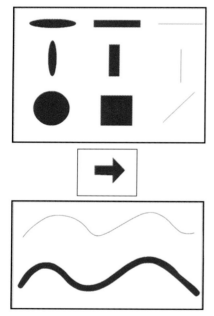

In this lesson, you will use several drawing tools to create various vector graphics.

Using Macromedia Flash Drawing and Editing Tools

When you point to a tool on the Tools panel, its name appears next to the tool. Figure 1 identifies the tools described below. Several of the tools have options that modify their use.

Selection—Used to select an object or parts of an object, such as the stroke or fill; and to reshape objects. The options available for the Selection tool are Snap to Objects (aligns objects), Smooth (smoothes lines), and Straighten (straightens lines).

Subselection—Used to select, drag, and reshape an object. Vector graphics are composed of lines and curves (each of which is a segment) connected by **anchor points**. Selecting an object with this tool displays the anchor points and allows you to use them to edit the object.

Free Transform—Used to transform objects by rotating, scaling, skewing, and distorting them.

Gradient Transform—Used to transform a gradient fill by adjusting the size, direction, or center of the fill.

Line—Used to draw straight lines. You can draw vertical, horizontal, and 45° diagonal lines by pressing and holding [Shift] while drawing the line.

Lasso—Used to select objects or parts of objects. The Polygon Mode option allows you to draw straight lines when selecting an object.

Pen—Used to draw lines and curves by creating a series of dots, known as anchor points, that are automatically connected.

Text—Used to create and edit text.

Oval—Used to draw oval shapes. Press and hold [Shift] to draw a perfect circle.

Rectangle—Used to draw rectangular shapes. Press and hold [Shift] to draw a perfect square. The Round Rectangle Radius option allows you to round the corners of a rectangle.

Pencil—Used to draw freehand lines and shapes. The options available for the Pencil tool are Straighten (draws straight lines), Smooth (draws smooth curved lines), and Ink (draws freehand with no modification).

Brush—Used to draw (paint) with brush-like strokes. Options allow you to set the size and shape of the brush, and to determine the area to be painted, such as inside or behind an object.

Ink Bottle—Used to apply line colors and thickness to the stroke of an object.

Paint Bucket—Used to fill enclosed areas of a drawing with color. Options allow you to fill areas that have gaps and to make adjustments in a gradient fill.

Eyedropper—Used to select stroke, fill, and text attributes so they can be copied from one object to another.

Eraser—Used to erase lines and fills. Options allow you to choose what part of the object to erase, as well as the size and shape of the eraser.

The Oval, Rectangle, Pencil, Brush, Line, and Pen tools are used to create vector objects.

Displaying Gridlines, Guides, and Rulers

Gridlines, guides, and rulers can be used to position objects on the stage. The Grid, Guides, and Rulers commands, found on the View menu, are used to turn on and off these features. You can modify the grid size and color, and you can specify the unit of measure for the rulers. In addition, Guide layers can be used to position objects on the stage.

FIGURE 1
Macromedia Flash tools

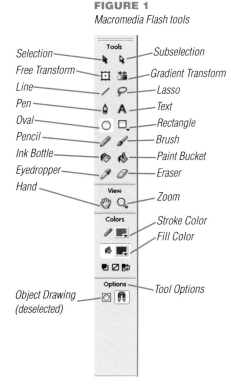

Show gridlines and check settings

1. Start Macromedia Flash, create a new Flash Document, then save it as **tools**.

2. Click **Window** on the menu bar, then click **Hide Panels**.

3. Click **Window** on the menu bar, then click **Tools**.

4. Click **Window** on the menu bar, point to **Properties**, then click **Properties**.

5. Click **View** on the menu bar, point to **Magnification**, then click **Fit in Window**.

6. Click the **Stroke Color tool** 🖊️ on the Tools panel, then click the **red color swatch** in the left column of the color palette (if necessary).

7. Click the **Fill Color tool** 🪣 on the Tools panel, then click the **blue color swatch** in the left column of the color palette (if necessary).

8. Click **View** on the menu bar, point to **Grid**, then click **Show Grid** to display the gridlines.

   A gray grid appears on the stage.

9. Point to several tools on the Tools panel, then read their names, as shown in Figure 2.

You started a new document, saved it, set up the workspace, changed the stroke and fill colors, then displayed the grid and viewed tool names on the Tools panel.

FIGURE 2
Tool name on the Tools panel

Point to a tool to display its name

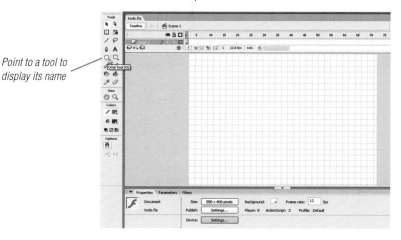

Use the Oval, Rectangle, and Line Tools

1. Click the **Oval tool** ○ on the Tools panel.

2. Verify that the **Object Drawing option** ◎ in the Options section of the Tools panel is deselected.

3. Using Figure 3 as a guide, draw the three oval shapes.

   TIP   Use the grid to approximate shape sizes and Hold down [Shift] to draw a circle, square and diagonal line. To undo an action, click the Undo command on the Edit menu.

4. Click the **Rectangle tool** ▢, then using Figure 3 as a guide, draw the three rectangle shapes.

5. Click the **Line tool** ╱, then, using Figure 3 as a guide, draw the three lines.

   Notice that the ovals and rectangles display both the stroke and fill colors, while the line tool displays only the stroke color.

You used the Oval, Rectangle, and Line tools to draw objects on the stage.

FIGURE 3
Objects created with drawing tools

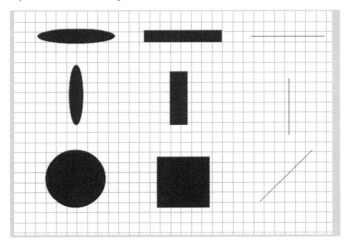

Use the Pen, Pencil, and Brush Tools

1. Click **Insert** on the menu bar, point to **Timeline**, then click **Layer**.

   A new layer—Layer 2—appears above Layer 1.

2. Click **Frame 5** on Layer 2.

3. Click **Insert** on the menu bar, point to **Timeline**, then click **Keyframe**.

   Since the objects were drawn in Frame 1, they are no longer visible when you insert a keyframe in Frame 5.

4. Click the **Zoom tool** on the Tools panel, point near the upper-left quadrant of the stage, then click to zoom in.

5. Click the **Pen tool** on the Tools panel, position it in the upper-left quadrant of the stage, as shown in Figure 4, then click to set an anchor point.

6. Using Figure 5 as a guide, click the remaining anchor points to complete drawing an arrow.

   | TIP   To close an object, be sure to re-click the first anchor point as your last action.

7. Click **View** on the menu bar, point to **Magnification**, then click **100%**.

8. Insert a new layer, Layer 3, then insert a keyframe in Frame 10.

9. Click the **Pencil tool** on the Tools panel.

10. Click the **Pencil Mode tool** in the Options section of the Tools panel, then click the **Smooth option**, as shown in Figure 6.

11. Draw the top image, as shown in Figure 7.

(continued)

FIGURE 4
Positioning the Pen Tool on the stage

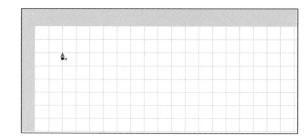

FIGURE 5
Setting anchor points to draw an arrow

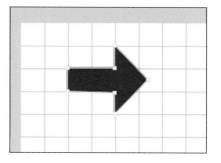

FIGURE 6
Pencil Tool options

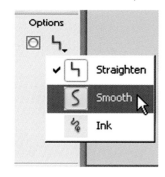

FIGURE 7
Images drawn using drawing tools

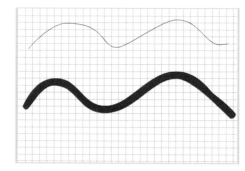

Drawing Objects in Macromedia Flash

12. Click the **Brush tool**  on the Tools panel.

13. Click the **Brush Size list arrow** in the Options section of the Tools panel, then click the 5th option from the top.

14. Repeat Step 11, drawing the bottom image. Notice the pencil tool displays the stroke color and the brush tool displays the fill color.

You added a layer, inserted a keyframe, then used the Pen Tool to draw an arrow; you selected the Smooth option for the Pencil tool and drew an object; you selected a brush size for the Brush tool and drew an object.

Modify an object using tool options

1. Click the **Selection tool** on the Tools panel, then drag a marquee around the top object to select it.

2. Click the **Smooth option** S. in the Options section of the Tools panel.

   The line becomes smoother.

3. Select the bottom object, then click the **Smooth option** S. in the Options section of the Tools panel.

   Your object should look similar to Figure 8. The object becomes smoother.

4. Save your work.

You smoothed objects using the tool options.

FIGURE 8
The dot pattern indicating the object is selected

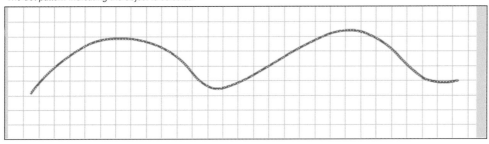

SELECT OBJECTS
AND APPLY COLORS

What You'll Do

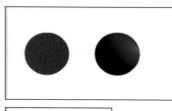

In this lesson, you will use several techniques to select objects, change the color of strokes and fills, and create a gradient fill.

Selecting Objects

Before you can edit a drawing, you must first select the object, or part of the object, on which you want to work. Objects are made up of a stroke(s) and a fill. Strokes can have several segments. For example, a rectangle will have four stroke segments, one for each side of the object. These can be selected separately or as a whole. Macromedia Flash highlights objects that have been selected, as shown in Figure 9. When the stroke of an object is selected, a colored line appears. When the fill of an object is selected, a dot pattern appears; and when objects are grouped, a bounding box appears.

Using the Selection Tool

You can use the Selection tool to select part or all of an object, and to select multiple objects. To select only the fill, click just the fill; to select only the stroke, click just the stroke. To select both the fill and the stroke, double-click the object or draw a marquee around it. To select part of an object, drag a marquee that defines the area you wish to

select, as shown in Figure 9. To select multiple objects or combinations of strokes and fills, press and hold [Shift], then click each item. To deselect an item(s), click a blank area of the stage.

Using the Lasso Tool

The Lasso tool provides more flexibility when selecting an area on the stage. You can use the tool in a freehand manner to select any size and shape of area. Alternately, you can use the Polygon Mode option to draw straight lines and connect them.

Object Drawing Model

Macromedia Flash provides two drawing modes, called models. In the Merge Drawing Model mode, the stroke and fill of an object are separate. Thus, as you draw an object such as a circle, the stroke and fill can be selected individually as described above. When using the Object Drawing Model mode, the stroke and fill are combined and cannot be selected individually. However, you can use the Break Apart option from the Modify menu to separate the stroke and fill so that they can be selected individually. In addition, you can turn off either the stroke or fill when drawing an object in either mode. You can toggle between the two modes using the Object Drawing icon in the options section of the Tools panel.

Working with Colors

Macromedia Flash allows you to change the color of the stroke and fill of an object. Figure 10 shows the Colors section of the Tools panel. To change a color, you click the Stroke Color tool or the Fill Color tool, and then select a color swatch on the color palette. The color palette, as shown in Figure 11, allows you to type in a six character code that represents the values of three colors (red, green, blue), referred to as RGB. When these characters are combined in various ways they can represent virtually any color. The values are in a hexadecimal format (base 16), so they include letters and digits (A-F + 0-9 = 16 options), and they are preceded by a pound sign (#). The first two characters represent the value for red, the next two for green, and the last two for blue. For example, #000000 represents black (lack of color); #FFFFFF represents white; #00FF00 represents green; and FFCC33 represents a shade of gold. You do not have to memorize the code for all colors. There are reference manuals available for looking up the codes, and many programs allow you to set the values visually by selecting a color from a palette.

You can set the desired colors before drawing an object, or you can change a color of a previously drawn object. You can use the Ink Bottle tool to change the stroke color, and you can use the Paint Bucket tool to change the fill color. You can also use the Property inspector to change the stroke and fill colors.

Working with Gradients

A gradient is a color fill that makes a gradual transition from one color to another. Gradients can be very useful for creating a 3-D effect, drawing attention to an object, and generally enhancing the appearance of an object. You can apply a gradient fill by using the Paint Bucket tool. The position of the Paint Bucket tool over the object is important because it determines the direction of the gradient fill.

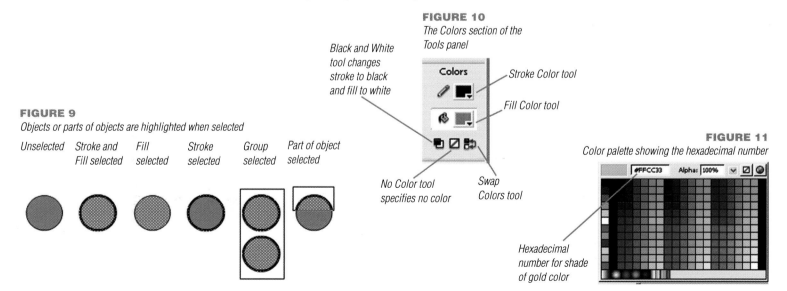

FIGURE 9
Objects or parts of objects are highlighted when selected

Unselected | Stroke and Fill selected | Fill selected | Stroke selected | Group selected | Part of object selected

FIGURE 10
The Colors section of the Tools panel

Black and White tool changes stroke to black and fill to white

Stroke Color tool

Fill Color tool

No Color tool specifies no color

Swap Colors tool

FIGURE 11
Color palette showing the hexadecimal number

Hexadecimal number for shade of gold color

Select a drawing using the mouse and the Lasso Tool

1. Click **Frame 1** on the timeline.

   TIP The actions you perform on the stage will produce very different results depending on whether you click a frame on the timeline or on a layer.

2. Click the **Selection tool** ⬉ on the Tools panel (if necessary), then drag the marquee around the circle to select the entire object (both the stroke and the fill).

3. Click anywhere on the stage to deselect the object.

4. Click inside the circle to select the fill only, then click outside the circle to deselect it.

5. Click the stroke of the circle to select it, as shown in Figure 12, then deselect it.

6. Double-click the **circle** to select it, press and hold **[Shift]**, double-click the **square** to select both objects, then deselect both objects.

7. Click the right border of the square to select it, as shown in Figure 13, then deselect it.

You used the Selection tool to select the stroke and fill of an object, and to select multiple objects.

FIGURE 12
Using the Selection tool to select the stroke of the circle

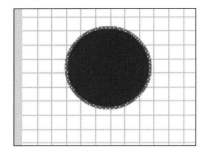

FIGURE 13
Using the Selection tool to select a segment of the stroke of the square

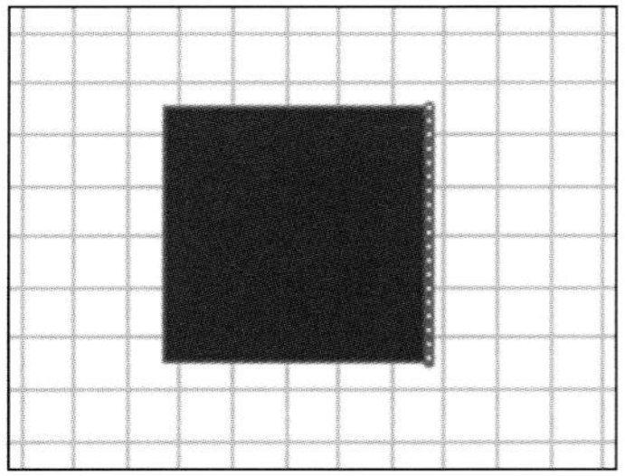

FIGURE 14
Circles drawn with the Oval tool

Change fill and stroke colors

1. Click **Layer 3**, click **Insert** on the menu bar, point to **Timeline**, then click **Layer**.

2. Click **Frame 15** of the new layer, click **Insert** on the menu bar, point to **Timeline**, then click **Keyframe**.

3. Click **View** on the menu bar, point to **Grid**, then click **Show Grid** to remove the gridlines.

4. Click the **Oval tool** ⬭ on the Tools panel, then draw two circles similar to those shown in Figure 14.

5. Click the **Fill Color tool** 🖌⬜ on the Tools panel, then click the **yellow color swatch** in the left column of the color palette.

6. Click the **Paint Bucket tool** 🪣 on the Tools panel, then click the fill of the right circle.

7. Click the **Stroke Color tool** ✏⬜ on the Tools panel, then click the **yellow color swatch** in the left column of the color palette.

8. Click the **Ink Bottle tool** 🍶 on the Tools panel, then click the stroke of the left circle, as shown in Figure 15.

You used the Ink Bottle and Paint Bucket tools to change the fill and stroke colors of an object.

FIGURE 15
Changing the stroke color

Create a gradient

1. Click the **Fill Color tool** on the Tools panel, then click the **red gradient color swatch** in the bottom row of the color palette, as shown in Figure 16.

2. Click the **Paint Bucket tool** on the Tools panel, then click the yellow circle.

3. Click different parts of the right circle, then click the right side, as shown in Figure 17.

4. Click the **Gradient Transform tool** on the Tools panel, then click the gradient-filled circle.

5. Drag each of the four handles, as shown in Figure 18, to determine their effects on the gradient, then click the stage to deselect the circle.

6. Click the **Fill Color tool** , click the **Hex Edit text box**, type **#0000FF**, then press **[Enter]** (Win) or **[return]** (Mac).

7. Save your work.

You applied a gradient fill and you used the Gradient Transform tool to alter the gradient.

FIGURE 16
Selecting the red gradient

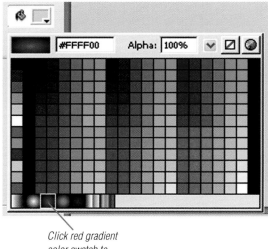

Click red gradient
color swatch to
select it

FIGURE 18
Gradient Transform handles

FIGURE 17
Clicking the right side of the circle

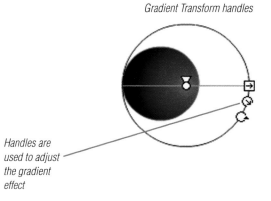

Handles are
used to adjust
the gradient
effect

Work with the Object Drawing Model Mode

1. Insert a new layer, then insert a keyframe on Frame 20.
2. Click the **Oval tool** ○ .
3. Click the **Stroke Color tool** ✐▢ , then click the red swatch.
4. Click the **Fill Color tool** ▧▢ , then click the black swatch.
5. Click the **Object Drawing option** ▢ in the Options section of the Tools panel to change the mode to the Object Drawing Model.
6. Draw a circle on the stage, as shown in Figure 19.

   Notice that when you use the Object Drawing Model mode, objects are automatically selected, and the stroke and fill areas are combined.
7. Click the **Selection tool** ▸ in the Tools panel, then click on a blank area of the stage to deselect the object.
8. Click once on the circle.

   The entire object is selected, including the stroke and fill areas.
9. Click **Modify** on the menu bar, then click **Break Apart**.

   Breaking apart an object drawn using the Object Drawing Model mode allows you to select the strokes and fills.
10. Click a blank area on the stage, then save your work.

You used the Object Drawing Model mode to draw an object, deselect it, and then break it apart to display the stroke and fill.

FIGURE 19
Circle drawn using the Object Drawing Model mode

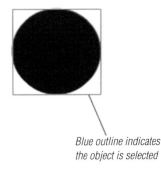

*Blue outline indicates
the object is selected*

WORK WITH OBJECTS

What You'll Do

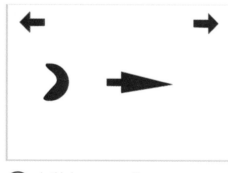

▶ *In this lesson, you will copy, move, and transform (resize, rotate, and reshape) objects.*

Copying and Moving Objects

To copy one or more objects, select them, then click the Copy command on the Edit menu. To paste the object, click the Paste command on the Edit menu. You can copy an object to another layer by selecting the frame and layer prior to pasting the object.

You can move an object by selecting it and dragging it to a new location. You can precisely position an object by selecting it and then pressing the arrow keys, which move the selection up, down, left, and right in small increments.

Transforming Objects

You can use the Free Transform tool to resize, rotate, skew, and reshape objects. After selecting an object, you can click the Free Transform tool to display eight square-shaped handles used to transform the object, and a circle-shaped transformation point located at the center of the object. The transformation point is the point around which the object can be rotated. You can also change its location. The Free Transform tool has four options: Rotate and Skew, Scale, Distort, and Envelope. These tool options restrict the transformations that can be completed; you can select only one option at a time.

Resizing an Object

You can enlarge or reduce the size of an object using the Scale option of the Free Transform tool. The process is to select the object and click the Free Transform tool, then click the Scale option in the Options section of the Tools panel. Eight handles appear around the selected object. You can drag the corner handles to resize the object without changing its proportions. That is, if the object starts out as a square, dragging a corner handle will change the size of the object, but it will still be a square. On the other hand, if you drag one of the middle handles, the object will be reshaped as taller, shorter, wider, or narrower.

Rotating and Skewing an Object

You can use the Rotate and Skew option of the Free Transform tool to rotate an object and to skew it. Select the object, click the Free Transform tool, then click the Rotate and Skew option in the Options section of the Tools panel. Eight square-shaped handles appear around the object. You can drag the corner handles to rotate the object, or you can drag the middle handles to skew the object, as shown in Figure 20. The Transform panel can be used to rotate and skew an object in a more precise way; select the object, display the Transform panel, enter the desired rotation of skew in degrees, then press [Enter] (Win) or [return] (Mac).

Distorting an Object

You can use the Distort and Envelope options to reshape an object by dragging its handles. The Envelope option provides more than eight handles to allow for more precise distortions.

Reshaping a Segment of an Object

You can use the Subselection tool to reshape a segment of an object. Click an edge of the object to display handles that can be dragged to reshape the object.

You can use the Selection tool to reshape objects. When you point to the edge of an object, the pointer displays an arc symbol. Using the Arc pointer, you can drag the edge of the object you want to reshape, as shown in Figure 21. If the Selection tool points to a corner of an object, the pointer displays an L-shaped symbol—dragging the pointer reshapes the corner of the object.

Flipping an Object

You can use an option under the Transform command to flip an object either horizontally or vertically. Select the object, click the Transform command on the Modify menu, and then choose Flip Vertical or Flip Horizontal. Other Transform options allow you to rotate and scale the selected object, and the Remove Transform command allows you to restore an object to its original state.

FIGURE 20
Using handles to manipulate an object

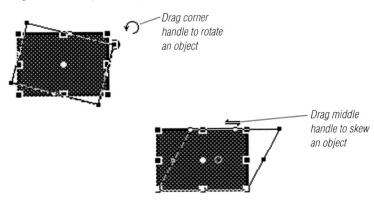

Drag corner handle to rotate an object

Drag middle handle to skew an object

FIGURE 21
Using the Selection tool to distort an object

Copy and move an object

1. Click **Frame 5** on the timeline.

2. Click the **Selection tool** on the Tools panel, then draw a marquee around the arrow object to select it.

3. Click **Edit** on the menu bar, click **Copy**, click **Edit** on the menu bar, click **Paste in Center**, then compare your image to Figure 22.

   A copy of the arrow is pasted on the center of the stage.

4. Drag and align the newly copied arrow under the original arrow, as shown in Figure 23.

You used the Selection tool to select an object, then you copied and moved the object.

FIGURE 22
A copy of the arrow on the stage

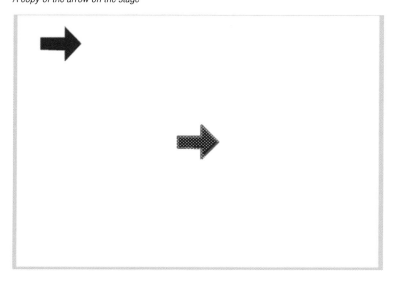

FIGURE 23
Aligning the arrows

FIGURE 24

Resizing an object using the corner handles

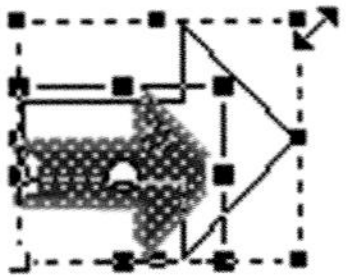

FIGURE 25

Reshaping an object using the middle handles

Resize and reshape an object

1. Verify that the bottom arrow is selected, then click the **Free Transform tool** on the Tools panel.
2. Click the **Scale option** in the Options section of the Tools panel.
3. Drag each corner handle towards and then away from the center of the object, as shown in Figure 24.

   As you drag the corner handles, the object's size is changed, but its proportions remain the same.
4. Click **Edit** on the menu bar, then click **Undo Scale.**
5. Repeat step 4 until the arrow returns to its original size.
6. Click the **Selection tool** (if necessary), then draw a marquee around the arrow to select it.
7. Drag each middle handle away and then toward the center of the object, as shown in Figure 25. As you drag the middle handles, the object's size and proportions are changed.
8. Click **Edit** on the menu bar, then click **Undo** to return the arrow to its original size.

You used the Free Transform tool and the Scale option to display an object's handles, and you used the handles to resize and reshape the object.

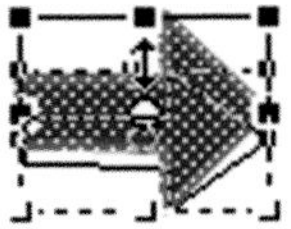

Rotate, skew, and flip an object

1. Verify that the arrow is selected (dot pattern displayed), click the **Free Transform tool** ⊡ , then click the **Rotate and Skew option** ⟲ in the Options section of the Tools panel.

2. Click the upper-right corner handle, then rotate the object clockwise.

3. Click the upper-middle handle, then drag it to the right.

   The arrow slants to the right.

4. Click **Edit** on the menu bar, click the **Undo** command, then repeat until the arrow is in its original shape and orientation.

5. Click the **Selection tool** ▶ on the Tools panel, verify that the bottom arrow is selected, click **Window** on the menu bar, then click **Transform**.

6. Double-click the **Rotate text box**, type **45**, then press **[Enter]** (Win) or **[return]** (Mac).

7. Click **Edit** on the menu bar, then click **Undo**.

8. Close the Transform panel.

9. Verify that the arrow is selected, click **Modify** on the menu bar, point to **Transform**, then click **Flip Horizontal**.

10. Move the arrows to the positions shown in Figure 26.

    | TIP   Drag a marquee around them to select the fill and the stroke.

11. Save your work.

You used Tools panel options, the Transform panel, and Modify menu commands to rotate, skew, and flip an object.

FIGURE 26
Moving objects on the stage

FIGURE 27
Using the Subselection tool to select an object

FIGURE 28
Using the Subselection tool to drag a handle to reshape the object

FIGURE 29
Using the Selection tool to drag an edge to reshape the object

Change view and reshape an object using the Subselection Tool

1. Select the arrow in the upper-right corner of the stage, click **Edit** on the menu bar, click **Copy**, click **Edit** on the menu bar, then click **Paste in Center**.
2. Click the **Zoom tool** on the Tools panel, then click the middle of the copied object to enlarge the view.
3. Click the **Subselection tool** on the Tools panel, then click the tip of the arrow to display the handles, as shown in Figure 27.

   | TIP   The handles allow you to change any segment of the object.

4. Click the handle at the tip of the arrow, then drag it, as shown in Figure 28.
5. Click the **Zoom tool** on the Tools panel, click the **Reduce option button** in the Options section of the Tools panel, then click the middle of the arrow.
6. Click the **Fill Color tool**, click the **blue color swatch**, click the **Oval tool** on the Tools panel, verify that the **Object Drawing option** in the Options section of the Tools panel is deselected, then draw a circle to the left of the middle arrow.
7. Click the **Selection tool** on the Tools panel, then point to the left edge of the circle until the Arc pointer is displayed.
8. Drag the pointer to the position shown in Figure 29.
9. Save your work.

You used the Zoom tool to change the view, and you used the Subselection and Selection tools to reshape objects.

WORK WITH TEXT
AND TEXT OBJECTS

What You'll Do

Classic Car Club

Join Us Now

We have great events
each year including a
Car Rally!

In this lesson, you will enter text using text blocks. You will also resize text blocks, change text attributes, and transform text.

Learning About Text

Macromedia Flash provides a great deal of flexibility when using text. Among other settings, you can select the typeface (font), size, style (bold, italic), and color (including gradients) of text. You can transform the text by rotating, scaling, skewing, and flipping it. You can even break apart a letter and reshape its segments.

Entering Text and Changing the Text Block

It is important to understand that text is entered into a text block, as shown in Figure 30. You use the Text tool to place a text block on the stage and to enter and edit text. A text block expands as more text is entered and may even extend beyond the edge of the stage. You can adjust the size of the text block so that it is a fixed width by dragging the handle in the upper- right corner of the block. Figure 31 shows the process of using the Text tool to enter text and resize the text block. Once you select the tool, you click the pointer on the stage where you want the text to appear. An

insertion point indicates where in the text block the next character will appear when typed. You can reshape the text block by pressing [Enter] (Win) or [return] (Mac) or by dragging the circle handle. After reshaping the text block, the circle handle changes to a square, indicating that the text block now has a fixed horizontal width. Then, when you enter more text, it automatically wraps within the text block. You can resize or move the text block at any time by selecting it with the Selection tool and dragging the section.

Changing Text Attributes

You can use the Properties panel to change the font, size, and style of a single character or an entire text block. Figure 32 shows the Properties panel when a text object is selected. You select text, display the Properties panel, and make the desired changes. You can use the Selection tool to select the entire text block by drawing a box around it. You can use the Text tool to select a single character or string of characters by dragging the

I-beam pointer over them, as shown in Figure 33.

Working with Paragraphs

When working on large bodies of text, such as paragraphs, Macromedia Flash provides many of the features found in a word processor. You can align paragraphs (left, right, center, justified) within a text block. You can use the Properties panel to set margins (space between the border of a text block and the paragraph text), indents for the first line of a paragraph, and line spacing (distance between paragraphs).

Transforming Text

It is important to understand that a text block is an object. Therefore, you can transform (reshape, rotate, skew, and so on) a text block as you would other objects. If you want to transform individual characters within a text block, you must first break it apart. Use the Selection tool to select the text block, and then click the Break Apart command on the Modify menu. Each character (or a group of characters) in the text block can now be selected and transformed.

FIGURE 30
A text block

FIGURE 31
Using the Text tool

FIGURE 32
The Properties panel when a text object is selected

FIGURE 33
Dragging the I-Beam pointer to select text

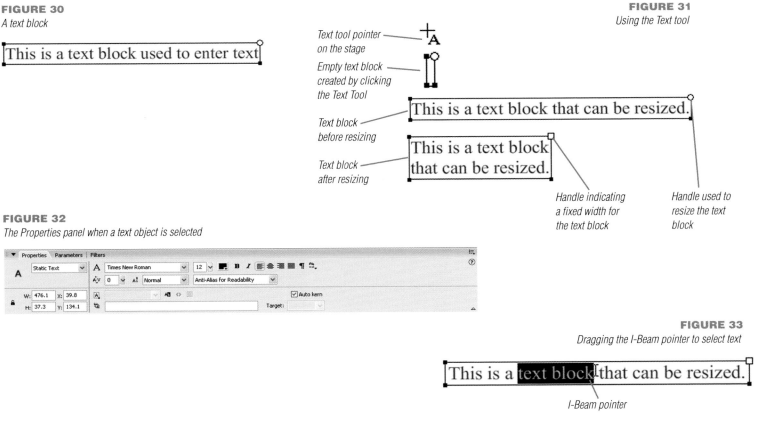

Enter text and change text attributes

1. Click **Layer 5**, insert a new layer, then insert a keyframe in Frame 25 of the new layer.

2. Click the **Text tool** **A** on the Tools panel, click the center of the stage, click in the **text box**, then type **We have great events each year including a Rally!**

3. Click the **I-Beam pointer** ⌶ before the word "Rally," as shown in Figure 34, then type **Car**.

4. Verify that the Property inspector panel is displayed, then drag the I-Beam pointer ⌶ across the text to select all the text.

5. Click the **Font list arrow**, click **Arial Black**, click the **Font Size list arrow**, then drag the slider to **16**.

6. Click the **Text (fill) color swatch** , click the **Hex Edit text box**, type **#990000**, then press **[Enter]** (Win) or **[return]** (Mac).

7. Position the **text pointer** +A over the circle handle until the pointer changes to a double arrow ↔, then drag the handle to the left, as shown in Figure 35.

8. Highlight the text using the text pointer +A, then click the **Align Center button** 🔳 in the Property inspector.

9. Click the **Selection tool** ▸ on the Tools panel, click the text object, then drag the object to the lower middle of the stage.

   TIP The Selection tool is used to select the text block, and the Text tool is used to select and edit the text within the text block.

You entered text, and also resized the text block and changed the font, type size, text color and text alignment.

FIGURE 34
Using the Text tool to enter text

We have great events each year including a |Rally!

FIGURE 35
Resizing the text block

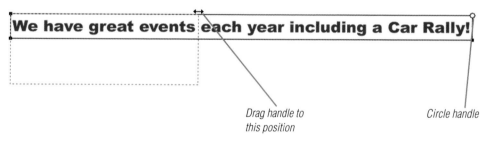

We have great events each year including a Car Rally!

Drag handle to this position

Circle handle

Using Filters

You can apply special effects, such as drop shadows, to text using the Filters option in the Property inspector. The process is to select the desired text, click the Filters tab in the Property inspector panel, choose the desired effect, and make any adjustments, such as changing the color of a gradient glow.

FIGURE 36
The Filters options in the Property inspector panel

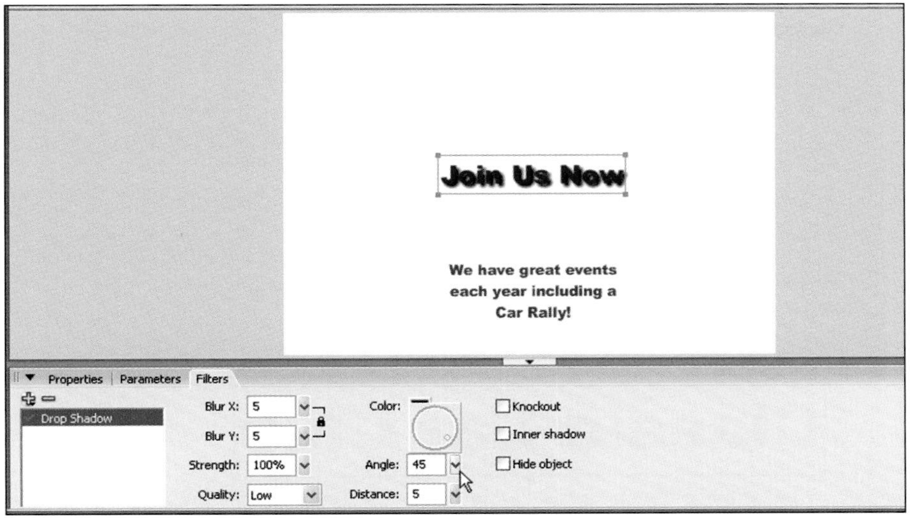

Add a Filter effect to text

1. Click the **Text tool A** on the Tools panel, click the center of the stage, click in the **text box**, then type **Join Us Now**.

2. Drag the **Text pointer** across the text to select it, then use the Property inspector to change the Font size to **30** and the Fill color to **#003399**.

3. Click **Filters** on the title bar of the Property inspector.

4. Click the **Add filter icon** , then click **Drop Shadow**.

5. Click the **Selection tool** in the Tools panel, then verify that the **text block** is selected.

6. Click the **Angle option list arrow** in the Filters section of the Property inspector, as shown in Figure 36.

7. Click and rotate the small circle within the larger circle and notice the changes in the drop shadow.

8. Set the angle to **50**.

9. Click the **Distance list arrow**, then move the slider and notice the changes in the drop shadow.

10. Set the Distance to **5**.

11. Save your work.

You used the Filter feature to create a drop shadow and then made changes to it.

Skew text

1. Verify that **Text tool** **A** is selected, click the pointer near the top middle of the stage, click in the **text box**, then type **Classic Car Club**.

   The attributes of the new text reflect the most recent settings changed in the Properties panel.

2. Drag the **I-Beam pointer** Ⅰ across the text to select it, then using the Property inspector change the font size to **40** and the fill color to **#990000**.

3. Click the **Selection tool** ▲ on the Tools panel, click the **Free Transform tool** ⊡ on the Tools panel, then click the **Rotate and Skew option** ⟳ in the Options section of the Tools panel.

4. Drag the top middle handle to the right to skew the text, as shown in Figure 37.

You entered a heading, changed the type size, and skewed text using the Free Transform tool.

FIGURE 37
Skewing the text

Classic Car Club

FIGURE 38

Reshaping a letter

*A portion of the letter
will extend outward.*

FIGURE 39

Applying a gradient fill to each letter

Reshape and apply a gradient to text

1. Click the **Selection tool** on the Tools panel, click the Classic Car Club text block to select it, click **Modify** on the menu bar, then click **Break Apart**.

 The words are now individual text blocks.

2. Click **Modify** on the menu bar, then click **Break Apart**.

 The letters are filled with a dot pattern, indicating that they can now be edited.

3. Click the **Zoom tool** on the Tools panel, click the **Enlarge option** in the Options section of the Tools panel, then click the **"C"** in Classic.

4. Click the **Subselection tool** on the Tools panel, then click the edge of the letter **"C"** to display the object's segment handles.

5. Drag a lower handle on the "C" in Classic, as shown in Figure 38.

6. Click the **Selection tool** , click the **Fill Color tool** on the Tools panel, then click the **red gradient color swatch** in the bottom row of the color palette.

7. Click the **Paint Bucket tool** on the Tools panel, then click the top of each letter to change the fill to a red gradient, as shown in Figure 39.

8. Click the **Selection tool** on the Tools panel, click **View** on the menu bar, point to **Magnification**, then click **Fit in Window**.

9. Click **Control** on the menu bar, click **Test Movie**, watch the movie, then close the Flash Player window.

10. Save your work, then close the movie.

You broke apart a text block, reshaped text, and added a gradient to the text.

WORK WITH LAYERS
AND OBJECTS

What You'll Do

▶ *In this lesson, you will create, rename, reorder, delete, hide, and lock layers. You will also display outline layers, use a Guide layer, distribute text to layers, and create a folder layer.*

Learning About Layers

Macromedia Flash uses two types of spatial organization. First, there is the position of objects on the stage, and then there is the stacking order of objects that overlap. An example of overlapping objects is text placed on a banner. Layers are used on the timeline as a way to organize objects. Placing objects on their own layer makes them easier to work with, especially when reshaping them, repositioning them on the stage, or rearranging their order in relation to other objects. In addition, layers are useful for organizing other elements such as sounds, animations, and ActionScript.

There are six types of layers:

Normal—The default layer type. All objects on these layers appear in the movie.

Guide (Standard and Motion)—Standard Guide layers serve as a reference point for positioning objects on the stage. Motion Guide layers are used to create a path for animated objects to follow.

Guided—A layer that contains an animated object, linked to a Motion Guide layer.

Mask—A layer that hides and reveals portions of another layer.

Masked—A layer that contains the objects that are hidden and revealed by a Mask layer.

Folder—A layer that can contain other layers.

Motion Guide and Mask layer types will be covered in a later chapter.

Working with Layers

The Layer Properties dialog box allows you to specify the type of layer. It also allows you to name, show (and hide), and lock them. Naming a layer provides a clue to the objects on the layer. For example, naming a layer Logo might indicate that the object on the layer is the company's logo. Hiding a layer(s) may reduce the clutter on the stage and make it easier to work with selected objects from the layer(s) that are not hidden. Locking a layer(s) prevents the objects from being accidentally edited. Other options in the Layer Properties dialog box allow you to view layers as outlines and change the outline color. Outlines can be used to help you determine which objects are on a layer. When you turn on this feature, each layer has a colored box that corresponds with the color of the objects on its layer, as shown in Figure 40. Icons on the Layers section of the timeline correspond to features in the Layer Properties dialog box, as shown in Figure 41.

FIGURE 40
Displaying outlines

Show Outline icon

Color of the outline box corresponds with the color of the objects on the layer

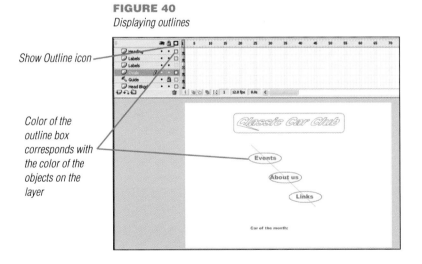

FIGURE 41
The Layers section of the timeline

Show/Hide All Layers

Show All Layers as Outlines

Lock/Unlock All Layers

Lock/Unlock This Layer

Insert a layer button

Show/Hide This Layer

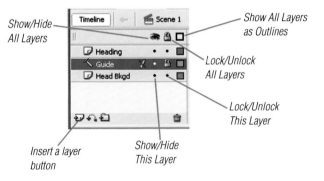

Using a Guide Layer

Guide layers are useful in aligning objects on the stage. Figure 42 shows a Guide layer that has been used to align three buttons along a diagonal path. The process is to insert a new layer, click the Layer command on the Modify menu to display the Layer Properties dialog box, select Guides as the layer type, then draw a path that will be used as the guide to align objects. You then display the Guides options from the View menu, turn on Snap to Guides, and drag the desired objects to the Guide line. Objects have a registration point that is used to snap when snapping to a guide. By default, this point is at the center of the object. Figure 43 shows the process.

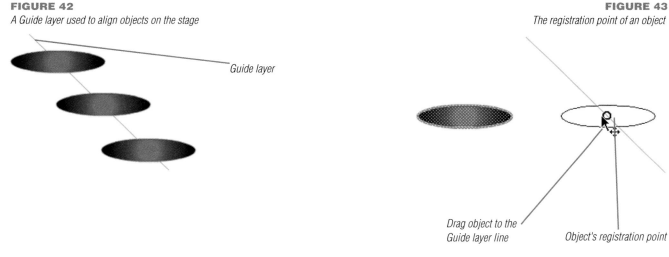

FIGURE 42
A Guide layer used to align objects on the stage

Guide layer

FIGURE 43
The registration point of an object

Drag object to the Guide layer line

Object's registration point

Distributing Text to Layers

Text blocks are made up of one or more characters. When you break apart a text block, each character becomes an object that can be edited independent of the other characters. You can use the Distribute to Layers command to cause each character to automatically be placed on its own layer. Figure 44 shows the seven layers created after the text block containing 55 Chevy has been broken apart and distributed to layers.

Using Folder Layers

As movies become larger and more complex, the number of layers increases. Macromedia Flash allows you to organize layers by creating folders and grouping other layers in them. Figure 45 shows a layers folder—Layer 6—with seven layers in it. You can click the Folder layer triangle next to Layer 6 to open and close the folder.

FIGURE 44
Distributing text to layers

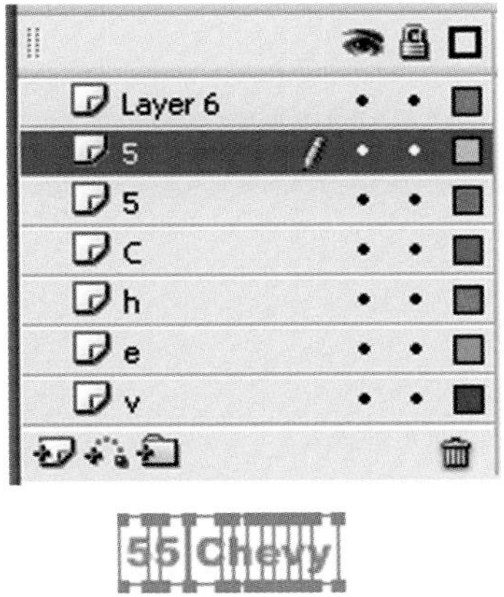

FIGURE 45
A folder layer

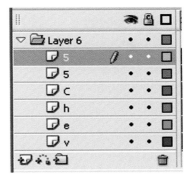

Create and reorder layers

1. Open fl2_1.fla from the drive and folder where your Data Files are stored, then save it as **layers2.fla**.

2. Click **View** on the menu bar, point to **Magnification**, then click **Fit in Window**.

3. Click the **Insert Layer icon** on the bottom of the timeline (below the layer names) to insert a new layer, Layer 2.

4. Click the **Rectangle tool** on the Tools panel, then click the **Set Corner Radius option** in the Options section of the Tools panel.

5. Type **10**, then click **OK**.

6. Click the **Fill Color tool** on the Tools panel, click the **Hex Edit text box**, type **#999999**, then press **[Enter]** (Win) or **[return]** (Mac).

7. Click the **Stroke Color tool** on the Tools panel, click the **Hex Edit text box**, type **#000000**, then press **[Enter]** (Win) or **[return]** (Mac).

8. Draw the rectangle shown in Figure 46 so it masks the text heading.

9. Drag Layer 1 above Layer 2 on the timeline, as shown in Figure 47.

You added a layer, drew an object on the layer, and reordered layers.

FIGURE 46
Drawing a rectangle with a rounded corner

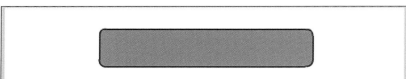

FIGURE 47
Dragging Layer 1 above Layer 2

Drag Layer 1
above Layer 2

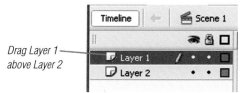

FIGURE 48
Renaming layers

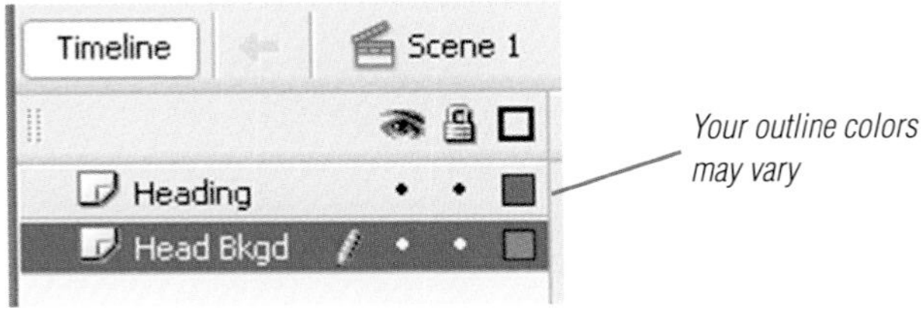

Timeline
Scene 1
Heading
Head Bkgd
Your outline colors may vary

Rename and delete layers on the timeline

1. Double-click **Layer 1** on the timeline, type **Heading** in the Layer Name text box, then press **[Enter]** (Win) or **[return]** (Mac).
2. Rename Layer 2 as **Head Bkgd**. Compare your timeline to Figure 48.
3. Click the **Heading layer**, then click the **Delete Layer icon** on the bottom of the timeline.
4. Click **Edit** on the menu bar, then click **Undo Delete Layer**.

You renamed layers to associate them with objects on the layers, then deleted and restored a layer.

Hide, lock, and display layer outlines

1. Click the **Show/Hide All Layers icon** 👁 to hide all layers, then compare your image to Figure 49.

2. Click the **Show/Hide All Layers icon** 👁 to show all the layers.

3. Click the **Heading layer**, then click the **Show/Hide icon** • twice to hide and show the layer.

4. Click the **Lock/Unlock All Layers icon** 🔒 to lock all layers.

5. With the layers locked, try to select and edit an object.

6. Click the **Lock/Unlock All Layers icon** 🔒 again to unlock the layers.

7. Click the **Show All Layers as Outlines icon** □ twice to display and turn off the outlines of all objects.

You hid and locked layers and displayed the outlines of objects in a layer.

FIGURE 49
Hiding all the layers

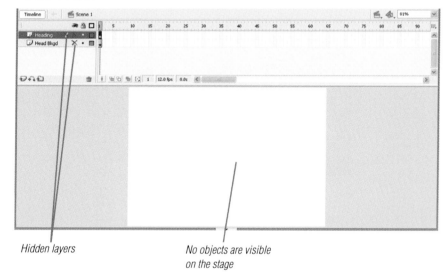

Hidden layers

No objects are visible on the stage

FIGURE 50
A diagonal line

Classic Car Club

Car of the month:

FIGURE 51
Layer 3 locked

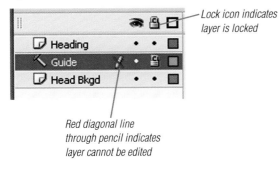

Lock icon indicates
layer is locked

Red diagonal line
through pencil indicates
layer cannot be edited

Create a guide for a Guide layer

1. Click the **Head Bkgd layer**, then click the **Insert Layer icon** on the timeline to add a new layer, Layer 3.

2. Rename the layer **Guide**.

3. Click **Modify** on the menu bar, point to **Timeline**, click **Layer Properties** to display the Layer Properties dialog box, click the **Guide option button**, then click **OK**.

4. Click the **Line tool** on the Tools panel, press and hold **[Shift]**, then draw the diagonal line, as shown in Figure 50.

5. Click the **Lock/Unlock This Layer icon** in Layer 3 to lock it, then compare your layers to Figure 51.

You created a guide for a Guide layer and drew a guide line.

Add objects to a Guide layer

1. Add a new layer on the timeline. Name it **Ovals**, then click **Frame 1** of the Ovals layer.

2. Click the **Fill Color tool**  on the Tools panel, then click the **red gradient color swatch** in the bottom row of the color palette, if necessary.

3. Click the **Oval tool** ○ on the Tools panel, then verify that the **Object Drawing option** ▣ in the Options section of the Tools panel is deselected.

4. Draw the oval, as shown in Figure 52.

5. Click the **Selection tool** ▶ on the Tools panel, then draw a marquee around the oval object to select it.

   TIP Make sure the entire object (stroke and fill) is selected and slowly drag the object so that its center is on the line.

6. Point to the center of the oval, click, then slowly drag it to the Guide layer line, as shown in Figure 53.

7. With the oval object selected, click **Edit** on the menu bar, then click **Copy**.

8. Click **Edit** on the menu bar, click **Paste in Center**, then, if necessary, align the copied object to the Guide layer line beneath the first oval.

9. Click **Edit** on the menu bar, click **Paste in Center**, then align the copied object to the bottom of the Guide layer line.

   TIP Objects are pasted in the center of the stage, and one object may cover up another object.

You created a Guide Layer and used it to align objects on the stage.

FIGURE 52
An oval object

FIGURE 53
Dragging an object to the Guide layer line

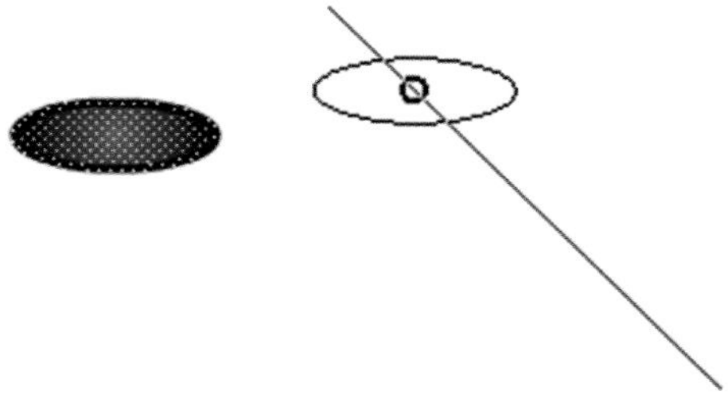

FIGURE 54

Adding text to the oval objects

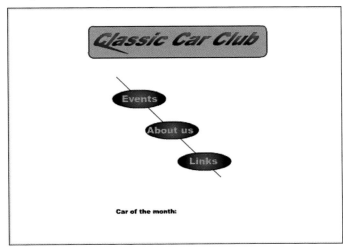

1. Insert a new layer on the timeline, then name it **Labels**.

2. Click Frame 1 of the Labels layer.

3. Click the **Text tool A** on the Tools panel, click the top oval, then type **Events**.

4. Drag the **I-Beam pointer** across Events to select the text, then using the Property inspector, set the font to **Arial Black**, the font size to **16**, and the fill color to **#999999**, if necessary.

5. Click the **Selection tool** on the Tools panel, click the text box to select it, then drag the text box to center it on the oval, as shown in Figure 54.

    TIP   Use the arrow keys on the keyboard to nudge the text in place, if necessary.

6. Repeat Steps 3 through 5, typing **About us** and **Links** text blocks.

7. Test the movie, then save and close the document.

8. Exit Flash.

You used the Text tool to create text blocks that were placed above objects.

Draw objects with the drawing tools.

1. Start Macromedia Flash, create a new Flash document, then save it as **skillsdemo2**.
2. Display the Grid.
3. Set the stroke color to black (Hex: 000000) and the fill color to blue (Hex: 0000FF).
4. Use the Oval tool to draw an oval on the left side of the stage, then draw a circle beneath the oval.
5. Use the Rectangle tool to draw a rectangle in the middle of the stage, then draw a square beneath the rectangle. If necessary, change the Round Rectangle Radius to 0.
6. Use the Line tool to draw a horizontal line on the right side of the stage, then draw a vertical line beneath the horizontal line and a diagonal line beneath the vertical line.
7. Use the Pen tool to draw an arrow-shaped object above the rectangle.
8. Use the Pencil tool to draw a freehand line above the oval, then use the Smooth option to smooth out the line.
9. Save your work.

Select and edit objects.

1. Use the Selection tool to select the stroke of the circle, then deselect the stroke.
2. Use the Selection tool to select the fill of the circle, then deselect the fill.
3. Use the Lasso tool to select several of the objects, then deselect them.
4. Use the Ink Bottle tool to change the stroke color of the circle to red (Hex #FF0000).
5. Use the Paint Bucket tool to change the fill color of the square to a red gradient.
6. Change the fill color of the oval to a blue gradient.
7. Save your work.

Work with objects.

1. Copy and paste the arrow object.
2. Move the copied arrow to another location on the stage.
3. Rescale both arrows to approximately half their original size.
4. Flip the copied arrow horizontally.
5. Rotate the rectangle to a 45° angle.
6. Skew the square to the right.
7. Copy one of the arrows and use the Subselection tool to reshape it, then delete it.
8. Use the Selection tool to reshape the circle to a crescent shape.
9. Save your work.

Enter and edit text.

1. Enter the following text in a text block at the top of the stage: **Gateway to the Pacific**.
2. Change the text to font: Tahoma, size: 24, color: red.
3. Use the gridlines to help align the text block to the top center of the stage.
4. Skew the text block to the right.
5. Save your work.

Work with layers.

1. Insert a layer into the document.
2. Change the name on the new layer to **Heading Bkgnd**.
3. Draw a rounded corner rectangle that covers the words Gateway to the Pacific.
4. Switch the order of the layers.
5. Lock all layers.
6. Unlock all layers.
7. Hide the Heading Bkgnd layer.
8. Show the Heading Bkgnd layer.
9. Show all layers as outlines.
10. Turn off the view of the outlines.
11. Create a Guide layer and move the arrows to it.
12. Add a layer and use the Text tool to type **SEATTLE** below the heading.
13. Break the text block apart and distribute the text to layers.
14. Create a Folder layer and add each of the SEATTLE text layers to it.
15. Save your work.

Use the Merge Drawing Model mode.

1. Insert a new layer and name it **MergeDraw**.
2. Click the Rectangle tool and verify that the Object Drawing option is deselected.
3. Draw a square, then use the Oval tool to draw a circle with a different color that covers approximately half of the square.
4. Use the Selection tool to drag the circle off of the square.

Use the Object Drawing Model mode.

1. Insert a new layer and name it **ObjectDraw**.
2. Click the Rectangle tool and click the Object Drawing option to select it.
3. Draw a square, then use the Oval tool to draw a circle with a different color that covers approximately half of the square.
4. Use the Selection tool to drag the circle off of the square.

5. Save your work, then compare your image to the example shown in Figure 55.
6. Test the movie, then save and close the document.
7. Exit Flash.

FIGURE 55
Completed Skills Review

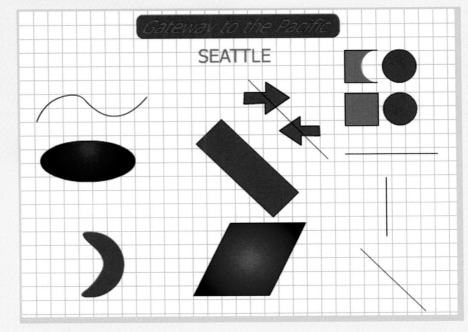

A local travel company, Ultimate Tours, has asked you to design several sample homepages for their new Web site. The goal of the Web site is to inform potential customers of their services. The company specializes in exotic treks, tours, and cruises. Thus, while their target audience spans a wide age range, they are all looking for something out of the ordinary.

1. Open a new Flash Document and save it as **ultimatetours2**.
2. Set the document properties, including the size and background color.
3. Create the following on separate layers and name the layers:
   - A text heading; select a font size and font color. Skew the heading, break it apart, then reshape one or more of the characters.
   - A subheading with a different font size and color.
   - A guide path.
   - At least three objects.
4. Snap the objects to the guide path.
5. On another layer, add text to the objects and place them on the guide path.
6. Lock all layers.
7. Compare your image to the example shown in Figure 56.
8. Save your work.
9. Test the movie, then close the movie.

FIGURE 56
Sample completed Project Builder 1

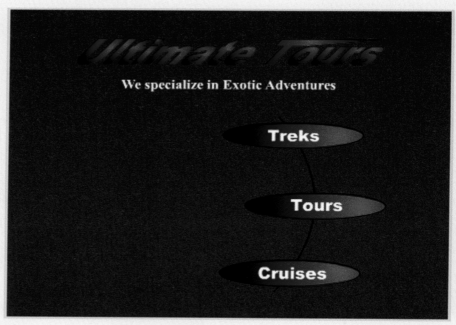

Drawing in Macromedia Flash

You have been asked to create several sample designs for the homepage of a new organization called The Jazz Club. The club is being organized to bring together music enthusiasts for social events and charitable fund-raising activities. They plan to sponsor weekly jam sessions and a show once a month. Because the club is just getting started, the organizers are looking to you for help in developing a Web site.

1. Plan the site by specifying the goal, target audience, treatment ("look and feel"), and elements you want to include (text, graphics, sound, and so on).
2. Sketch out a storyboard that shows the layout of the objects on the various screens and how they are linked together. Be creative in your design.
3. Open a new movie and save it as **thejazzclub2**.
4. Set the document properties, including the size and background color, if desired.
5. Display the gridlines and rulers and use them to help align objects on the stage.
6. Create a heading with a background, text objects, and drawings to be used as links to the categories of information provided on the Web site.
7. Hide the gridlines and rulers.
8. Save your work, then compare your image to the example shown in Figure 57.

FIGURE 57
Sample completed Project Builder 2

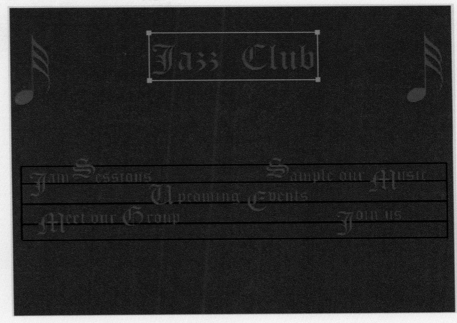

Drawing in Macromedia Flash

Figure 58 shows the homepage of a Web site. Study the figure and complete the following. For each question indicate how you determined your answer.

1. Connect to the Internet, go to *www.course.com*, navigate to the page for this book, click the Online Companion link, then click the link for this chapter.

2. Open a document in a word processor or open a new Macromedia Flash document, save the file as **dpc2**, then answer the following questions. (*Hint*: Use the Text tool in Macromedia Flash.)

   - Whose Web site is this?
   - What is the goal(s) of the site?
   - Who is the target audience?
   - What is the treatment ("look and feel") that is used?
   - What are the design layout guidelines being used (balance, movement, and so on)?
   - What may be animated on this homepage?
   - Do you think this is an effective design for the company, its products, and its target audience? Why or why not?
   - What suggestions would you make to improve on the design and why?

FIGURE 58
Design Project

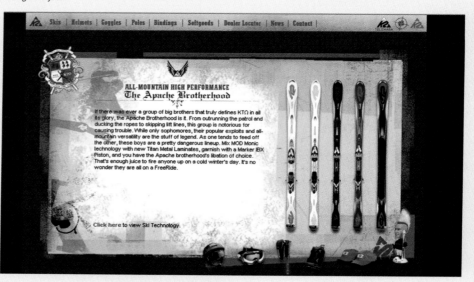

After weeks of unsuccessful job hunting, you have decided to create a personal portfolio of your work. The portfolio will be a Web site done completely in Macromedia Flash.

1. Research what should be included in a portfolio.
2. Plan the site by specifying the goal, target audience, treatment ("look and feel"), and elements you want to include (text, graphics, sound, and so on).
3. Sketch out a storyboard that shows the layout of the objects on the various screens and how they are linked together. Be creative in your design.
4. Design the homepage to include personal data, contact information, previous employment, education, and samples of your work.
5. Open a new Flash document and save it as **portfolio2**.
6. Set the document properties, including the size and background color, if desired.
7. Display the gridlines and rulers and use them to help align objects on the stage.
8. Add a border the size of the stage. (*Hint*: Use the Rectangle tool and set the fill color to none.)

9. Create a heading with its own background, then create other text objects and drawings to be used as links to the categories of information provided on the Web site. (*Hint*: In this file, the Tahoma font is used. You can replace this font with Impact or any other appropriate font on your computer.)
10. Hide the gridlines and rulers.
11. Save your work, then compare your image to the example shown in Figure 59.

FIGURE 59
Sample completed Portfolio Project

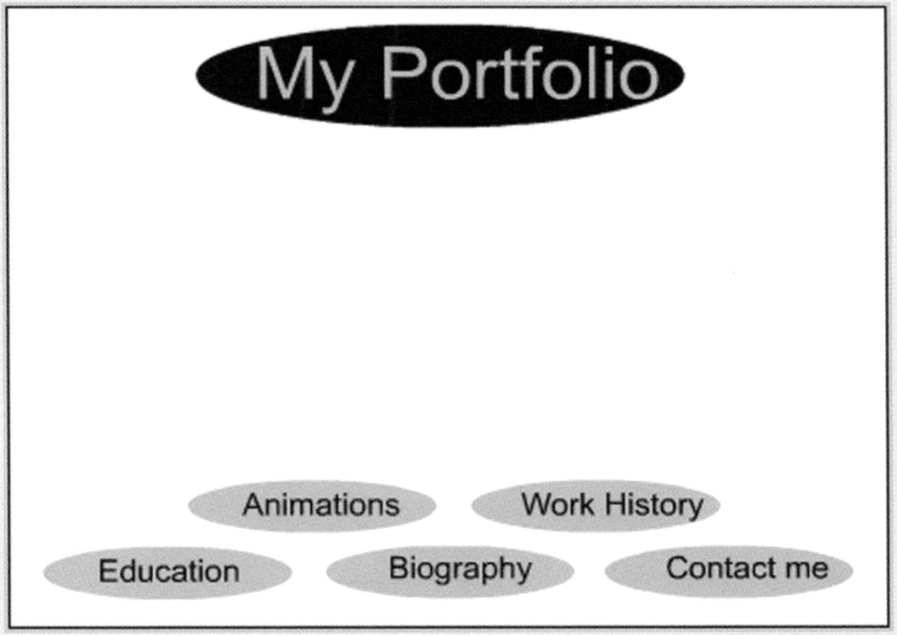

Drawing in Macromedia Flash

chapter

WORKING WITH SYMBOLS
AND INTERACTIVITY

1. Create symbols and instances.

2. Work with Libraries.

3. Create buttons.

4. Assign actions to buttons.

3 WORKING WITH SYMBOLS
AND INTERACTIVITY

Introduction

An important benefit of Macromedia Flash is its ability to create movies with small file sizes. This allows the movies to be delivered from the Web more quickly. One way to keep the file sizes small is to create reusable graphics, buttons, and movie clips. Macromedia Flash allows you to create a graphic (drawing) and then make unlimited copies, which you can use in other movies. Macromedia Flash calls the original drawing a **symbol** and the copied drawings **instances**. Using instances reduces the movie file size because Macromedia Flash needs to store only the symbol's information (size, shape, color). When you want to use a symbol in a movie, Macromedia Flash creates an instance (copy), but does not save the instance in the Macromedia Flash movie; this keeps down the movie's file size. What is especially valuable about this process is that you can change the attributes (such as color and shape) for each instance. For example, if your Web site contains drawings of cars, you have to create just one drawing, insert as many instances of the car as you like, and then change the instances accordingly. Macromedia Flash stores symbols in the Library panel—each time you need a copy of the symbol, you can open the Library panel and drag the symbol to the stage, creating an instance of the symbol.

There are three categories of symbols: graphic, button, and movie clip. A graphic symbol is useful because you can reuse a single image and make changes in each instance of the image. A button symbol is useful because you can create buttons for interactivity, such as starting or stopping a movie. A movie clip symbol is useful for creating complex animations because you can create a movie within a movie. Movie clips will be covered in a later chapter.

Tools You'll Use

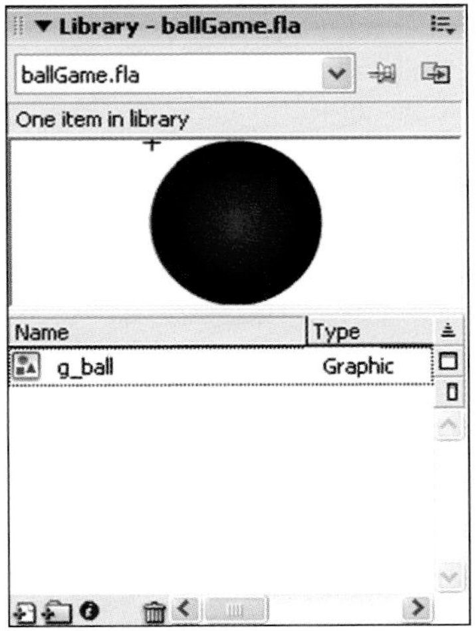

Convert to Symbol

Name: [Symbol 1]

Type: ○ Movie clip   Registration: ▪□□
○ Button   □□□
⊙ Graphic

OK
Cancel
Advanced

▼ **Library - ballGame.fla**

ballGame.fla

One item in library

Name	Type	
g_ball	Graphic	

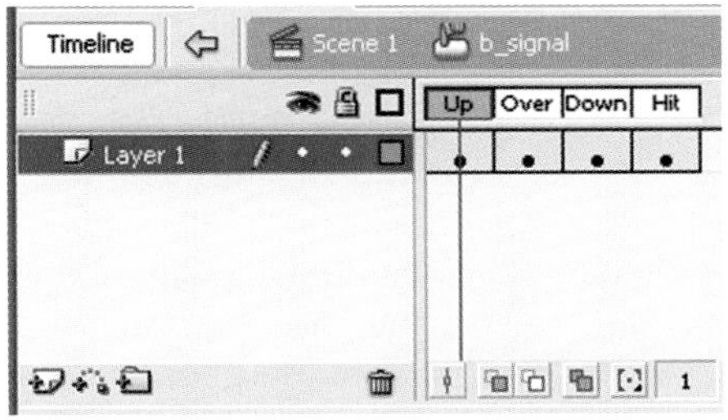

Timeline ⇦ Scene 1 b_signal

Up | Over | Down | Hit

Layer 1

1

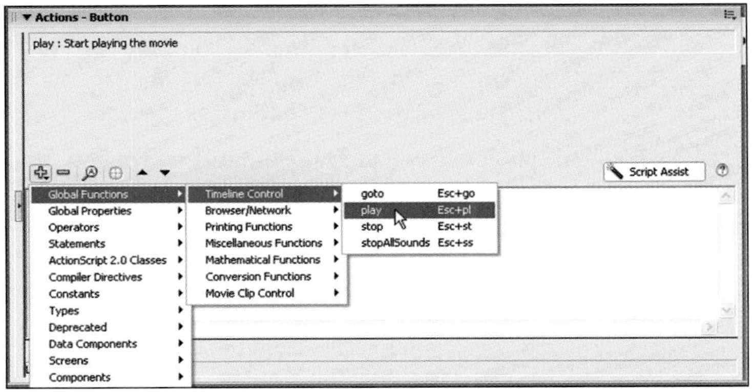

▼ **Actions - Button**

play : Start playing the movie

Global Functions ▶	Timeline Control ▶	goto	Esc+go
Global Properties ▶	Browser/Network ▶	play	Esc+pl
Operators ▶	Printing Functions ▶	stop	Esc+st
Statements ▶	Miscellaneous Functions ▶	stopAllSounds	Esc+ss
ActionScript 2.0 Classes ▶	Mathematical Functions ▶		
Compiler Directives ▶	Conversion Functions ▶		
Constants ▶	Movie Clip Control ▶		
Types ▶			
Deprecated ▶			
Data Components ▶			
Screens ▶			
Components ▶			

Script Assist

CREATE SYMBOLS
AND INSTANCES

What You'll Do

▶ *In this lesson, you will create graphic symbols, turn them into instances, and then edit the instances.*

Creating a Graphic Symbol

You can use the New Symbol command on the Insert menu to create and then draw a symbol. You can also draw an object and then use the Convert to Symbol command on the Modify menu to convert the object to a symbol. The Convert to Symbol dialog box, shown in Figure 1, allows you to name the symbol and specify the type of symbol you want to create (Movie Clip, Button, or Graphic). When naming a symbol, it's a good idea to use a naming convention that allows you to quickly identify the type of symbol and to group like symbols together. For example, you could identify all graphic symbols by naming them g_*name* and all buttons as b_*name*.

After you complete the Convert to Symbol dialog box, Macromedia Flash places the symbol in the Library panel, as shown in Figure 2. To create an instance of the symbol, you simply drag a symbol from the Library panel to the stage. To edit a symbol, you select it from the Library panel or use the Edit Symbol command on the Edit menu. When you edit a

symbol, the changes are reflected in all instances of that symbol in your movie. For example, you can draw a car, convert the car to a symbol, and then create several instances of the car. You can uniformly change the size of all the cars by selecting the car symbol from the Library panel and then rescaling it to the desired size.

Working with Instances

You can have as many instances as needed in your movie, and you can edit each one to make it somewhat different than the others. You can rotate, skew (slant), and resize graphic and button instances. In addition, you can change the color, brightness, and transparency. However, there are some limitations. An instance is a single object with no segments or parts, such as a stroke and a fill—you cannot select a part of an instance. Therefore, any changes to the color of the instance are made to the entire object. Of course, you can use layers to stack other objects on top of an instance to change its appearance. In addition, you can use the Break Apart command on the Modify menu to break the link between an instance and a symbol. Once the link is broken, you can make any changes to the object, such as changing its stroke and fill color. However, because the link is broken, the object is no longer an instance, and any changes you make to the original symbol would not affect the object.

The process for creating an instance is to open the Library panel and drag the desired symbol to the stage. You select an instance by using the Selection tool to draw a box around it. A blue border indicates that the object has been selected. Then, you can use the Free Transform tool options (such as Rotate and Skew, or Scale) to modify the entire image, or you can break apart the instance and edit individual lines and fills.

QUICKTIP

You need to be careful when editing an instance. Use the Selection tool to draw a box around the instance, or click the object once to select it. Do not double-click the instance; otherwise, you will open an edit window that is used to edit the symbol, not the instance.

FIGURE 1

Using the Convert to Symbol dialog box to convert a symbol

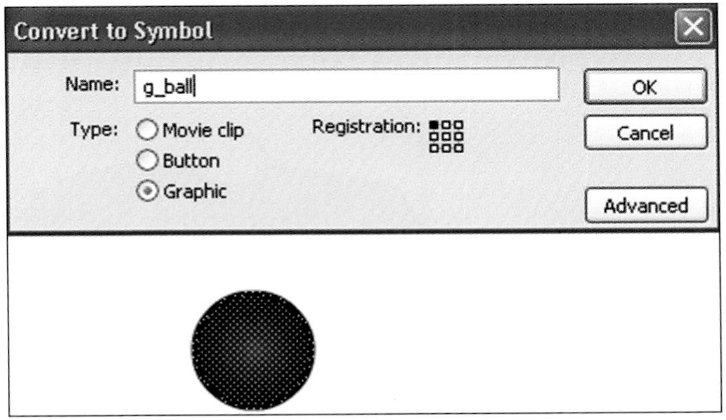

Convert to Symbol
Name:
g_ball
OK
Type:
Movie clip
Button
Graphic
Registration:
Cancel
Advanced

FIGURE 2

A graphic symbol in the Library panel

Library - ballGame.fla
ballGame.fla
One item in library
Name
Type
g_ball
Graphic

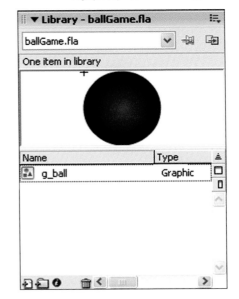

Create a symbol

1. Open fl3_1.fla from the drive and folder where your Data Files are stored, then save it as **coolcar**.

2. Hide all panels, display the Property inspector, the Library panel, and the Tools panel, then set the magnification to **Fit in Window**.

3. Click the **Selection tool** on the Tools panel, then drag the marquee around the car to select it.

4. Click **Modify** on the menu bar, then click **Convert to Symbol**.

5. Type **g_car** in the Name text box.

6. Click the **Graphic option button**, as shown in Figure 3, then click **OK**.

7. Click the **g_car symbol** in the Library panel to display the car, as shown in Figure 4.

You opened a file with an object, converted the object to a symbol, and displayed the symbol in the Library panel.

g_car symbol

FIGURE 5
Creating an instance

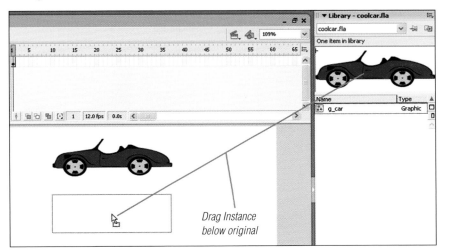

Drag Instance below original

FIGURE 6
The alpha set to 50%

Create and edit an instance

1. Point to the car image in the Item Preview window, then drag the image to the stage beneath the first car, as shown in Figure 5.

   TIP You can also drag the name of the symbol from the Library panel to the stage.

2. Click the **Selection tool** on the Tools panel (if necessary), verify that the bottom car is selected, click **Modify** on the menu bar, point to **Transform**, then click **Flip Horizontal**.

3. Expand the Property inspector, if necessary.

4. Click the **Color list arrow** on the Property inspector, then click **Alpha**.

5. Click the **Alpha Amount list arrow**, then drag the slider to **50%**, and notice how the transparency changes.

   Figure 6 shows the transparency set to 50%.

6. Click a blank area of the stage.

   Changing the alpha setting gives the car a more transparent look.

You created an instance of a symbol and edited the instance on the stage.

Edit a symbol in symbol-editing mode

1. Double-click the **g_car symbol icon** 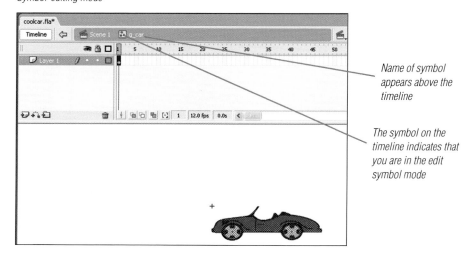 in the Library panel to enter symbol-editing mode, then compare your screen to Figure 7.

   The g_car symbol appears on the stage above the timeline, indicating that you are editing the g_car symbol.

   TIP You can also edit a symbol by clicking Edit on the menu bar, then clicking Edit Symbols.

2. Click a blank area of the stage to deselect the car.

3. Verify that the **Selection tool** ▶ is selected, then click the **light gray hubcap** inside the front wheel to select it.

4. Press and hold **[Shift]**, then click the **hubcap** inside the back wheel to select the fills of both hubcaps.

5. Click the **Fill Color tool** on the Tools panel, click the **blue color swatch** in the left column of the color palette, then compare your image to Figure 8.

   Changes you make to the symbol affect every instance of the symbol on the stage. The hubcap color becomes blue in the Library panel and on the stage.

6. Click **Scene 1** above the Timeline layers to return to the main timeline.

   The hubcap color of the instances on the stage reflects the color changes you made to the symbol.

You edited a symbol in symbol-editing mode that affected all instances of the symbol.

FIGURE 7
Symbol-editing mode

The symbol on the timeline indicates that you are in the edit symbol mode

Name of symbol appears above the timeline

FIGURE 8
Edited symbol

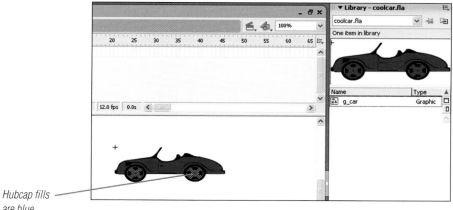

Hubcap fills are blue

FIGURE 9
The car with the maroon body selected

FIGURE 10

Changing the symbol affects only the one instance of the symbol

Instance of the symbol —————

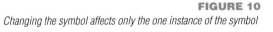

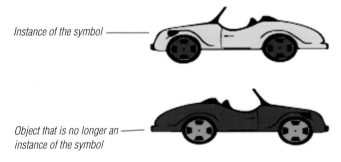

Object that is no longer an —————
instance of the symbol

Break apart an instance

1. Click the **Selection tool** ![pointer] on the Tools panel, then drag the marquee around the bottom car to select it.
2. Click **Modify** on the menu bar, then click **Break Apart**.

   The object is no longer linked to the symbol, and its parts (strokes and fills) can now be edited.
3. Click a blank area of the stage to deselect the object.
4. Click the **blue front hubcap**, press and hold **[Shift]**, then click the **blue back hubcap** to select both hubcaps.
5. Click the **Fill Color tool** ![icon] on the Tools panel, then click the **green color swatch** in the left column of the color palette.
6. Double-click the **g_car symbol icon** ![icon] in the Library window to enter symbol-editing mode.
7. Click the **maroon front body** of the car to select it, press and hold **[Shift]**, then click the **maroon back body** of the car, as shown in Figure 9.
8. Click the **Fill Color tool** ![icon], then click the **yellow color swatch** in the left column of the color palette.
9. Click **Scene 1** above the timeline layers, then compare your image to Figure 10.

   The body color of the car in the original instance is a different color, but the one to which you applied the Break Apart command remains unchanged.
10. Save your work.

You used the Break Apart command to break the link of the instance to its symbol, then you edited the object and the symbol.

WORK WITH
LIBRARIES

What You'll Do

In this lesson, you will use the Library panel to organize the symbols in a movie.

Understanding the Library

The Library in a Macromedia Flash movie contains the movie symbols. The Library provides a way to view and organize the symbols, and allows you to change the symbol name, display symbol properties, and add and delete symbols. Figure 11 shows the Library panel for a movie. Refer to this figure as you read the following description of the parts of the Library.

Title bar—Names the movie with which the Library is associated. The list box below the title bar can be used to display the Library panel of any open document. This allows you to use the objects from other movies in the current movie by simply dragging them to the stage from any Library panel. In addition to the movie libraries, you can create permanent libraries that are available whenever you start Macromedia Flash. Macromedia Flash also has sample libraries that contain buttons and other objects. The permanent and sample libraries are accessed through the Common Libraries command on the Windows menu. All of the assets in all of the libraries are available for use in any movie.

Options menu—Shown in Figure 12; provides access to several features used to edit symbols (such as renaming symbols) and organize symbols (such as creating a new folder).

Item Preview window—Displays the selected symbol. If the symbol is a movie clip, a control button appears allowing you to preview the movie.

Toggle Sorting Order icon—Allows you to reorder the list of folders and symbols within folders.

Wide Library View and Narrow Library View icons—Used to expand and collapse the Library window to display more or less of the symbol properties.

Name text box—Lists the folder and symbol names. Each symbol type has a different icon associated with it. Clicking a symbol name or icon displays the symbol in the Item Preview window.

New Symbol icon—Displays the Create New Symbol dialog box, allowing you to create a new symbol.

New Folder icon—Allows you to create a new folder.

Properties icon—Displays the Symbol Properties dialog box for the selected symbol.

Delete Item icon—Deletes the selected symbol or folder.

FIGURE 11
The Library panel

Title bar

Options menu

Click to list Library panel of any open document

Item Preview window

Toggle Sorting Order icon

Wide Library View icon

Name text box

Narrow Library View icon

Delete icon

New Symbol icon

New Folder icon

Properties icon

FIGURE 12
The Options menu

New Symbol...
New Folder
New Font...
New Video...
Rename
Move to New Folder...
Duplicate...
Delete
Edit
Edit with...
Properties...
Linkage...
Component Definition...
Select Unused Items
Update...
Play
Expand Folder
Collapse Folder
Expand All Folders
Collapse All Folders
Shared Library Properties...
Keep Use Counts Updated
Update Use Counts Now
Help
Group Library with ▸
Close Library
Rename panel group...
Maximize panel group
Close panel group

Create folders in the Library panel

1. Open fl3_2.fla, then save it as **carRace**.

2. Hide all panels, display the Property inspector and the Tools panel, then set the magnification to **Fit in Window**.

3. Click **Window** on the menu bar, then click **Library** to open the Library panel, as shown in Figure 13.

4. Click the **New Folder icon** in the Library panel.

5. Type **Graphics** in the Name text box, then press **[Enter]** (Win) or **[return]** (Mac).

6. Click the **New Folder icon** in the Library panel.

7. Type **Buttons** in the Name text box, then press **[Enter]** (Win) or **[return]** (Mac).

   Your Library panel should resemble Figure 14.

You opened a Macromedia Flash movie and created folders in the Library panel.

FIGURE 13
The open Library panel

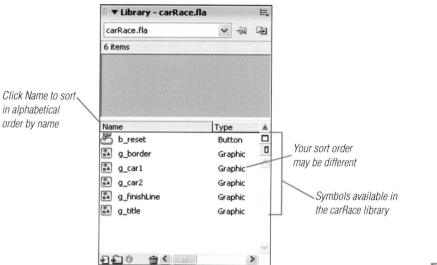

Click Name to sort in alphabetical order by name

Your sort order may be different

Symbols available in the carRace library

FIGURE 14
The Library panel with the folders added

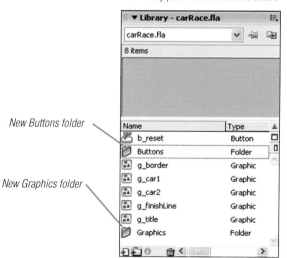

New Buttons folder

New Graphics folder

FIGURE 15

The Library panel after moving the symbols to the folders

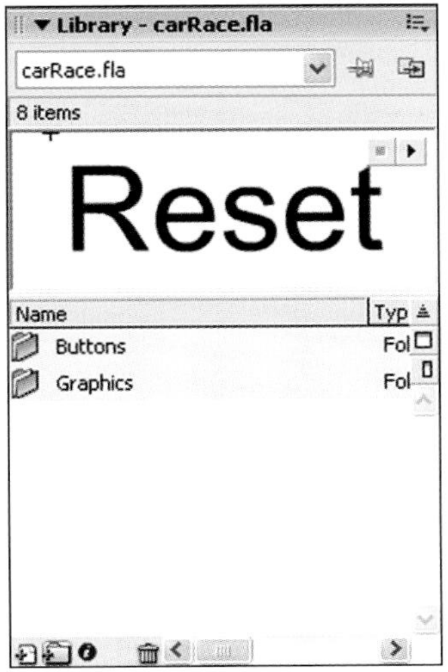

Organize symbols within Library panel folders

1. Drag the **g_title symbol** in the Library panel to the Graphics folder.

2. Drag the other graphic symbols to the Graphics folder.

3. Drag the **b_reset symbol** to the Buttons folder, then compare your Library panel to Figure 15.

4. Double-click the **Graphics folder** to open it and display the symbols.

5. Double-click the **Graphics folder** to close the folder.

You organized the symbols within the folders and opened and closed the folders.

Display the properties of a symbol, rename and delete symbols

1. Double-click the **Graphics folder icon** to display the symbols.

2. Click the **g_car1 symbol**, then click the **Properties icon** ❷ to display the Symbol Properties dialog box.

3. Type **g_redCar** in the Name text box, as shown in Figure 16, then click **OK**.

4. Repeat steps 2 and 3 renaming the g_car2 symbol to **g_blueCar**.

   TIP Double-click the name to rename it without opening the Symbol Properties dialog box.

5. Click **g_border** in the Library panel to select it.

6. Click the **Delete icon** 🗑 at the bottom of the Library panel.

7. If necessary, click **Yes** to complete the delete process.

   TIP You can also select an item and press [Delete], or use the Options menu in the Library panel to remove an item from the library.

You used the Library panel to display the properties of a symbol and rename and delete symbols.

FIGURE 16
Renaming a symbol

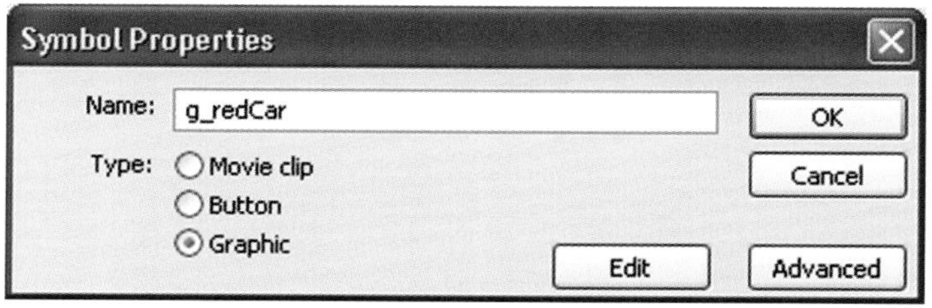

FIGURE 17

The carRace.fla document and the coolcar.fla Library panel

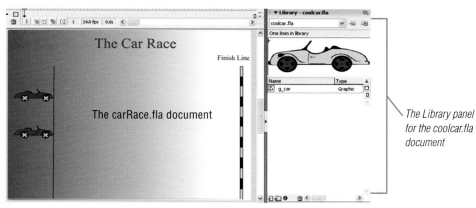

The Car Race

Finish Line

The carRace.fla document

The Library panel for the coolcar.fla document

Use multiple Library panels

1. Click the **Library panel text box list arrow** ⌄ near the top of the Library panel to display the open documents.

2. Click **coolcar.fla**.

   The Library panel for the coolcar document is displayed. However, the carRace document remains open, as shown in Figure 17.

3. Drag the **car** from the Library panel to the center of the stage.

4. Click the **Library panel text box list arrow** ⌄ to display the open documents.

5. Click **carRace.fla** to view the carRace document's Library panel.

   Notice the g_car symbol is automatically added to the Library panel of the carRace document.

6. Click the **g_car symbol** in the Library panel.

7. Click the **Delete icon** 🗑 at the bottom of the Library panel, then (if necessary) click **Yes** to delete the symbol.

   You deleted the g_car symbol from the carRace Library but it still exists in the coolcar library.

8. Save your work.

9. Click **coolcar.fla** above the timeline to display the document.

10. Close the coolcar document.

You used the Library panel to display the contents of a Library and added an object from the Library to the current document.

CREATE
BUTTONS

What You'll Do

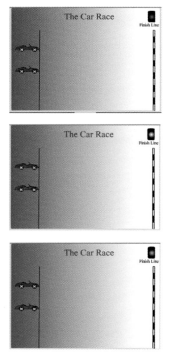

 In this lesson, you will create buttons, edit the four button states, and test a button.

Understanding Buttons

Button symbols are used to provide interactivity. When you click a button, an action occurs, such as starting an animation or jumping to another frame on the timeline. Any object, including Macromedia Flash drawings, text blocks, and imported graphic images, can be made into buttons. Unlike graphic symbols, buttons have four states: Up, Over, Down, and Hit. These states correspond to the use of the mouse and recognize that the user requires feedback when the mouse is pointing to a button and when the button has been clicked. This is often shown by a change in the button (such as a different color or different shape). These four states are explained below and shown in Figure 18.

Up—Represents how the button appears when the mouse pointer is not over it.

Over—Represents how the button appears when the mouse pointer is over it.

Down—Represents how the button appears after the user clicks the mouse.

Hit—Defines the area of the screen that will respond to the click. In most cases, you will want the Hit state to be the same or similar to the Up state in location and size.

When you create a button symbol, Macromedia Flash automatically creates a new timeline. The timeline has only four frames, one for each state. The timeline does not play; it merely reacts to the mouse pointer by displaying the appropriate button state and performing an action, such as jumping to a specific frame on the main timeline.

The process for creating and previewing buttons is as follows:

Create a button symbol—Draw an object or select an object that has already been created and placed on the stage. Use the Convert to Symbol command on the Modify menu to convert the object to a button symbol and to enter a name for the button.

Edit the button symbol—Select the button and choose the Edit Symbols command on the Edit menu or double-click the button symbol in the Library panel. This displays the button timeline, shown in Figure 19, which allows you to work with the four button states. The Up state is the original button symbol that Macromedia Flash automatically places in Frame 1. You need to determine how the original object will change for the other states. To change the button for the Over state, click Frame 2 and insert a keyframe. This automatically places a copy of the button in Frame 1 into Frame 2. Then, alter the button's appearance for the Over state. Use the same process for the Down state. For the Hit state, you insert a keyframe on Frame 4 and then specify the area on the screen that will respond to the pointer.

Return to the main timeline—Once you've finished editing a button, choose the Edit Document command on the Edit menu, or click Scene 1 above the timeline layers, to return to the main timeline.

Preview the button—By default, Macromedia Flash disables buttons so that you can manipulate them on the stage. You can preview a button by choosing the Enable Simple Buttons command on the Control menu. You can also choose the Test Movie command on the Control menu to play the movie and test the buttons.

FIGURE 18
The four button states

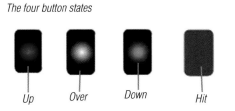

Up   Over   Down   Hit

FIGURE 19
The button timeline

Create a button

1. Insert a layer above the top layer in the carRace document timeline, then name the layer **signal**.

2. Click the **Rectangle tool** on the Tools panel, click the **Stroke Color tool** on the Tools panel, then click the **black color swatch** in the left column of the color palette.

3. Click the **Fill Color tool** on the Tools panel, then click the **red gradient color swatch** in the bottom row of the color palette.

4. Click the **Set Corner Radius icon** in the Options section of the Tools panel, type **5**, then click **OK**.

5. Draw the rectangle shown in Figure 20.

6. Click the **Zoom tool** on the Tools panel, then click the **rectangle** to enlarge it.

7. Click the **Gradient Transform tool** in the Tools panel, then click the **rectangle**.

8. Drag the diagonal arrow towards the center of the rectangle, as shown in Figure 21.

9. Click the **Selection tool** on the Tools panel, then drag the marquee around the rectangle to select it.

10. Click **Modify** on the menu bar, then click **Convert to Symbol**.

11. Type **b_signal** in the Name text box, click the **Type Button option button**, then click **OK**.

12. Drag the **b_signal symbol** to the Buttons folder in the Library panel.

You created a button symbol on the stage and dragged it to the Buttons folder in the Library panel.

FIGURE 20
The rectangle object

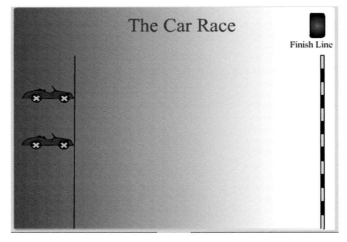

FIGURE 21
Adjusting the gradient

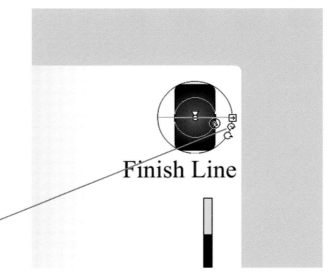

Drag the diagonal arrow from the outside ring towards the center of the rectangle

Working with Symbols and Interactivity

FIGURE 22

Specifying the hit area

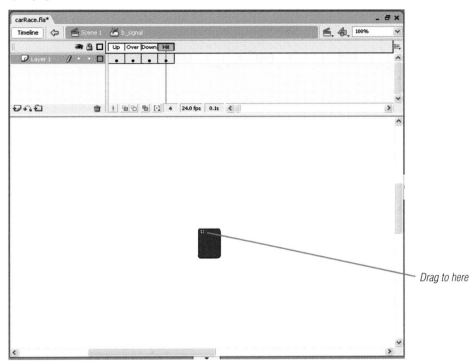

Drag to here

Edit a button and specify a Hit area

1. Open the Buttons folder, right-click (Win) or control-click (Mac) **b_signal** in the Library panel, then click **Edit**.

   Macromedia Flash switches to symbol-editing mode, and the timeline contains four button states.

2. Click the blank **Over frame** on Layer 1, then insert a keyframe.

   TIP   The [F6] key inserts a keyframe in the selected frame.

3. Click the **Fill Color tool** on the Tools panel, then click the **grey gradient color swatch** on the bottom of the color palette.

4. Insert a keyframe in the Down frame on Layer 1.

5. Click the **Fill Color tool** , then click the **green gradient color swatch** on the bottom of the color palette.

6. Insert a keyframe in the Hit frame on Layer 1.

7. Click the **Rectangle tool** on the Tools panel, click the **Fill Color tool** , then click the **blue color swatch** in the left column of the color palette.

8. Draw a rectangle that covers the button.

   Your screen should resemble Figure 22.

   | TIP   The Hit area is not visible on the stage.

9. Click **Scene 1** above the Timeline layers to return to the main timeline.

You edited a button by changing the color of its Over and Down states, and you specified the Hit area.

Test a button

1. Click the **Selection tool** , then click a blank area of the stage.

2. Click **Control** on the menu bar, then click **Enable Simple Buttons**.

3. Point to the signal button on the stage; the pointer changes to 👆, and the button changes to a grey gradient, the color you selected for the Over state. Compare your image to Figure 23.

4. Press and hold the mouse button, then notice that the button changes to a green gradient, the color you selected for the Down state, as shown in Figure 24.

(continued)

FIGURE 23
The button's Over state

FIGURE 24
The button's Down state

FIGURE 25

The button's Up state

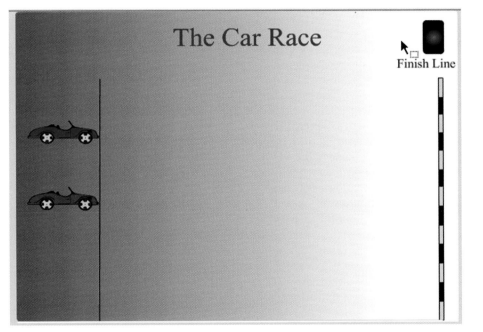

5. Release the mouse and notice that the button changes to the Over state color.

6. Move the mouse away from the signal button, and notice that the button returns to a red gradient, the Up state color, as shown in Figure 25.

7. Click **Control** on the menu bar, then click **Enable Simple Buttons** to turn it off.

8. Click **Window** on the menu bar, then click **Library** to close the Library panel.

9. Click **View** in the menu bar, point to **Magnification**, then click **Fit in Window**.

10. Save your work.

You used the mouse to test a button and view the button states.

ASSIGN ACTIONS
TO BUTTONS

What You'll Do

In this lesson, you will use ActionScripts to assign actions to frames and buttons.

Understanding Actions

In a basic movie, Macromedia Flash plays the frames sequentially, repeating the movie without stopping for user input. However, you may often want to provide users with the ability to interact with the movie by allowing them to perform actions such as starting and stopping the movie or jumping to a specific frame in the movie. One way to provide user interaction is to assign an action to the Down state of a button or preferably to the instance of a button. Then, whenever the user clicks the button, the action occurs. Macromedia Flash provides a scripting language, called ActionScript, that allows you to add actions to buttons and frames within a movie. For example, you can place a stop action in a frame that pauses the movie and then assign a play action to a button that starts the movie when the user clicks the button.

Analyzing ActionScript

ActionScript is a powerful scripting language that allows those with even limited programming experience to create complex actions. For example, you can create order forms that capture user input, or volume controls that display when sounds are played. A basic ActionScript involves an event (such as a mouse click) that causes some action to occur by triggering the script. The following is an example of a basic ActionScript:

```
on (release) {
        gotoAndPlay(10);
}
```

In this example, the event is a mouse click (indicated by the word release) that causes the movie's playback head to go to Frame 10 and play the frame. This is a simple ActionScript and is easy to follow. Other ActionScripts can be quite complex and may require programming expertise to understand. Fortunately, Macromedia Flash provides an easy way to use ActionScripts without having to learn the scripting language. The Script Assist feature within the Actions panel allows you to assign basic actions to frames and objects, such as buttons. Figure 26 shows the Actions panel displaying an ActionScript indicating that when the user clicks on the selected object (a button), the movie plays.

The process for assigning actions to buttons, shown in Figure 27, is as follows.

■ Select the desired button on the stage.
■ Display the Actions panel.
■ Select the Script Assist button to display the Script Assist panel within the ActionScript panel.
■ Click the Add a new item to the script icon to display a list of Action categories.
■ Select the appropriate category from a drop-down list. Macromedia Flash provides several Action categories. The Timeline Control category within the Global Functions allows you to create scripts for controlling movies and navi-gating within movies. You can use these actions to start and stop movies, jump to specific frames, and respond to user mouse movements and key-strokes.

■ Select the desired action, such as play.
■ Specify the event that triggers the action.

Button actions respond to one or more mouse events, including:

Release—With the pointer inside the button Hit area, the user presses and releases (clicks) the mouse button. This is the default event.

Key Press—With the Macromedia Flash button displayed, the user presses a prede-termined key on the keyboard.

Roll Over—The user moves the pointer into the button Hit area.

Drag Over—The user holds down the mouse button, moves the pointer out of the button Hit area and then back into the Hit area.

Using Frame Actions—In addition to assigning actions to buttons which require some user interaction, you can assign actions to frames. Actions that are assigned to frames are executed when the playhead reaches the frame. A common frame action is stop, which is often assigned to the first and last frame in the timeline.

FIGURE 26
The Actions panel displaying an ActionScript

FIGURE 27
The process for assigning actions to buttons

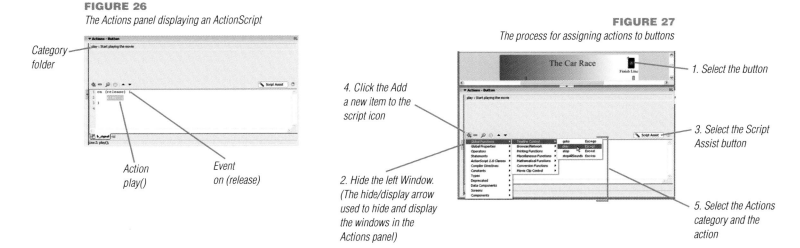

Category folder

4. Click the Add a new item to the script icon

1. Select the button

3. Select the Script Assist button

Action play()

Event on (release)

2. Hide the left Window. (The hide/display arrow used to hide and display the windows in the Actions panel)

5. Select the Actions category and the action

Assign a stop action to frames

1. Click **Control** on the menu bar, then click **Test Movie**.

   The movie plays and continues to loop.

2. Close the test movie window.

3. Hide all panels, then display the Tools panel.

4. Insert a new layer, name it **stopmovie**, then click **Frame 1** of the layer.

5. Click **Window** on the menu bar, then click **Actions** to display the Actions panel, as shown in Figure 28.

6. Drag the **Actions panel top border** down to display the stage, click the **hide/display arrow** to close the left window of the Actions panel, then click the **Script Assist button** 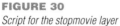 to turn on this feature.

7. Click the **Add a new item to the script button** to display the Script categories, point to **Global Functions**, point to **Timeline Control**, then click **stop**, as shown in Figure 29.

8. Insert a keyframe in Frame 66 on the stopmovie layer, then repeat step 7. Compare your screen to Figure 30.

9. Test the movie.

   The movie does not play because there is a stop action assigned to Frame 1.

10. Close the test movie window.

You inserted a layer and assigned a stop action to the first and last frames on the layer.

FIGURE 28

The Actions panel with both windows displayed

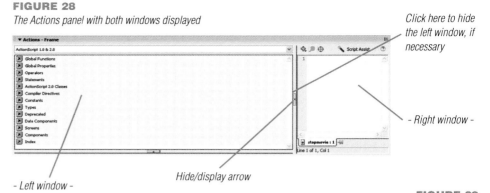

Click here to hide the left window, if necessary

- Right window -

- Left window -

Hide/display arrow

FIGURE 29

Assigning an action to Frame 1 on the stopmovie layer

FIGURE 30

Script for the stopmovie layer

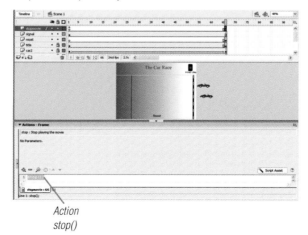

Action stop()

FIGURE 31

Assigning a play action to a button

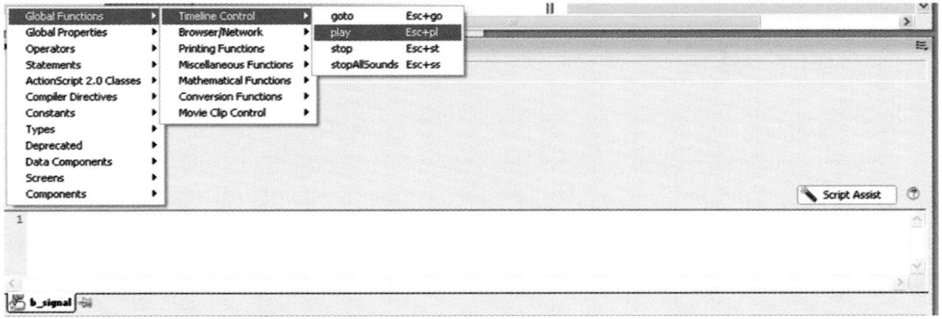

Understanding the Actions panel

The Actions panel has two windows. The left window uses folders to display the Action categories. The right window uses lists to display the categories. The right window, called the Script pane, is used with the Script Assist feature and it displays the ActionScript code as the code is being generated. When using the Script Assist feature, it is best to close the left window. This is done by clicking the hide/display arrow.

1. Click **View** on the menu bar, point to **Magnification**, then click **Fit in Window**.

   TIP   If you want a larger view of the stage, you can use the Selection tool to drag the bottom border of the timeline up to hide more layers.

2. Click **Frame 1** of the Signal layer.

3. Click the **button** on the stage. Verify that b_signal is displayed in the lower left of the Actions panel.

   TIP   To select the button, click it with the Selection tool.

4. Click ⊞ to display the Script categories, point to **Global Functions**, point to **Timeline Control**, then click **play**, as shown in Figure 31.

5. Click **Control** on the menu bar, then click **Test Movie**.

6. Click the **signal button**.

   The movie plays and stops. The reset button appears but it does not have an action assigned to it.

7. Close the test movie window.

You used the Actions panel to assign a play action to a button.

Assign a goto frame action to a button

1. Click **Frame 66** of the reset layer to display the Reset button.

2. Click the **Reset button** on the stage to select it.

3. Click 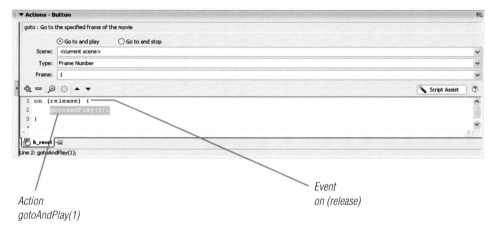 to display the Script categories, point to **Global Functions**, point to **Timeline Control**, then click **goto**.

   The Script Assist window displays options that allow you to specify the frame number to go to and play, as shown in Figure 32. Frame 1 is the default frame number.

4. Click **Control** on the menu bar, then click **Test Movie**.

5. Click the **signal button** to start the movie, then when the movie stops, click the **Reset button**.

6. Close the test movie window.

You used the Actions panel to assign an action to a button.

FIGURE 32
Assigning a goto action to a button

*Event
on (release)*

*Action
gotoAndPlay(1)*

FIGURE 33

Assigning a keypress action to a button

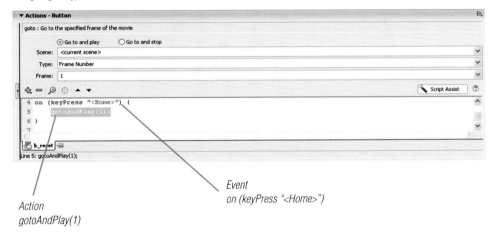

Event
on (keyPress "<Home>")

Action
gotoAndPlay(1)

1. Click after the **right curly bracket** (}) in the Actions panel to highlight the bracket in step 3 of the ActionScript.

2. Click ⊕ in the Script Assist window, point to **Global Functions**, point to **Movie Clip Control**, then click **on**.

   The Script Assist window displays several event options. Release is selected.

3. Click the **Release check box** to deselect the option.

4. Click the **Key Press check box** to select it, then press [**Home**].

5. Click ⊕ in the Script Assist window, point to **Global Functions**, point to **Timeline Control**, then click **goto**.

   The ActionScript now indicates that pressing the [Home] key will cause the playhead to go to Frame 1, as shown in Figure 33.

6. Click **File** on the menu bar, point to **Publish Preview**, then click **Default – (HTML)**.

   The movie opens in your default browser.

7. Click the **signal button** to start the movie, then when the movie stops, press the [**Home**] key.

8. Close the browser window, then save and close the movie.

9. Exit Flash.

You added an event that triggers a goto frame action.

Create a symbol.

1. Start Flash, open fl3_3.fla, then save it as **skillsdemo3**.
2. Change the background color of the document to **#CCCCCC**.
3. Change the title, Color Spin, to font size **30**.
4. Insert a new layer above the ballspin layer and name it **titlebkgnd**.
5. Draw a black rectangle behind the Color Spin title text using the Set Corner Radius option, and set the Corner radius points to **10**.
6. Select the rectangle, convert it to a graphic symbol, then name it **g_bkgnd**.
7. Save your work.

Create and edit an instance.

1. Insert a new layer above the title layer and name it **vballs-sm**.
2. Display the Library panel, if necessary.
3. Drag the g_vball-sm symbol to the upper-left corner of the stage.
4. Drag the g_vball-sm symbol three more times to each of the remaining corners of the stage.
5. Double-click the g_vball-sm symbol icon in the Library panel to switch to symbol-editing mode.
6. Change the color of the ball to red.
7. Return to the document and notice how all instances have been changed to red.
8. Select the ball in the upper-right corner of the stage and break apart the object.

9. Change the color to a blue gradient.
10. Select, break apart, and change the bottom-left ball to a green gradient and the bottom-right ball to white.
11. Save your work.

Create a folder in the Library panel.

1. Use the Options menu in the Library panel to create a new folder.
2. Name the folder **Graphics**.
3. Move the three graphic symbols to the Graphics folder.
4. Expand the Graphics folder.
5. Save your work.

Work with the Library window.

1. Rename the g_bkgnd symbol to **g_title-bkgnd** in the Library panel.
2. Collapse and expand the folder.
3. Save your work.

Create a button.

1. Insert a new layer above the vballs-sm layer and name it **start**.
2. Drag the g_title-bkgnd symbol from the Library panel to the bottom center of the stage.
3. Create a white, bold, 30-pt Arial text block on top of the g_title-bkgnd object, then type **Start**. (*Hint*: Center the text block in the background object.)

4. Select the rectangle and the text. (*Hint*: Click the Selection tool, then press and hold [Shift].)
5. Convert the selected objects to a button symbol and name it **b_start**.
6. Create a new folder named **Buttons** in the Library panel and move the b_start button symbol to the folder.
7. Display the b_start button timeline.
8. Insert a keyframe in the Over frame.
9. Select the text and change the color to gray.
10. Insert a keyframe in the Down frame.
11. Select the text and change the color to blue.
12. Insert a keyframe in the Hit frame.
13. Draw a rectangular object that covers the area for the Hit state.
14. Return to movie-editing mode.
15. Save your work.

Test a button.

1. Turn on Enable Simple Buttons.
2. Point to the button and notice the color change.
3. Click the button and notice the other color change.

Stop a movie.

1. Insert a new layer and name it **stopmovie**.
2. Insert a keyframe in Frame 40 on the new layer.
3. With Frame 40 selected, display the Actions panel.
4. Assign a stop action to the frame.
5. Click Frame 1 on the new layer.
6. Assign a stop action to Frame 1.
7. Save your work.

Assign an action to a button.

1. Click Control on the menu bar, then click Enable Simple Buttons to turn off this feature.
2. Use the Selection tool to select the button on the stage.
3. Use Script Assist in the Actions panel to assign an event and a play action to the button.
4. Test the movie.
5. Save your work, then compare your image to Figure 34.
6. Exit Flash.

FIGURE 34
Completed Skills Review

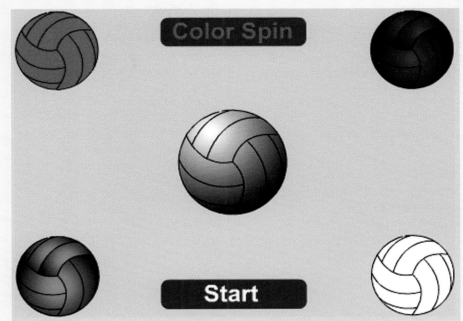

The Ultimate Tours travel company has asked you to design a sample navigation scheme for its Web site. The company wants to see how its homepage will link with one of its main categories (Treks). Figure 35 shows a sample homepage and Treks screen. Using these or the homepage you created in Chapter 2 as a guide, you will add a Treks screen and link it to the homepage. (*Hint*: Assume that all of the drawings on the homepage are on Frame 1, unless noted.)

1. Open ultimatetours2.fla (the file you created in Chapter 2 Project Builder 1), then save it as **ultimatetours3**.

2. Insert a layer above the Subheading layer, name it **logo**, then type logo as a place-holder in the upper-left corner of the stage.

3. Select the layer that the Ultimate Tours text block is on, then insert a keyframe on a frame at least five frames further along the timeline.

4. Insert a new layer, name it **treks headings**, insert a keyframe on the last frame of the movie, then create the Treks screen, except for the home graphic.

5. Convert the Treks graphic on the homepage to a button symbol, then edit the symbol so that different colors appear for the different states.

6. Assign a goto action that jumps the play-head to the Treks screen when the Treks button is clicked.

7. Insert a new layer and name it **stopmovie**. Add stop actions that cause the movie to stop after displaying the homepage and after displaying the Treks page.

8. Insert a new layer and name it **homeButton**, insert a keyframe on the appropriate frame, then draw the home button image with the Home text.

9. Convert the image to a button symbol, then edit the symbol so that different colors appear for the different states. Assign a goto action for the button that jumps the movie to Frame 1.

10. Test the movie.

11. Save your work, then compare your Web page to the sample shown in Figure 35.

FIGURE 35
Sample completed Project Builder 1

You have been asked to assist the International Student Association (ISA). The association sponsors a series of monthly events, each focusing on a different culture from around the world. The events are led by a guest speaker who makes a presentation, followed by a discussion. The events are free and they are open to everyone. ISA would like you to design a Macromedia Flash movie that will be used with its Web site. The movie starts by providing information about the series, and then provides a link to the upcoming event.

1. Open a new Flash document and save it as **isa3**.
2. Create an initial Information screen with general information about the association's series.
3. Assign an action that stops the movie.
4. Add a button on the general information screen that jumps the movie to a screen that presents information about the next event.
5. Add a button on the information screen that jumps the movie to a screen that lists the series (all nine events for the school year-September through May).
6. On the next event and series screens, add a Return button that jumps the movie back to the general information screen.
7. Specify different colors for each state of each button.
8. Test the movie.
9. Save your work, then compare your movie to the sample shown in Figure 36.

FIGURE 36

Sample completed Project Builder 2

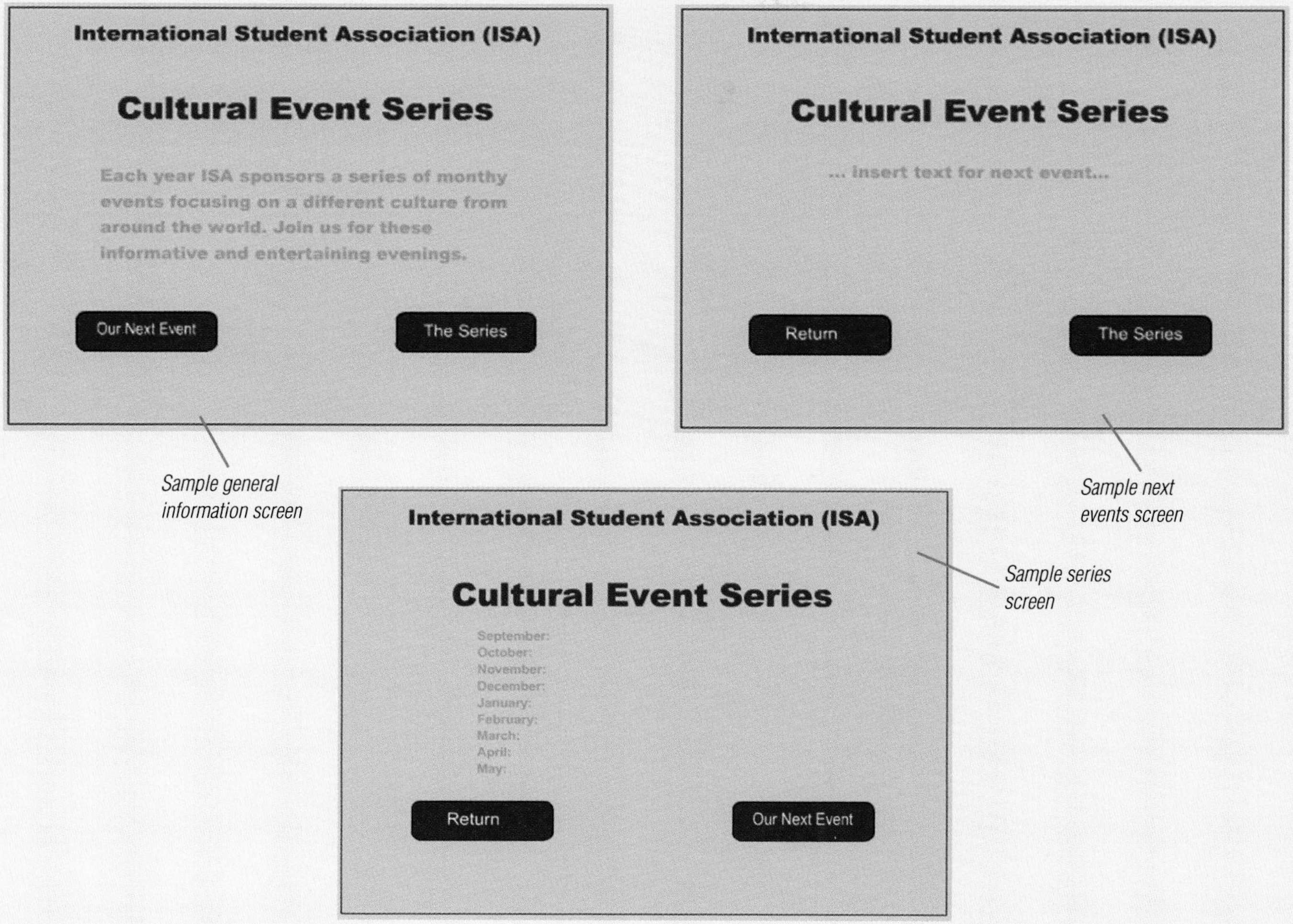

Sample general
information screen

Sample next
events screen

Sample series
screen

Figure 37 shows the homepage of a Web site. Study the figure and complete the following questions. For each question, indicate how you determined your answer.

1. Connect to the Internet, go to *www.course.com*, navigate to the page for this book, click the Online Companion link, then click the link for this chapter.

2. Open a document in a word processor or open a new Macromedia Flash document, save the file as **dpc3**, then answer the following questions. (*Hint*: Use the Text tool in Macromedia Flash.)

   - Whose Web site is this?
   - What is the goal(s) of the site?
   - Who is the target audience?
   - What is the treatment ("look and feel") that is used?
   - What are the design layout guidelines being used (balance, movement, and so on)?
   - What may be animated in this home page?
   - Do you think this is an effective design for the company, its products, and its target audience? Why or why not?
   - What suggestions would you make to improve on the design, and why?

FIGURE 37
Design Project

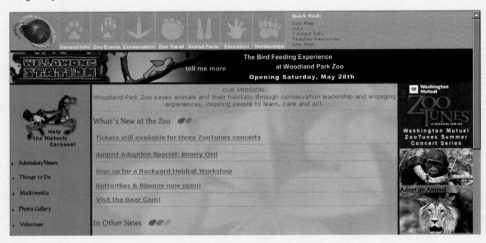

This is a continuation of Portfolio Project in Chapter 2, which is the development of a personal portfolio. The homepage has several categories, including the following:

- Personal data
- Contact information
- Previous employment
- Education
- Samples of your work

In this project, you will create a button that will be used to link the homepage of your portfolio to the animations page. Next, you will create another button to start the animation.

1. Open portfolio2.fla (the file you created in Portfolio Project, Chapter 2), then save it as **portfolio3**. (*Hint*: When you open the file, you may receive a warning message that the font is missing. You can replace this font with the default, or with any other appropriate font on your computer.)
2. Unlock the layers as needed.
3. Change the My Portfolio text to **#003366** and the oval background to **#CCCCCC**.
4. Insert a new layer, insert a keyframe on Frame 3 (or one frame past the last frame of the movie), then create an animation using objects that you create.
5. Insert a new layer, insert a keyframe on Frame 2 (or one frame before the

animation frame), then create a Sample Animation screen.
6. Convert the title into a button symbol, then edit the symbol so that different colors appear for the different states. Assign an action that jumps to the frame that plays an animation.
7. Change the Animations graphic on the homepage to a button, then edit the symbol

so that different colors appear for the different states. Assign an action that jumps to the Sample Animation screen.
8. Insert a new layer, then name it **stopmovie**. Insert keyframes and assign stop actions to the appropriate frames.
9. Test the movie.
10. Save your work, then compare your movie to the sample shown in Figure 38.

FIGURE 38
Sample completed Portfolio Project

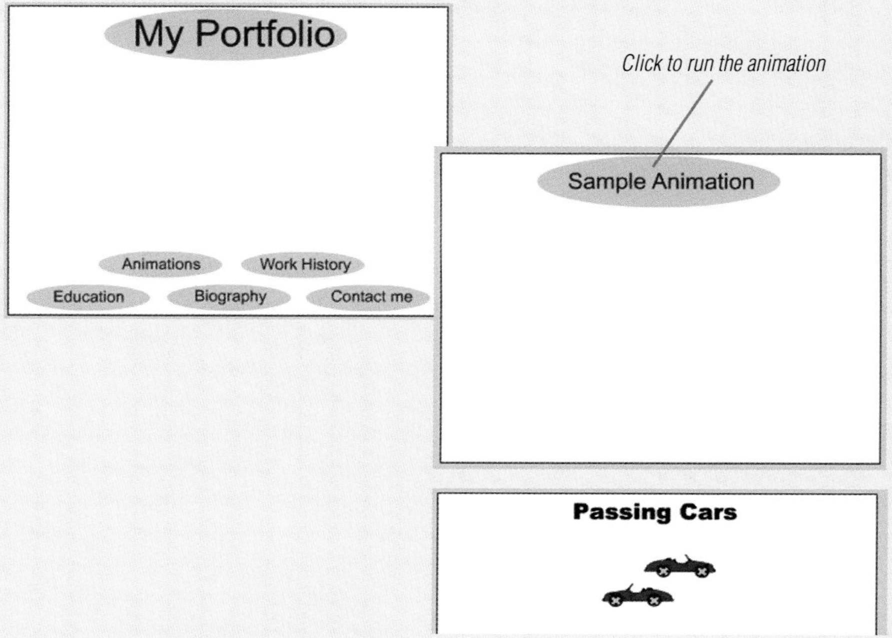

Click to run the animation

chapter

4 CREATING ANIMATIONS

1. Create frame-by-frame animations.

2. Create motion-tweened animation.

3. Work with motion guides.

4. Create animation effects.

5. Animate text.

4 CREATING ANIMATIONS

Introduction

Animation can be an important part of your Web site, whether the site focuses on e-commerce (attracts attention and provides product demonstrations), education (simulates complex processes such as DNA replication), or entertainment (provides interactive games).

How Does Animation Work?

The perception of motion in an animation is actually an illusion. Animation is like a motion picture in that it is made up of a series of still images. Research has found that our eye captures and holds an image for one-tenth of a second before processing another image. By retaining each impression for one-tenth of a second, we perceive a series of rapidly displayed still images as a single, moving image. This phenomenon is known as persistence of vision and provides the basis for the frame rate in animations. Frame rates of 10–12 frames-per-second (fps) generally provide an acceptably smooth computer-based animation. Lower frame rates result in a jerky image, while higher frame rates may result in a blurred image. Macromedia Flash uses a default frame rate of 12 fps.

Macromedia Flash Animation

Creating animation is one of the most powerful features of Macromedia Flash, yet developing basic animations is a simple process. Macromedia Flash allows you to create animations that can move and rotate an object around the stage, and change its size, shape, or color. You can also use the animation features in Macromedia Flash to create special effects, such as an object zooming or fading in and out. You can combine animation effects so that an object changes shape and color as it moves across the stage. Animations are created by changing the content of successive frames. Macromedia Flash provides two animation methods: frame-by-frame animation and tweened animation.

Tools You'll Use

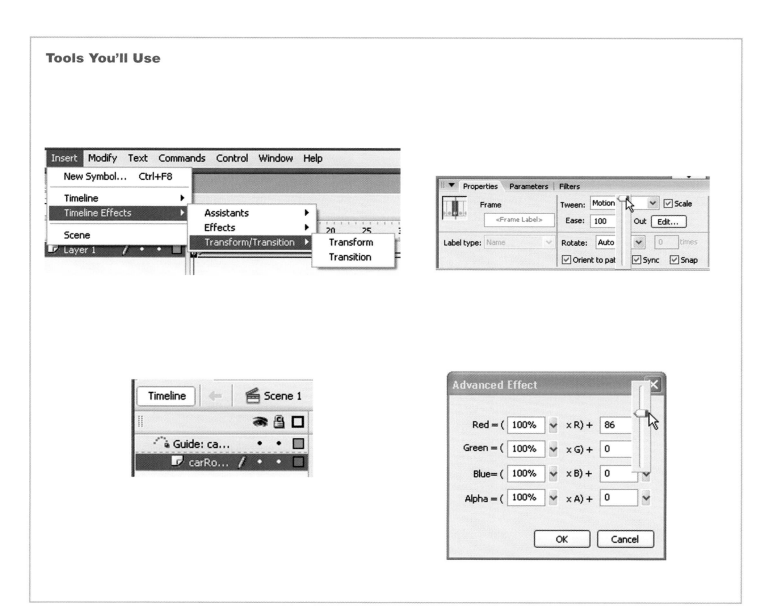

CREATE FRAME-BY-FRAME ANIMATIONS

What You'll Do

In this lesson you will create frame-by-frame animations.

Understanding Frame-by-Frame Animations

A frame-by-frame animation (also called a frame animation) is created by specifying the object that is to appear in each frame of a sequence of frames. Figure 1 shows three images that are variations of a cartoon character. In this example the head and body remain the same, but the arms and legs change to represent a walking motion. If these individual images are placed into succeeding frames (with keyframes), an animation is created.

Frame-by-frame animations are useful when you want to change individual parts of an image. The images in Figure 1 are simple—only three images are needed for the animation. However, depending on the complexity of the image and the desired movements, the time needed to display each change can be substantial. When creating a frame-by-frame animation, you need to consider the following points:

■ The number of different images. The more images there are, the more effort

is needed to create them. However, the greater the number of images, the less change you need to make in each image. Therefore, the movement in the animation may seem more realistic.

■ The number of frames in which each image will appear. If each image appears in only one frame, the animation may appear rather jerky, since the changes are made very rapidly. In some instances, you may want to give the impression of a rapid change in an object, such as rapidly blinking colors. The number of frames creates varied results.

■ The movie frame rate. Frame rates below 10 may appear jerky, while those above 30 may appear blurred. The frame rate is easy to change, and you should experiment with different rates until you get the desired effect.

Keyframes are critical to the development of frame animations because they signify a change in the object. Because frame animations are created by changing the object, all frames in a frame animation may need to be keyframes. The exception is when you want an object displayed in several frames before it changes.

Creating a Frame-by-Frame Animation

To create a frame animation, select the frame on the layer where you want the animation to begin, insert a keyframe, and then place the object on the stage. Next, select the frame where you want the change to occur, insert a keyframe, then change the object. You can also add a new object in place of the original one. Figure 2 shows the first six frames of an animation in which the front end of a car raises up and down in place. The movement of the animation is visible because the Onion Skin feature is turned on; this feature will be discussed later in this chapter. In this case, the car stays in place during the animation. A frame animation can also involve movement of the object around the stage.

FIGURE 1
Three images used in an animation

FIGURE 2
The first six frames of an animation

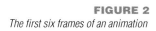

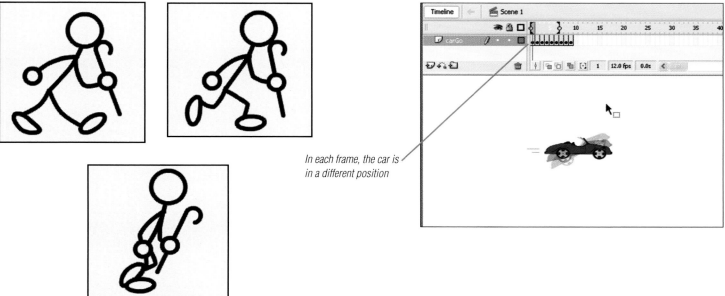

In each frame, the car is in a different position

Create an in-place frame-by-frame animation

1. Open fl4_1.fla from the drive and folder where your Data Files are stored, then save it as **frameAn**.

2. Hide all panels, then open the Tools panel, Property inspector and Library panel.

3. Click **View** on the menu bar, point to **Magnification**, then click **Fit in Window**.

4. Click Frame 2 on the carGo layer, then press [**F6**] to insert a keyframe.

5. Verify that the car is selected, click the **Free Transform tool** on the Tools panel, then click the **Rotate and Skew option** in the Options section of the Tools panel.

6. Drag the top-right handle up one position, as shown in Figure 3.

7. Insert a keyframe in Frame 3 on the carGo layer.

8. Drag the top-right handle up one more position.

9. Insert a keyframe in Frame 4 on the carGo layer, then drag the top-right handle down one position.

10. Insert a keyframe in Frame 5 on the carGo layer, then drag the top-right handle down to position the car to its original horizontal position.

11. Insert a keyframe in Frame 6 on the carGo layer, then compare your timeline to Figure 4.

You created an in-place frame animation by inserting several keyframes and adjusting an object in each of the frames.

FIGURE 3
Rotating the car

Click handle and
drag up

FIGURE 4
The timeline with keyframes

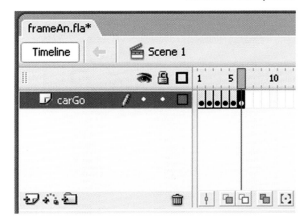

Add detail to the animation

1. Click the **Pencil tool** 🖉 on the Tools panel.

2. Click the **Stroke Color tool** 🖉⬛ on the Tools panel, then click the **black color swatch** in the left column of the color palette (if necessary).

   | TIP Adjust the Zoom settings as needed using the View menu or Zoom tool.

3. Verify Frame 6 is selected, then draw the two lines shown in Figure 5.

   | TIP Press and hold [Shift] to draw straight lines.

4. Click **Control** on the menu bar, then click **Play**.

You added lines to the animation that indicate motion.

FIGURE 5

Adding lines to the object

Create a moving frame animation

1. Insert a keyframe in Frame 7 on the carGo layer.
2. Click the **Selection tool** ![cursor] on the Tools panel, drag a marquee around the car and the lines to select them.
3. Drag the car and the two lines to the right approximately half the distance to the right edge of the stage, as shown in Figure 6.
4. Insert a keyframe in Frame 8 on the carGo layer.
5. Click the **Pencil tool** ![pencil] on the Tools panel, then draw a third line, as shown in Figure 7.
6. Click the **Selection tool** ![cursor], drag a marquee around the car and lines, then drag the car and the three lines to the right edge of the stage.
7. Insert a keyframe in Frame 9 on the carGo layer, then drag the car and the three lines completely off the right side of the stage, as shown in Figure 8.
8. Play the movie.

You created a moving frame animation by dragging the object across the stage.

FIGURE 6
Positioning the car

FIGURE 7
The car with a third line

FIGURE 8
Positioning the car off the stage

FIGURE 9

Changing the frame rate

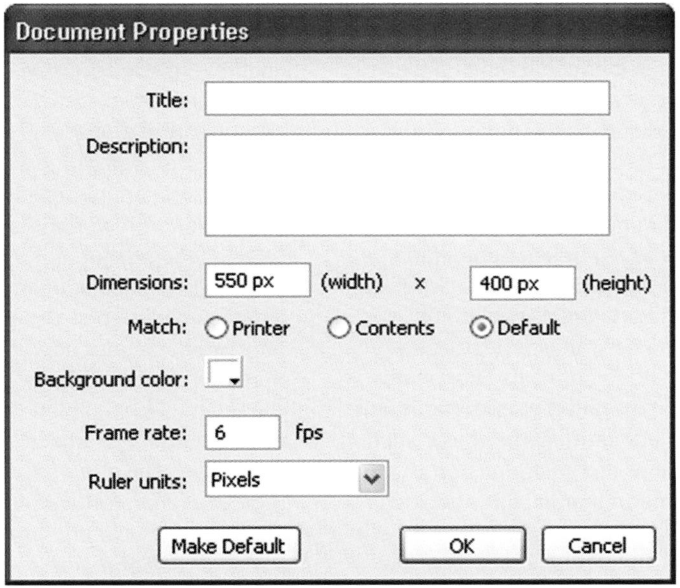

Change the frame rate

1. Double-click the **Frame Rate icon** `12.0 fps` on the timeline to display the Document Properties dialog box.

2. Type **6** in the Frame Rate text box, as shown in Figure 9, then click **OK**.

3. Click **Control** on the menu bar, then click **Play** to play the movie.

4. Repeat Steps 1 through 3, typing **18** in the Frame Rate text box.

5. Change the frame rate to 12.

6. Save your work.

7. Play the movie, then close the movie.

You changed the frame rate for the movie to see its effect on the movement of the object.

CREATE MOTION-TWEENED ANIMATION

What You'll Do

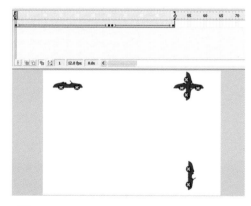

 In this lesson, you will create motion-tweened animations.

Understanding Motion Tweening

Frame-by-frame animation can be a tedious process, especially if you have to alter an object's position an infinitesimal amount in every frame. Fortunately, once you create start and end frames, Macromedia Flash can fill in the in-between frames, a process called **tweening**. In tweened animation, Macromedia Flash stores only the attributes that change from frame to frame. For example, if you have an object that moves across the stage, Macromedia Flash stores the location of the object in each frame, but not the other attributes of the object, such as its dimensions and color. In contrast, for frame-by-frame animation, all of the attributes for the object need to be stored in each frame. Frame animations have larger file sizes than tweened animations.

There are two types of tweened animation: shape and motion. Shape animations are similar to the process of image morphing in which one object slowly turns into another—often unrelated—object, such as a robot that turns into a man. Shape-tweened animations will be covered in the next chapter. You can use **motion tweening** to create animations in which objects move and in which they are resized, rotated, and recolored. Figure 10 shows a motion-tweened animation of a car moving diagonally across the screen. There are only two keyframes needed for this animation: a keyframe in Frame 1 where the car starts, and a keyframe in Frame 30 where the car ends. Macromedia Flash automatically fills in the other frames. In Figure 10 the Onion Skin feature is enabled so that outlines of the car are displayed for each frame of the animation.

To create a motion-tweened animation, select the starting frame and, if necessary, insert a keyframe. Position the object on the stage and verify that it is selected. Next, choose the Create Motion Tween command from the Timeline option on the Insert menu, then insert a keyframe in the ending frame of the animation. Figure 10 shows the timeline after creating a Motion Tween and specifying an ending keyframe. Motion tweening is represented by black dots displayed in the keyframes and a black arrow linking the keyframes against a light blue background. The final step is to move the object and/or make changes to the object, such as changing its size or rotating it. Keep in mind the following points as you create motion-tweened animations.

■ If you change the position of the object, it will move in a direct line from the

starting position to the ending position. To move the object on a predetermined path, you can create several motion-tweened animations in succeeding frames, or you can use a motion guide as explained in the next lesson.

■ If you reshape an object in the ending keyframe, the object will slowly change from the starting to the ending keyframes. If this is not the effect you want, you can add a keyframe immediately after the tweened animation and reshape the object at that point.

■ When you select an object and create a motion tween, Macromedia Flash automatically creates a symbol,

names it Tween 1, and places it in the Library panel.

■ You can remove a motion tween animation by selecting a frame within the tween and using the Remove Tween command from the Timeline option in the Insert menu.

FIGURE 10
Sample motion-tweened animation

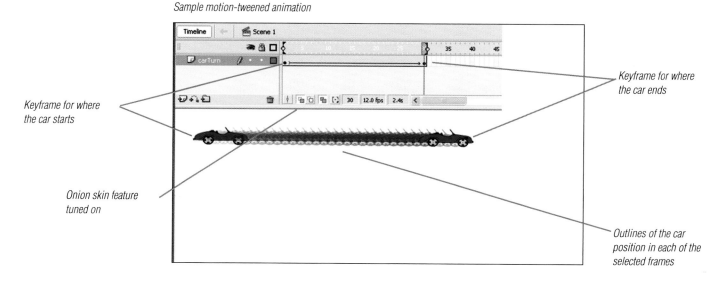

Keyframe for where
the car starts

Onion skin feature
tuned on

Keyframe for where
the car ends

Outlines of the car
position in each of the
selected frames

Create a motion-tweened animation

1. Open fl4_2.fla, then save it as **carAn**.

2. Click **Frame 1** on the carTurn layer, click **Insert** on the menu bar, point to **Timeline**, then click **Create Motion Tween**.

3. Insert a keyframe in Frame 30 on the carTurn layer.

4. Click the **Selection tool** 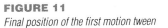 on the Tools panel (if necessary), select the car, then drag the car to the position on the stage shown in Figure 11.

5. Play the movie.

You created a motion-tweened animation, causing an object to move across the stage.

FIGURE 11
Final position of the first motion tween

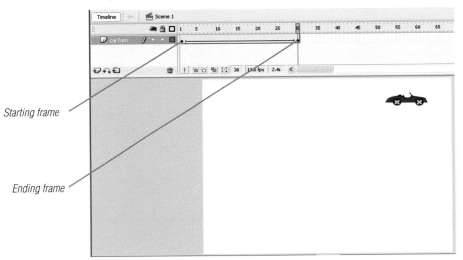

Starting frame

Ending frame

Creating Animations

FIGURE 12

Final position of the combined motion tweens

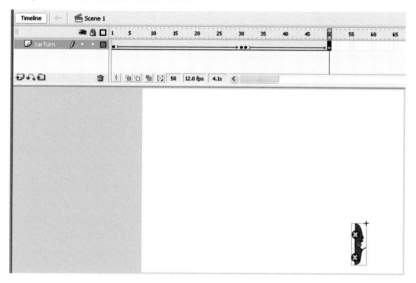

1. Click **View** on the menu bar, point to **Magnification**, then click **Fit in Window**.

2. Insert a keyframe in Frame 31 on the carTurn layer.

3. Verify that the car is selected, click **Modify** on the menu bar, point to **Transform**, then click **Rotate 90° CW**.

   | TIP CW means clockwise.

4. Insert a keyframe in Frame 50 on the carTurn layer.

   A motion-tween is automatically inserted in the timeline because of the previous motion-tween that was created for the object.

   | TIP If you did not want another motion tween to be automatically inserted, you could add a Blank Keyframe to the frame following the animation. You use the Timeline option from the Insert menu.

5. Click the **Selection tool** on the Tools panel (if necessary), then drag the car to the location shown in Figure 12.

6. Play the movie.

7. Save your work, then close the movie.

You combined two motion-tweened animations with a rotation between the animations.

WORK WITH MOTION GUIDES

What You'll Do

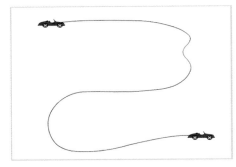

In this lesson, you will create a motion guide and attach an animation to it.

Understanding Motion Guides

In the previous lesson, you combined two animations to cause an object to change directions. Macromedia Flash provides a way for you to create a path that will guide moving objects around the stage in any direction, as shown in Figure 13 (Note: the onion skin feature is turned on to show how the car follows the path). **Motion guide layers** allow you to draw a motion guide path and attach motion-tweened animations to the path. The animations are placed on their own layer beneath the motion guide layer. There are two ways to work with motion guides. One way is to insert a guide layer, draw a path, then create an animation and attach the animated object to the path. The second way is to create an animation, insert a motion guide layer and draw a path, then attach the animated object to the path. The process for using the second method is as follows:

- Create a motion-tweened animation.
- Select the layer the animation is on and insert a motion guide layer. The selected layer is indented below the motion guide layer, as shown in Figure 14. This indicates that the selected layer is associated with the motion guide layer.
- Draw a path using the Pen, Pencil, Line, Circle, Rectangle, or Brush tools.
- Attach the object to the path by dragging the object by its registration point to the beginning of the path in the first frame, and to the end of the path in the last frame.

Depending on the type of object you are animating and the path, you may need to orient the object to the path. This means that the object will rotate in response to the direction of the path. The Property inspector is used to specify that the object will be oriented to the path. The advantages of using a motion guide are that you can have an object move along any path, including a path that intersects itself, and you can easily change the shape of the path, allowing you to experiment with different motions. A consideration when using a motion guide is that, in some instances, orienting the object along the path may result in an unnatural-looking animation. You can fix this by stepping through the animation one frame at a time until you reach the frame where the object is positioned poorly. You can then insert a keyframe and adjust the object as desired.

Working with the Property Inspector When Creating Motion-Tweened Animations

The Property inspector provides the following options when creating motion-tweened animations:

- Tween—specifies Motion, Shape, or None.
- Scale—tweens the size of an object. Select this option when you want an object to grow smaller or larger.
- Ease—specifies the rate of change between tweened frames. For

example, you may want to have an object—such as a car—start out slowly and accelerate gradually. Ease values are between –100 (slow) to 100 (fast).

- Rotate—specifies the number of times an object rotates clockwise (CW) or counterclockwise (CCW).
- Orient to path—orients the baseline of the object to the path.
- Sync—ensures that the object loops properly.
- Snap—attaches the object to the path by its transformation point.

Transformation Point and Registration Point

Each symbol has a transformation point (O) that is used to orient the object when it is being animated. For example,

when you rotate a symbol, the transformation point is the pivot point around which the object rotates. The transformation point is also the point that snaps to a motion guide, as shown in Figure 13. When attaching an object to a path you can drag the transformation point to the path. The default position for a transformation point is the center of the object. You can reposition the transformation point while in the symbol edit mode by dragging the transformation point to a different location in the object. Objects also have a registration point (+) that is used to position the object on the stage using ActionScript code. The transformation and registration points can overlap—this is displayed as a plus sign within a circle.

FIGURE 14
A motion guide layer

FIGURE 13
A motion guide with an object (car) attached

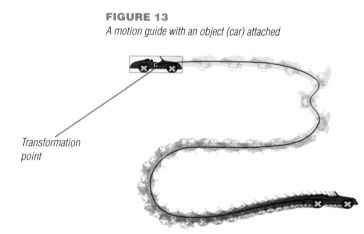

Transformation point

Motion guide layer

Indented layer containing the animation that will follow the path created on the guide layer

Create an animation without a motion guide

1. Open fl4_3.fla, then save it as **carPath**.

2. Set the View to Fit in Window.

3. Click **Frame 1** of the carRoute layer.

4. Make sure that the car is selected, click **Insert** on the menu bar, point to **Timeline**, then click **Create Motion Tween**.

5. Insert a keyframe in Frame 40 on the carRoute layer.

6. Drag the **car** to the lower-right corner of the stage, as shown in Figure 15.

7. Play the movie.

   The car moves diagonally down to the corner of the stage.

You created a motion animation that moves an object in a diagonal line across the stage.

FIGURE 15
Positioning the car

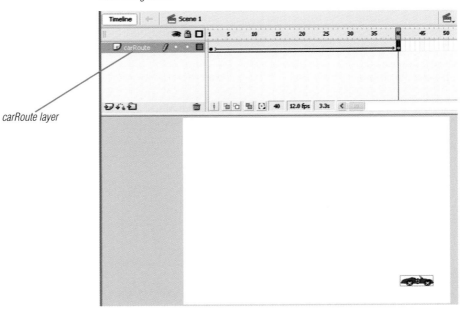

carRoute layer

FIGURE 16
The completed motion path

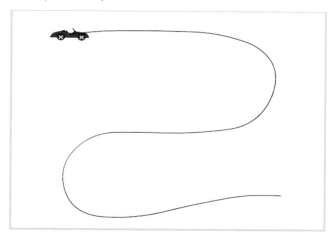

FIGURE 17
Snapping an object to the path

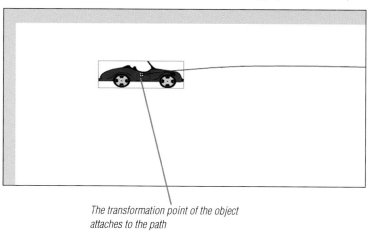

The transformation point of the object
attaches to the path

Add a motion guide to an animation

1. Click **Frame 1** on the carRoute layer.

2. Click **Insert** on the menu bar, point to **Timeline**, then click **Motion Guide**.

   The carRoute layer is indented beneath the guide layer on the timeline.

3. Click **Frame 1** of the Guide layer, click the **Pencil tool** on the Tools panel, click the **Smooth option** in the Options section of the Tools panel, then draw a path starting at the transformation point inside the car similar to the one shown in Figure 16.

4. Click the **Selection tool** on the Tools panel.

5. Click **Frame 1** of the carRoute layer. If the transformation point is not on the path, click the transformation point of the car, then drag it to the beginning of the path, as shown in Figure 17.

   > TIP An object is snapped to the beginning or end of a motion path when the start or end point of the motion path intersects the car's transformation point.

6. Click **Frame 40** on the carRoute layer.

7. If the car does not snap to the end of the path, click the **Selection tool**, click the transformation point of the car, then drag it to the end of the path.

8. Play the movie.

You created a motion guide on a path and attached an animation to it.

Orient an object to the path

1. Play the movie again and notice how the car does not turn front-first in response to the turns in the path.

2. Make sure the Property inspector is displayed, then click **Frame 1** on the carRoute layer.

3. Make sure the car is selected, then click the **Orient to path check box**.

4. Play the movie.

   Notice the car is oriented front-first to the turns in the path.

You used the Property inspector to specify that the object is oriented to the path.

Alter the path

1. Click **Frame 1** on the carRoute layer.

2. Click the **Selection tool**, if necessary.

3. Point to the middle of the right curve line of the path.

4. When the pointer changes to the arc pointer 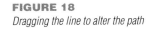, drag the line up, as shown in Figure 18.

   Your path may be different.

5. Play the movie.

You altered the motion guide path.

FIGURE 18
Dragging the line to alter the path

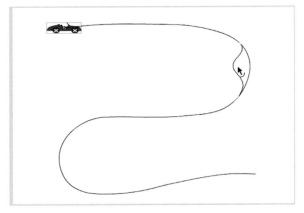

FIGURE 19
Setting the Ease value

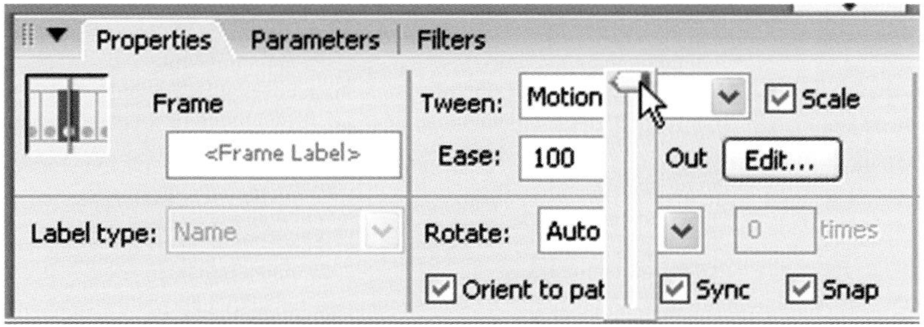

Accelerate an animated object

1. Play the movie and notice the speed of the car is constant.
2. Click **Frame 1** on the carRoute layer.
3. Click the **Ease list arrow** in the Property inspector, then drag the slider up to **100**, as shown in Figure 19.
4. Play the movie and notice how the car starts out fast and decelerates as it moves toward the end of the path.
5. Click **Frame 1** on the carRoute layer.
6. Click the **Ease list arrow** in the Property inspector, drag the slider down to **–100**, then click a blank area outside the stage.
7. Play the movie and notice how the car starts out slow and accelerates as it moves toward the end of the path.
8. Click **Control** on the menu bar, then click **Test Movie.**
9. View the movie, then close the test movie window.
10. Save your work.

You set Ease values to alter the starting and ending speed of the car.

CREATE ANIMATION EFFECTS

What You'll Do

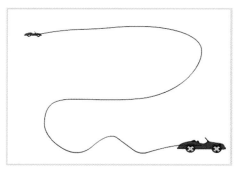

In this lesson, you will use motion tweening to resize, rotate, and change the color of animated objects.

Creating Motion Animation Effects

Up to this point, you have created motion-tweened animations that cause an object to move around the stage. There are several other effects that you can create using motion tweening, including resizing, rotating, and changing the color of an object as it is in motion.

Resizing an Object Using a Motion Tween

The simplest process for resizing an object during a motion tween is to select a frame as the starting frame, draw or place an object on the stage, then create a motion tween. You can select an ending frame and resize the object using the resize handles that are displayed when you select the Free Transform tool and the Scale option on the Tools panel. The results of this process are shown in Figure 20. By moving and resizing an object, you can create the effect that it is moving away from you or toward you. If you have the object remain stationary while it is being resized, the effect is similar to zooming in or out.

Rotating an Object Using a Motion Tween

You have several options when rotating an object using a motion tween. You can cause the object to rotate clockwise or counterclockwise any number of degrees and any number of times. You can also stipulate an Ease value to cause the rotation to accelerate or decelerate. These effects can be specified using the Free Transform tool and the Rotate option on the Tools panel, adjusting settings in the Property inspector, or clicking a Transform option on the Modify menu. The Transform options include Flip Vertical and Flip Horizontal. Choosing these options causes the object to slowly flip throughout the length of the animation. You can combine effects so that they occur simultaneously during the animation. For example, you can have a car rotate and get smaller as it moves across the stage. The Scale and Rotate dialog box allows you to specify a percentage for scaling and a number of degrees for rotating.

Changing an Object's Color Using a Motion Tween

Macromedia Flash provides several ways in which you can alter the color of objects using a motion tween. The most basic change involves starting with one color for the object and ending with another color. The tweening process slowly changes the color across the specified frames. When the movie is played, the colors are blended as the object moves across the stage. If you start with a red color and end with a blue color, at the middle of the animation the object's color is purple with equal portions of the blue and red colors mixed together.

More sophisticated color changes can be made using the Property inspector. You can adjust the brightness; tint the colors; adjust the transparency (Alpha option); and change the red, green, and blue values of an object. One of the most popular animation effects is to cause an object to slowly fade in. You can accomplish this by motion tweening the object, setting the Alpha value to 0 (transparent) in the starting frame, and then setting it to 100 in the ending frame. To make the object fade out, just reverse the values.

Using the Onion Skin Feature

Figure 21 displays the animation using the Onion Skin feature. Normally, Macromedia Flash displays one frame of an animation sequence at a time on the stage. Turning on the Onion Skin feature allows you to view an outline of the object(s) in any number of frames. This can help in positioning animated objects on the stage. The Edit Multiple Frames feature is also turned on allowing you to view the objects in the Keyframes in a non-outline form.

FIGURE 20
Resizing an object during a motion tween

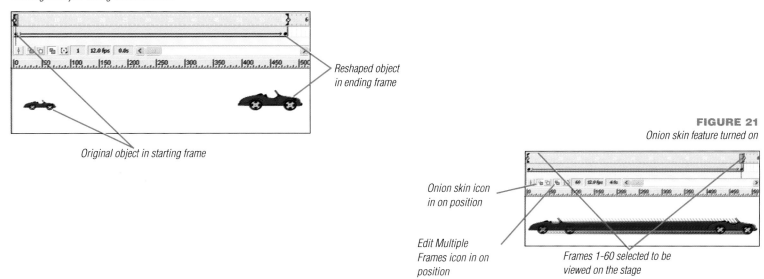

Reshaped object in ending frame

Original object in starting frame

FIGURE 21
Onion skin feature turned on

Onion skin icon in on position

Edit Multiple Frames icon in on position

Frames 1-60 selected to be viewed on the stage

Combining Various Animation Effects

Macromedia Flash allows you to combine the various motion-tween effects so that you can rotate an object as it moves across the stage, changes color, and changes size. Macromedia Flash allows you to combine motion-tweened animations to create various effects. For example, if you create an airplane object, you can apply the following aerial effects:

- enter from off stage and perform a loop;
- rotate the plane horizontally to create a barrel roll effect;
- grow smaller as it moves across the screen to simulate the effect of the plane speeding away;

- change colors on the fuselage to simulate the reflection of the sun.

Creating Timeline Effects

Macromedia Flash provides several pre-built Timeline effects, such as having an object fade-in, that allow you to create complex animations with only a few steps. You simply select an object, select an effect, then specify the settings. You can apply Timeline effects to the following objects:

- Text
- Graphics, including shapes, groups, and graphic symbols
- Bitmap images
- Button symbols

When you apply a Timeline effect to an object, Macromedia Flash creates a layer and transfers the object to the new layer. The object is placed inside the effect graphic, and all tweens and transformations required for the effect reside in the graphic on the new layer. The new layer automatically receives the same name as the effect, with a number appended that represents the order in which the effect is applied. An effect symbol is created and placed in an Effects Folder that is added to the Library panel. Also, the effect graphic is added to the Library panel.

Adding an Effect to an Object

To add an effect to an object, you select the object, then choose Timeline Effects from

FIGURE 22

The Timeline Effects options on the Insert menu

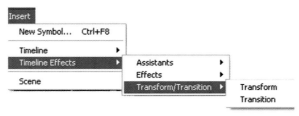

Creating Animations

the Insert menu. Three options appear that are used to display categories of effects available for the type of object you've selected, as shown in Figure 22. When you choose an effect a dialog box appears, illustrating the effect and allowing you to modify the default settings. Figure 23 shows the default settings for the Fade effect. These settings allow you to:

- Specify the duration of the effect in number of frames
- Specify the direction (In or Out)
- Specify a motion ease

When you select the object on the stage, you can view properties for the effect in the Property inspector.

Editing a Timeline Effect

To edit a Timeline effect you select the object associated with the effect on the Stage and click Edit in the Property inspector. This displays the appropriate Effects Setting dialog box.

Deleting a Timeline Effect

The context menu is used to delete Timeline effects. On the Stage, right-click (Win) or control click (Mac) the object and select Timeline Effects from the context menu, then select Remove Effect.

FIGURE 23

Default settings for the Fade In effect

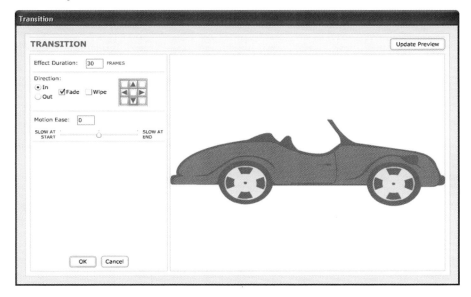

Use motion tweening to resize an object

1. Make sure that the carPath.fla movie is open.

2. Click **Frame 1** on the carRoute layer.

3. Make sure the car is selected, click the **Free Transform tool** ⊞ on the Tools panel, then click the **Scale option** ⊡ in the Options section of the Tools panel.

4. Drag the upper-left corner handle 🖈 inward until the car is approximately half the original size, as shown in Figure 24.

   | TIP Use the Zoom tool to enlarge the view of the car, if desired.

5. Click **Frame 40** on the carRoute layer.

6. Make sure the car is selected, then click the **Scale option** ⊡.

7. Drag the upper-right corner handle 🖈 outward until the car is approximately twice the original size, as shown in Figure 25.

8. Play the movie and notice how the car is resized.

9. Save your work, then close the movie.

You used the Scale option to resize an object in a motion animation.

FIGURE 24
Using the handles to reduce the size of the car

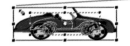

Click and drag the handle toward the car

FIGURE 25
Using the handles to increase the size of the car

Click and drag the handle away from the car

Creating Animations

FIGURE 26
Specifying the rotate settings

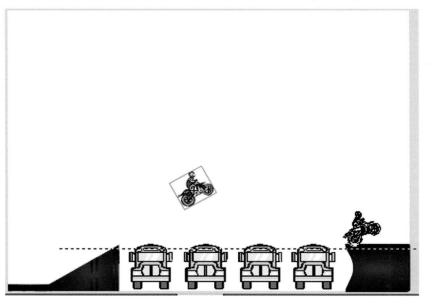

▼	Properties	Parameters	Filters	
	Frame		Tween: Motion ✓ ☑ Scale	
		<Frame Label>	Ease: 0 ✓ Edit... ⚠	
	Label type: Name ✓		Rotate: CCW ✓ 1 times	
			☐ Orient to path ☑ Sync ☑ Snap	

Rotation will be counter clockwise

FIGURE 27
Repositioning the motorbike

Use motion tweening to rotate an object

1. Open fl4_4.fla, then save it as **mBikeRotate**, then play the movie.

2. Click **Frame 10** on the motorBike layer.

3. Make sure the motorbike is selected, click **Insert** on the menu bar, point to **Timeline**, then click **Create Motion Tween**.

4. Click the **Rotate list arrow** on the Property inspector, click **CCW**, then verify 1 is entered into the times box, as shown in Figure 26.

5. Insert a keyframe in Frame 20 on the motorbike layer.

6. Play the movie; notice the motorbike moves forward, then rotates in place in the middle of the buses.

7. Click **Frame 20** on the motorBike layer, then drag the motorbike across the stage to the edge of the landing area, as shown in Figure 27.

8. Insert a Keyframe in Frame 21 on the motorbike layer.

9. Verify the motorbike is selected, click **Modify** on the menu bar, point to **Transform**, then click **Scale and Rotate**.

10. Type **30** for the Rotate value, then click **OK**.

11. Insert a keyframe in Frame 22, then drag the motorbike to the edge of the stage.

12. Play the movie; notice that the motorbike rotates as it moves over the buses to the landing area in the new location.

13. Save your work.

You created a motion animation and used the Property inspector to rotate the object.

Use motion tweening to change the color of an object

1. Click **Frame 20** on the motorBike layer.

2. Click the **Selection tool** ![selection tool icon] on the Tools panel, then click the motorbike to select it.

3. Click the **Color list arrow** in the Property inspector, click **Advanced**, then click the **Settings button** [Settings...].

4. Click the **xR)+ list arrow**, then drag the slider to **86**, as shown in Figure 28.

5. Click **OK**.

6. Click **Frame 1** on the timeline, then play the movie. You can see how the color slowly changes to a red shade.

   > TIP   Because motion tweening is performed on instances of symbols and text blocks, changing the color of a motion-tweened object affects the entire object. To make changes in individual areas of an object, you must first select the object and choose the Break Apart command from the Modify menu.

You used the Property inspector to change the color of an object as it was being animated.

FIGURE 28
Changing the color settings

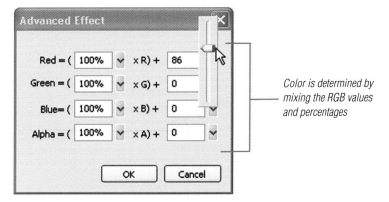

Color is determined by mixing the RGB values and percentages

Display the Onion Skin feature

1. Click **Frame 1** on the motorBike layer, then click the **Onion Skin icon** on the timeline.

2. Click the **Edit Multiple Frames icon** on the timeline.

3. Drag the **End Onion Skin slider** in the time-line to Frame 22, then compare your timeline to Figure 29.

   Each frame of the animation is visible on the stage.

4. Play the movie and notice that the animation is not affected by the onion skin feature being turned on.

5. Click the **Onion Skin icon** and the **Edit Multiple Frames icon** on the timeline to turn off these features.

6. Save and close the movie.

You displayed the animation using the Onion Skin feature, allowing you to view the object as it appears in each frame of the animation.

FIGURE 29
Using the Onion Skin feature

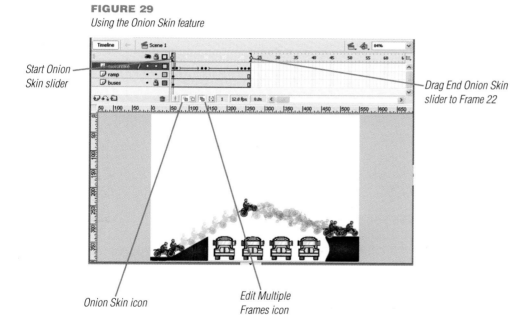

Start Onion Skin slider

Drag End Onion Skin slider to Frame 22

Onion Skin icon

Edit Multiple Frames icon

Create a Timeline Effect

1. Open fl4_5.fla, then save it as **carEffects**.

2. Click **Window** on the menu bar, then click **Library** to display the Library panel.

   Notice that there is only one item, a graphic named g_car, in the Library.

3. Click the **Selection tool** ![selection] on the Tools panel (if necessary), then drag the car from the Library panel to the upper-left corner of the stage, as shown in Figure 30.

4. Click **Modify** on the menu bar, then click **Break Apart**.

5. Click **Insert** on the menu bar, point to **Timeline Effects**, point to **Transform/ Transition**, then click **Transition**.

   The Transition dialog box opens allowing you to change the settings for Fade and Wipe effects. The preview shows how the default settings will affect the object on the stage, including a fade, a wipe and a duration of 30 frames.

6. Click the **Wipe check box** to turn off this effect, then click **Update Preview**. Notice that fade is the only effect.

7. Click **OK** to close the dialog box.

   A new layer was created and given the same name (Transition 1) as the effect, as shown in Figure 31. Note: the number after the word Transition may vary.

8. Play the movie.

You created a Fade in Timeline Effect.

FIGURE 30
Positioning the car on the stage

FIGURE 31
The layer name displays the effect name

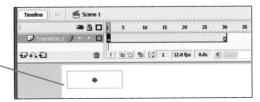

Car is not visible because the fade in transition effect starts in Frame 1

FIGURE 32

The Library panel displaying the Transition Effect

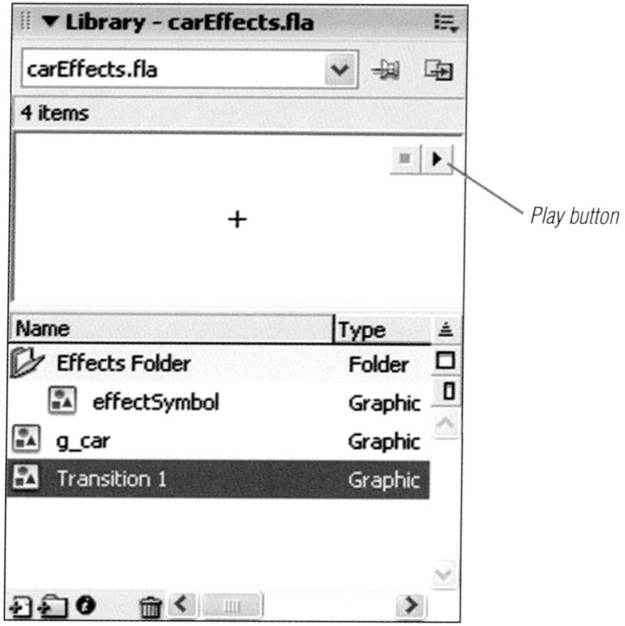

Play button

1. Double click the **Effects Folder icon** in the Library panel, then click **effectSymbol** to display the graphic symbol in the Item preview window of the Library panel.

   The effectSymbol was created and added to an Effects Folder in the Library panel when the Timeline effect was specified.

2. Click the **Transition symbol1** in the Library panel.

   The Transition graphic was created and added to the Library panel when the Timeline effect was specified. This graphic holds the effect which can be viewed in the Library panel.

3. Click the **Play button** in the Item preview window of the Library panel, as shown in Figure 32.

You viewed the effectSymbol and played the transition using the graphic within the Library panel.

Edit and remove a Timeline Effect

1. Display the Property inspector panel, if necessary.

2. Click **Frame 30** on the timeline, click the **Selection tool** , then click the **car**.

3. Click the **Edit button**  on the Properties panel to open the Transition dialog box.

4. Click the **Out option button** to change the direction.

5. Drag the **Motion Ease slider** to the right to set the Motion Ease to **100**, then compare your screen to Figure 33.

6. Click **Update Preview**, then click **OK**.

7. Play the movie.

8. Click **Frame 1** on the Timeline.

9. Right-click (Win) or control click (Mac) the car, point to **Timeline Effects**, then click **Remove Effect**.

10. Play the movie.

You edited a timeline effect using an Effect Settings dialog box, then removed the effect.

FIGURE 33
The completed Transition dialog box

Fade

Direction

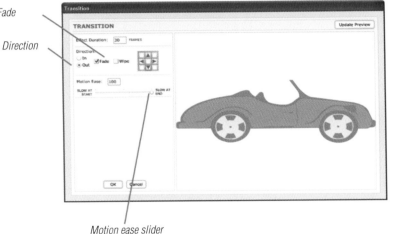

Motion ease slider

FIGURE 34
The completed Transform dialog box

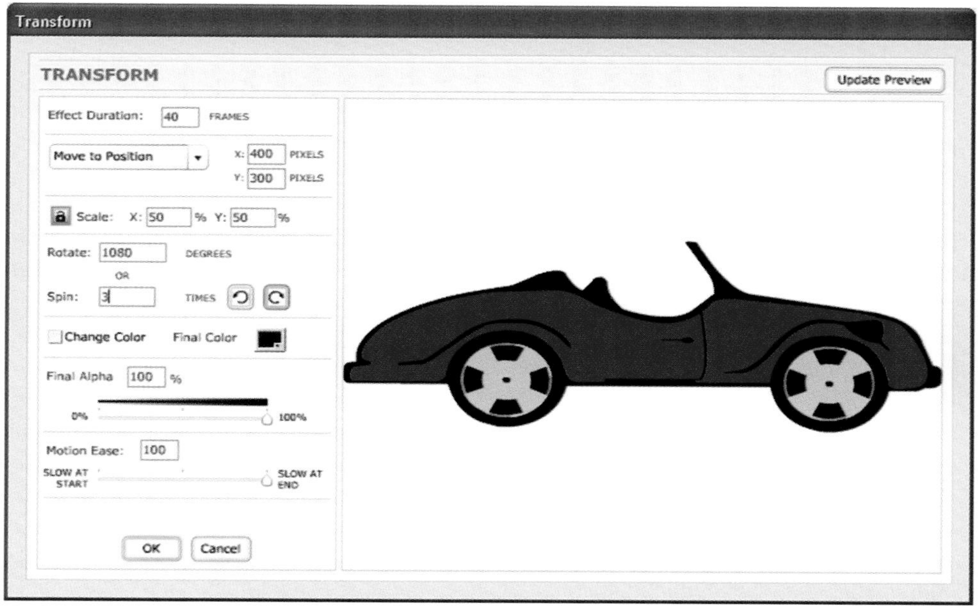

Apply several Timeline Effects to one object

1. Click the **Selection tool** ▸ on the Tools panel, then drag a marquee around the car to select it.

2. Click **Insert** on the menu bar, point to **Timeline Effects**, point to **Transform/ Transition**, then click **Transform**.

3. Change the effect duration to **40** frames.

4. Click the **Change Position by list arrow**, then click **Move to Position**.

5. Double-click **0** in the X Position text box, then type **400**.

6. Double-click **0** in the Y Position text box, then type **300**. X and Y are the coordinates (in pixels) for the position of the object on the stage. If the stage dimensions are 800x600, then 400(X-width) and 300(Y-height) would position the object in the middle of the stage.

7. Click the **Scale Lock icon** 🔒 to unlock it.

8. Double-click **100** in the X Scale text box, then type **50**.

9. Double-click **100** in the Y Scale text box, then type **50**.

10. Change the spin times to **3**.

11. Change the Motion Ease value to **100**, then compare your screen to Figure 34.

12. Click **Update Preview**, then click **OK**.

13. Play the movie, then save and close the movie.

You used the Effect Settings dialog box to apply several effects to a single object.

ANIMATE TEXT

What You'll Do

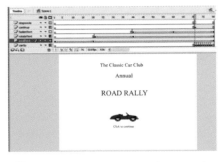

 In this lesson, you will animate text by scrolling, rotating, zooming, and resizing it.

Animating Text

You can motion tween text block objects just as you do graphic objects. You can resize, rotate, reposition, and change their colors. Figure 35 shows three examples of animated text with the Onion Skin feature turned on. When the movie starts, each of the following can occur one after the other:

- The Classic Car Club text block scrolls in from the left side to the top center of the stage. This is done by positioning the text block off the stage and creating a motion-tweened animation that moves it to the stage.
- The Annual text block appears and rotates five times. This occurs after you create the Annual text block, position it in the middle of the stage under the heading, and use the Property inspector to specify a clockwise rotation that repeats five times.

Creating Animations

- The ROAD RALLY text block slowly zooms out and appears in the middle of the stage. This occurs after you create the text block and use the Free Transform tool handles to resize it to a small block. You use the Property inspector to specify a transparent value. Finally, the text block is resized to a larger size at the end of the animation.

Once you create a motion animation using a text block, the text block becomes a symbol and you are unable to edit individual characters within the text block. You can, however, edit the symbol as a whole.

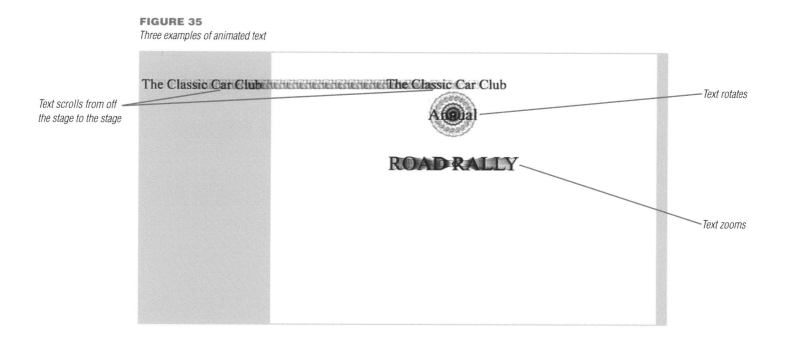

FIGURE 35
Three examples of animated text

Text scrolls from off the stage to the stage

Text rotates

Text zooms

Select, copy, and paste frames

1. Open frameAn.fla (the file you created earlier in this chapter), then save the movie as **textAn**.

2. Click **Frame 10** on the carGo layer, press and hold **[Shift]**, then click **Frame 1** to select all the frames, as shown in Figure 36.

3. Click **Edit** on the menu bar, point to **Timeline**, then click **Cut Frames**.

4. Click **Frame 71** on the carGo layer.

5. Click **Edit** on the menu bar, point to **Timeline**, then click **Paste Frames**.

6. Play the movie, then save your work.

7. Click **Frame 1** of the carGo layer.

You selected frames, and moved them from one location on the timeline to another location on the timeline.

FIGURE 36
Selecting frames

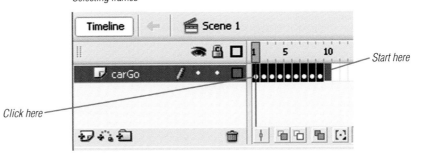

Creating Animations

FIGURE 37
Positioning the Text tool pointer outside the stage

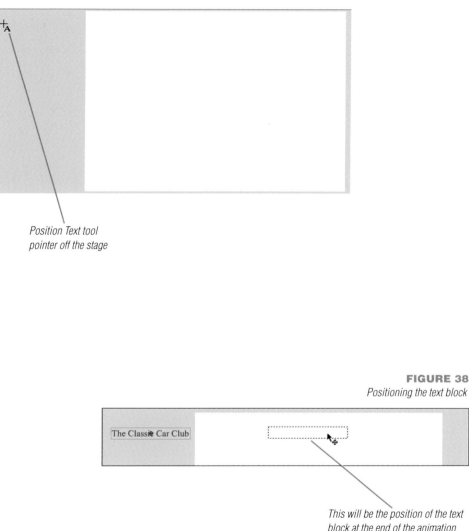

*Position Text tool
pointer off the stage*

FIGURE 38
Positioning the text block

The Classic Car Club

*This will be the position of the text
block at the end of the animation*

Create animated text

1. Insert a new layer, then name it **scrollText**.

2. Click **Frame 1** on the scrollText layer, then verify that the Property inspector is displayed.

3. Click the **Text tool A** on the Tools panel, click the ⁺A pointer outside the stage in the upper-left corner of the workspace, as shown in Figure 37, then click to display a text box.

4. Click the **Font list arrow** in the Property inspector, then click **Times New Roman**, if necessary.

5. Click the **Font Size list arrow** in the Property inspector, then drag the slider to **20**.

6. Click the **Text (fill) color swatch** ▮, click the **blue color swatch** on the left column of the color palette, then click the **Left Align button** ▤ in the Property inspector.

7. Type **The Classic Car Club**.

8. Click the **Selection tool ▶** on the Tools panel, click the **text block**, click **Insert** on the menu bar, point to **Timeline**, then click **Create Motion Tween**.

9. Insert a keyframe in Frame 20 on the scrollText layer.

10. Drag the text block horizontally to the top center of the stage, as shown in Figure 38.

11. Insert a keyframe in Frame 80 on the scrollText layer.

12. Play the movie.

   The text moves to center stage from offstage left.

You created a text block object and applied a motion tween animation to it.

Create rotating text

1. Insert a new layer, then name it **rotateText**.

2. Insert a keyframe in Frame 21 on the rotateText layer.

3. Click the **Text tool**  on the Tools panel, position the pointer beneath the "a" in "Classic," then click to display a blank text box.

4. Click the **Font Size list arrow** on the Property inspector, drag the slider to **24**, click in the new text box, type **Annual**, then compare your image to Figure 39.

5. Click the **Selection tool** on the Tools panel, click **Insert** on the menu bar, point to **Timeline**, then click **Create Motion Tween**.

6. Click **Frame 21** on the rotateText layer, click the **Rotate list arrow** in the Property inspector, click **CW**, then type **2** in the times text box.

7. Insert keyframes in Frames 40 and 80 on the rotateText layer.

8. Play the movie.

   The Annual text rotates clockwise two times.

You inserted a new layer, created a rotating text block, and used the Property inspector to rotate the text box.

FIGURE 39
Positioning the Annual text block

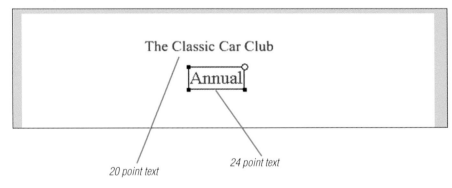

The Classic Car Club

Annual

20 point text

24 point text

FIGURE 40

Using the Text Tool to type ROAD RALLY

> The Classic Car Club
>
> Annual
>
> ROAD RALLY

FIGURE 41

Resizing and repositioning the text block

> The Classic Car Club
>
> Annual
>
> ▰◉▰

FIGURE 42

The enlarged text block

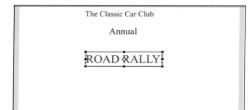

> The Classic Car Club
>
> Annual
>
> ROAD RALLY

Resize and fade in text

1. Insert a new layer, name it **fadeinText**, then insert a keyframe in Frame 40 on the fadeinText layer.

2. Click the **Text tool A** on the Tools panel, position the pointer beneath the Annual text box aligning with the "T" in "The", then type **ROAD RALLY**, as shown in Figure 40.

3. Click the **Free Transform tool** ⊞ on the Tools panel, then click the **Scale option** ⊡ in the Options section.

4. Drag the upper-left corner handle ⌐ inward to resize the text block, then position the text block, as shown in Figure 41.

5. Click **Insert** on the menu bar, point to **Timeline**, then click **Create Motion Tween**.

6. Click the **Color list arrow** on the Property inspector, click **Alpha**, click the **Alpha Amount list arrow**, then drag the slider to **0**.

7. Insert a keyframe in Frame 60 on the fadeinText layer, then click the object.

8. Click the **Alpha Amount list arrow** in the Property inspector, then drag the slider to **100**.

9. Click the **ROAD RALLY** text block, click the **Free Transform tool** ⊞, click the **Scale option** ⊡, drag the upper-left corner handle ⌐ outward to resize the text block, then position it, as shown in Figure 42.

10. Insert a keyframe in Frame 80 on the fadeinText layer.

11. Play the movie.

You created a motion animation that caused a text block to fade in and zoom out.

Make a text block into a button

1. Insert a new layer, then name it **continue**.

   | TIP Scroll up the timeline to view the new layer.

2. Insert a keyframe in Frame 71 on the continue layer.

3. Click the **Text tool A** on the Tools panel, position the **Text Tool pointer** beneath the back wheel of the car, then type **Click to continue**.

4. Drag the pointer over the text to select it, click the **Font Size list arrow** in the Property inspector, drag the slider to **12**, click the **Selection tool** on the Tools panel, then compare your image to Figure 43.

5. Verify that the text box is selected, click **Modify** on the menu bar, click **Convert to Symbol**, type **b_continue** in the Name text box, click the **Type Button option button** (if necessary), then click **OK**.

6. Click the **Selection tool** (if necessary), then double-click the **text block** to edit the button.

7. Insert a keyframe in the Over frame, click the **Fill Color tool** on the Tools panel, then click the **black color swatch** in the left column of the color palette.

8. Insert a keyframe in the Down frame, click the **Fill Color tool**, then click the **bright green color swatch** in the left column of the color palette.

9. Insert a keyframe in the Hit frame, click the **Rectangle tool** on the Tools panel, then draw a rectangle that covers the text block and the car, as shown in Figure 44.

10. Click **Scene 1** above the Timeline layers to return to the main timeline.

You made the text block into a button.

FIGURE 43
Adding a button

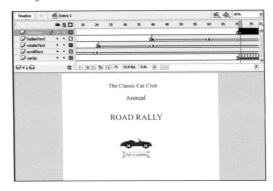

FIGURE 44
The rectangle that defines the hit area

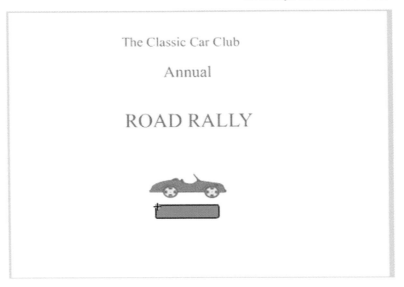

FIGURE 45
Add a play action

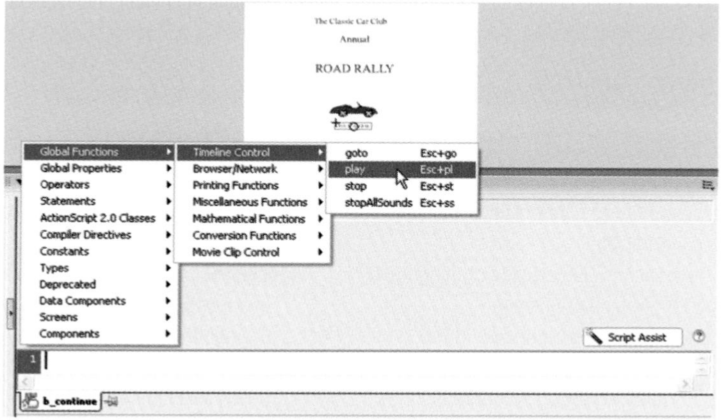

Add an action to the button

1. Display the Actions panel.

2. Click the **Selection tool** ![arrow] on the Tools panel, then click the **continue button** on the stage.

3. Click the **ScriptAssist button** [Script Assist] to turn it on, then verify the b_continue button symbol is displayed in the lower left corner of the Actions panel.

4. Click the **Add a new item to the script button** ![plus] in the Script Assist window, point to **Global Functions**, point to **Timeline Control**, then click **play**, as shown in Figure 45.

5. Insert a new layer, name it **stopmovie**, then insert a keyframe in Frame 71.

6. Click the **Add a new item to the script button** ![plus] in the Script Assist window, point to **Global Functions**, point to **Timeline Control**, then click **stop**.

7. Click **Control** on the menu bar, then click **Test Movie**.

   The movie plays the animated text blocks, then plays the animated car when you click the ActionScript text.

8. Close the test movie window, then save and close the movie.

9. Exit Flash.

You inserted a play button and added a stop action to it.

Create a frame animation.

1. Start Flash, openfl4_6.fla, then save it as **skillsdemo4**.
2. Add a background color of **#006666**.
3. Insert a keyframe in Frame 22 on the v-ball layer.
4. Resize the object to approximately one-fourth its original size.
5. Insert a keyframe in Frame 23 on the v-ball layer.
6. Resize the object back to approximately its original size.
7. Insert a keyframe in Frame 24 on the v-ball layer, then drag the object to the upper-left corner of the stage.
8. Insert a keyframe in Frame 25 on the v-ball layer, then drag the object to the lower-left corner of the stage.
9. Insert a keyframe in Frame 26 on the v-ball layer, then drag the object to the upper-right corner of the stage.
10. Insert a keyframe in Frame 27 on the v-ball layer, then drag the object to the lower-right corner of the stage.
11. Change the movie frame rate to 3 frames per second, then play the movie.
12. Change the movie frame rate to 12 frames per second, play the movie, then save your work.

Create a motion-tweened animation.

1. Insert a new layer and name it **ballAn**.
2. Insert a keyframe in Frame 28 on the ballAn layer.
3. Display the Library panel, then drag the g_vball graphic symbol to the lower-left corner of the stage.
4. Make sure the object is selected, then create a Motion Tween.
5. Insert a keyframe in Frame 60 on the ballAn layer.
6. Drag the object to the lower-right corner of the stage.
7. Play the movie, then save your work.

Create a motion guide.

1. Click Frame 28 on the ballAn layer.
2. Insert a Motion Guide layer.
3. Use the Pencil tool to draw a motion path in the shape of an arc, then alter the path to resemble Figure 46.
4. Attach the object to the left side of the path in Frame 28 on the ballAn layer.
5. Attach the object to the right side of the path in Frame 60 on the ballAn layer.
6. Use the Property inspector to orient the object to the path.
7. Play the movie, then save your work.

Accelerate the animated object.

1. Click Frame 28 on the ballAn layer.
2. Use the Property inspector to change the Ease value to **−100**.
3. Play the movie, then save your work.

Create motion animation effects.

1. Click Frame 60 on the ballAn layer, and use the Free Transform tool and the Scale tool option handles to resize the object to approximately one-fourth its original size.
2. Click Frame 28 on the ballAn layer, and use the Property inspector to specify a clock-wise rotation that plays five times.
3. Play the movie.
4. Select Frame 60 on the ballAn layer, then select the ball.
5. Use the Advanced Color option in the Property inspector to change the color of the object to green by specifying **143** as the green value.
6. Play the movie, then save your work.

Animate text.

1. Click the Guide: ballAn layer, then insert a new layer and name it **heading**.
2. Click Frame 1 on the heading layer.
3. Use the Text tool to type **Having fun with a** in a location off the top-left of the stage.
4. Change the text to Arial, 20 point, gray, and boldface.
5. Insert a motion tween.
6. Insert a keyframe in Frame 10 on the heading layer.
7. Drag the text to the top center of the stage.
8. Insert a keyframe in Frame 60 on the heading layer.
9. Play the movie and save your work.
10. Insert a new layer and name it **zoom**.
11. Insert a keyframe in Frame 11 on the zoom layer.
12. Use the Text Tool to type **Volleyball** below the heading, then center it as needed.

13. Create a motion tween.
14. Insert a keyframe in Frame 20 on the zoom layer.
15. Click Frame 11 on the zoom layer and select the text block.
16. Use the Property inspector to set the Alpha color option to **0**.

17. Resize the text block to **7** pixels in height in Frame 11 on the zoom layer.
18. Select Frame 20 on the zoom layer, and resize the text block to approximate the size shown in Figure 46.

19. Insert a keyframe in Frame 60 of the zoom layer.
20. Test the movie, then save your work.
21. Exit Flash.

FIGURE 46
Completed Skills Review

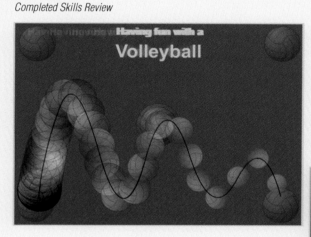

The Ultimate Tours travel company has asked you to design several sample animations for their Web site. Figure 47 shows a sample homepage and the Cruises screen. Using these (or one of the homepages you created in Chapter 3) as a guide, complete the following:

For the Ultimate Tours homepage:

1. Open ultimatetours3.fla (the file you created in Chapter 3 Project Builder 1) and save it as **ultimatetours4**.
2. Animate the heading **Ultimate Tours** so that it zooms out from a transparent text block.
3. After the heading appears, make the subheading **We Specialize in Exotic Adventures** appear.
4. Make each of the buttons (Treks, Tours, Cruises) scroll from the bottom of the stage to their positions on the stage. Stagger the buttons so that each one scrolls after the other.
5. Make the logo text appear.

6. Assign a stop action after the homepage appears.
7. Assign a go-to action to the Cruises button to jump to the frame that has the Cruises screen.
8. Add a Cruises screen, then display the heading, subheading, and logo.
9. To the Library panel, import the graphic file ship.gif from the drive and folder where your Data Files are stored, then rename the graphic file **g_ship**.
10. Create a motion-tweened animation that moves the ship across the screen.
11. Add a motion path that has a dip in it.
12. Attach the boat to the motion path, and orient it to the path.

13. Add a new layer, name it **cruise placeholder**, then add three placeholders (Cruise 1, Cruise 2, Cruise 3) to the last frame of the timeline.
14. Add the Home button.
15. Test the movie, then compare your movie to the example shown in Figure 47.

FIGURE 47
Sample completed Project Builder 1

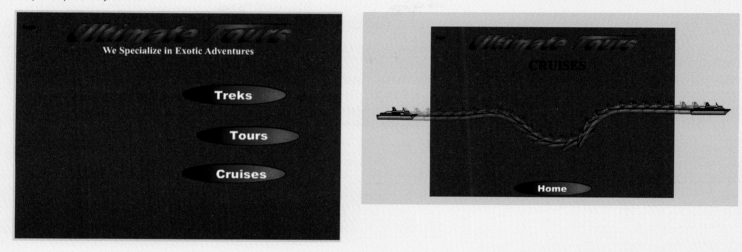

You have been asked to develop a Web site for the school's summer basketball camp. The camp caters to kids aged 6 to 12 years old. Participants are grouped by ability and given instruction on the fundamentals of basketball such as dribbling, passing, and shooting; the rules of the game; teamwork; and sportsmanship. A tournament is played at the end of the two-week camp.

Include the following on the Web site:

1. An initial screen with information about the camp (you provide the camp name, dates, and so on).
2. A black border around the stage, and add a colored background.
3. A frame-by-frame animation.
4. A motion-tweened animation.
5. One or more animations that has an object(s) change location on the stage, rotate, change size, and change color.
6. One or more animations that has a text block(s) change location on the stage, rotate, change size, change color, zoom in or out, and fade in or out.
7. An animation that uses a motion guide.
8. An animation that changes the Ease setting.
9. Save the movie as **summerBB4**, then compare your image to the example shown in Figure 48.

FIGURE 48

Sample completed Project Builder 2

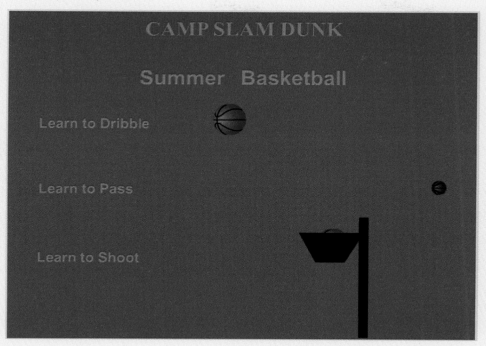

DESIGN PROJECT

Figure 49 shows a Web site for kids. Study the figure and complete the following. For each question, indicate how you determined your answer.

1. Connect to the Internet, go to *www.course.com*, navigate to the page for this book, click the Online Companion link, then click the link for this chapter.

2. Open a document in a word processor or open a new Macromedia Flash document, save the file as **dpc4**, then answer the following questions. (*Hint*: Use the Text tool in Macromedia Flash.)

   ■ What seems to be the purpose of this site?

   ■ Who would be the target audience?

   ■ How might a frame animation be used in this site?

   ■ How might a motion-tweened animation be used?

   ■ How might a motion guide be used?

   ■ How might motion animation effects be used?

   ■ How might the text be animated?

FIGURE 49
Design Project

This is a continuation of the Portfolio Project in Chapter 3, which is the development of a personal portfolio. The homepage has several categories, including the following:

- Personal data
- Contact information
- Previous employment
- Education
- Samples of your work

In this project, you will create several buttons for the sample animations screen and link them to the animations.

1. Open portfolio3.fla (the file you created in Portfolio Project, Chapter 3) and save it as **portfolio4**.
2. Display the Sample Animation screen and change the heading to Sample Animations.
3. Add layers and create buttons for the tweened animation, frame-by-frame animation, motion path animation, and animated text.
4. Create a tweened animation or use the passing cars animation from Chapter 3, and link it to the appropriate button on the Sample Animations screen.

5. Create a frame-by-frame animation, and link it to the appropriate button on the Sample Animations screen.
6. Create a motion path animation, and link it to the appropriate button on the Sample Animations screen.
7. Create several text animations, using scrolling, rotating, and zooming; link them to the appropriate button on the Sample Animations screen.

8. Add a layer and create a Home button that links the Sample Animations screen to the Home screen.
9. Create frame actions that cause the movie to return to the Sample Animations screen after each animation has been played.
10. Test the movie.
11. Save your work, then compare sample pages from your movie to the example shown for two of the screens in Figure 50.

FIGURE 50
Sample completed Portfolio Project

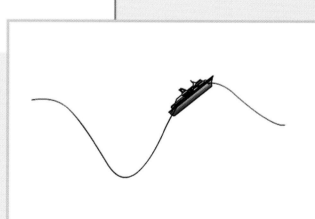

5

CREATING SPECIAL
EFFECTS

1. Create shape-tweened animations.

2. Create a mask effect.

3. Add sound.

4. Add scenes.

5. Create an animated navigation bar.

5 CREATING SPECIAL EFFECTS

Introduction

Now that you are familiar with the basics of Macromedia Flash, you can begin to apply some of the special features that can enhance a movie. Special effects can provide variety and add interest to a movie, as well as draw the viewer's attention to a location or event in the movie. One type of special effect is an animation that changes the shape of an object. This can be done using the shape tween feature of Flash. Another, related, type of special effect is morphing. The process of morphing makes one shape appear to change into another shape over time, such as an airplane changing into a hot air balloon as it flies across the sky. Another special effect is a spotlight that highlights an area(s) of the movie or reveals selected contents on the stage. You can use sound effects to enhance a movie by creating moods and dramatizing events. Another type of special effect is an animated navigation bar. For example, one that causes a drop down menu when the user rolls over a button. This effect can be created using masks and invisible buttons.

In addition to working with special effects, you now have experience in developing several movies around one theme, Classic Car Club, and are ready to incorporate these individual movies into a single movie with several scenes. Scenes provide a way to organize a large movie that has several parts, such as a Web site.

Tools You'll Use

CREATE SHAPE TWEEN
ANIMATIONS

What You'll Do

▶ *In this lesson, you will create a shape-tweened animation and specify shape hints.*

Shape Tweening

In Chapter 4, you learned that you can use motion tweening to change the shape of an object. You accomplish this by selecting the Free Transform tool and then dragging the handles. This process allows you to resize and skew the object. While this is easy and allows you to include motion along with the change in shape, there are two drawbacks. First, you are limited in the type of changes (resizing and skewing) that can be made to the shape of an object. Second, you must work with the same object throughout the animation. When you use **shape tweening**, however, you can have an animation change the shape of an object to any form you desire, and you can include two objects in the animation with two different shapes. As with motion tweening, you can use shape tweening to change other properties of an object, such as the color, location, and size.

Using Shape Tweening to Create a Morphing Effect

Morphing involves changing one object into another, sometimes unrelated, object.

For example, you could turn a robot into a man, or turn a football into a basketball. The viewer sees the transformation as a series of incremental changes. In Macromedia Flash, the first object appears on the stage and changes into the second object as the movie plays. The number of frames included from the beginning to the end of this shape-tweened animation determines how quickly the morphing effect takes place. The first frame in the animation displays the first object and the last frame displays the second object. The in-between frames display the different shapes that are created as the first object changes into the second object.

When working with shape tweening you need to keep the following points in mind:

- Shape tweening can be applied only to editable graphics. To apply shape tweening to instances, groups, symbols, text blocks, or bitmaps, you can use the Break Apart command on the Modify menu to break apart an object and make it editable. When you break apart an instance of a symbol, it is no longer linked to the original symbol.

- You can shape tween more than one object at a time as long as all the objects are on the same layer. However, if the shapes are complex and/or if they involve movement in which the objects cross paths, the results may be unpredictable.
- You can use shape tweening to move an object in a straight line, but other options, such as rotating an object, are not available.
- You can use the settings in the Property inspector to set options (such as acceleration or deceleration) for a shape tween.
- Shape hints can be used to control more complex shape changes.

Properties Panel Options

Figure 1 shows the Property inspector options for a shape tween. The options allow you to adjust several aspects of the animation, as described below.

- Adjust the rate of change between frames to create a more natural appearance during the transition by setting an ease value. Setting the value between -1 and -100 will begin the shape tween gradually and accelerate it toward the end of the animation. Setting the value between 1 and 100 will begin the shape tween rapidly and decelerate it toward the end of the animation. By default, the rate of change is set to 0, which causes a constant rate of change between frames.
- Choose a blend option. The Distributive option creates an animation in which the in-between shapes are smoother and more irregular. The Angular option preserves the corners and straight lines and works only with objects that have these features. If the objects do not have corners, Macromedia Flash will default to the Distributive option.

Shape Hints

You can use shape hints to control the shape's transition appearance during animation. Shape hints allow you to specify a location on the beginning object that corresponds to a location on the ending object. Figure 2 shows two shape animations of the same objects, one using shape hints and the other not using shape hints. The figure also shows how the object being reshaped appears in one of the in-between frames. Notice that with the shape hints the object in the in-between frame is more recognizable.

FIGURE 1

The Property inspector options for a shape tween

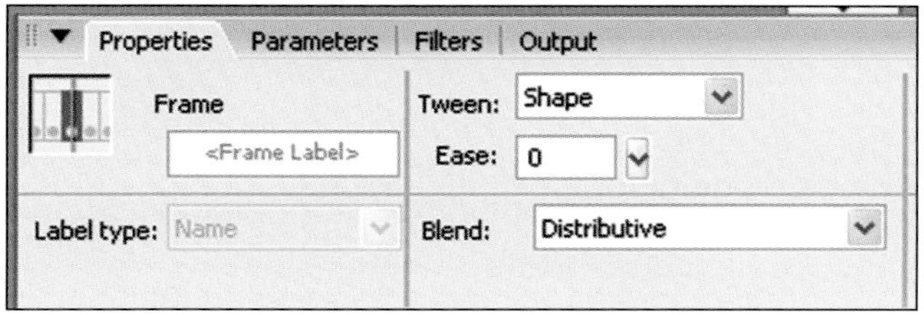

FIGURE 2

Two shape animations: with and without shape hints

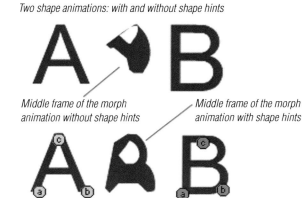

Middle frame of the morph animation without shape hints

Middle frame of the morph animation with shape hints

Create a shape tween animation

1. Open fl5_1.fla from the drive and folder where your Data Files are stored, then save it as **antiqueCar**.

2. Hide all panels, open the Tools and Property inspector panels, then change the view to Fit in Window.

3. Click **Frame 30** on the shape layer, then press **[F6]** to insert a keyframe.

4. Click a blank area outside the stage to deselect the car.

5. Point to the right side of the top of the car, then use the arc pointer ⮎ to drag the car top to the shape, as shown in Figure 3.

6. Click anywhere on the shape layer between Frames 1 and 30.

7. Make sure the Property inspector is displayed, click the **Tween list arrow**, ˅ then click **Shape**.

8. Click **Frame 1** on the shape layer, then play the movie.

9. Click **Frame 30** on the shape layer.

10. Click the **Selection tool** ▸ (if necessary) on the Tools panel, then drag a marquee around the car to select it.

11. Drag the car to the right side of the stage.

12. Play the movie, then save and close it.

You created a shape-tweened animation, causing an object to change shape as it moves over several frames.

FIGURE 3
The reshaped object

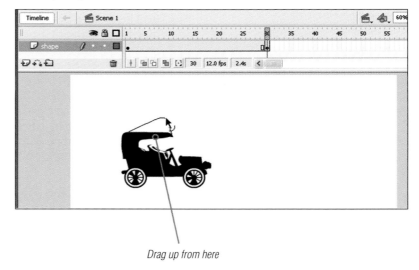

Drag up from here

Create a morphing effect

1. Open fl5_2.fla from the drive and folder where your Data Files are stored, then save it as **morphCar**.

2. Click **Frame 40** on the morph layer.

3. Click **Insert** on the menu bar, point to **Timeline**, then click **Blank Keyframe**.

   TIP   Inserting a blank keyframe prevents the object in the preceding keyframe from automatically being inserted into the blank frame.

4. Click the **Edit Multiple Frames icon** on the timeline.

   Turning on the Edit Multiple Frames feature will allow you to align the two objects to be morphed.

5. Open the Library panel.

6. Drag the **g_antiqueCarTopDown graphic** symbol from the Library panel directly on top of the car on the stage, as shown in Figure 4.

   TIP   Use the arrow keys to move the object in small increments.

7. Make sure that the **g_antiqueCarTopDown** object is selected, click **Modify** on the menu bar, then click **Break Apart**.

8. Click the **Edit Multiple Frames icon** to turn off the feature.

9. Click anywhere between Frames 1 and 40 on the morph layer, click the **Tween list arrow** on the Property inspector, then click **Shape**.

10. Click **Frame 1** on the timeline, then play the movie.

    The first car morphs into the second car.

11. Save the movie.

You created a morphing effect, causing one object to change into another.

FIGURE 4
Positioning the car instance on the stage

Line up both cars so it appears that there is only one car

Adjust the rate of change in a shape-tweened animation

1. Click **Frame 40** on the morph layer.

2. Click the **Selection tool** ▸ (if necessary) on the Tools panel, then drag a marquee around the car to select it.

3. Drag the **car** to the right side of the stage.

4. Click **Frame 1** on the morph layer.

5. Click the **Ease list arrow** on the Property inspector, then drag the slider down to **−100**, as shown in Figure 5.

6. Play the movie.

   The car starts out slow and speeds up as the morphing process is completed.

7. Repeat Steps 4 and 5, but change the Ease value to **100**.

8. Click **Frame 1** on the timeline, then play the movie.

   The car starts out fast and slows down as the morphing process is completed.

9. Save your work, then close the movie.

You added motion to a shape-tweened animation and changed the Ease values.

FIGURE 5

Changing the Ease value for the morph

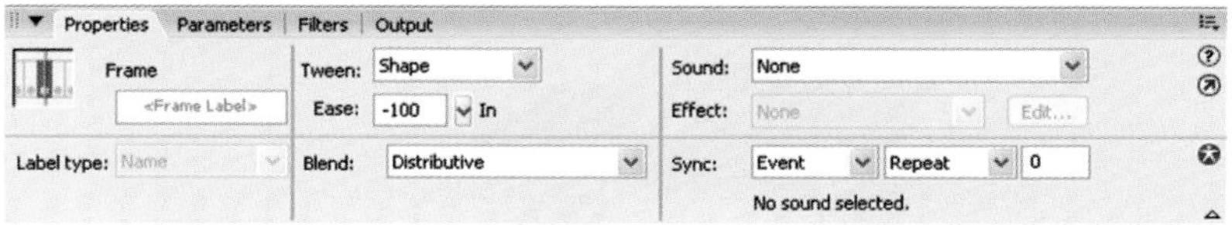

FIGURE 6
Positioning a shape hint

FIGURE 7
Adding shape hints

FIGURE 8
Matching shape hints

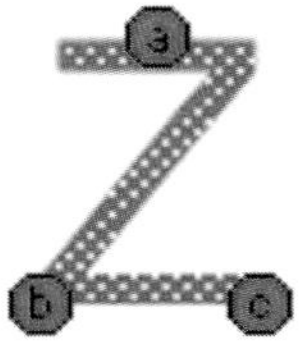

Use shape hints

1. Open fl5_3.fla from the drive and folder where your Data Files are stored, then save it as **shapeHints**.

2. Play the movie and notice how the L morphs into a Z.

3. Click **Frame 15** on the timeline, the midpoint of the animation, then notice the shape.

4. Click **Frame 1** on the hints layer to display the first object.

5. Make sure the object is selected, click **Modify** on the menu bar, point to **Shape**, then click **Add Shape Hint**.

6. Drag the **Shape Hint icon** to the location shown in Figure 6.

7. Repeat Steps 5 and 6 to set a second and third Shape Hint icon, as shown in Figure 7.

8. Click **Frame 30** on the hints layer. The shape hints are stacked on top of each other.

9. Drag the **Shape Hint icons** to match Figure 8.

10. Click **Frame 15** on the hints layer, then notice how the object is more recognizable now that the shape hints have been added.

11. Click **Frame 1** on the timeline, then play the movie.

12. Save your work, then close the movie.

You added shape hints to a morph animation.

CREATE A
MASK EFFECT

What You'll Do

Cla ssic Car lub

▶ *In this lesson, you will apply a mask effect.*

Understanding Mask Layers

A **mask layer** allows you to cover up the objects on one or more layers and, at the same time, create a window through which you can view various objects on the other layer. You can determine the size and shape of the window and specify whether it moves around the stage. Moving the window around the stage can create effects such as a spotlight that highlights certain contents on the stage, drawing the viewer's attention to a specific location. Because the window can move around the stage, you can use a mask layer to reveal only the area of the stage and the objects you want the viewer to see.

You need at least two layers on the timeline when you are working with a mask layer. One layer, called the mask layer, contains the window object through which you view the objects on the second layer below. The second layer, called the masked layer, contains the object(s) that are viewed through the window. Figure 9 shows how a mask layer works: The top part of the figure shows the mask

layer with the window in the shape of a circle. The next part of the figure shows the layer to be masked. The last part of the figure shows the results of applying the mask. Figure 9 illustrates the simplest use of a mask layer. In most cases, you want to have other objects appear on the stage and have the mask layer affect only a certain portion of the stage.

Following is the process for using a mask layer:

- Select an original layer that will become the masked layer—it contains the objects that you want to display through the mask layer window.
- Insert a new layer above the masked layer that will become the mask layer. A mask layer always masks the layer(s) immediately below it.
- Draw a filled shape, such as a circle, or create an instance of a symbol that will become the window on the mask layer. Macromedia Flash will ignore bitmaps, gradients, transparency colors, and line styles on a mask layer. On a mask layer, filled areas become

transparent and non-filled areas become opaque.

- Select the new layer and open the Layer Properties dialog box using the Timeline option from the Modify menu. Then select Mask. Macromedia Flash converts the layer to become the mask layer.

- Select the original layer and open the Layer Properties dialog box after selecting the Layer command on the Modify menu, then choose Masked. Macromedia Flash converts the layer to become the masked layer.
- Lock both the mask and masked layers.
- To mask additional layers: Drag an existing layer beneath the mask layer,

or create a new layer beneath the mask layer and use the Layer Properties dialog box to convert it to a masked layer.

- To unlink a masked layer: Drag it above the mask layer, or select it and select Normal from the Layer Properties dialog box.

FIGURE 9
A mask layer with a window

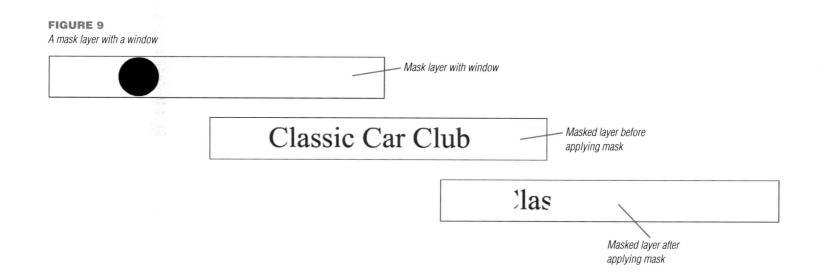

Mask layer with window

Classic Car Club

Masked layer before applying mask

Clas

Masked layer after applying mask

Create a mask layer

1. Open fl5_4.fla, then save it as **classicCC**.

2. Insert a new layer, name it **mask**, then click **Frame 1** of the mask layer.

3. Click the **Oval tool** ○ on the Tools panel, click the **Stroke Color tool** ✐ ▢ on the Tools panel, then click the **No Stroke icon** ▢ on the top row of the color palette.

4. Click the **Fill Color tool** ▧ ▢ on the Tools panel, then click the black color swatch in the left column of the color palette.

5. Draw the circle shown in Figure 10, click the **Selection tool** ▸ on the Tools panel, draw a marquee around the circle to select it, click **Insert** on the menu bar, point to **Timeline**, then click **Create Motion Tween**.

6. Insert a keyframe in Frame 40 on the mask layer, then drag the circle to the position shown in Figure 11.

7. Click the **mask layer** on the timeline to select it, click **Modify** on the menu bar, point to **Timeline**, then click **Layer Properties**.

8. Verify that the **Show check box** is selected in the Name section, click the **Lock check box** to select it, click the **Mask option button** in the Type section, then click **OK**.

   The mask layer has a shaded mask icon next to it on the timeline.

9. Play the movie from Frame 1 and notice how the circle object covers the text in the heading layer as it moves across the stage.

You created a mask layer containing an oval object that moves across the stage.

FIGURE 10
Object to be used as the window on a mask layer

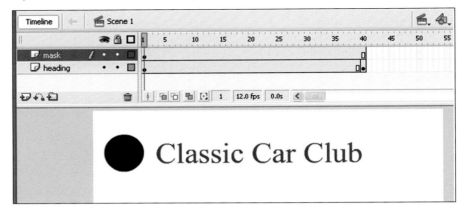

FIGURE 11
Repositioning the circle

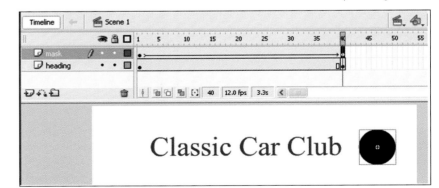

Creating Special Effects

FIGURE 12
The completed Layer Properties dialog box

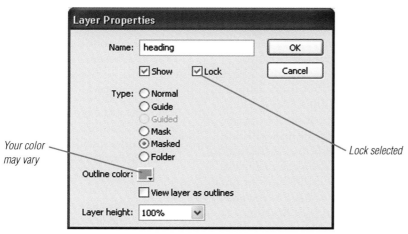

Your color
may vary

Lock selected

Create a masked layer

1. Click the **heading layer** to select it, click **Modify** on the menu bar, point to **Timeline**, then click **Layer Properties** to open the Layer Properties dialog box.

2. Verify that the **Show check box** is selected in the Name section, click the **Lock check box** to select it, click the **Masked option button** in the Type section, compare your dialog box to Figure 12, then click **OK**.

   The heading layer appears indented and has a shaded masked icon next to it on the timeline.

3. Play the movie and notice how the circle object acts as a window to display the text on the heading layer.

4. Save your work, then close the movie.

You used the Layer Properties dialog box to create a masked layer.

ADD
SOUND

What You'll Do

In this lesson, you will add sound to an animation.

Incorporating Animation and Sound

Sound can be extremely useful in a Macromedia Flash movie. Sounds are often the only effective way to convey an idea, elicit an emotion, dramatize a point, and provide feedback to a user's action, such as clicking a button. How would you describe in words or show in an animation the sound a whale makes? Think about how chilling it is to hear the footsteps on the stairway of a haunted house. Consider how useful it is to hear the pronunciation of "Buenos Dias" as you are studying Spanish. All types of sounds can be incorporated into a Macromedia Flash movie: for example, CD-quality music that might be used as background for a movie; narrations that help explain what the user is seeing; various sound effects, such as a car horn beeping; and recordings of special events, such as a presidential speech or a rock concert.

Following is the process for adding a sound to a movie:

- Import a sound file into the movie; Macromedia Flash places the sound into the movie's Library.
- Create a new layer.
- Select the desired frame in the new layer and drag the sound symbol to the stage.

You can place more than one sound file on a layer, and you can place sounds on layers with other objects. However, it is recommended that you place each sound on a separate layer as though it were a sound channel. In Figure 13, the sound layer shows a wave pattern that extends from Frame 1 to Frame 14. The wave pattern gives some indication of the volume of the sound at any particular frame. The higher spikes in the pattern indicate a louder sound. The wave pattern also gives some indication of the pitch. The denser the wave pattern, the lower the pitch. You can alter the sound by adding or removing frames.

However, removing frames may create undesired effects. It is best to make changes to a sound file using a sound-editing program.

You can use options in the Property inspector, as shown in Figure 14, to synchronize a sound to an event—such as clicking a button—and to specify special effects—such as fade in and fade out. You can import the following sound file formats into Macromedia Flash:

- WAV (Windows only)
- AIFF (Macintosh only)
- MP3 (Windows or Macintosh)

If you have QuickTime 4 or later installed on your computer, you can import these additional sound file formats:

- AIFF (Windows or Macintosh)
- Sound Designer II (Macintosh only)
- Sound Only QuickTime Movies (Windows or Macintosh)
- Sun AU (Windows or Macintosh)
- System 7 Sounds (Macintosh only)
- WAV (Windows or Macintosh)

FIGURE 13
A sound symbol displayed on the timeline

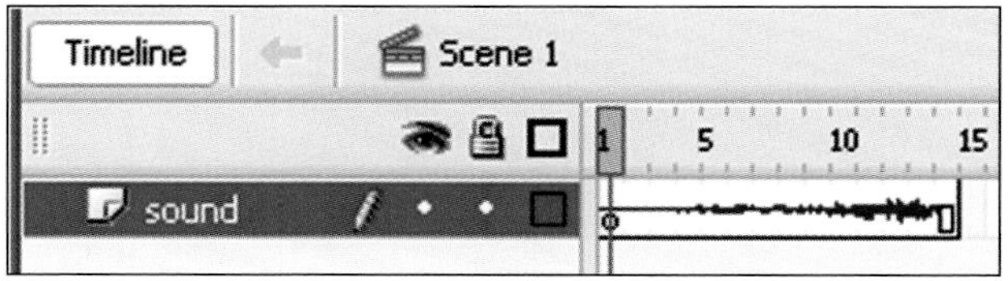

FIGURE 14
The sound options in the Property inspector

Add sound to a movie

1. Open fl5_5.fla, then save it as **rallySnd**.

2. Play the movie and notice that there is no sound.

3. Click the **stopmovie layer**, insert a new layer, then name it **carSnd**.

4. Insert a keyframe in Frame 72 on the carSnd layer.

5. Click **File** on the menu bar, point to **Import**, then click **Import to Library**.

6. Use the Import to Library dialog box to navigate to the drive and folder where your Data Files are stored, click the **CarSnd.wav file**, then click **Open** (Win) or **Import to Library** (Mac).

7. Open the Library Panel, if necessary.

8. Click **Frame 72** of the CarSnd layer.

9. Drag the **CarSnd sound symbol** 🔊 to the stage, as shown in Figure 15.

10. Click **Control** on the menu bar, then click **Test Movie**.

11. Click the **Click to continue text button** to test the sound, then close the test movie window.

You imported a sound and added it to a movie.

FIGURE 15
Dragging the CarSnd symbol to the stage

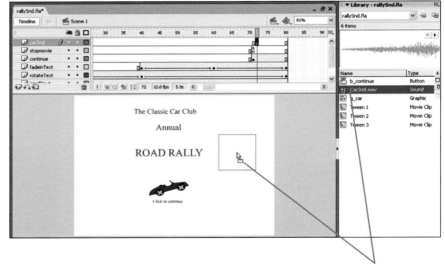

Drag the CarSnd
symbol to the stage

FIGURE 16

The button timeline with the sound layer

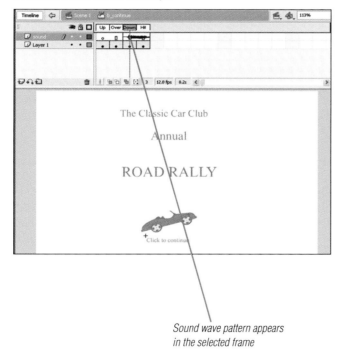

Sound wave pattern appears
in the selected frame

Add sound to a button

1. Click **Frame 71** on the carSnd layer.

2. Click the **Selection tool** ![cursor] on the Tools panel, drag a marquee around "Click to continue" to select the button, then double-click the selection to display the button's timeline.

3. Insert a new layer above Layer 1, then name it **sound**.

4. Click the **Down frame** on the sound layer, click **Insert** on the menu bar, point to **Timeline**, then click **Blank Keyframe**.

5. Click **File** on the menu bar, point to **Import**, then click **Import to Library**.

6. Use the Import to Library dialog box to navigate to the drive and folder where your Data Files are stored, click the **beep.wav file,** then click **Open** (Win) or **Import to Library** (Mac).

7. Drag the **beep.wav sound symbol** to the stage, then compare your timeline to Figure 16. Dragging the sound symbol to the stage causes the sound to be inserted into the selected frame.

8. Click **Scene 1** above the Timeline layers to display the main Timeline.

9. Click **Control** on the menu bar, click **Test Movie** to test the movie, then close the test movie window.

10. Save your work, then close the movie.

You added a sound layer to a button, imported a sound, then attached the sound to the button.

ADD SCENES

What You'll Do

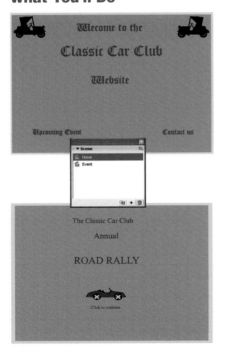

 In this lesson, you will add scenes to a movie and combine scenes from multiple movies into one movie.

Understanding Scenes

Until now you have been working with relatively short movies that have only a few layers and less than 100 frames. However, movies can be quite complex and extremely large. One way to help organize large movies is to use scenes. Just as with their celluloid equivalent, Macromedia Flash scenes are discrete parts of a movie. They have their own timeline and they can be played in any order you specify, or they can be linked through an interactive process that lets the user navigate to a desired scene.

QUICKTIP

There are no guidelines for the length or number of scenes appropriate for any size movie. The key is to determine how best to break down a large movie so that the individual parts are easier to develop, edit, and combine.

Working with Scenes

To add a scene to a movie, you choose Scene from the Insert menu or use the Scene panel. The Scene panel option is found in the Windows menu. The Scene panel can be used to accomplish the following:

- Rename a scene by double-clicking the scene name, then typing in the new name.
- Duplicate a scene by selecting it, then clicking the Duplicate Scene icon.
- Add a scene by clicking the Add Scene icon.
- Delete a scene by selecting it, then clicking the Delete scene icon.
- Reorder the scenes by dragging them up or down the list of scenes.

When a movie is played, the scenes are played in the order they are listed in the Scene panel. You can use the interactive features of Flash, such as a stop action and buttons with goto actions to allow the user to jump to various scenes.

Following is the process for combining scenes from several movies into one movie:
- Open the movie that will be used as Scene 1.
- Insert a new scene into the movie.
- Open the movie that will be used as Scene 2.

- Copy the frames from the second movie into Scene 2 of the first movie.
- Continue the process until the scenes for all the movies have been copied into one movie.

The home page for the Classic Car Club Web site, shown in Figure 17, will become the first scene of a multi-scene movie.

FIGURE 17
The Classic Car Club home page

Add and name a scene

1. Open fl5_6.fla, then save it as **cccHome**.

2. Click **Window** on the menu bar, point to **Other Panels**, then click **Scene** to open the Scene panel.

3. Double-click **Scene 1** in the Scene panel, type **Home**, then press **[Enter]** (Win) or **[return]** (Mac).

4. Click the **Add scene icon** ＋ , double-click **Scene 2**, type **Event**, press **[Enter]** (Win) or **[return]** (Mac), then compare your Scene panel with Figure 18.

   When the new scene, Event, is created, the stage and timeline are blank.

5. Click **Home** in the Scene panel and notice that the timeline changes to the Home scene.

6. Click **Event** in the Scene panel and notice that the timeline changes to the Event scene, which is blank.

7. Click **Control** on the menu bar, then click **Test Movie** to test the movie and notice how the movie moves from Scene 1 to the blank Scene 2.

   There is no content or stop action scripts in the Events scene, so the movie just jumps from one scene to another.

8. Close the test movie window.

You added a scene and used the Scene panel to rename the scenes.

FIGURE 18
Changes to the Scene panel

FIGURE 19

Selecting all the frames

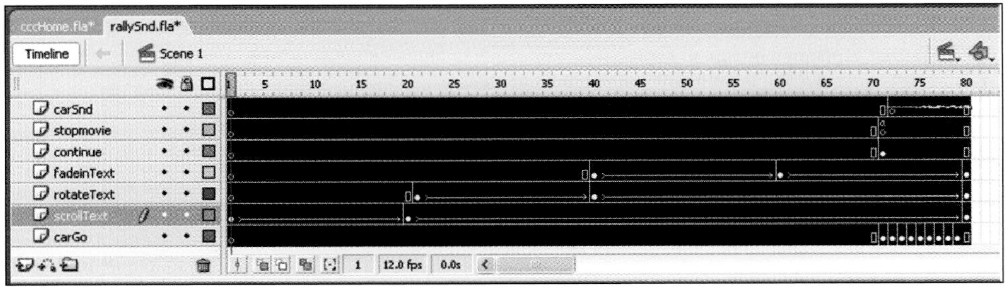

Copying frames to add to a scene

1. Open rallySnd.fla.

   | TIP: rallySnd.fla is the file you created in Lesson 3.

2. Click **Edit** on the menu bar, point to **Timeline**, then click **Select All Frames** to select all the frames in all the layers, as shown in Figure 19.

3. Click **Edit** on the menu bar, point to **Timeline**, then click **Copy Frames**.

4. Close rallySnd.fla without saving the changes.

5. Click **Window** on the menu bar, then click **cccHome.fla**, if necessary.

6. Make sure that the Event scene is selected.

7. Click **Frame 1** on Layer 1 of the Event scene.

8. Click **Edit** on the menu bar, point to **Timeline**, then click **Paste Frames**.

   The layers and frames from rallySnd.fla appear in the timeline of the Event scene.

9. Click **Home** in the Scene panel.

10. Test the movie and notice how the Home scene is played, followed by the Event scene.

11. Click the **Click to continue button** to complete the Events scene.

12. Close the test movie window.

You copied frames from one movie into a scene of another movie.

Add interactivity to scenes

1. Make sure that the Home scene is displayed.

2. Drag the **Scene panel** to display the entire stage, if necessary.

3. Click the **Selection tool**  on the Tools panel, then click the **Upcoming Event text button** on the stage.

4. Open the Actions panel, if necessary.

5. Verify the **Script Assist button** is selected and the script window is in view.

6. Verify the b_event button symbol is displayed in the lower left corner of the Actions panel.

7. Click the **Add a new item to the script icon** ⊕, point to **Global Functions**, point to **Movie Clip Control**, then click **on**.

8. Verify **Release** is selected, click the **Add a new item to the script icon** ⊕, point to **Global Functions**, point to **Timeline Control**, then click **goto**.

9. Click the **Scene list arrow** ∨, then click **Event**.

10. Compare your Actions panel with Figure 20.

You used the Actions panel to assign a goto action to a button that caused the movie to jump to another scene.

FIGURE 20
The completed Actions panel

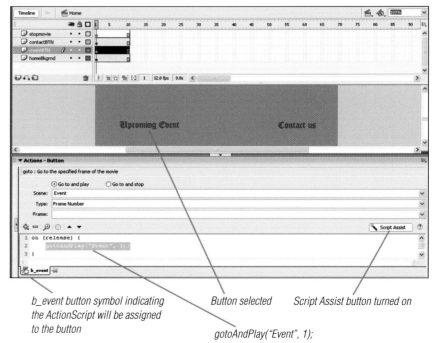

b_event button symbol indicating
the ActionScript will be assigned
to the button

Button selected   Script Assist button turned on

gotoAndPlay("Event", 1);

Add a Stop Action to a Frame

1. Click **Frame 1** of the stopmovie layer.

2. Click the **Add a new item to the script icon** ⊕ , point to **Global Functions**, point to **Timeline Control**, then click **stop**.

3. Compare your Actions panel to Figure 21.

4. Test the movie, click the **Upcoming Event button**, then notice how the Event scene plays.

5. Close the Scene panel.

6. Close the test movie window.

7. Save your work, then close the movie.

You added a stop action to a frame to cause the movie to stop playing.

FIGURE 21

Adding a stop action

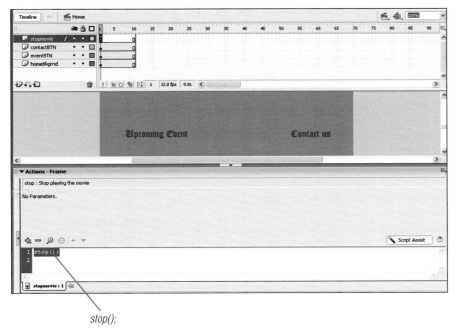

stop();

CREATE AN ANIMATED
NAVIGATION BAR

What You'll Do

In this lesson you will work through this process to create one drop down menu. The Web site is similar to the one in the previous lesson, however a navigation bar has been provided as well as the necessary buttons.

Understanding Animated Navigation Bars

A common navigation scheme for a Web site is a navigation bar with drop down menus such as the one shown in Figure 22. This scheme has several advantages. First, it allows the developer to provide several menu options to the user without cluttering the screen, thereby, providing more screen space for the Web site content. Second, it allows the user to go quickly to a location on the site without having to navigate through several screens to find the desired content. Third, it provides consistency in function and appearance making it easy for users to learn and work with the navigation scheme.

There are several ways to create drop down menus using the animation capabilities of Macromedia Flash. One common technique allows you to give the illusion of a drop down menu by using masks that reveal the menu. When the user points to (rolls over) an option in the navigation bar, a list or "menu" of buttons is displayed ("drops down"). Then the user can click a button to go to another location in the Web site or trigger some other action. The dropping down of the list is actually an illusion created by using a mask to "uncover" the menu options.

The process is:
- Create a navigation bar.
  This could be as basic as a background graphic in the shape of a rectangle with navigation bar buttons.
- Position the drop down buttons.
  Add a layer beneath the navigation bar layer. Then place the buttons below the navigation bar beneath their respective menu items on the stage. If the navigation bar has an Events button with two choices, Road Rally and Auction, that you want to have appear on a drop down menu, you would position these two buttons below the Events button on this drop down buttons layer.
- Add the animated mask.
  Add a mask layer above the drop down buttons layer and create an animation

of an object that starts above the drop down buttons and moves down to reveal them. Then change the layer to a mask layer and the button layers to masked layers.

- Assign actions to the drop down buttons. Select each drop down button and assign an action, such as "on release go to a Frame".
- Assign a roll over action to the navigation bar button.

The desired effect is to have the drop down buttons appear when the user points to a navigation bar button. Therefore, you need to assign a "on rollOver" action to the navigation bar button that causes the playhead to go to the frame that plays the animation on the mask layer. This can be done using the Script Assist feature.

- Create an invisible button.

When the user points to a navigation bar button, the drop down menu appears showing the drop down buttons. There needs to be a way to have the menu disappear when the user points away from the navigation bar button. This can be done by creating a button on a layer below the masked layers. This button would be slightly larger than the drop down buttons and their navigation bar button as shown in Figure 23. A rollOver action would be assigned to this button so that when the user rolls off the drop down or navigation bar buttons, they will roll on to this button and the action would be carried out. This button should be made transparent so the user does not see it.

Using Frame Labels

Until now you have been working with frame numbers in ActionScript code when creating a go to action. Frame labels can also be used in the code. You can assign a label to a frame as an identifier. For example, you could assign the label home to frame 10 and then create a goto home action that will cause the playhead to jump to frame 10. One advantage of using frame labels is that if you insert frames in the timeline the label adjusts for the added frames. So, you do not have to change the ActionScript that uses the frame label. Another advantage is that the descriptive labels help you identify parts of the movie as you work with the timeline. You assign a frame label by selecting the desired frame and typing a label in the Frame text box in the Property inspector.

FIGURE 23
A button that will be assigned a rollOver action

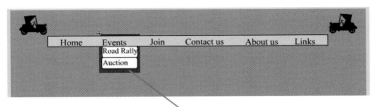

When the user's pointer rolls over the blue button a script will be executed that causes the drop down menu to disappear

FIGURE 22
A Web site with a navigation bar with drop down menus

Position the Drop Down Buttons

1. Open fl5_7.fla from the drive and folder where your Data Files are stored, then save it as **navBar**.

2. Hide all panels, then open the Tools, Library, and Property inspector panels.

3. Set the view to **Fit in Window**.

4. Click the **homeBkgrnd layer**, insert a new layer, then name it roadRally.

5. Click **Frame 2** of the roadRally layer, then press **[F6]** to insert a Keyframe.

6. Expand the Library panel, double-click the **Buttons folder**, then drag the **b_roadRally button** to the position just below the Events button on the Navigation bar, as shown in Figure 24.

7. Insert a layer above the homeBkgrnd layer, then name it **auction**.

(continued)

FIGURE 24

Positioning the b_roadRally button

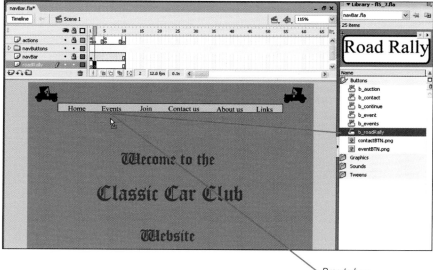

Drag to here

FIGURE 25
Positioning the buttons

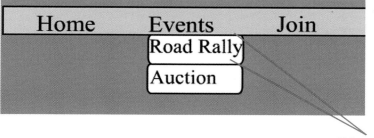

Make sure the button
borders overlap

8. Click **Frame 2** of the auction layer, then press **[F6]** to insert a Keyframe.

9. Drag the **b_auction button** from the Library panel and position it below the b_roadRally button.

10. Click the **Zoom tool** on the Tools panel, then click the **Events button** on the stage to enlarge the view.

11. Click the **Selection tool** on the Tools panel, then click each button and use the arrow keys to position them, as shown in Figure 25.

    The top line of the Road Rally button must overlap with the bottom border of the navigation bar. And the bottom border of the Road Rally button must overlap with the top border of the Auction button.

You placed the drop down button on the stage and repositioned them.

Add a Mask Layer

1. Click the **roadRally layer**, insert a new layer above the roadRally layer, then name it **mask**.

2. Click **Frame 2** of the mask layer, then press **[F6]** to insert a Keyframe.

3. Click the **Rectangle tool** ▢ on the Tools panel, set the Stroke Color to none ◙, then set the Fill Color to black.

4. Draw a rectangle that covers the buttons, as shown in Figure 26.

5. Click the **Selection tool** ▶ on the Tools panel, then drag the **rectangle** to above the buttons, as shown in Figure 27.

6. Verify the rectangle is selected, click **Insert** on the menu bar, point to **Timeline**, then click **Create Motion Tween**.

7. Click **Frame 5** on the mask layer, then press **[F6]** to insert a Keyframe.

(continued)

FIGURE 26
The drawn rectangle that covers the buttons

FIGURE 27
Dragging the rectangle above the buttons

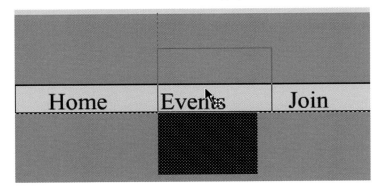

Creating Special Effects

FIGURE 28
The rectangle positioned over the buttons

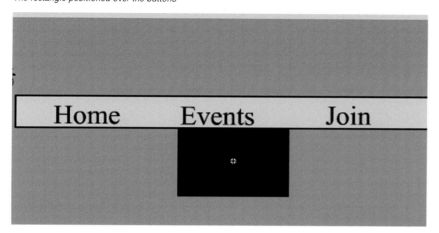

8. Click the **Selection tool** on the Tools panel, then drag the **rectangle** down to cover the buttons, as shown in Figure 28.

9. Click **mask** on the Timeline, click **Modify** on the menu bar, point to **Timeline**, click **Layer Properties**, click the **Mask option button**, then click **OK**.

10. Click **roadRally** on the Timeline, click **Modify** on the menu bar, point to **Timeline**, then click **Layer Properties**, click the **Masked option button**, then click **OK**.

11. Click **auction** on the Timeline, click **Modify** on the menu bar, point to **Timeline**, then click **Layer Properties**, click the **Masked option button**, then click **OK**.

12. Drag the **playhead** in the Timeline and notice how the mask hides and reveals the buttons.

13. Save your work.

You added a mask that animates to hide and reveal the menu buttons.

Assign an Action to a Drop Down Button

1. Click **Frame 2** of the roadRally layer, then click the **Road Rally button** to select it.

2. Open the Actions panel and verify the Script Assist window is visible and the b_roadRally button symbol is displayed, as shown in Figure 29.

3. Click the **Add a new item to the script icon**, point to **Global Functions**, point to **Timeline Control**, then click **goto**.

4. Click the **Scene list arrow**, then click **Scene 2**, as shown in Figure 30.

5. Set the Type to **Frame Number** and the Number to **1**.

You used the Script Assist window to assigned a goto action to a menu button.

FIGURE 29
The Actions panel with the b_roadRally button selected

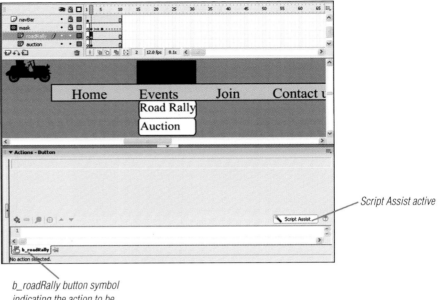

Script Assist active

b_roadRally button symbol indicating the action to be created will be assigned to the button

FIGURE 30
Selecting the scene to go to

Creating Special Effects

FIGURE 31

Specifying a frame label

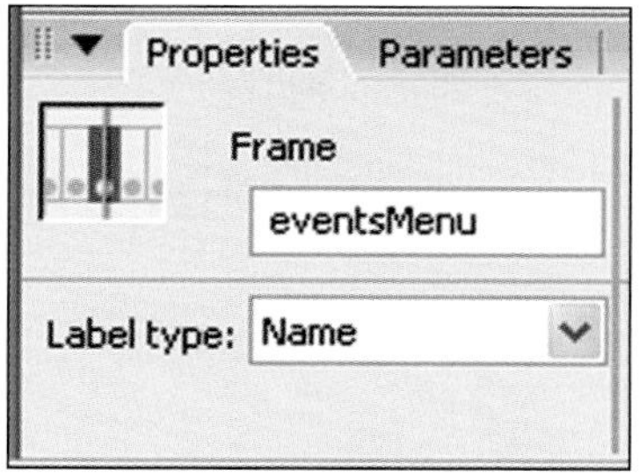

Properties   Parameters

Frame

eventsMenu

Label type: Name

FIGURE 32

The completed Actions panel

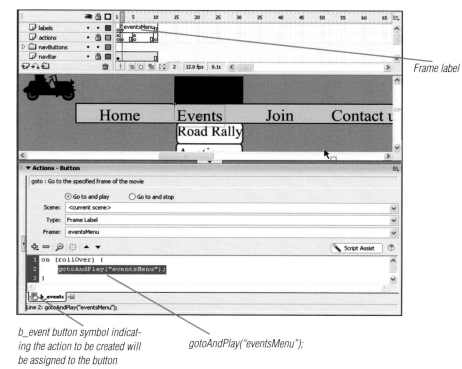

Frame label

*b_event button symbol indicat-
ing the action to be created will
be assigned to the button*

gotoAndPlay("eventsMenu");

Add a Frame Label and Assign a Rollover Action

1. Insert a layer at the top of the Timeline, name it **labels**, then insert a Keyframe in Frame 2 of the labels layer.

2. Verify that the Property inspector panel is open, click inside the **Frame text box**, then type **eventsMenu**, as shown in Figure 31.

3. Collapse the Property inspector panel, then click the **Events button** on the stage to select it.

4. Verify the b_events button symbol is displayed in the lower left corner of the Actions panel.

5. Click the **Add a new item to the script icon** 🔁, point to **Global Functions**, point to **Movie Clip Control**, then click **on**.

6. Click the **Release check box** to deselect it, then click the **Roll Over check box** to select it.

7. Click the **Add a new item to the script icon** 🔁, point to **Global Functions**, point to **Timeline Control**, then click **goto**.

8. Click the **Type list arrow** ✓, then click **Frame Label**.

9. Click the **Frame list arrow** ✓, then click **eventsMenu**. Your screen should resemble Figure 32.

10. Click **Control** on the menu bar, then click **Test Movie**.

11. Point to **Events**, then click **Road Rally**.

12. Close the test window, then save your work.

You added a frame label and assigned a rollOver action using the frame label.

Add an Invisible Button

1. Click **Control** on the menu bar, click **Test Movie**, move the pointer over Events on the navigation bar, then move the pointer away from Events.

   Notice that when you point to Events the drop down menu appears, however, when you move the pointer away from the menu it does not disappear.

2. Close the test window.

3. Insert a layer above the homeBkgrnd layer, then name it **rollOver**.

4. Click the **Rectangle tool** 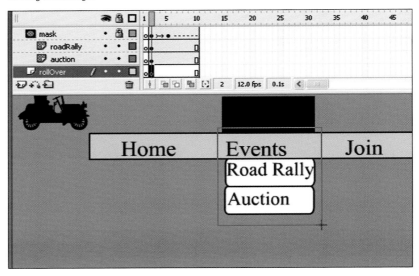 on the Tools panel, verify that the Stroke Color is set to none, then set the Fill Color to blue.

5. Insert a Keyframe in Frame 2 of the rollover layer.

6. Draw a rectangle, as shown in Figure 33.

7. Click the **Selection tool** on the Tools panel, then click the blue rectangle to select it.

8. Click **Modify** on the menu bar, then click **Convert to Symbol**.

9. Type **b_rollOver** for the name, click the **Button option button**, then click **OK**.

(continued)

FIGURE 33
Drawing the rectangle

FIGURE 34

The Actions panel displaying the b_rollOver button symbol

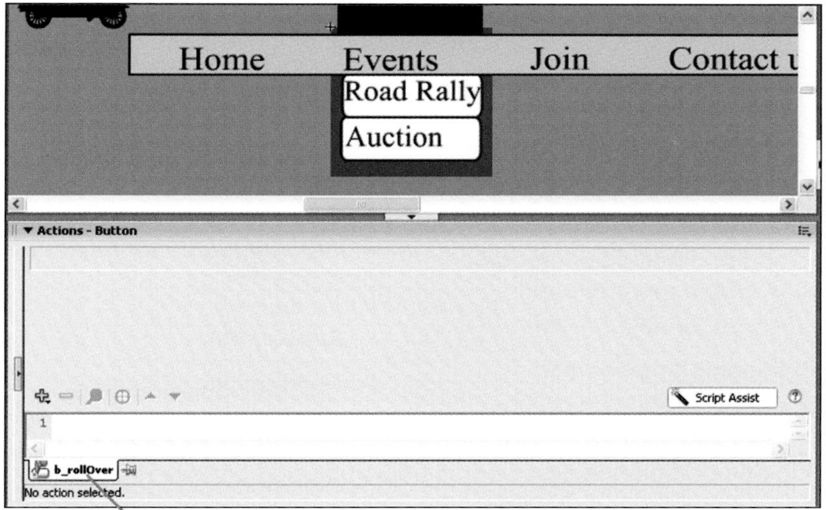

b_roadRally button symbol indicating the action to be created will be
assigned to the button

10. Verify the button is selected and the
b_rollOver button symbol is displayed in the
Actions panel, as shown in Figure 34.

11. Click the **Add a new item to the script
icon** 🔁, point to **Global Functions**, point
to **Movie Clip Control**, then click **on**.

12. Click the **Release check box** to deselect it,
then click the **Roll Over check box** to select it.

13. Click the **Add a new item to the script
icon** 🔁, point to **Global Functions**, point
to **Timeline Control**, then click **goto**.

14. Verify Frame 1 is specified.

15. Display the Property inspector, click the
Color list arrow, click **Alpha**, then set the
percentage to 0.

16. Click **Control** on the menu bar, then click
Test Movie.

17. Point to **Events** to display the drop down menu,
then move the pointer away from Events and
notice the drop down menu disappears.

18. Close the test window, then save and close
the movie.

19. Exit Flash.

*You added a button and assigned a rollOver action
to it, then made the button transparent.*

Create a shape-tweened animation.

1. Start Flash, open f15_8.fla, save it as **skillsdemo5**.
2. Insert keyframes in Frames 45 and 65 on the face2 layer.
3. In frame 65, use the Selection tool to drag and reshape the mouth of face2 into a smile.
4. Display the Properties panel.
5. Click anywhere between Frames 45 and 65.
6. Use the Properties panel to specify a Shape Tween.
7. Play the movie.
8. Save your work.

Create a morphing effect.

1. Insert a keyframe in Frame 65 on the number1 layer.
2. Use the Selection Tool to select 1, then break it apart twice.
3. Insert a blank keyframe in Frame 85 on the number1 layer.
4. Display the Library panel.
5. Click the Edit Multiple Frames icon on the timeline to turn on this feature.
6. Drag the g_number2 symbol and place it directly over the 1 so that both graphics are visible.
7. Break apart the 2 symbol twice.
8. Turn off the Edit Multiple Frames feature.
9. Click anywhere between Frames 65 and 85 on the number1 layer.

10. Use the Properties panel to specify a Shape tween.
11. Play the movie, then save your work.

Use shape hints.

1. Click Frame 65 of the number1 layer.
2. With the 1 selected, add two shape hints, one at the top and one at the bottom of the 1.
3. Click Frame 85 of the number1 layer, then position the shape hints accordingly.
4. Play the movie, then save your work.

Create and apply a mask layer.

1. Insert a new layer above the heading layer, then name it **mask**.
2. Click Frame 1 on the mask layer.
3. Drag the g_face graphic from the Library panel to the left side of the word "How".
4. Insert a Motion tween.
5. Insert a keyframe in Frame 45 on the mask layer.
6. Drag the face to the right side of the word "faces?".
7. Click the mask layer on the timeline, click Modify on the menu bar, point to Timeline, then click Layer Properties.
8. Use the Layer Properties dialog box to specify a Mask layer that is locked.
9. Click heading in the timeline, then use the Layer Properties dialog box to specify a Masked layer that is locked.
10. Play the movie, then save your work.

Add and name a scene.

1. Display the Scene panel.
2. Rename Scene 1 **faces**.
3. Add a new scene, then name it **correct**.
4. Type a heading, **That's correct**, with a red, Arial, 72 pt font, and center it near the top of the stage.
5. Change the name of Layer 1 to **heading**.
6. Insert a keyframe in Frame 30 on the heading layer.
7. Test the movie.
8. Save your work.

Add interactivity to a scene.

1. Display the faces scene, insert a new layer above the face2 layer, and name it **stopmovie**.
2. Insert a keyframe in Frame 85 on the stopmovie layer and add a stop action to it.
3. Use the Selection Tool to select the Continue button on the stage.
4. Use the Actions panel to assign a goto action to the Continue button that jumps the movie to the scene named correct.
5. Test the movie.
6. Save your work.

Add sound to a movie.

1. Use the Scene panel to display the correct scene.
2. Insert a new layer and name it **applause**.
3. Click Frame 1 on the applause layer.
4. Display the Library panel and drag the applause sound symbol to the stage.
5. Test the movie.
6. Save your work.

Add a transition effect.

1. Display the correct scene, if necessary.
2. Insert a new layer above the heading layer, name it **mask,** then specify it as a mask layer.
3. Draw a rectangle, then create a motion tween that causes the rectangle to move from above the stage to covering the stage.
4. Verify that the heading layer is a masked layer.
5. Test the movie.
6. Save your work, then compare your images to Figure 35.
7. Exit Flash.

FIGURE 35

Completed Skills Review

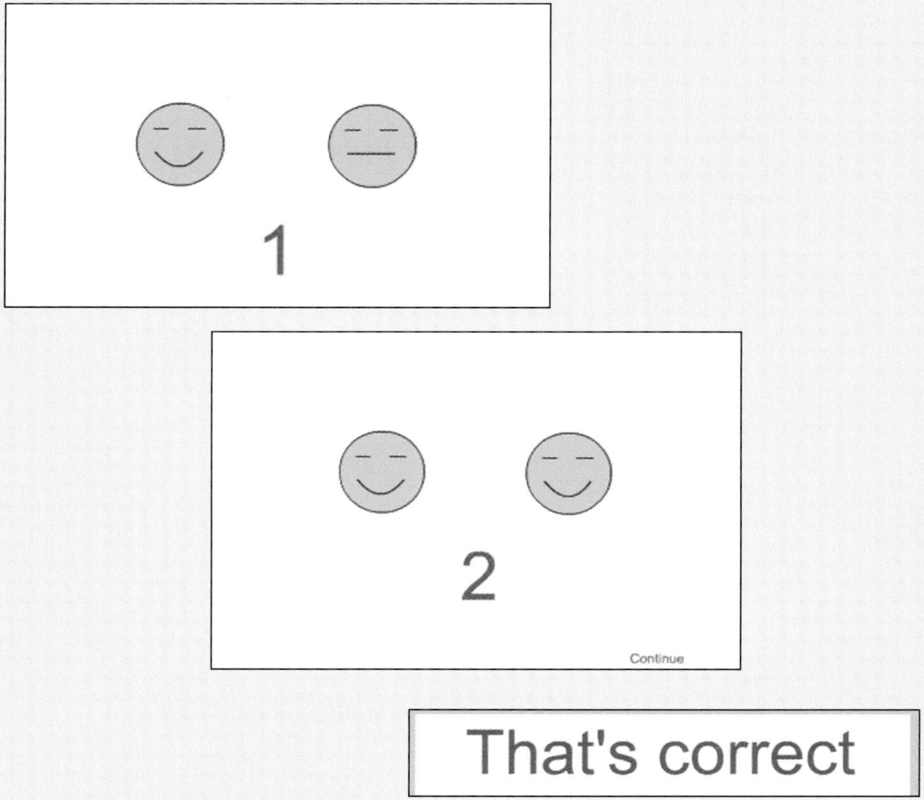

The Ultimate Tours travel company has asked you to design several sample animations for their Web site. Figure 36 shows a sample Cruises screen with morphed and shape-tweened animations, as well as a mask effect. Using these or one of the sites you created in Chapter 4 as a guide, complete the following for the Cruises screen of the Ultimate Tours Web site:

1. Open ultimatetours4.fla (the file you created in Chapter 4 Project Builder 1) and save it as **ultimateTours5**.
2. Create a morph animation.
3. Create a shape-tweened animation.
4. Create a button that goes to another scene.

For the new scene:

5. Create a scene and give it an appropriate name.

6. Rename Scene 1.
7. Create an animation using a mask effect in the new scene.
8. Add a sound to the scene (foghorn.wav is provided for you).
9. Add an action to go to the Cruises screen when the animation is done and the viewer clicks a button.
10. Test the movie, then compare your image to the example shown in Figure 36.

FIGURE 36

Sample completed Project Builder 1

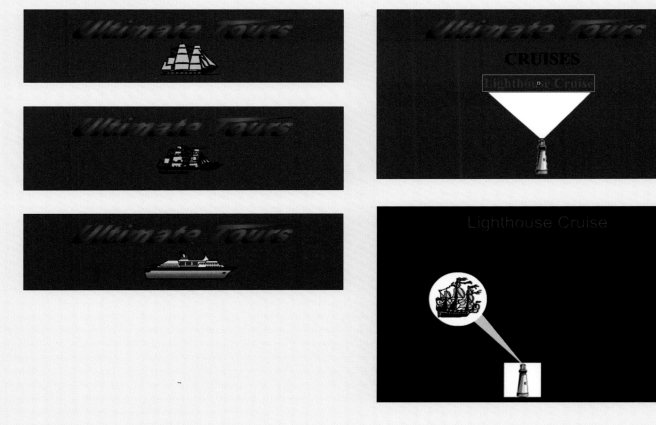

You have been asked to develop a Web site illustrating the signs of the zodiac. The introductory screen will have a heading with a mask effect and links to the 12 zodiac signs. Clicking a sign will display another screen with a different graphic to represent the sign and information about the sign, as well as special effects such as sound, shape animation, and morphing. Each information screen will be linked to the introductory screen.

1. Open a new Flash document, then save it as **zodiac5**.
2. Create an introductory screen for the Web site with the following:
   - A heading
   - A mask layer that creates a spotlight effect
   - Several graphics
   - Two graphics that are buttons that jump to another scene when clicked
3. Create a second scene that has
   - A morph animation using two graphics
   - A sound
   - A Home button with a sound when clicked
4. Create a third scene that has
   - A shape animation using shape hints
   - A Home button with a sound when clicked
5. Rename all of the scenes.
6. Test the movie.
7. Save the movie, then compare your image to the example shown in Figure 37.

FIGURE 37
Sample completed Project Builder 2

Figure 38 shows the homepage of a Web site. Study the figure and complete the following questions. For each question, indicate how you determined your answer.

1. Connect to the Internet, go to *www.course.com*, navigate to the page for this book, click the Online Companion link, then click the link for this chapter.

2. Open a document in a word processor or open a new Macromedia Flash document, save the file as **dpc5**, then answer the following questions. (*Hint*: Use the Text tool in Macromedia Flash.)

   - What seems to be the purpose of this site?
   - Who would be the target audience?
   - How might a shape-tweened animation be used in this site?
   - How might a morph animation be used?
   - How might a mask effect be used?
   - How might sound be used?
   - What suggestions would you make to improve the design and why?

FIGURE 38
Design Project

This is a continuation of Portfolio Project in Chapter 4, which is the development of a personal portfolio. The homepage has several categories, including the following:

- Personal data
- Contact information
- Previous employment
- Education
- Samples of your work

In this project, you will create several buttons for the Sample Animations screen and link them to the animations.

1. Open portfolio4.fla (the file you created in Portfolio Project, Chapter 4) and save it as **portfolio5**.
2. Display the Sample Animations screen.
3. Add layers and create buttons for a shape-tweened animation, morph animation, and an animation using shape hints.
4. Add a new scene and create the morph animation in this scene.
5. Rename the new scene and Scene 1 using appropriate names.
6. Add a sound to the scene.
7. Add a new scene with a navigation bar animation and name the scene appropriately. Add a button on the Sample Animations screen that links to this scene.

8. Create frame actions that cause the movie to return to the Sample Animations screen after each animation has been played.
9. Test the movie.

FIGURE 39
Sample completed Portfolio Project

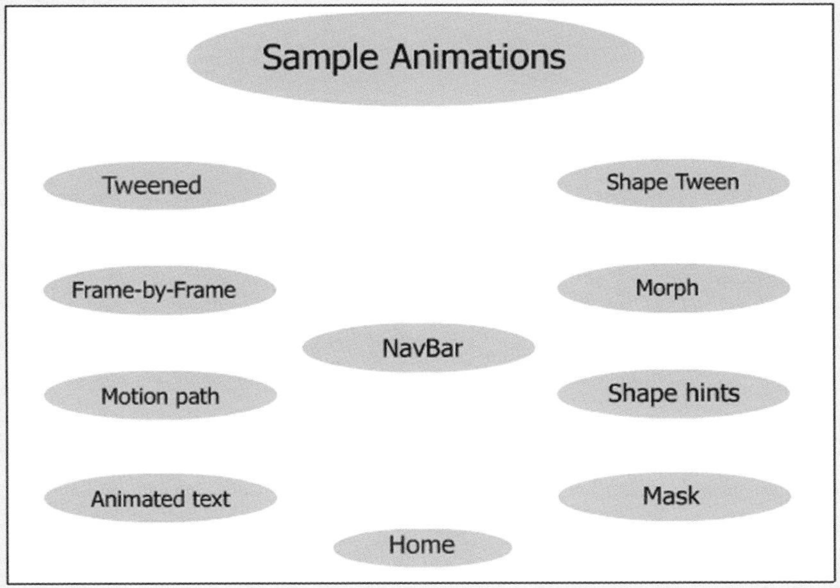

10. Save your work, then compare your image to the example shown in Figure 39.

6

PREPARING AND
PUBLISHING MOVIES

1. Publish movies.

2. Reduce file size to optimize a movie.

3. Create a Preloader.

4. Use HTML Publish Settings.

6 PREPARING AND PUBLISHING MOVIES

Introduction

During the planning process for a Macromedia Flash movie, you are concerned with, among other things, how the target audience will view the movie. The most common use of Macromedia Flash is to develop movies that provide Web content and applications. Macromedia Flash provides several features that help you generate the files that are necessary for delivering movies over the Internet. When you deliver content over the Internet, you want to provide compelling movies. However, it is important that you keep the file size down so that the movies play smoothly regardless of the user's connection speed. Macromedia Flash allows you to test movies to determine where problems might arise during download and to make changes to optimize the movies.

Tools You'll Use

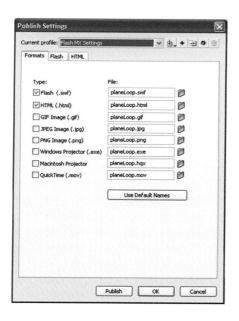

PUBLISH
MOVIES

What You'll Do

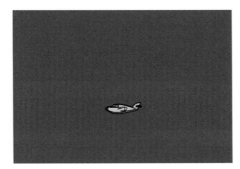

▶ *In this lesson, you will use the Publish Settings feature of Macromedia Flash to publish a movie, create a GIF animation, and create a JPEG image from a movie.*

Using Publish Settings

The Publish feature in Macromedia Flash generates the files necessary to deliver the movies on the Web. When you publish a movie using the default settings, a Macromedia Flash (.swf) file is created that can be viewed using the Macromedia Flash Player. In addition, an HTML file is created with the necessary code to instruct the browser to play the Macromedia Flash file using the Macromedia Flash Player. If you are not distributing the movie over the

Internet, or if a Macromedia Flash Player is not available, you can use the Publish feature to create alternate images and stand-alone projector files.

Figure 1 shows the Publish Settings dialog box with a list of the available formats for publishing a Macromedia Flash movie. You can choose a combination of formats, and you can specify a different name (but not file extension) for each format. The GIF, JPEG, and PNG formats create still images that can be delivered on the Web. The projector formats are executable files and the QuickTime format requires a QuickTime player. After selecting a format(s), a tab appears allowing you to display a dialog box with settings specifically for the format.

Figure 2 shows the Flash tab of the Publish Settings dialog box. You can choose settings for the following options:

- The version of the Macromedia Flash Player

- The Load Order (for example, Bottom up starts loading from Frame 1 of the bottom layer)
- Other options, such as compressing the movie
- The quality for JPEG images and audio

FIGURE 1
The Publish Settings dialog box

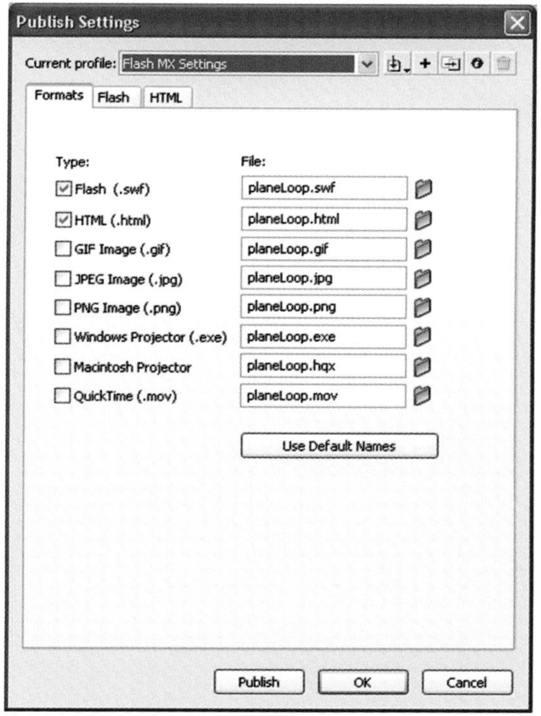

FIGURE 2
The Flash tab

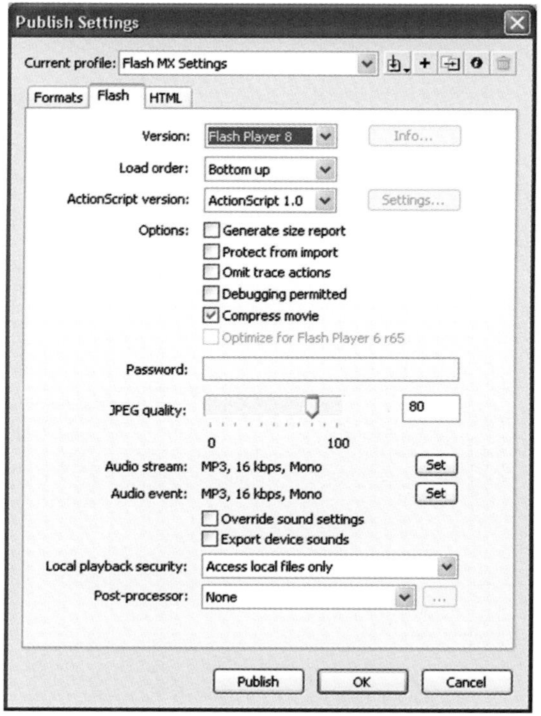

Figure 3 shows the Publish Settings dialog box for the GIF format. GIF files, which are compressed bitmaps, provide an easy way to create images and simple animations for delivery on the Web. GIF animations are frame-by-frame animations created from Flash movie frames. Using this dialog box, you can change several settings, including these:

- Specifying the dimensions in pixels (or you can match the movie dimensions)
- Specifying a static image or animated GIF
- Selecting from a range of appearance settings, such as optimizing colors and removing gradients

Using Publish Preview

You can use the Publish Preview command on the File menu to publish a movie and display the movie in either your default browser or the Macromedia Flash Player. In addition, you can use this command to view HTML, GIF, JPEG, PNG, Projector, and QuickTime files.

FIGURE 3
The GIF tab

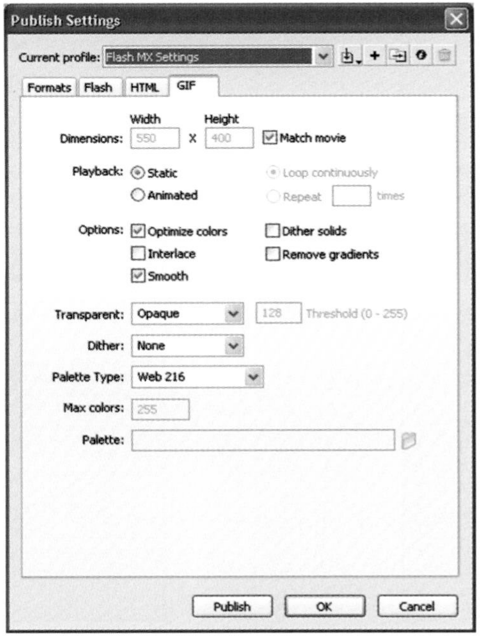

FIGURE 4
The three planeLoop files

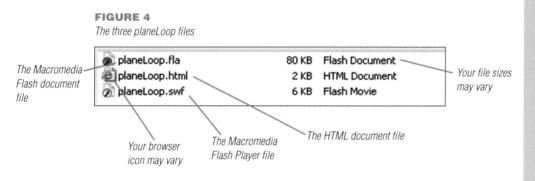

The Macromedia
Flash document
file

planeLoop.fla   80 KB   Flash Document
planeLoop.html   2 KB   HTML Document
planeLoop.swf   6 KB   Flash Movie

Your file sizes
may vary

Your browser
icon may vary

The Macromedia
Flash Player file

The HTML document file

Publish using the default settings

1. Open fl6_1.fla from the drive and folder where your Data Files are stored, save it as **planeLoop**, then play the movie.

2. Click **File** on the menu bar, click **Publish Settings**, then click the **Formats tab** (if necessary).

3. Verify that the **Flash** and **HTML check boxes** are the only ones selected, then click the **Flash tab**.

4. Click the **Version list arrow**, click **Flash Player 8**, verify that the Load Order is **Bottom up**, and that the **Compress movie check box** is selected.

5. Accept the remaining default settings, click **Publish**, then click **OK**.

6. Navigate to the drive and folder where you save your Macromedia Flash movies, click the **Files of type list arrow** (Win) or **Show list arrow** (Mac), click **All Files** (if necessary), then notice the three files whose file names start with "planeLoop", as shown in Figure 4.

7. Display the Macromedia Flash program, click **File** on the menu bar, point to **Publish Preview**, then click **Default - (HTML)**. The movie plays in a browser or in an HTML editor.

   TIP Netscape users may have difficulty viewing the files, depending on the version of Netscape that is installed on the computer.

8. Close the browser or the HTML editor.

You published a movie using the default publish settings and viewed it in a browser.

Create a GIF animation from a movie

1. Click **File** on the menu bar, click **Publish Settings**, then click the **Formats tab**.

2. Click the **GIF Image (.gif) check box**, then click the **GIF tab**.

3. Click the **Match movie check box** to turn off this setting, double-click the **Width text box**, type **275,** double-click the **Height text box**, then type **200**.

4. Click the **Animated option button**, accept the remaining default settings, then compare your dialog box with Figure 5.

5. Click **Publish**, then click **OK**.

6. Navigate to the folder where you save your Macromedia Flash movies, click the **Files of type list arrow** (Win) or **Show list arrow** (Mac), click **All Files** (if necessary), then locate the planeLoop.gif file.

7. Open your browser, open **planeLoop.gif**, then notice the GIF animation plays in the browser with the modified settings.

   Because the GIF file is not a Macromedia SWF file, it does not require Macromedia Flash Player in order to play—it can be displayed directly in a Web browser.

8. Close the browser.

You changed the publish settings for a GIF image, then created a GIF animation and viewed it in your Web browser.

FIGURE 5
The completed GIF format dialog box

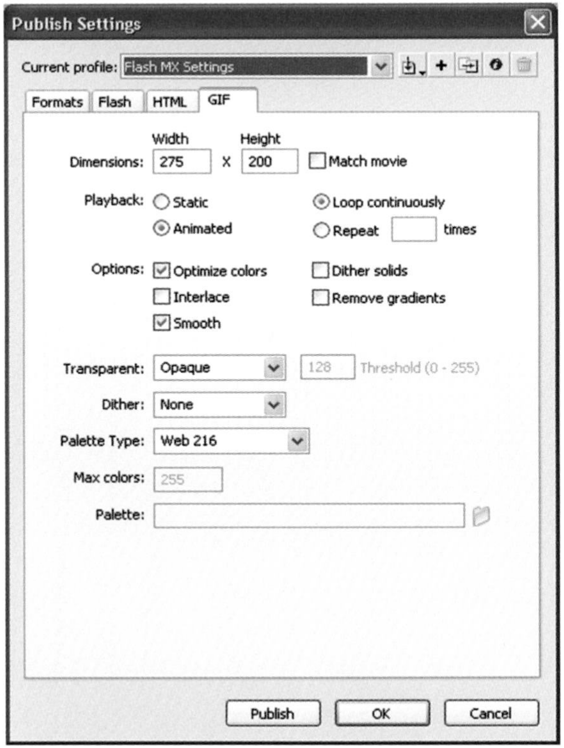

FIGURE 6

The JPEG image displayed in the browser

Your browser
may vary

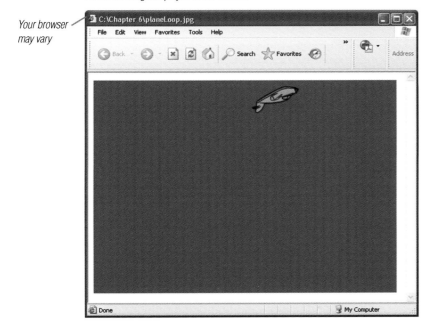

1. Display the Macromedia Flash program, click **Frame 10** on the plane layer.

2. Click **File** on the menu bar, then click **Publish Settings**.

3. Click the **Formats tab**, click the **GIF Image check box** to deselect it, then click the **JPEG Image check box**.

4. Click the **JPEG tab**, accept the default settings, click **Publish**, then click **OK**.

5. Navigate to the folder where you save your Macromedia Flash movies, click the **Files of type list arrow** (Win) or **Show list arrow** (Mac), click **All Files** (if necessary), then notice the planeLoop.jpg file.

6. Open your browser, open **planeLoop.jpg**, then notice that the static JPEG image appears in the browser, as shown in Figure 6.

7. Close your browser.

8. Save your work, then close the movie.

You changed the publish settings for a JPEG image, then created a JPEG image and viewed it in your Web browser.

REDUCE FILE SIZE TO
OPTIMIZE A MOVIE

What You'll Do

In this lesson, you will test a movie and reduce its file size.

Testing a Movie

The goal in publishing a movie is to provide the most effective playback for the intended audience. This requires that you pay special attention to the download time and play-back speed. Users are turned off by long waits to view content, jerky animations, and audio that skips. These events can occur as the file size increases in relation to the user's Internet connection speed.

Macromedia Flash provides various ways to test a movie to determine where changes can improve its delivery. The following are guidelines for optimizing movies:

- Use symbols and instances for every element that appears in a movie more than once.
- When possible, use tweened anima-tions rather than frame-by-frame animations.
- For animation sequences, use movie clips rather than graphic symbols.
- Confine the area of change to a keyframe so that the action takes place in as small an area as possible.

- Use bitmap graphics as static elements rather than in animations.
- Group elements, such as related images.
- Limit the number of fonts and font styles.
- Use gradients and alpha transparencies sparingly.

When you publish a movie, Macromedia Flash optimizes it using default features, including compressing the entire movie, which is later decompressed by the Macromedia Flash Player.

Using the Bandwidth Profiler

When a movie is delivered over the Internet, the contents of each frame are sent to the user's computer. The Macromedia Flash Player tries to match the movie's frame rate. However, depend-ing on the amount of data in the frame and the user's connection speed, the movie may pause while the frame's con-tents download. The first step in optimiz-ing a movie is to test the movie and determine which frames may create a pause during playback. The test should be done using a simulated Internet connection speed that is representative of the speed of your target audience. You can set a simulated speed using the Bandwidth Profiler, shown in Figure 7. The Bandwidth Profiler allows you to view a graphical representation of the size of each frame. Each bar represents a frame of the movie, and the height of the bar corresponds to the frame's size. If a bar extends above the red baseline, the movie may need to pause to allow the frame's contents to be downloaded. Figure 7 shows the following:

- Movie information: dimensions, frame rate, file size, duration, and preload
- Settings: simulated bandwidth (specified in the Debug menu option)
- State: selected frame number and size of contents in the frame

The Bandwidth Profiler indicates that downloading the contents of Frame 38 may result in a pause because of the large size of the contents in this frame in relationship to the connection speed and the frame rate. If the specified connection speed is correct for your target audience and the frame rate is needed to ensure acceptable animation quality, then the only change that can be made is in the contents of the frame.

Using the Simulate Download feature

When testing a movie you can simulate downloading Flash movies using different connection speeds. The most common connections are Dial-up, DSL, cable, and T1. Dial-up is a phone connection that provides a relatively slow download speed. Broadband is a type of data transmission in which a wide band of frequencies is available to transmit more information at the same time. DSL provides a broadband Internet connection speed that is available through phone lines. DSL is widely used by homes and businesses. A cable connection to the Internet provides connection speeds comparable to DSL. T1 provides an extremely fast connection speed and is widely used in businesses, especially for intranet (a computer network within a company) applications. You can test the movie that you are developing at the different speeds to evaluate the download experience for potential users.

FIGURE 7
The Bandwidth Profiler

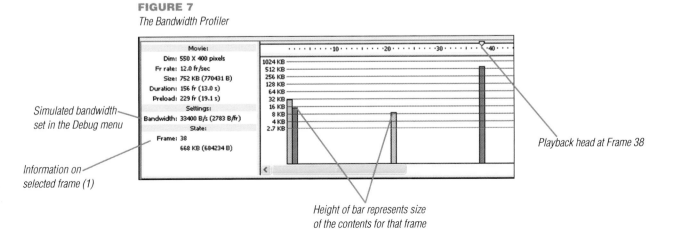

Simulated bandwidth set in the Debug menu

Information on selected frame (1)

Playback head at Frame 38

Height of bar represents size of the contents for that frame

Play a movie stored on your computer in a browser

1. Open fl6_2.fla, then save it as **planeFun**.

2. Hide all the panels, then display the Tools and Property inspector panels.

3. Change the view to **Fit in Window**.

4. Click **File** on the menu bar, then click **Publish Settings**.

5. Make sure the **Flash** and **HTML check boxes** on the Formats tabs are selected, click **Publish**, then click **OK**.

6. Navigate to the drive and folder where you save your Macromedia Flash movies, click the **Files of type list arrow** (Win) or **Show list arrow** (Mac), click **All Files** (if necessary), then locate the planeFun.html file.

7. Double-click the **planeFun.html** file to open it in your browser.

8. Click the **Start button** and notice how the animation runs smoothly until the middle of the morphing animation, where there is a noticeable pause, as shown in Figure 8.

   The pause is caused by the browser waiting for the remaining contents of the movie to be down-loaded. The pause may not be very long because the movie file is located on your computer (or a local network computer) and not being down-loaded from a remote Web server. A user view-ing this movie over a dial-up connection from a Web site would probably have a very long pause.

9. Close your browser, then return to the Macromedia Flash program.

You played a movie in a browser and viewed the pause that occurs in the middle of the movie.

FIGURE 8
A pause in the movie

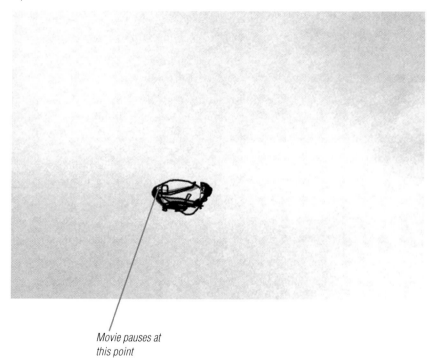

Movie pauses at this point

FIGURE 9

FIGURE 9

Selecting the connection speed for a simulated download

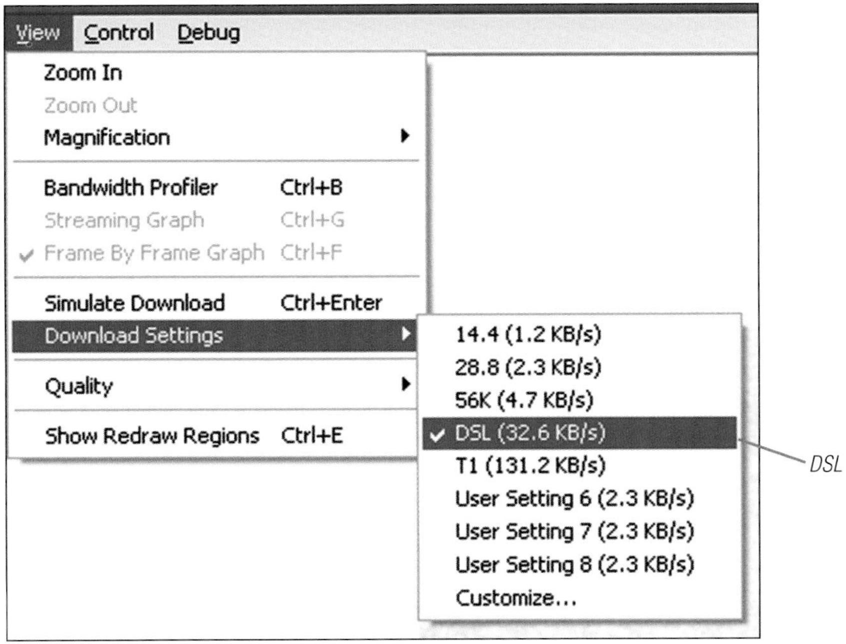

View	Control	Debug
Zoom In		
Zoom Out		
Magnification	▶	
Bandwidth Profiler	Ctrl+B	
Streaming Graph	Ctrl+G	
✓ Frame By Frame Graph	Ctrl+F	
Simulate Download	Ctrl+Enter	
Download Settings	▶	
Quality	▶	
Show Redraw Regions	Ctrl+E	

- 14.4 (1.2 KB/s)
- 28.8 (2.3 KB/s)
- 56K (4.7 KB/s)
- ✓ DSL (32.6 KB/s) ——— *DSL*
- T1 (131.2 KB/s)
- User Setting 6 (2.3 KB/s)
- User Setting 7 (2.3 KB/s)
- User Setting 8 (2.3 KB/s)
- Customize...

Test the download time for a movie

1. Click **Control** on the menu bar, click **Test Movie**, then maximize the test movie window, if necessary.

2. Click **View** on the menu bar, point to **Download Settings**, then click **DSL(32.6 KB/s)**, as shown in Figure 9.

3. Click **View** on the menu bar, then click **Simulate Download**.

4. Click **Start**, then notice the pause in the movie when the plane morphs into the hot air balloon.

   You may have to wait several moments for the movie to continue.

5. Click **View** on the menu bar, point to **Download Settings**, then click **T1 (131.2KB/s)**.

6. Click **View** on the menu bar, then click **Simulate Download** to turn off the feature, if necessary.

7. Click **View** on the menu bar, then click **Simulate Download** to turn on the feature.

   You need to turn off the Simulate Download feature and turn it on again to start the simulation.

8. Click **Start** then notice the pause in the movie is shorter with the simulated T1 line speed.

You used the test movie window to simulate the download time for a movie using different connection speeds.

Use the Bandwidth Profiler

1. Verify that the test movie window is still open.

2. Click **View** on the menu bar, point to **Download Settings**, then click **DSL(32.6 KB/s)**.

3. Click **View** on the menu bar, then click **Bandwidth Profiler**.

4. Click **View** on the menu bar, then click **Frame By Frame Graph** to select it, if necessary.

5. Click **View** on the menu bar, then click **Simulate Download**.

   Notice the green bar as it scrolls at the top of the Bandwidth profiler to indicate the frames being downloaded. The bar pauses at Frame 38, as shown in Figure 10.

6. Click **Frame 37** on the Timeline, then notice that the only object in the frame is the morphing balloon and its size is less than 1 KB.

7. Click **Frame 38** on the Timeline, then notice the large color photograph.

   The state settings indicate that the file size is over 512 KB. This image's large file size takes several moments to download and causes the pause in the movie.

8. Close the test movie window.

You used the Bandwidth Profiler to determine which frame causes a pause in the movie.

FIGURE 10
The Bandwidth Profiler indicating the pause at Frame 38

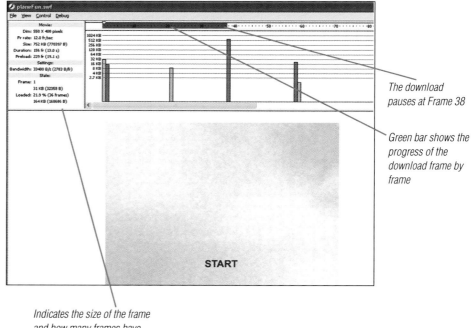

The download pauses at Frame 38

Green bar shows the progress of the download frame by frame

Indicates the size of the frame and how many frames have been loaded

FIGURE 11
Positioning the cloud image

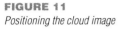

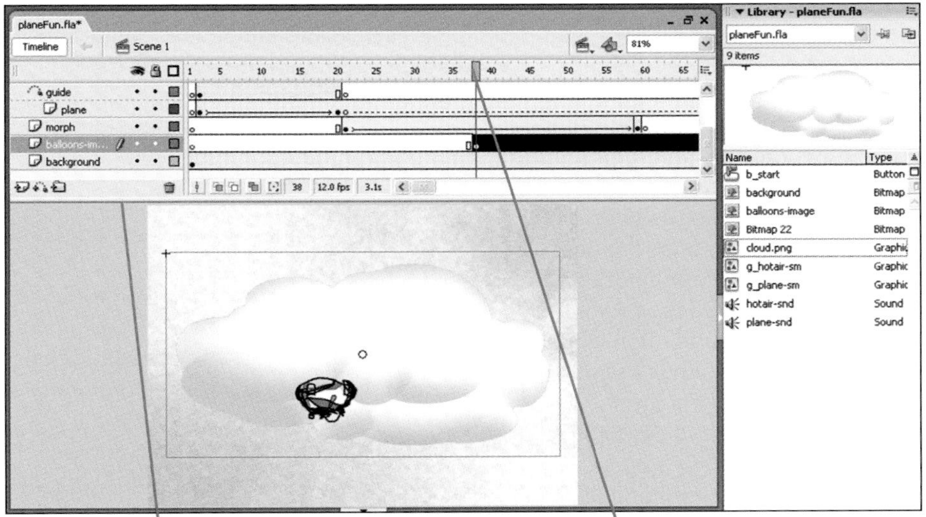

Drag the border down to view more layers

Frame 38 selected

Optimize a movie by reducing file size

1. Point to the **bottom border** of the Timeline, then, when the pointer changes to a double-arrow, drag the **border down** to view the balloons-image layer.
2. Click **Frame 38** on the balloons-image layer to view the image on the stage.

   TIP If the layer name appears cut off, position the mouse over the right border of the layer section, then drag the border to the right until the name is fully visible.

3. Click the **balloon photographic image** on the stage, click **Edit** on the menu bar, then click **Cut**.

   The balloon image is no longer visible on the stage.

4. Click **Window** on the menu bar, then click **Library**.
5. Drag the **cloud graphic symbol** from the Library panel to the center of the stage, as shown in Figure 11.
6. Click **Control** on the menu bar, then click **Test Movie**.
7. Click **View** on the test movie window menu bar, click **Simulate Download**, then click **Start**.

   Notice the movie no longer pauses.

8. Click **Frame 38** on the timeline in the test movie window and notice that the file size is now just above the 8KB line.
9. Close the test movie window.
10. Save your work, then close the movie.

You replaced an image that had a large file size with one having a small file size to help optimize a movie.

CREATE A PRELOADER

What You'll Do

Loading

In this lesson, you will create a preloader for the planeFun movie. Ten frames have been added to the beginning of the movie and labels have been added to the start and ending frames of the movie.

Preloading a movie

One way to improve the playback performance of large or complex movies is to preload the movie frames. Preloading frames prevents the browser from playing a specified frame or series of frames until all of the frames have been downloaded. Commonly, a preloader frame includes a simple animation that starts in Frame 1 and loops until the rest of the movie has been downloaded. The animation could consist of the word "Loading" flashing on the screen, the words "Please wait" with a series of scrolling dots, or the hand of a clock sweeping around in a circle. The purpose of the animation is to indicate to the viewer that the movie is being loaded. The animation is placed on its own layer. A second layer contains the ActionScript code that checks to see if the movie has been loaded and, if not, causes a loop which continues until the last frame of the movie has been loaded.

For example, assume a movie has 155 frames. An additional 10 frames could be added to the beginning of the movie for the preloader, and the preloader animation would run from Frames 1 to 10. A label, such as **startofMovie**, would be added to Frame 11 (the first frame of the actual movie). Another label, such as **endofMovie** would be added to frame 165, the last frame of the entire movie. Then the following ActionScript code would be placed in Frame 1 of the movie on the preloaderScript layer.

```
ifFrameLoaded ("endofMovie") {
    gotoAndPlay ("startofMovie");
}
```

Preparing and Publishing Movies

This is a conditional statement that checks to see if the Frame labeled endofMovie is loaded. If the statement is true then the next line of the script is executed and the playhead goes to the Frame labeled startofMovie. This script is placed in Frame 1. So each time the playhead is on Frame 1 there is a check to see if the entire movie has been downloaded. If the condition is false, the playhead moves on to Frames 2, 3, 4, and so on. Then the following ActionScript code would be placed in Frame 10.

gotoAndPlay (1);

This creates a loop. When the movie first starts the playhead is on Frame 1 and there is a check to see if the movie has been loaded. If not, the playhead continues to Frame 10 (playing the animation) where this script causes it to loop back to Frame 1 for another check. The looping process will continue until all frames have been loaded.

Figure 12 shows the Timeline that displays the two preloader layers after the preloader has been created.

FIGURE 12

The completed preloader with the animation and ActionScript

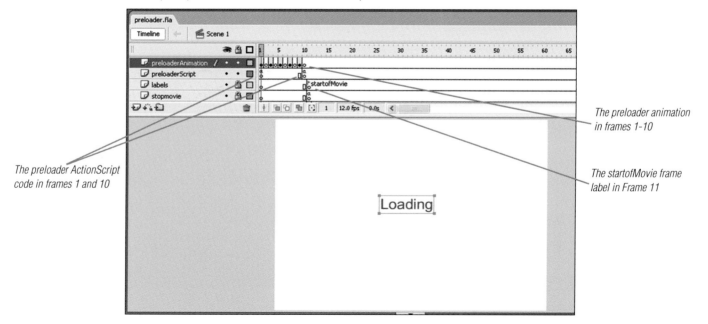

The preloader animation in frames 1-10

The preloader ActionScript code in frames 1 and 10

The startofMovie frame label in Frame 11

Add Layers for a Preloader

1. Open fl6_3.fla, then save it as **preloader**.

2. Hide all panels, then open the Tools and Property inspector panels.

3. Change the view to **Fit in Window**.

4. Click the **labels layer** at the top of the Timeline, then click the **Insert Layer icon** to insert a new layer.

5. Name the new layer **preloaderScript**.

6. Insert a new layer, above the preloaderScript layer, then name it **preloaderAnimation**.

7. Click **Frame 10** of the preloaderAnimation layer, then insert a keyframe.

8. Insert a keyframe in Frame 10 of the preloaderScript layer.

   Your screen should resemble Figure 13.

You added two layers that will be used to create a preloader. One layer will contain the ActionScript and the other layer will contain the animation for the preloader.

FIGURE 13
The preloader layers added to the Timeline

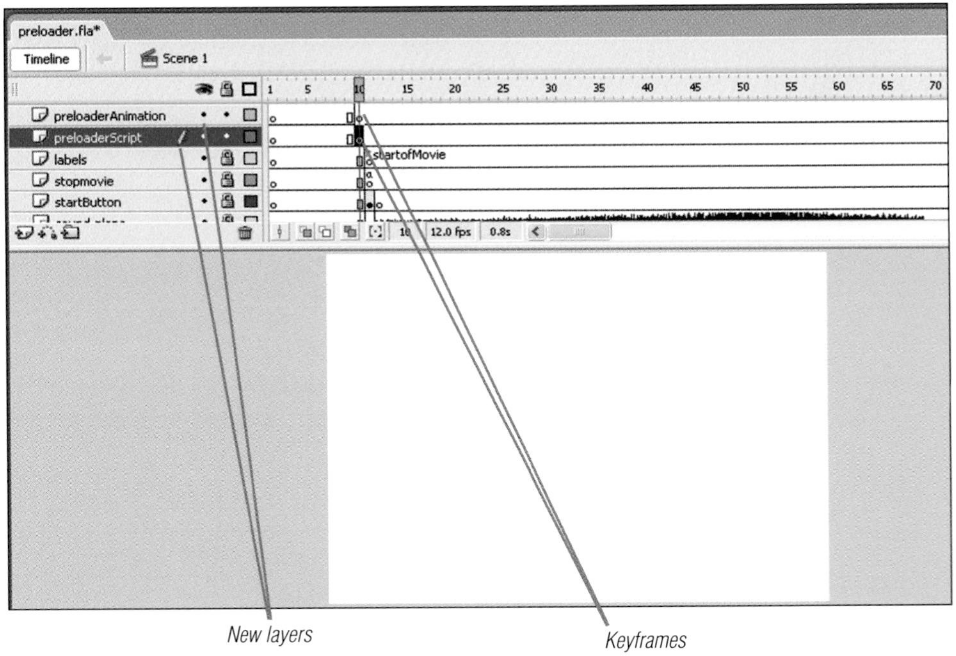

New layers   Keyframes

FIGURE 14

The Actions panel displaying preloaderscript:1

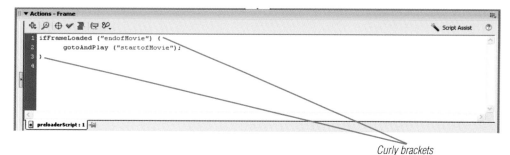

preloaderscript:1 indicates that the ActionScript
that is to be developed will be applied to Frame 1
of the preloaderscript layer

Script Assist feature is off
when the button does not have
a white background

FIGURE 15

The ActionScript code to check if the last frame in the movie has been downloaded

```
1  ifFrameLoaded ("endofMovie") {
2        gotoAndPlay ("startofMovie");
3  }
4
```

Curly brackets

Add Actions to the Preloader

1. Open the **Actions panel**, then turn off the Script Assist feature (if necessary).

2. Click **Frame 1** of the preloaderScript layer.

3. Verify the preloaderscript:1 is displayed in the lower left corner of the Action panel, as shown in Figure 14.

   This indicates that the ActionScript that is to be developed will be applied to Frame 1 of the preloaderscript layer.

4. Click inside the **Action panel script window**, then type the following code into the Actions panel, as shown in Figure 15.

   ifFrameLoaded ("endofMovie") {
   gotoAndPlay ("startofMovie");
   }

5. Click **Frame 10** of the preloaderScript layer, then verify preloaderscript:10 is displayed in the lower left corner of the Action panel.

6. Click inside the **Action panel script window**, then type the following code into the Actions panel.

   gotoAndPlay (1);

7. Collapse the Action panel.

You added Actions to frames in the preloaderScript layer that creates a loop. The loop includes a check to see if the entire movie has been loaded and, if so, jumps to a starting place in the movie.

Create the Preloader Animation

1. Click **Frame 1** of the preloaderAnimation layer.

2. Click the **Text tool** A on the Tools menu, click in middle of the stage, then type **Loading**.

3. Double-click to select the **Loading** text, then use the Property inspector to set the font to **Arial**, the size to **30** and the color to blue, as shown in Figure 16.

4. Click the **Selection tool** ▸ on the Tools panel, then insert keyframes in Frames 3, 5, 7, and 9 of the preloaderAnimation layer.

5. Click **Frame 2** on the preloaderAnimation layer, click **Insert** on the menu bar, point to **Timeline**, then click **Blank Keyframe**.

   Inserting a blank keyframe prevents the contents of the previous frame from being inserted into the frame.

6. Insert blank keyframes for Frames 4, 6, and 8 on the preloaderAnimation layer.

7. Drag the playhead back and forth across Frames 1 through 10 and view the animation.

   This animation causes the word Loading to flash. You can create any animation for the preloader and use as may frames as desired.

You created an animation that will play as the playhead loops waiting for the movie to load.

FIGURE 16
The text used in the animation

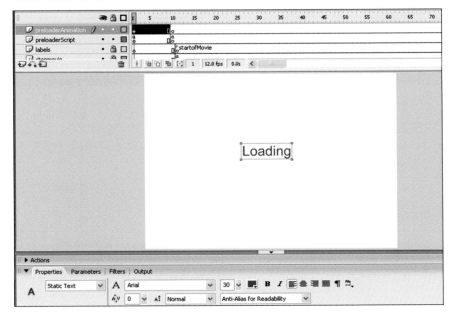

FIGURE 17

The Bandwidth Profiler showing the delay in downloading Frame 48

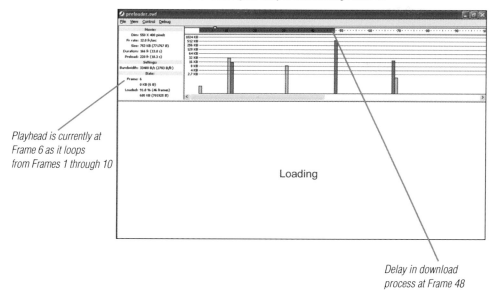

Playhead is currently at
Frame 6 as it loops
from Frames 1 through 10

Loading

Delay in download
process at Frame 48

Testing the Preloader

1. Click **Control** on the menu bar, then click **Test Movie**.

2. Maximize the test movie window, if necessary.

3. Click **View** on the menu bar, then click **Bandwidth Profiler** to display it, if necessary.

4. Click **View** on the menu bar, point to **Download Settings**, then verify that **DSL (32.6 KB/s)** is selected.

5. Click **View** on the menu bar, then click **Simulate Download**.

   Notice the playhead loops causing the animation to play over and over as the frames are loaded. There is a delay at Frame 48 as the large jpg file is loaded, as shown in Figure 17.

6. Repeat step 5 twice to run the simulation again, then drag the scroll bar on the Bandwidth Profiler to the right to view the last frames of the movie.

   Notice the information in the left panel of the Bandwidth Profiler, showing the percentage of frames loaded.

7. Close the test movie window.

8. Save and close the movie.

You tested the preloaded by simulating a download and you viewed the information on the Bandwidth Profiler during the simulation.

USE HTML
PUBLISH SETTINGS

What You'll Do

Having PlaneFun!!!

In this lesson, you will use the HTML Publish Settings to align the movie window in a browser window and change the code of an HTML document.

Understanding HTML Publishing Options

During the publishing process, Macromedia Flash automatically creates an HTML document that allows a Macromedia Flash movie to be displayed on the Web. The HTML document specifies, among other things, the movie's background color, its size, and its placement in the browser. In addition, the attributes for the OBJECT (Internet Explorer for Win) and EMBED (all other browsers for Win and Mac) tags are specified in the HTML document. These tags are used to direct the browser to load the Macromedia Flash Player. The HTML options from the Publish Settings dialog box can be used to change these settings.

Following is a description of the HTML options:

Template—Macromedia Flash provides several templates that create different HTML coding. For example, selecting Flash for Pocket PC creates HTML coding suitable for Pocket PC browsers and screens.

Dimensions—This option sets the values for the WIDTH and HEIGHT attributes in the OBJECT and EMBED tags and is used to set the size of the movie display window in the browser. You can choose to match the size of the movie, enter the size in pixels, or set the movie dimensions as a percentage of the browser window.

Playback—These options control the movie's playback and features, including:
- Paused at Start—pauses the movie until the user takes some action.
- Loop—repeats the movie.
- Display Menu—displays a shortcut menu (with options such as zoom in and out, step forward and back, rewind, and play) when the user right-clicks (Win) or [control] clicks (Mac) the movie in the browser.
- Device Font (Win)—allows you to substitute system fonts for fonts not installed on the user's computer.

Quality—This option allows you to specify the quality of the appearance of objects within the frames. Selecting low quality increases playback speed, but reduces image quality, while selecting high quality results in the opposite effect.

Window Mode—This option allows you to specify settings for transparency, positioning, and layering.

HTML Alignment—This option allows you to position the movie in the browser.

Scale—If you have changed the movie's original width and height, you can use this option to place the movie within specified boundaries.

Flash Alignment—This option allows you to align the movie within the movie window.

Determining Movie Placement in a Browser

When you publish a movie for delivery on the Internet, you need to be concerned with where in a browser window the movie will appear. The placement is controlled by settings in the HTML document. You can specify the settings when you publish the movie. A Macromedia Flash movie is displayed within a movie window. You can have the movie window match the size of the movie or use the HTML panel in the Publish Settings dialog box to specify a different size. Figure 18 shows the relationships among the movie dimensions, the movie display window, the browser window, and the HTML settings. In this example, the user's screen resolution is set

to Width: 800 pixels, Height: 600 pixels. The movie dimensions are Width: 400 pixels, Height: 400 pixels. You can adjust the following settings in the HTML Publish Settings dialog box:

- Movie window width: 400 pixels, Height: 100 pixels
- HTML alignment: right
- Flash alignment: right

When you reduce the size of one movie window dimension below the size of the corresponding movie dimension, the other movie dimension is reduced in order to keep the same aspect ratio. In this example, the movie window height of 100 causes the movie height to be resized to 100. Then, the movie width is resized to 100 to maintain the same 1:1 aspect ratio.

FIGURE 18

Relationships among the movie dimensions, movie and browser windows, and the HTML settings

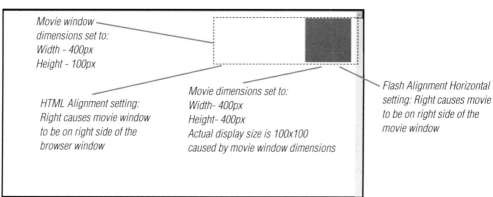

Movie window dimensions set to:
Width - 400px
Height - 100px

HTML Alignment setting: Right causes movie window to be on right side of the browser window

Movie dimensions set to:
Width- 400px
Height- 400px
Actual display size is 100x100 caused by movie window dimensions

Flash Alignment Horizontal setting: Right causes movie to be on right side of the movie window

Change HTML publish settings

1. Open planeFun.fla, click **File** on the menu bar, then click **Publish Settings**.

2. Click the **HTML tab**.

3. Click the **Dimensions list arrow** ˅, then click **Percent**.

4. Double-click the **Height text box**, type **30**, then compare your dialog box to Figure 19.

   Specifying 100 percent for the width and 30 percent for the height causes the Macromedia Flash Player window to be as wide as the browser window and approximately one-third the height.

5. Click **Publish**, then click **OK**.

6. Click **File** on the menu bar, point to **Publish Preview**, then click **Default-(HTML)**.

7. Click the **Start button**, then view the movie.

   TIP The movie is centered within the Macromedia Flash Player window because both the horizontal and vertical alignments were specified as centered in the HTML settings.

8. Close the browser.

You resized the Macromedia Flash Player window by changing the HTML publish settings.

FIGURE 19
Changing the HTML publish settings

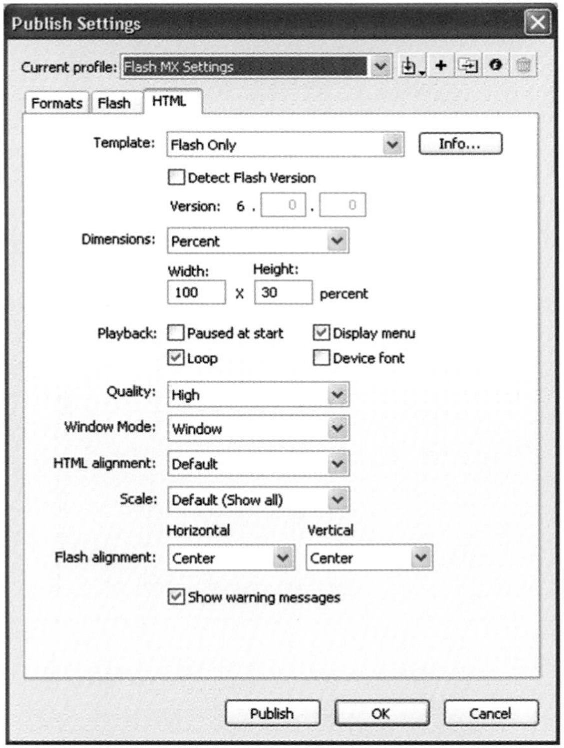

FIGURE 20
Changing the HTML code

Your code may vary

1. Open a text editor such as Notepad (Win) or TextEdit (Mac).

2. Click **File** on the text editor menu bar, click **Open**, change the Files of type to **All Files** (if necessary), then open **planeFun.html** in the text editor window.

3. Click to the left of </body> near the bottom of the text, then press **[Enter]** to insert a blank line above the second tag from the bottom, </body>.

4. Click on the blank line, type **
, then press **[Enter] (Win) or **[return]** (Mac).

5. Type ** <font color="red"> Having PlaneFun!!!</font> **, then compare the text you typed with the boxed text in Figure 20.

6. Save the file, then close the text editor.

7. Navigate to the folder where you save your Macromedia Flash movies, then double-click **planeFun.html** to open the movie in your browser.

   The text you added appears centered on the screen in red.

8. Close your browser.

9. Save your work, then close the movie.

10. Exit Flash.

You edited an HTML document to display format-ted text below the Flash movie.

Publish using default settings.

1. Start Flash, open fl6_4.fla, then save it as **skillsdemo6**.
2. Open the Publish Settings dialog box.
3. Verify that the Formats tab is selected and the Flash and HTML options are the only Format types checked.
4. Click Publish, then click OK to close the dialog box.
5. Navigate to the drive and folder where your Data Files are stored to view the folder with the skillsdemo6.swf and skillsdemo6.html files.
6. Return to the Macromedia Flash program.
7. Use the Publish Preview feature to display the movie in a browser or HTML editor.
8. Close your browser or HTML editor.
9. Save your work.

Create a GIF animation.

1. Open the Publish Settings dialog box.
2. Display the formats.
3. Select the GIF Image (.gif) format, then click the GIF tab to open the GIF format options.
4. Change the width to **275** and the height to **200**.
5. Click the Animated option button, then set the Palette type to Adaptive.
6. Publish the movie, then click OK to close the dialog box.
7. Open your browser.
8. Navigate to the folder with the GIF animation and play it in the browser.

9. Close the browser.
10. Save your work.

Create a JPEG image.

1. Select the last frame in the timeline.
2. Open the Publish Settings dialog box.
3. Click the Formats tab, click the JPEG check box, then click the JPEG tab.
4. Click Publish, then click OK to close the dialog box.
5. Navigate to the folder with the JPEG image.
6. Open your browser and open the JPEG file.
7. Close the browser.
8. Save your work.

Test a movie.

1. Use the Publish Preview feature to view the movie in your browser and note the pause.
2. Close the browser.
3. Click Control on the menu bar, then click Test Movie to view the movie in the Macromedia Flash Player window.
4. Turn off the loop feature.
5. Set the Download Setting to 28.8.
6. Display the Bandwidth Profiler, click View on the menu bar, then click Frame By Frame Graph.
7. Determine the frame where the movie pauses, display the frame, and view the image.
8. Close the Macromedia Flash Player window.

Optimize a movie.

1. Select the frame on the mountains layer with the large image.
2. Replace the image with the mountains-sm bitmap symbol in the Library panel. (*Hint*: Unlock the layer to delete the existing image.)
3. Center the mountains-sm image below the heading.
4. Save the movie.
5. Use the Publish Preview feature to view the movie in a browser.
6. Close the browser.

Change HTML publish settings.

1. Click the HTML tab in the Publish Settings dialog box.
2. Change the Dimensions to Percent, then change the width to **100%** and the height to **40%**.
3. Click OK to close the dialog box.
4. Use the Publish Preview feature to view the movie in a browser.
5. Close the browser.
6. Save your work.

Edit an HTML document.

1. Open a text editor.
2. Open the skillsdemo6.html file.
3. Insert a blank line above the </BODY> tag.
4. Type **</br>** then press [Enter] to insert a new line.

5. Type **<center><font color="green">Beautiful Northern Arizona</font></center>**.
6. Save your work.
7. Display skillsdemo6.html in your browser.
8. Close the browser.
9. Close the text editor.

Add a background.

1. Insert a new layer and move it below the mountains layer.
2. Name the new layer **background**.
3. Select Frame 1 on the background layer.
4. Display the Library panel, if necessary.
5. Drag the g_background graphic symbol to the center of the stage.
6. Compare the last frame of your movie to Figure 21.
7. Save your work, then publish the movie.

Add a preloader.

1. Add a Scene to the movie and name it **preloader**, then rename Scene 1 as **home**.
2. Move the preloader Scene above the home Scene so that it plays first.
3. Create a preloader in the preloader Scene timeline.
4. Test the move.
5. Save your work.
6. Exit Flash.

FIGURE 21
Completed Skills Review

The Ultimate Tours travel company has asked you to create a Web site, a GIF animation, and a JPEG image using movies you created in previous chapters.

1. Open ultimatetours5.fla (the file you created in Chapter 5 Project Builder 1) and save it as **ultimatetours6**.
2. Use the Publish Settings dialog box to publish the movie using the default setting for the Flash and HTML formats.
3. Use the Publish Preview feature to display the movie in the browser.
4. Display the GIF format tab in the Publish Settings dialog box, and make a change in the dimensions.
5. Create a GIF animation.
6. Display the GIF animation in your browser.
7. Create a JPEG image of the last frame of the home scene, as shown in Figure 22.
8. Display the JPEG image in your browser.
9. Make a change in the HTML publish settings, then display the movie in your browser.
10. Edit the HTML document and display the movie in your browser.
11. Save your work.

FIGURE 22
Sample completed Project Builder 1

You have been asked to test a previously developed Macromedia Flash movie, optimize the movie, and publish it. Then create a remote Web site and upload the files to the site. Figure 23 shows an image from Chapter 4. You may choose a different chapter.

1. Open a previously developed movie and save it as **publish6**.
2. Use the Publish Settings dialog box to publish the movie using the default setting for the Flash and HTML formats.
3. Use the Publish Preview feature to display the movie in the browser.
4. Display the GIF format tab in the Publish Settings dialog box, and make a change in the dimensions.
5. Create a GIF animation.
6. Display the GIF animation in your browser.
7. Create a JPEG image of the last frame of the movie.
8. Display the JPEG image in your browser.
9. Make a change in the HTML publish settings, then display the movie in your browser.
10. Edit the HTML document and display the movie in your browser.
11. Save your work.

FIGURE 23
Sample completed Project Builder 2

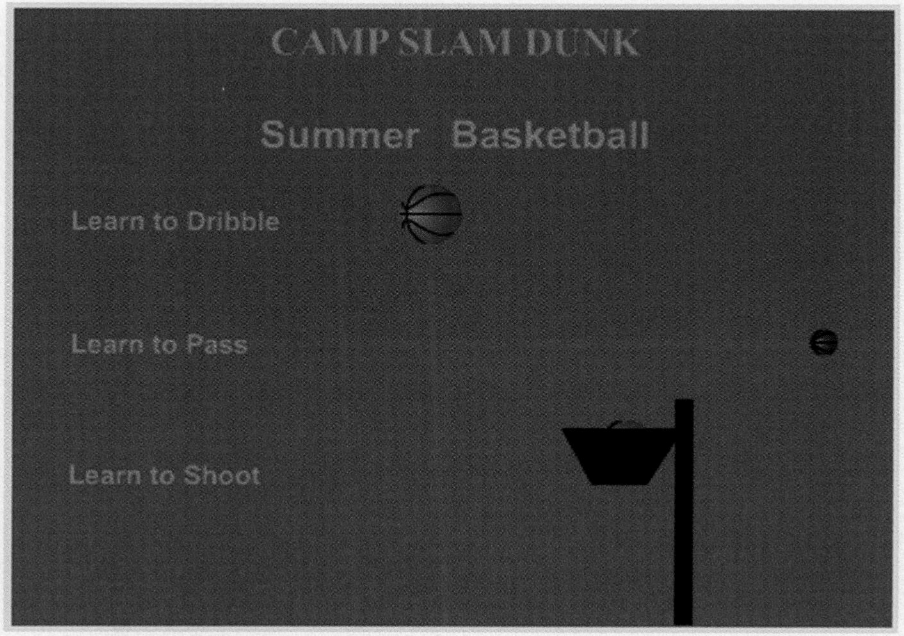

Preparing and Publishing Movies

Figure 24 shows the homepage of a Web site. Study the figure and complete the following questions. For each question, indicate how you determined your answer.

1. Connect to the Internet, go to *www.course.com*, navigate to the page for this book, click the Online Companion link, then click the link for this chapter.
2. Open a document in a word processor or open a new Macromedia Flash movie, save the file as **dpc6**, then answer the following questions. (*Hint*: Use the Text tool in Macromedia Flash.)
   - What seems to be the purpose of this site?
   - Who would be the target audience?
   - How might the Bandwidth Profiler be used when developing this site?
   - Assuming there is a pause in the playing of a Flash movie on the site, what suggestions would you make to eliminate the pause?
   - What would be the value of creating a GIF animation from one of the animations on the site?

- What would be the value of creating a JPEG image from one of the animations on the site?

- What suggestions would you make to improve on the design, and why?

FIGURE 24
Design Project

This is a continuation of Portfolio Project in Chapter 5, which is the development of a personal portfolio. In this project, you will create a Web site, a GIF animation, and a JPEG image with the movies you have created.

1. Open portfolio5.fla (the file you created in Portfolio Project, Chapter 5) and save it as **portfolio6**.
2. Use the Publish Settings dialog box to publish the movie using the default settings for the Flash and HTML formats.
3. Use the Publish Preview feature to display the movie in the browser.
4. Display the GIF format tab in the Publish Settings dialog box and make a change in the dimensions.
5. Create a GIF animation.
6. Display the GIF animation in your browser.
7. Create a JPEG image of the first frame of the home scene.
8. Display the JPEG image in your browser.
9. Use the Bandwidth Profiler to display a frame-by-frame graph of the movie and to determine which frame may cause a pause in the movie at a 28.8K connection speed.
10. Make a change in the movie to help optimize it.

11. Make a change in the HTML publish settings, then display the movie in your browser.
12. Edit the HTML document and display the movie in your browser.

13. Save your work, then compare your JPEG image to the example shown in Figure 25.

FIGURE 25
Sample completed Portfolio Project

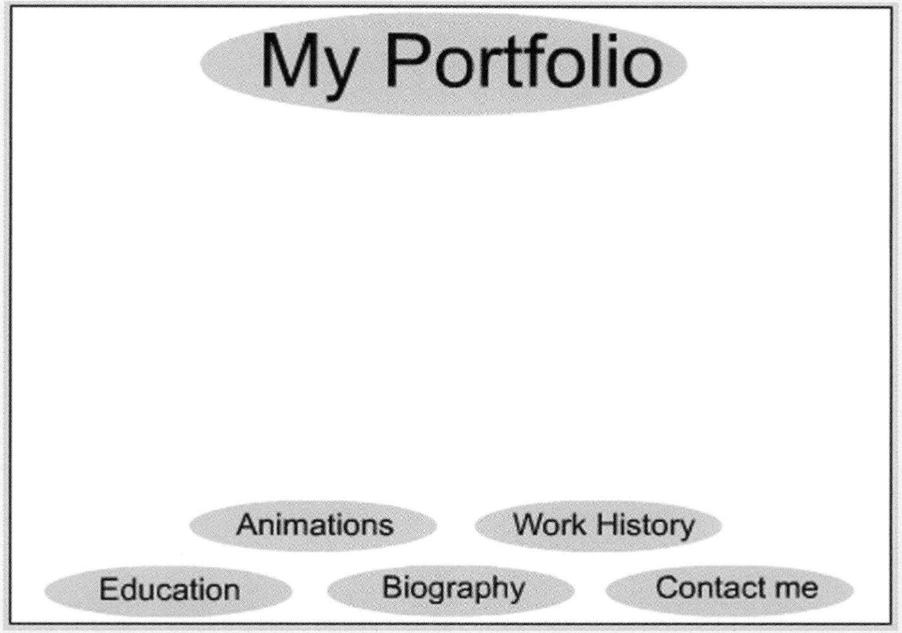

chapter

7

IMPORTING AND
MODIFYING GRAPHICS

1. Understand and import graphics.

2. Break apart bitmaps and use bitmap fills.

3. Trace bitmap graphics.

4. Use imported graphics in a scene.

7 IMPORTING AND
MODIFYING GRAPHICS

Introduction

Within your movies, you may often find yourself wanting to use a logo or image that originated in another application. In previous chapters, you learned to create images using the drawing tools on the Tools panel. However, you are not limited to just what you can draw within your movie. You can import and even animate bitmap and vector graphics that have been created or modified in other applications.

Importing vector images from an application such as Macromedia Fireworks or Adobe Illustrator is easy—the vector images are treated almost the same as if you created them in Macromedia Flash. While importing bitmap images is easy, working with them can be more difficult.

Using bitmaps can increase the file size of your movies dramatically, resulting in slower download times. Therefore, it is most efficient to use vector images or to create images directly within Macromedia Flash.

In this chapter, you will practice importing graphics that have been created outside of the Macromedia Flash environment. For those who are "artistically-challenged," bringing in graphics from other applications can often help to make up for less-than-perfect drawing skills. You can import a wide variety of vector and bitmap graphics, and even video. Once the graphics are inside your Library, you can trace them, break them apart, use them to fill an object, optimize them, and animate them.

Tools You'll Use

UNDERSTAND AND
IMPORT GRAPHICS

What You'll Do

▶ In this lesson, you will import graphics from several different drawing and image-editing programs.

Understanding the Formats

Because Macromedia Flash is a vector-based application, all images and motion within the application are calculated according to mathematical formulas. This vector-based format results in smaller file size, as well as a robust ability to resize movies without a notable loss in quality.

When you introduce bitmapped images, some of the vector-based benefits change dramatically. A bitmap or raster image is based on pixels, not on a mathematical formula. Importing multiple bitmaps will increase the file size of your movie and decrease flexibility in terms of resizing the movie.

You have the ability to import both vector and bitmap images from applications such as Macromedia Fireworks, Macromedia Freehand, Adobe Illustrator, Adobe Photoshop, and Adobe ImageReady. In many cases, you can retain features such as layers, transparency, and animation.

Importing Different Graphic Formats: Overview

There are several ways of getting external graphics into your movie. Generally, the best way to use a graphic in your movie is to **import** it by selecting the Import option on the File menu. Then you can choose the Import to Stage command to have the image placed on the stage or choose the Import to Library command to have the image placed only in the Library. Next, you navigate to the graphic of your choice. Figure 1 displays the Import to Library dialog box with the All Files option selected. Once you import a graphic, you will see it on the stage or inside the Library panel. If the original graphic has layers in it, Macromedia Flash might create new layers in your document, depending on the file type and what you specify when you import the graphic. Macromedia Flash will automatically place the additional layers on the stage or inside a movie clip symbol, when applicable. Movie clips are movies within a movie. They have their own Timeline and they can be used to organize the contents of a movie, as well as create complex animations, as covered in a later chapter.

For some file formats, you can also cut and paste across applications, although with less flexibility than importing provides. If you are importing large numbers of graphics, you can import a batch of images, all of which will automatically use the same settings, enabling you to choose your import preferences once.

QUICKTIP
All imported graphics must be at least 2 pixels by 2 pixels.

Using Macromedia Fireworks PNG files

You can import Macromedia Fireworks PNG files as flattened images or as editable objects. If you choose to import a flattened image, Macromedia Flash will automatically bitmap the image. To import a PNG file as a bitmap, choose the Import into new layer in current scene option. Macromedia Flash will create a new layer in your movie that contains the flattened layers from the original PNG file. You can also choose the Import as a single flattened bitmap option to add the image to the current layer.

FIGURE 1
Import to Library dialog box

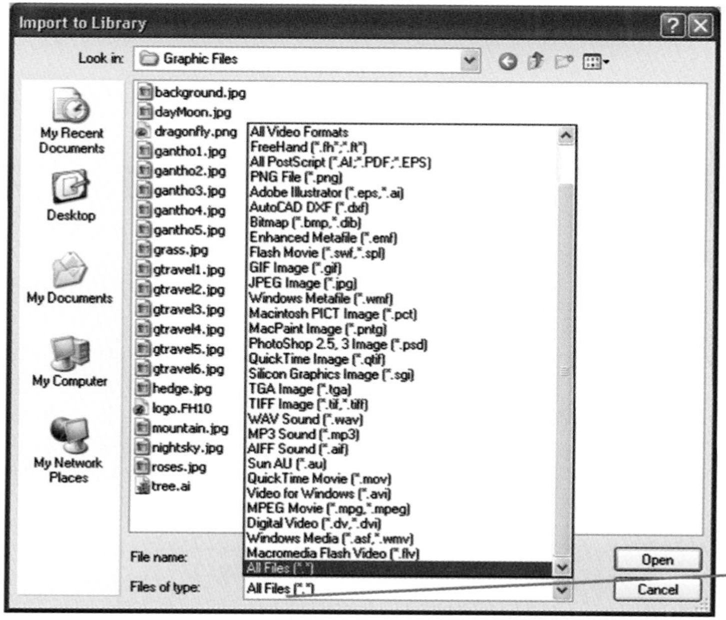

All Files

When you insert a PNG file as an editable object, it retains its vector format as well as its layers and transparency features. If you click the Import as movie clip and retain layers option, all the features of the PNG file will appear inside a movie clip symbol that is stored in the Library. This will include layers, animation, and transparency, where applicable. Figure 2 shows the Fireworks PNG Import Settings dialog box in which these settings appear.

Importing Macromedia Freehand Files

When importing Macromedia Freehand files, you can preserve layers, text blocks, symbols, and pages, as well as choose certain pages within a document to import. Macromedia Flash will automatically convert cyan, magenta, yellow, and black (CMYK) files to red, green, and blue (RGB) files. Remember to place all Macromedia Freehand objects on their own layers when you want to preserve layers. As you import the file, choose the Layers option, which will preserve your objects and your layers. If you import a Macromedia Freehand file with overlapping objects on one layer, Macromedia Flash will treat the file as if it had overlapping objects. However, in Macromedia Freehand, each object remains intact, even when overlapped. In Macromedia Flash, selection and groups of elements are based on color. If two shapes of the same color are overlapped, they will become one shape. Keep the following points in mind as you import files from Macromedia Freehand to Macromedia Flash:

- Macromedia Flash will support only up to eight colors in a gradient fill.
- Macromedia Flash will import blends in separate paths; the more paths you have, the greater the file size.
- Macromedia Flash will import both CMYK and Grayscale Macromedia Freehand images as RGB, which in some cases might increase the file size.

FIGURE 2
Fireworks PNG Import Settings dialog box

Retains layers from the original file

Maintains drawn shapes and editable paths

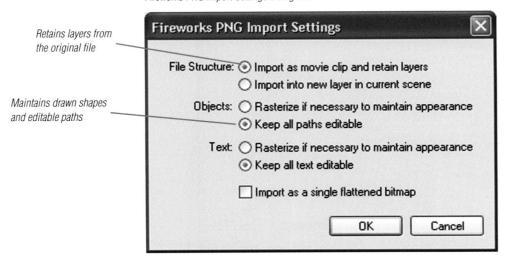

Importing Adobe Illustrator Files

Similar to Macromedia Freehand files, most Adobe Illustrator files are vector-based. However, importing Illustrator files can be problematic. You should remember to ungroup any grouped elements in the Illustrator file before starting to import. In Illustrator, you again have the ability to preserve layers on import. You can use layers in two ways: first with each layer as a keyframe, and second with each layer as its own layer in Macromedia Flash. Figure 3 shows the importing while preserving layers option.

Importing Bitmaps from Adobe Photoshop/Adobe ImageReady

Macromedia Flash allows you to use and modify imported bitmaps in a variety of ways. You can control the size, compression, and anti-aliasing of an imported bitmap. You can also use a bitmap as a fill or convert a bitmap to a vector by tracing it or breaking it apart.

When using Photoshop or ImageReady, you must have QuickTime 4.0 or later installed on your computer in order to use the following file types: .psd, .pic, .pct, or .tif. QuickTime must be installed on your computer in the recommended or complete method; otherwise, you can import Photoshop/ImageReady documents only if they are saved in a .gif, .jpg, or .png format. When importing a flattened bitmap format, such as a .gif or .jpg, it is a good idea to compress the bitmap before you import it.

Once you import a bitmap, it becomes an element in the Library. To edit the graphic from the Library panel, double-click the object to open the Bitmap Properties dialog box. Inside these properties, you can compress the image even more and allow for smoothing (anti-aliasing) on the image.

If an instance of a bitmap symbol is on the stage, you can use the Property inspector to numerically change the dimensions of the image on the stage as well as swap it for another image and edit the bitmap in an outside application.

FIGURE 3
Import dialog box

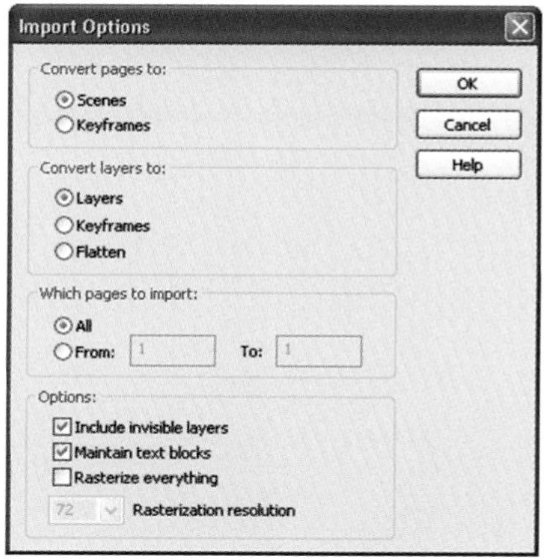

Import a layered PNG file as a movie clip symbol

1. Start Flash, create a new Flash document, save it as **gsamples**, then verify that the size is **550 × 400 pixels**.

2. Make sure that the Library panel is open.

   TIP You can also open the Library panel by pressing [F11] (Win) or [command][L] (Mac).

3. Click **File** on the menu bar, point to **Import**, click **Import to Stage**, then navigate to the drive and folder where your Data Files are stored.

4. Click the **Files of type list arrow** ⌄ (Win) or **Enable list arrow** (Mac), click **PNG File (*.png)** (if necessary), click **dragonfly.png**, then click **Open** (Win) or **Import** (Mac).

5. In the Fireworks PNG Import Settings dialog box, verify that the **Import as a single flattened bitmap check box** is deselected, then verify that the **Import as movie clip and retain layers option button** in the File Structure section is selected.

   TIP If you click the Import into new layer in current scene option button instead, the PNG file will be flattened into a single layer.

6. Click the **Keep all paths editable option button** in the Objects section, if necessary.

7. Click the **Keep all text editable option button** in the Text section (if necessary), click **OK**, set the view to Fit in Window, then compare your stage and Library panel to Figure 4.

   The dragonfly appears on the stage and a new folder appears in the Library, which contains the dragonfly movie clip.

8. Name Layer 1 as **dragonfly**.

You imported a Fireworks PNG file as a movie clip in the Library panel.

FIGURE 4
Imported movie clip symbol

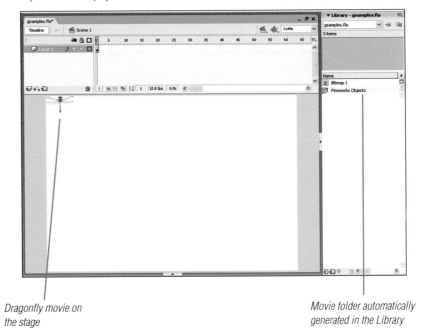

Dragonfly movie on
the stage

Movie folder automatically
generated in the Library

FIGURE 5
Tree on the stage after importing

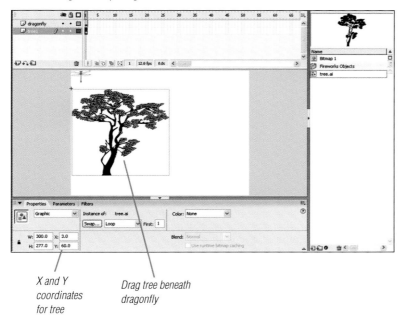

X and Y
coordinates
for tree

Drag tree beneath
dragonfly

1. Click **File** on the menu bar, point to **Import**, then click **Import to Library**.

   TIP   The Import to Library option imports the graphic into the Library panel as a symbol, but not to the stage.

2. Click the **Files of type list arrow** ⌄ (Win) or **Enable list arrow** (Mac), click **Adobe Illustrator (*.eps, *.ai)**, click **tree.ai**, then click **Open** (Win) or **Import to Library** (Mac).

3. Click the **Layers option button** in the Convert layers to section of the Illustrator Import dialog box (if necessary) to convert each layer in the original graphic to a layer in the symbol.

   TIP   If you select the Key Frames option instead of Layers, the layers will import as separate keyframes. This option might be useful if you are importing an animation.

4. Verify that the **Include invisible layers check box** is selected, then click **OK**.

   A new graphic symbol, tree.ai, appears in the Library panel.

5. Insert a new layer, name it **tree1**, then drag the **tree1 layer** beneath the dragonfly layer.

6. Verify that **Frame 1** of the tree1 layer is selected, then drag the **tree.ai graphic symbol** from the Library panel to the left side of the stage beneath the dragonfly.

7. Open the Property inspector, double-click the W: text box, type **300**, double-click the H: text box, type **277**, then press **[Enter]** (Win) or **[return]** (Mac).

8. Position the tree, as shown in Figure 5.

You imported an Illustrator file with layers intact to the Library panel and dragged the symbol to the stage.

Import an Adobe Photoshop file saved in JPG format

1. Click **File** on the menu bar, point to **Import**, then click **Import to Library**.

2. Click the **Files of type list arrow** ⌄ (Win) or **Enable list arrow** (Mac), click **JPEG Image** (*.jpg), click **background.jpg**, then click **Open** (Win) or **Import to Library** (Mac).

   The background.jpg file imports as a flattened bitmap image into the Library panel.

3. Insert a new layer, move the **new layer** to the bottom of the timeline, then name it **background**.

4. Verify that **Frame 1** of the background layer is selected, then drag the **background graphic symbol** from the Library panel to the center of the stage.

5. Click the **background graphic** on the stage to select it, then use the Property inspector to change the width to **550** and the height to **400**.

6. Drag the graphic into position X: **0.0** and Y: **0.0** so that the graphic covers the entire stage, as shown in Figure 6.

7. Click the **Lock/Unlock layer icon** 🔒 to lock the background layer. Your screen should resemble Figure 7.

8. Save your work.

You imported a JPG file to the Library panel and dragged it to the stage.

FIGURE 6
Setting the width and height for the graphic

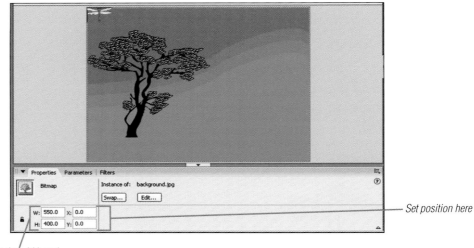

Set position here

Set the width and height here

FIGURE 7
The imported graphics placed on the stage

The layer locked

FIGURE 8

Bitmap Properties dialog box

Bitmap Properties

background.jpg

C:\A - FLASH 8\Chapter
7\HEE\FL8-HEE-Ch7-DataFiles\background.jpg

Thursday, July 28, 2005 4:47:36 PM

400 x 300 pixels at 32 bits per pixel

☑ Allow smoothing

Compression: Photo (JPEG)

☐ Use imported JPEG data

Quality: 50   (100=highest)

Imported JPEG: original = 480.0 kb,
compressed = 575.7 kb, 119% of original

OK
Cancel
Update
Import...
Test
Advanced

*Remove check mark from
the Use imported JPEG
data check box*

*Compressed size
of the graphic*

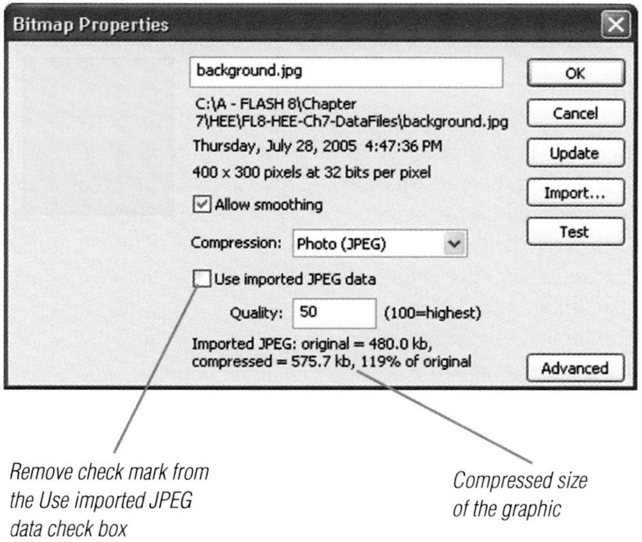

Change the compression settings of a bitmap

1. Right-click (Win) or [control] click (Mac) the **background bitmap symbol** in the Library panel, then click **Properties** to open the Bitmap Properties dialog box.

2. Click the **Allow smoothing check box** to select it, if necessary.

3. Verify that **Photo (JPEG)** is selected for Compression.

4. Click the **Use imported JPEG data check box** to deselect it, then verify that the Quality is set to **50**, as shown in Figure 8.

   The compressed size of the graphic is displayed at the bottom of the dialog box.

5. Click **Test**.

   Notice the compressed size of the graphic with the quality reduced.

6. Click **OK**.

7. Save your work.

You compared the file sizes of different compressions and then compressed a bitmap file.

BREAK APART BITMAPS
AND USE BITMAP FILLS

What You'll Do

In this lesson, you will break apart bitmap images and manipulate bitmap fill images to create new effects.

Breaking Apart Bitmaps

Breaking apart a bitmap image allows increased flexibility in how you can use it within a movie. If you are planning to use unmanipulated photographs or images, there is no need to break apart a bitmap image. Once you do break apart a bitmap image, you can click different areas of the image to manipulate them separately from the image as a whole, including changing color, cropping, and scaling. You can also sample a bitmap image you break apart with the Eyedropper tool on the Tools panel, and then use the image as a fill for a drawn shape or as the fill for text.

Breaking apart an image effectively makes each area of color a discrete element that you can manipulate separately from the rest of the image. When selected, a stage-level object appears as a series of pixels, whereas a symbol is selected with a blue outline surrounding it. A **stage-level object** is a vector object that you draw directly on the stage, unlike a symbol, which you place on the stage from the Library panel. You manipulate an image that you break apart the same as you would a stage-level object.

QUICKTIP

Introducing bitmaps will always increase the file size of your movie, resulting in slower download times for the users.

Using Bitmap Fills

Until now, you have been applying solid colors and gradient fills to objects. Macromedia Flash allows you to apply a bitmap fill to any drawn shape or text that has been broken apart. A **bitmap fill** is created by taking one image and using it to fill another image.

Figure 9 shows different bitmap fill effects. You can apply a bitmap fill to any drawn shape. If necessary, Macromedia Flash will tile (repeat) the bitmap to fill the shape. You can use the Fill Transform tool to change the size, shape, rotation, and skew of your fill, which allows you to position the original image exactly as you want it in the new shape.

In addition to filling shapes with a bitmap, you can also apply your images as a fill by using the Paintbrush tool. This process involves breaking apart the image, selecting it with the Eyedropper tool, then choosing a paintbrush and brush size. When you begin painting, you will see your image as a fill. You can also use the Fill Transform tool with the paintbrush fill.

Selecting a Bitmap Fill with the Color Mixer Panel
If the bitmap image you want to use for a fill is not on the stage, you can use the Color Mixer to select it. The process is similar to clicking a new color in the color picker, but instead of choosing a solid color or gradient, you choose Bitmap, and then select the bitmap of your choice. If you select a bitmap fill through the Color Mixer, you do not have to break apart the bitmap. Figure 10 shows the Color Mixer panel with a bitmap fill selected.

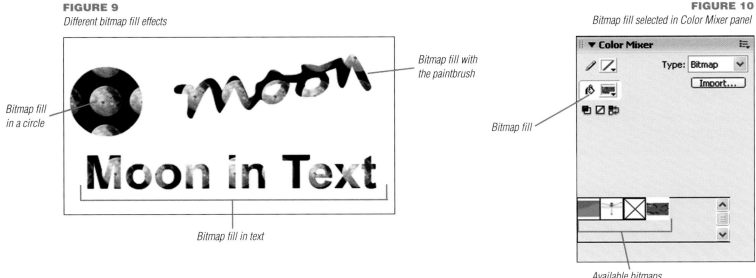

FIGURE 9
Different bitmap fill effects

Bitmap fill in a circle

Bitmap fill with the paintbrush

Bitmap fill in text

FIGURE 10
Bitmap fill selected in Color Mixer panel

Bitmap fill

Available bitmaps from Library

Break apart a bitmap

1. Verify that the **gsamples.fla** document is open, click **File** on the menu bar, point to **Import**, then click **Import to Library**.

2. Click the **Files of type list arrow** ∨ (Win) or **Enable list arrow** (Mac), click **JPEG Image (*.jpg)** (if necessary), click **dayMoon**, then click **Open** (Win) or **Import to Library** (Mac).

3. Insert a new layer, move it to just above the background layer, then name it **moon**.

4. Drag the **dayMoon graphic symbol** from the Library panel to the top right corner of the stage, as shown in Figure 11.

5. Verify the moon is selected, click **Modify** on the menu bar, click **Break Apart**, then compare your image to Figure 12.

6. Click any gray area around the stage to deselect the moon image.

7. Click the **Lasso tool** ℘ on the Tools panel, then click the **Magic Wand Settings tool** in the Options section of the Tools panel.

8. Click the **Smoothing list arrow** ∨, click **Pixels**, then click **OK**.

9. Zoom in on the moon, click the **Magic Wand tool** in the Options section of the Tools panel, then click any part of the black background of the moon image.

10. Click **Edit** on the menu bar, click **Cut**, then set the view to Fit in Window.

    The selected black area no longer appears on the stage, as shown in Figure 13.

11. Click the **Selection tool** ᛕ on the Tools panel.

You broke apart and edited a bitmap image.

FIGURE 11
Moon on stage after importing

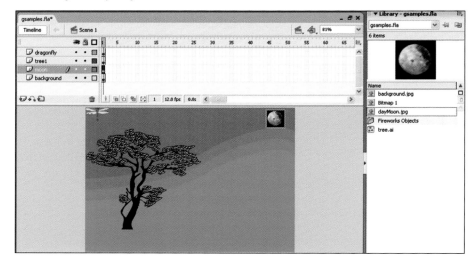

FIGURE 12
Moon pixels after being broken apart

Individual pixels appear as a grid

FIGURE 13
The image after deleting the black area

FIGURE 14

Selecting a bitmap Fill with the Eyedropper Tool

Bitmap displayed
for fill color

FIGURE 15

Filling a shape with a bitmap

Hedge bitmap tiles
to fill the rectangle

Using the Lasso Tool and the Magic Wand Tool

The Lasso tool lets you select an irregularly shaped part of a graphic, which you can then move, scale, rotate, or reshape. The Magic Wand option extends the Lasso tool so you can select areas of similar color in a bitmap you have broken apart. With the Magic Wand Properties tool, you can specify a color similarity threshold for the Magic Wand (a higher number means more matching colors will be selected) and the type of smoothing that will be applied to the selection.

Use and edit a bitmap fill

1. Click **File** on the menu bar, point to **Import**, click **Import to Library**, then open **hedge.jpg**.

2. Insert a new layer, move it to just above the dragonfly layer on the timeline, then name it **hedge**.

3. Drag the **hedge graphic symbol** from the Library panel to the center of the stage.

4. Click **Modify** on the menu bar, then click **Break Apart**.

5. Click the **Eyedropper tool** 🖊 on the Tools panel, click the **hedge image** on the stage, then compare your screen to Figure 14.

   TIP The Eyedropper tool lets you select a fill from an existing object so you can apply it to another object.

6. Click the **Selection tool** ▶ on the Tools panel, then click the **hedge image** on the stage to select it.

7. Click **Edit** on the menu bar, then click **Cut** to remove the graphic from the stage.

8. Click the **Rectangle tool** ▭ on the Tools panel, click the **Stroke color tool** 🖊▭ on the Tools panel, then click the **None button** ▨.

9. Using Figure 15 as a guide, draw a rectangle just below the tree trunk across the bottom half of the stage.

   The rectangle fills with a tiling bitmap of the hedge.

   TIP To change the size or skew, or to move the bitmap fill image, click the Free Transform tool on the Tools panel, then click the images.

10. Save your work.

You used the Eyedropper tool to select a fill from an object, then applied the fill to another object.

TRACE BITMAP
GRAPHICS

What You'll Do

In this lesson, you will trace a bitmap graphic to create vectors and special effects.

Understanding Tracing

Tracing is an outstanding feature for the illustration-challenged, or if you need to convert a bitmap image into a vector image for animation purposes. When you apply the trace functions, you turn a pure bitmap into vector paths and fills with varying degrees of detail. If you keep all the detail in an image, you end up with very detailed, intricate vector paths, which tend to increase file size. If you remove some of the detail, you can turn a photograph into a more abstract-looking drawing, which usually requires less file size. Once traced, you can remove the original image from the Library panel and work with only the traced paths and shapes, thereby reducing the movie's file size. The traced shapes act just like shapes you have drawn, with fills, lines, and strokes that you can manipulate and change. Tracing allows an image to act as a graphic drawn directly in Macromedia Flash, which is why you are able to select paths based on color and to use paths to manipulate the shape of an image.

QUICKTIP

Tracing bitmaps can often take a long time, especially if it is a detailed trace or a large image.

One of the challenges with using the trace feature comes when you try to animate a traced image. Tracing creates paths and shapes, but every piece of the original image remains on one layer. To animate or tween between pieces of the shape, you often have to isolate parts of the object onto their own layers. Figure 16 shows the before and after effects of tracing an image. In this example, you can see how tracing makes the original photograph appear more abstract. Figure 17 shows the traced image cut up for animation.

Using the Trace Settings

It is possible to trace an image using very detailed or less detailed settings. Your traced image will look more like the original graphic if you retain more detail. If you want the traced image to look more abstract, use less detail. However, the greater the detail, the greater the file size.

In Figure 18, three different trace effects are created by adjusting the trace values.

There are four options that affect how detailed the trace will appear: Color Threshold, Minimum Area, Curve Fit, and Corner Threshold. Color Threshold compares two side-by-side pixels; if the difference is less than the color threshold, the two are considered the same color. Color Threshold options include integers between 1 and 500. Minimum Area sets the number of surrounding pixels to consider, with options between 1 and 1000. Curve Fit determines how smoothly outlines are drawn. Corner Threshold works with sharp edges to retain them or smooth them out. Figure 19 shows the Trace Bitmap dialog box.

QUICKTIP
You can no longer trace an image once you break it apart.

FIGURE 17
Dividing a traced image by color

FIGURE 16
Before and after tracing a bitmap

Sections of the moon selected by color and moved

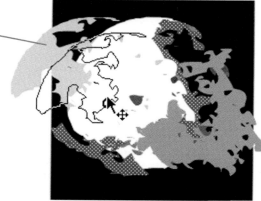

FIGURE 18
Three different effects with different trace settings

FIGURE 19
Trace Bitmap dialog box

Trace Bitmap	
Color threshold: 100	OK
Minimum area: 8 pixels	Cancel
Curve fit: Normal	
Corner threshold: Normal	

Trace a bitmap image

1. Click the **Selection tool** ▶ on the Tools panel, click the **moon image** on the stage to select it, then press **[Delete]**.

2. Drag the **dayMoon.jpg graphic** from the Library panel to the upper right corner of the stage.

3. Verify that the **moon** is selected, click **Modify** on the menu bar, point to **Bitmap**, then click **Trace Bitmap**.

4. Verify that **100** appears in the Color threshold text box, click the **Minimum area text box**, type **8** (if necessary), then review the default Normal settings for Curve fit and Corner threshold.

5. Click **OK**, click the gray area around the stage to deselect the moon, then compare your image to Figure 20.

6. Click the **Zoom tool** 🔍 on the Tools panel, then click the **moon** to enlarge it, as shown in Figure 21.

You traced a bitmap image and zoomed in on it.

FIGURE 20
The traced bitmap image

Bitmap image traced

FIGURE 21
Zooming in on the moon

Importing and Modifying Graphics

FIGURE 22
Selecting the black edge of the bitmap

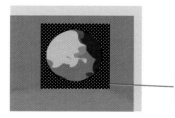

Click anywhere on
the black edge

FIGURE 23
Changing the fill color

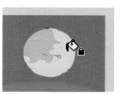

FIGURE 24
The completed screen

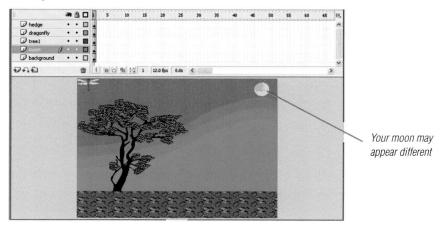

Your moon may
appear different

Edit a traced bitmap image

1. Click the **Selection tool** ↖ on the Tools panel.

2. Click the black edge of the traced moon image to select the black color as shown in Figure 22, then press **[Delete]**.

3. Click the **Paint Bucket tool** 🪣 on the Tools panel.

4. Click the **Fill Color tool** 🪣▢ on the Tools panel, change the color to **#B7DEFF**, then press **[Enter]**.

5. Click various parts of the **moon image** with the **Paint Bucket tool** 🪣 to change the color to resemble Figure 23.

   Note: Click Edit on the menu bar, then click Undo to use the undo command, as needed.

6. Click the **Selection tool** ↖ on the Tools panel.

7. Click **View** on the menu bar, point to **Magnification**, then click **Fit in Window**.

   Your screen should resemble Figure 24.

8. Save your work.

You edited a traced bitmap image by changing the color of parts of the bitmap.

USE IMPORTED GRAPHICS
IN A SCENE

What You'll Do

 In this lesson, you will optimize your Library of imported graphics and manipulate instances of symbols on the stage.

Mixing Graphic Formats

In the previous lessons, you combined importing graphics, filling with bitmaps, tracing bitmaps, and manipulating imported images. You can use all of these techniques in tandem to create a cohesive Macromedia Flash movie without having to be an artist or an illustration expert. Tracing also allows a way to tie together different photo styles without ruining the integrity of the movie.

In your sample file, the sky is a bitmap fill from a JPG file, the grass is an imported and traced Photoshop file, the dragonfly is a Macromedia Fireworks file, and the trees are Illustrator files. All of these combine to create an outdoor scene. Depending on the effect you are trying to achieve, you might use one or more of these techniques to create your own movies.

Optimizing Your Library

Because all the library elements have to be saved with the movie, make sure you do not have any extraneous bitmaps or imported images in the Library panel. If you broke apart an image, it is still necessary to keep the original image inside the Library. When an image is traced, the original image can be removed from the Library panel. If you import any images that you do not use, you should remove them from the Library panel before publishing. If you don't manipulate an imported image at all, it is still required to be in the Library panel. Taking the time to clean up your Library will result in a better-optimized Macromedia Flash movie.

A well-optimized movie means that you are not using any symbols gratuitously

---

DESIGNTIP   **Cropping images before importing**

It is always a good idea to crop images prior to importing them into the Library. It is best to import only what you will use to help keep the file size down. If you are using an image more than once, and one version is cropped and the second version is not, then you would need to import the entire image and crop one instance of it.

and that all symbols have been optimized. Generally, it is also a good idea to group your symbols into folders in the Library panel. Grouping is commonly done by symbol type, as displayed in Figure 25, or by the piece of the movie with which a symbol is associated.

Importing Idiosyncrasies

In addition to the applications mentioned above, you can also import graphics that are from AutoCAD, MacPaint, Silicon

Graphics Image, and QuickTime. Table 1 on the following page details the file formats, applications, and platforms that Macromedia Flash supports for importing. All the file formats have slightly different behavior when imported. Many of these files rely on QuickTime 4 or higher for support. Generally, if Macromedia Flash does not know what to do with a bitmap file or if QuickTime is not installed, it will import even a complex layered file as one single, flattened layer.

Animating Imported Graphics

One of the most powerful features and benefits to Macromedia Flash is its ability to animate. You can animate any type of imported graphic, from moving a photograph across a scene to separating the pieces of a PNG file and animating them.

Once the images are inside Macromedia Flash, you can manipulate them the way you would any other object by utilizing Library elements, tweening animation, and other animation techniques to bring still images to life.

FIGURE 25
A well-organized Library

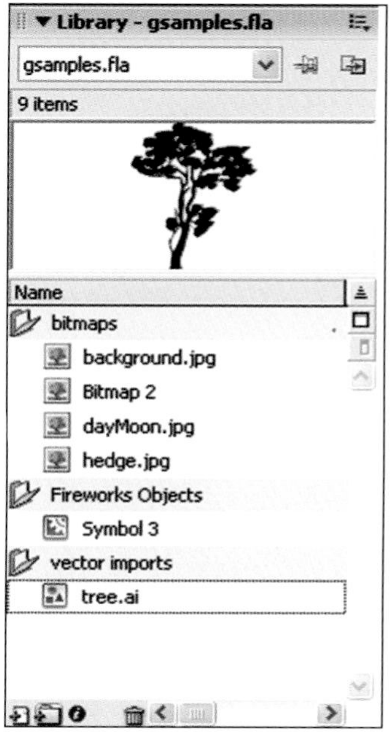

TABLE 1: File Formats for Imported Graphics

file type	extension	supported on Windows/Macintosh	file type	extension	supported on Windows/Macintosh
Adobe Illustrator (version 10 or earlier)	.eps, .ai, .pdf	Windows Macintosh	Photoshop*	.psd	Windows Macintosh
AutoCAD DXF	.dxf	Windows Macintosh	PICT*	.pic, .pct	Windows Macintosh
Bitmap	.bmp	Windows Macintosh (using QuickTime)	PNG	.png	Windows Macintosh
Enhanced Windows Metafile	.emf	Windows	QuickTime Image*	.qtif	Windows Macintosh
Macromedia FreeHand	.fh7, .fh8, .fh9, .fh10, .fh11	Windows Macintosh	Silicon Graphics Image	.sgi	Windows Macintosh
Flash Player 6	.swf	Windows Macintosh	FutureSplash Player	.sp1	Windows Macintosh
GIF and animated GIF	.gif	Windows Macintosh	TGA*	.tga	Windows Macintosh
JPEG	.jpg	Windows Macintosh	TIFF*	.tif	Windows Macintosh
MacPaint*	.pntg	Windows Macintosh	Windows Metafile	.wmf	Windows

*requires QuickTime 4 or later

Importing and Modifying Graphics

FIGURE 26
Positioning the dragonfly

1. Drag the **dragonfly image** over the center of the tree, as shown in Figure 26.
2. Insert a new layer above the hedge layer in the timeline, then name it **tree2**.
3. Click **Frame 1** of the tree2 layer, then drag the **tree symbol** from the Library panel to the middle of the stage.
4. Use the Property inspector to change the width of the tree to **96** and the height to **88**.
5. Position the tree, as shown in Figure 27.
6. Save your work, then close gsamples.fla.
7. Exit Flash.

You used traced images, bitmap fills, and imported PNG files to build a still scene that you can animate.

FIGURE 27
Positioning the tree

Positioning the second tree

Understand and import graphics.

1. Create a new Flash document with a size of **550 × 400** pixels and no background color, then save it as **skillsdemo7**.
2. Make sure the Library panel is open.
3. Import the Freehand file logo.FH10 to the Library with the following settings:
   Mapping Pages: Scenes
   Layers: Flatten
   Pages: All
   Options: (select all three)
4. Import roses.jpg to the Library.
5. Import mountain.jpg to the Library.

6. Import nightsky.jpg to the Library.
7. Name Layer 1 **red-roses** and drag the roses symbol to the upper-right corner of the stage.
8. Create a layer named **logo** and drag the logo symbol to the upper-left corner of the stage.
9. Create a layer named **mountain** and drag the mountain symbol to the bottom-center of the stage.
10. Use the Property inspector to change the width of the mountain so that it is as wide as the stage, 550 pixels. If necessary, move the mountain image so it is centered and flush with the bottom of the stage.
11. Save your work.

Break apart bitmaps and use bitmap fills.

1. Break apart the roses image.
2. Click the roses image with the Eyedropper tool, then delete the roses image from the stage.
3. Use the Rectangle tool to create a rectangle behind the logo that spans the width of the stage.
4. Create a new layer above the mountain layer named **more roses**.
5. Paint a line of roses along the bottom of the mountain image. (*Hint*: Use the Brush tool.)
6. Save your work.

Trace bitmap graphics.

1. Trace the mountain image, using settings of **100** for Color Threshold, **10** for Minimum Area, and Normal for Curve Fit and Corner Threshold.
2. Deselect the image.
3. Select the nightsky image as a bitmap fill, then use the Paint Bucket tool to change the blue sky and clouds, in the background of the mountain, to stars. (*Hint:* You can either move the nightsky image to the stage and break it apart to create the bitmap fill, or try using the Color Mixer.)
4. Draw a rectangle on a separate layer to fill in the white space between the roses and the sky.
5. Save your work.

Use imported graphics.

1. Delete the image you traced (mountain) from the Library panel to decrease file size.
2. Compare your movie to Figure 28, then save your work.
3. View the movie.
4. Exit Flash.

FIGURE 28
Completed Skills Review

Ultimate Tours is rolling out a new "summer in December" promotion in the coming months and wants a Macromedia Flash Web site to showcase a series of tours to Florida, Bermuda, and the Caribbean. The Web site should use bright, "tropical" colors and have a family appeal. Though you will eventually animate this site, Ultimate Tours would first like to see still pictures of what you are planning to do.

1. Open a new Flash document, then save it as **ultimatetours7**.
2. Set the movie properties, including the size and background color if desired.
3. Create the following text elements on separate layers:
   - A primary headline **Ultimate Tours Presents…** with an appropriate font and treatment.
   - A subheading **Our new "Summer in December" Tour Packages!** in a smaller font size.
4. Import the following JPG files to the Library panel (alternately, you can create your own images, obtain images from your computer or the Internet, or create images from scanned media):
   gtravel1.jpg
   gtravel2.jpg
   gtravel3.jpg
   gtravel4.jpg
   gtravel5.jpg
   gtravel6.jpg

5. Move three of the images to the stage to create an appealing vacation collage, arranging and resizing the images as appropriate. (*Hint*: Some of the sample files have a white background. If you want to include one of these images and your stage has a different background color, try breaking the image apart, then using the Magic Wand tool to erase the background of the image.)
6. Trace one of the images on the stage to create an artistic effect and reduce file size, then delete the traced image from the Library panel.

FIGURE 29
Sample completed Project Builder 1

7. Create three round or square buttons using an image from the Library panel as a bitmap fill. Resize or skew the bitmap fill as appropriate.
8. Apply a bitmap fill to some or all the letters in the title. (*Hint*: To add a bitmap fill to text, you must first convert the characters to shapes by breaking apart the text two times.)
9. Lock all the layers.
10. Save your work, then compare your image to the example shown in Figure 29.

Importing and Modifying Graphics

You have been asked to create several sample designs for the homepage of a new student art, poetry, and fiction anthology called AnthoArt. This Web site will showcase artwork that includes painting, woodcuts, and photography, as well as writing (including poetry and fiction).

1. Open a new movie and save it as **anthoart7**.
2. Set the movie properties, including the size and background color if desired.
3. Import the following JPG files to the Library panel (alternately, you can create your own images, obtain images from your computer or the Internet, or create images from scanned media):
   gantho1.jpg
   gantho2.jpg
   gantho3.jpg
   gantho4.jpg
   gantho5.jpg

4. Using a combination of tracing and breaking apart images, create a collage on the stage from at least four images.
5. Create a title of **AnthoArt**, using a bitmap fill for some or all of the letters.

6. Create an Enter button, using one of the images as a bitmap fill.
7. Save your work, then compare your movie image to the example shown in Figure 30.

FIGURE 30
Sample completed Project Builder 2

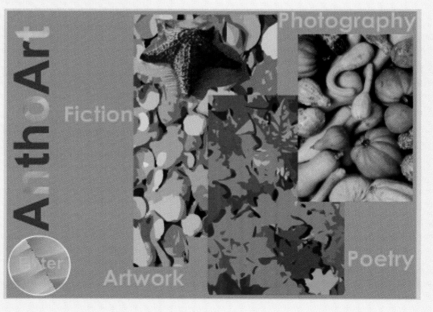

DESIGN PROJECT

Figure 31 shows the homepage of the NASA Web site. Study the figure and complete the following. For each question, indicate how you determined your answer.

1. Connect to the Internet, go to *www.course.com*, navigate to the page for this book, click the Online Companion link, then click the link for this chapter.

2. Open a document in a word processor or open a new Macromedia Flash document, save the file as **dpc7**, then answer the following questions. (*Hint*: Use the Text tool in Macromedia Flash.)

   ■ Are photographs used well in this Web site, why or why not?

   ■ Could the goals and intent of the Web site be accomplished without the use of photographs?

   ■ Do the images contribute to the design of the site? If so, how?

   ■ Which file format do you think was used for the images?

   ■ Can you guess what file format the logo was before it was brought into Macromedia Flash? Or, do you think it was recreated in the application?

   ■ Do you think the graphics in this site should be changed in any way? How?

   ■ Who do you think is the target audience for this Web site?

FIGURE 31
Design Project

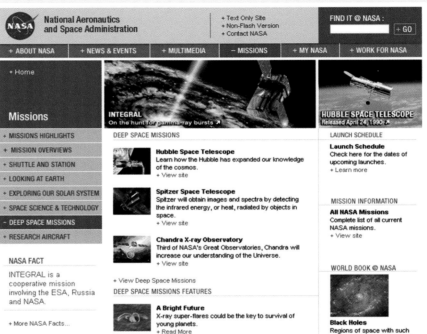

To showcase your broad range of skills, you want to add some Web-related work to your portfolio. This will allow you to improve upon and continue to use Web sites and artwork you previously created. First, you will need to take screen captures of the Web sites you have built and scan any artwork or design work that is in print. Try to create at least four samples of your work. Using an image editor, convert these images into JPEGs.

1. Open a new Flash document, then save it as **portfolio7**.
2. Add a heading and colors as desired.
3. Import to the Library panel at least four samples of your work in a variety of file formats, if necessary.
4. Place the samples on the stage.
5. Resize the images so you can fit all four of them on the stage at one time.
6. Add a sentence below or next to each image describing the image.
7. Save your work, then compare your movie to the example shown in Figure 32.

FIGURE 32
Sample completed Portfolio Project

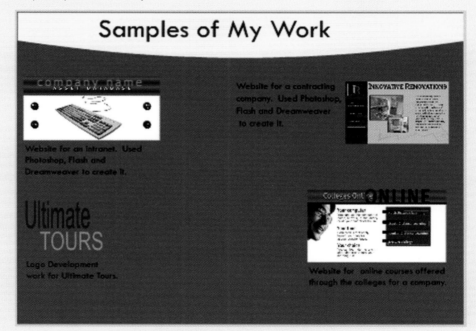

chapter

8

BUILDING COMPLEX
ANIMATIONS

1. Plan for complex movies and animations.

2. Create an animated graphic symbol.

3. Create a movie clip symbol.

4. Animate buttons with movie clip symbols.

8 BUILDING COMPLEX
ANIMATIONS

Introduction

As your movies become more complex and you begin utilizing more advanced features of Macromedia Flash, planning your work is critical. Part of the planning process is figuring out how to develop a clean timeline, with objects that are easy to recognize and manipulate, and how to optimize file size by reusing symbols as much as possible.

Creating animated graphic symbols and movie clip symbols can help meet both goals. A well-built movie consists of many small pieces of animation put together and often, of movies nested within movies. While the concept of movies within

movies might sound confusing, it is actually very logical from a file management, media management, and animation perspective. Building scenes with 40 layers and 200 keyframes can be unwieldy. The alternative is to split the many animations on the stage into smaller, reusable pieces, and then insert these smaller pieces as needed. When added up, you probably have an equal number of keyframes and layers, but they are never visible in a scene at the same time. Creating animated graphic symbols and movie clip symbols also allows you greater flexibility in adding ActionScript to elements, as well as with bringing elements on and off the stage.

Tools You'll Use

PLAN FOR COMPLEX MOVIES
AND ANIMATIONS

What You'll Do

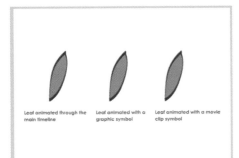

Leaf animated through the   Leaf animated with a   Leaf animated with a movie
main timeline   graphic symbol   clip symbol

▶ *In this lesson, you will work with and compare animated graphic and movie clip symbols.*

Making Effective Use of Symbols and the Library Panel

It is important to sketch out in advance what you are trying to accomplish in a movie. In addition to making development work easier, planning ahead will also allow you to organize your Library panel with more accuracy. Consider the following questions as you plan your project:

- Are there any repeated elements on the stage? If yes, you should make them into graphic symbols. Graphic symbols should include any still element that is used on the stage more than once. Graphic symbols might also be elements that you want to be able to tween. Keep in mind a graphic symbol can contain other graphic symbols.
- Are there any repeating or complex animations, or elements on screen that animate while the rest of the scene is still? If so, make these animated graphic symbols or movie clip symbols.

- What kind of interactivity will your Macromedia Flash movie have? You can assign ActionScript to button symbols and to movie clip symbols, but not to graphic symbols. You should use button symbols for any element used for navigation or an element that you want to be clickable. Button symbols can contain both graphic and movie clip symbols inside them.

Remember, your Library panel should house all of the building blocks for your movies. In order to build a logical Library panel, you should have a solid plan in place for the different elements you expect to use.

Understanding Animated Graphic Symbols

Just as you can create a graphic symbol from multiple objects on the stage, you can convert an entire multiple-frame, multiple-layer animation into a single **animated graphic symbol** that you can store in the Library panel. Creating a single animated graphic symbol removes all of the associated keyframes, layers, and tweening of the animation from your timeline, which results in a much cleaner timeline. Animated graphic symbols can also reduce file size if you expect to use the animation in more than one place in a movie.

Compare the two timelines in Figure 1. On the left is a tree animated through the main timeline; each individual leaf on the tree has its own layer. On the right is a timeline for a movie with the same animation, but with the leaves grouped into an animated graphic symbol and appearing on a single layer.

An animated graphic symbol remains tied to the timeline of the movie in which you place the symbol. This means there must be enough frames on the timeline for the animation to run, and that if the movie stops, so does the animation.

Understanding Movie Clip Symbols

A **movie clip symbol** is a more robust way to store complex animations in the Library panel: essentially a movie within a movie. The biggest difference between a movie clip symbol and an animated graphic symbol is

FIGURE 1
Comparing timelines

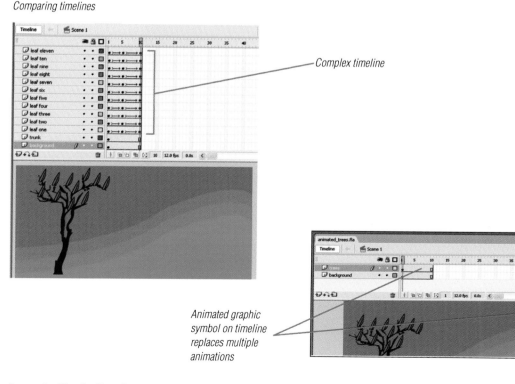

Complex timeline

Animated graphic symbol on timeline replaces multiple animations

that the movie clip symbol retains its own independent timeline when you insert an instance of the symbol into a movie. Even if the main timeline stops, the movie clip keeps going, endlessly repeating like a film loop.

Consider Figure 2: This scene looks like a drawing of a still living room. However, if it were animated, the fire could be crackling and the candles flickering. Each one of these animated elements might reside in a movie clip symbol. That way, when placed on the stage in a scene, each of the movie clip symbols would move according to its own independent timeline, as well as only taking up one layer and, potentially, only one keyframe on the timeline. Not only does this help to organize the different pieces of a movie, it also allows you to isolate animated elements and have animations repeat at their own pace. In this lesson you will view the same animation (animated leaf) created in three different ways: using the main timeline, a graphic symbol, and a movie clip.

FIGURE 2
Using movie clip symbols

You could create one movie clip symbol of a flickering flame, and use it to animate all three candles

The fire could be its own movie clip symbol, continuously crackling and moving as fires do

FIGURE 3
Adding an animated graphic symbol to the stage

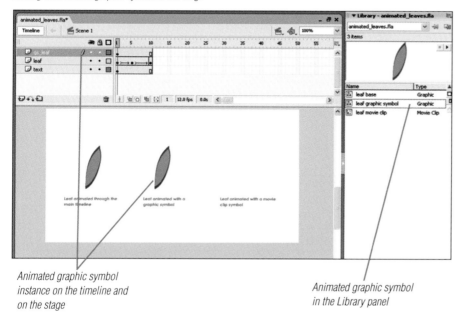

Animated graphic symbol
instance on the timeline and
on the stage

Animated graphic symbol
in the Library panel

Work with an animated graphic symbol

1. Open fl8_1.fla, then save it as **animated_leaves**.
2. Open the Library panel.
3. Press [**Enter**] (Win) or [**return**] (Mac) to play the animation. The motion tween in the leaf layer of the timeline causes the leaf to move.
4. Right-click (Win) or [control] click (Mac) the **leaf graphic symbol** in the Library panel, then click **Edit**.
5. Press [**Enter**] (Win) or [**return**] (Mac) to play the animation.

    This is the same animation as the one on the main timeline. It was developed by creating a new graphic symbol (named leaf graphic symbol) of the leaf, copying the frames of the animation on the main timeline, and pasting them into the timeline of this leaf graphic symbol.

6. Click **Scene 1** near the top of the timeline to return to the main timeline.
7. Insert a new layer above the leaf layer, then name it **gs_leaf**.
8. Click **Frame 1** of the gs leaf layer, drag the **leaf graphic symbol** from the Library panel to the stage above the text, as shown in Figure 3.

    The animated graphic symbol version of the leaf still takes up 10 frames on the timeline, but the symbol's motion tween does not display because it is saved as part of the symbol.

9. Press [**Enter**] (Win) or [**return**] (Mac) to view the animations.

You moved an instance of an animated graphic symbol to the stage and compared it to an animation created through the main timeline.

Work with a movie clip symbol

1. Insert a new layer above the gs leaf layer, name it **mc leaf**, then drag the **leaf movie clip symbol** from the Library panel to the stage above the text, as shown in Figure 4.

2. Click **Frame 1** of the mc leaf layer, then press **[Enter]** (Win) or **[return]** (Mac) to view the animations.

   The movie clip symbol version of the leaf does not move because movie clips on the stage play only when you export, publish, or test the movie.

3. Click **Control** on the menu bar, then click **Test Movie** to test the movie.

   All three leaves animate in place continually.

4. Close the test movie window.

You placed an instance of a movie clip symbol on the stage, then tested the movie.

FIGURE 4
Adding a movie clip symbol to the stage

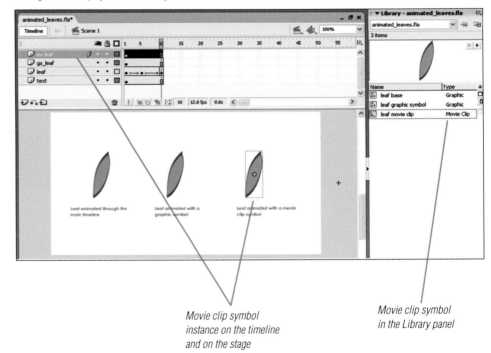

Movie clip symbol instance on the timeline and on the stage

Movie clip symbol in the Library panel

FIGURE 5
Inserting a stop *action with the Actions panel*

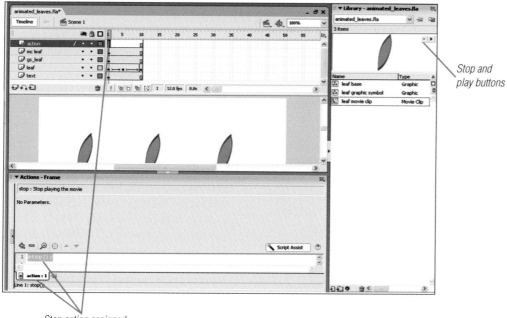

Stop and play buttons

Stop action assigned to Frame 1 of the action layer

1. Insert a new layer above the mc leaf layer, then name it **action**.

2. Open the **Actions panel**, then click **Frame 1** on the action layer.

3. Click the **Script Assist button** [Script Assist] to turn on this feature.

4. Verify that action :1 is displayed in the lower left of the Actions panel.

   This indicates that the ActionScript code will be assigned to Frame 1 of the action layer.

5. Click **Add a new item to the script button** in the Script Assist window, point to **Global Functions**, point to **Timeline Control**, then click **stop**.

   Your screen should resemble Figure 5.

6. Click **Control** on the menu bar, then click **Test Movie**.

   Only the movie clip symbol moves because it has an independent timeline; the stop action stopped the main timeline, upon which the other two instances of the leaf are dependent.

7. Close the test movie window.

8. Collapse the Actions panel.

9. Save your work, then close the movie.

You assigned a stop action to the timeline and tested the movie.

CREATE AN ANIMATED
GRAPHIC SYMBOL

What You'll Do

▶ In this lesson, you will convert an animation on the timeline into an animated graphic symbol.

Using Graphic Symbols for Animations

Most of the time, you will want to use movie clip symbols instead of animated graphic symbols to store animations. However, there are some situations where creating an animated graphic symbol is useful, such as a sequential animation you want to play only one time, rather than repeat continuously as a movie plays. Or, you might want an animation to synchronize with other elements on the stage, and since animated graphic symbols use the main timeline, it can be easier to achieve this effect. Also, you can preview animated graphic symbols you place on the stage right from the Macromedia Flash editing environment by dragging the playhead back and forth across the timeline (also called scrubbing). This makes animated graphic symbols easier to test within Macromedia

Flash than movie clip symbols, which play only when you export the movie.

You create an animated graphic symbol in the same way you create a static graphic symbol, by choosing the Graphic option in the Create New Symbol dialog box. An animated graphic symbol looks the same as a static graphic symbol in the Library panel. However, when you select the animated graphic symbol or a movie clip symbol, it displays with Stop and Play buttons in the Library panel. You can click these buttons for testing purposes, as shown in Figure 6.

Copying Frames and Layers from the Timeline

Despite good preliminary planning, you may end up drawing and animating objects in a scene and decide later that the animation would be better placed inside an animated graphic or movie clip symbol. Fortunately, it is easy to copy frames and layers from the main timeline and paste them into a new symbol.

To move multiple layers and frames from within a scene to a symbol, first select the layers and keyframes that you want to copy. To select multiple frames in one or more layers, click and hold in the first frame you want to select, then drag to the last frame. Also, you can click the first frame, press and hold [Shift], then click the last frame to select the frames and those in-between.

To select non-contiguous layers, press and hold [Ctrl] (Win) or [command] click (Mac), then click each layer name. To select contiguous layers, click the first layer name, then press and hold [Shift] and click the last layer name to select the layers and all in-between layers. Figure 7 shows a selection across multiple frames and layers. Once you select the keyframes, click Edit on the menu bar, point to Timeline, then click Cut Frames. Create or open the symbol, then place your cursor in a frame, click Edit on the menu bar, point to Timeline, then click Paste Frames.

Macromedia Flash pastes each individual layer from the original scene into the symbol, and even maintains the layer names.

Note that you cannot copy sound or interactivity in an animation from the main timeline to an animated graphic symbol. If you want to include sound or interactivity with an animation that you are using in the Library panel, you should create a movie clip symbol.

FIGURE 6
Stop and Play buttons in the Library panel

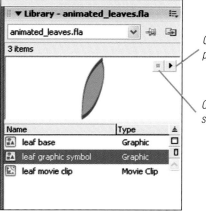

Click this button to play the animation

Click this button to stop the animation

FIGURE 7
Multiple frames and layers selected

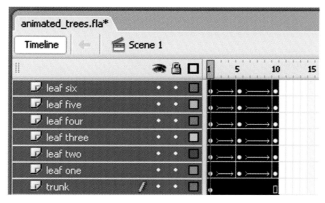

Delete objects from the timeline

1. Open fl8_2.fla, then save it as **animated_trees**.

2. Verify the Library panel is open, drag the border down to display the leaf and trunk layers of the timeline, then set the View to **Fit in Window**.

3. Play the movie.

   The leaves animate on 11 separate layers.

4. Select all of the numbered **leaf** and **trunk layer frames** on the timeline, as shown in Figure 8.

   TIP You can press and hold [Ctrl], then click one or more layer names to select all frames in the layers.

5. Click **Edit** on the menu bar, point to **Timeline**, then click **Cut Frames**.

   The tree is no longer visible on the stage.

You selected and then cut the frames of the layers on the timeline that made up the tree.

Move frames to create an animated graphic symbol

1. Click **Insert** on the menu bar, then click **New Symbol**.

2. Type **animated tree** in the Name text box, click the **Graphic option button** (if necessary), as shown in Figure 9, then click **OK**.

   You are now in the graphic object-editing screen.

3. Click **Frame 1** on Layer 1, click **Edit** on the menu bar, point to **Timeline**, then click **Paste Frames**.

   The tree trunk and leaves appear on the stage.

   (continued)

FIGURE 8
Selecting frames in the main timeline

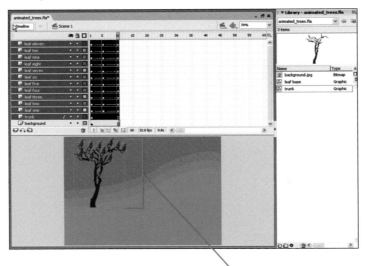

Selecting the frames in the timeline also selects the elements on the stage

FIGURE 9
The Create New Symbol dialog box

Building Complex Animations

FIGURE 10

Moving an instance of the tree symbol to the stage

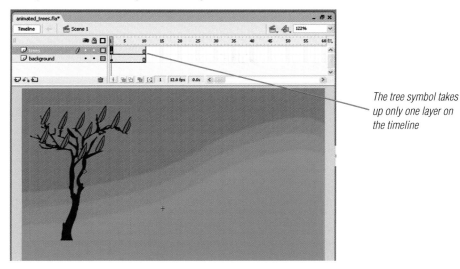

The tree symbol takes up only one layer on the timeline

FIGURE 11

Resizing the second instance of the tree symbol

Hover over one of the corners of the tree until the cursor appears as a two-headed arrow, then drag to resize

4. Click **Scene 1** on the timeline to return to the main timeline.

5. Click the **leaf eleven layer**, then click the **Delete Layer icon** 🗑 on the bottom of the timeline.

6. Repeat Step 5 to delete the remaining leaf layers and the trunk layer.

You pasted frames from the main timeline and converted them into an animated graphic symbol. You then deleted the layers from the main timeline.

Move an animated graphic symbol to the stage

1. Insert a new layer above the background layer, then name it **trees**.

2. Click **Frame 1** on the trees layer, then drag the **animated tree graphic symbol** from the Library panel to the left side of the stage, as shown in Figure 10.

3. Play the movie.

4. Click **Frame 1** of the trees layer, then drag another instance of the **animated tree graphic symbol** from the Library panel to the right side of the stage.

5. Click the **Free Transform tool** ⊡ on the Tools panel, click the **Scale option icon** ⊡ in the Options section of the timeline, click a corner sizing handle on the tree, then drag to resize the tree to the size shown in Figure 11.

6. Play the movie and watch the leaves animate on the stage.

7. Save your work, then close the movie.

You created two instances of an animated graphic symbol on the stage.

CREATE A MOVIE
CLIP SYMBOL

What You'll Do

▶ *In this lesson, you will create a movie clip symbol and nest movie clips symbols within one another.*

Using Movie Clip Symbols for Animations

Movie clip symbols are usually the most efficient choice for creating and storing complex animations. The main advantage of movie clip symbols is that they maintain their own independent timeline, which is especially useful for animating continuous or looping actions. Movie clip symbols require only one layer and one frame in the main movie, regardless of the complexity of the animation, which can make it easier to work with the timeline.

Movie clip symbols offer many other sophisticated features not available with animated graphic symbols. For example, you can add sound and associate ActionScript statements to movie clip symbols, or create an animation for a movie clip in the main timeline (such as a motion tween) while the movie clip continues to play its own animation on its independent timeline. In addition, you can use movie clip symbols to animate a button.

To start building a movie clip symbol, create a new symbol and then choose Movie Clip in the Create New Symbol dialog box. You can create the movie clip animation from scratch, or cut and copy frames and layers from the main timeline, as you did with the animated graphic symbol in the previous lesson.

QUICKTIP

While you're working in editing mode, you can see only a static image of the first frame of a movie clip symbol on the stage. To view the full animation, you must export, publish, or test the movie.

Nesting Movie Clips

A movie clip symbol is often made up of many other movie clips, a process called **nesting**. You can nest as many movie clip symbols inside another movie clip as you like. You can also place a symbol, graphic, or button inside of a movie clip symbol. Figure 12 shows a diagram of nesting.

Nesting movie clips creates a **parent-child relationship** that will become increasingly important as you enhance the interactivity of your movies and begin to deploy more sophisticated ActionScript statements. When you insert a movie clip inside another movie clip, the inserted clip is considered the child and the original clip the parent. These relationships are hierarchical, similar to folders that contain files on your computer or in your file cabinet. Keep in mind that if you place an instance of

a parent clip into a scene and change it, you will also affect the nested child clip. Any time you change the instance of a parent clip, the associated child clips update automatically.

The Movie Explorer panel, shown in Figure 13, allows you to inspect the nesting structure of your entire movie. This is a useful reference to print out as you work on a movie, so you can easily view the movie's structure and see which elements are nested inside each other. You can also

apply a filter to view just the elements you want. To access the Movie Explorer, click Window on the menu bar, then click Movie Explorer.

The Options menu lets you perform a variety of actions on the elements listed in the Movie Explorer. For example, you can go to the element on the stage and timeline, find the element in the Library panel, or open all panels relevant to the element so you can edit it.

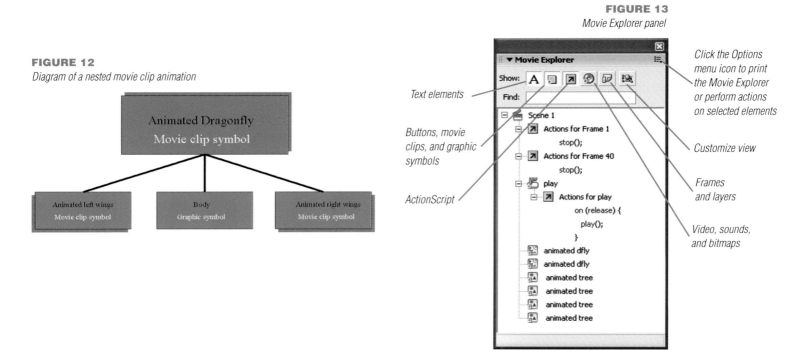

FIGURE 12
Diagram of a nested movie clip animation

FIGURE 13
Movie Explorer panel

Create a movie clip symbol

1. Open fl8_3.fla, then save it as **dragonfly**.

2. Verify that the Library panel is open, then notice the symbols.

   The Library panel contains the dfly body, left wings, and right wings graphic symbols, as well as the animated left wings movie clip symbol. These symbols will form the basis of your movie clip.

3. Click the **animated left wings movie clip symbol** in the Library panel, then click the **Play button** ▶ .

   The wings appear to flutter. Next, you will create another movie clip symbol to animate a set of right wings for the dragonfly.

4. Click **Insert** on the menu bar, then click **New Symbol**.

5. Type **animated right wings** in the Name text box, click the **Movie clip option button**, then click **OK**.

6. Click **Frame 1** on Layer 1 on the timeline, then drag the **right wings graphic symbol** from the Library panel to the center of the stage, so that the circle is above the centering cross hair, as shown in Figure 14.

   Note: There are two cross hairs. One is the registration point for the wings and the other is the registration point for the movie clip.

7. Insert keyframes in Frames 5 and 10 on the timeline.

8. Click **Frame 5** on Layer 1, open the Property inspector (if necessary), click the **wings object** on the stage, double-click the **W:** text box, type **47**, then press [**Enter**] (Win) or [**return**] (Mac).

(continued)

FIGURE 14

Positioning the wings in the Edit window

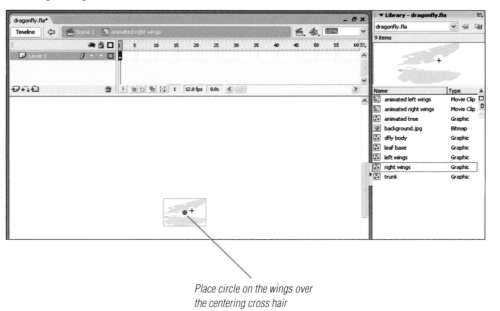

Place circle on the wings over the centering cross hair

Building Complex Animations

FIGURE 15
Animated timeline

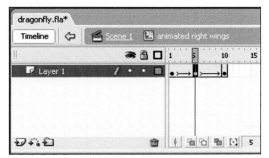

FIGURE 16
Assembled animated dragonfly

9. Click **Frame 1** on Layer 1, click **Insert** on the menu bar, point to **Timeline**, then click **Create Motion Tween**.

10. Click **Frame 5** on Layer 1, click **Insert** on the menu bar, point to **Timeline**, click **Create Motion Tween**, then compare your timeline to Figure 15.

11. Click **Control** on the menu bar, then click **Play** to play the movie clip, then return to the main timeline.

You created a movie clip symbol containing two motion-tween animations.

Nest movie clip symbols

1. Click **Insert** on the menu bar, then click **New Symbol**.

2. Type **animated dfly** in the Name text box, click the **Movie clip option button** (if necessary), then click **OK**.

3. Drag the **dfly body graphic symbol** from the Library panel to the center of the stage.

4. Drag the **animated left wings movie clip symbol** from the Library panel to the stage, then attach it to the upper left side of the dragonfly's body.

5. Drag the **animated right wings** to the upper right side of the body.

   Compare your image to Figure 16.

6. Click **Scene 1** on the timeline to return to the main timeline.

You nested two movie clips inside a new movie clip symbol.

Move the movie clip symbol to the stage, rotate, and resize it

1. Insert a new layer above the trees layer, then name it **dragonfly**.

2. Click **Frame 1** on the dragonfly layer, then drag the **animated dfly movie clip symbol** from the Library panel on top of the left tree on the stage, as shown in Figure 17.

3. Click the **dragonfly graphic** on the stage to select it.

4. Click **Modify** on the menu bar, point to **Transform**, then click **Scale and Rotate**.

5. Type **180** for the Rotate value, then click **OK**.

6. Display the Property inspector, then verify that the **dragonfly** on the stage is selected.

7. Change the width to **43** and the height to **32** in the Property inspector.

8. Insert a keyframe in Frame 30 on all the layers on the timeline.

You added an instance of a movie clip symbol to the stage, rotated it 180 degrees, and resized it.

FIGURE 17
Animated dragonfly instance placed on the stage

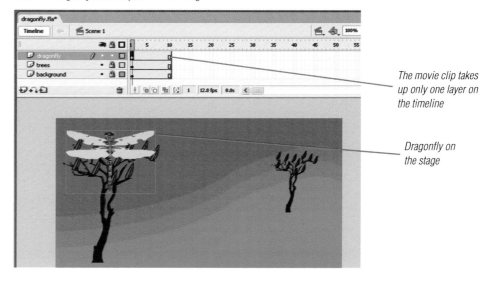

The movie clip takes up only one layer on the timeline

Dragonfly on the stage

FIGURE 18

Motion guide path for the dragonfly

The color of your
motion guide path
may vary

FIGURE 19

Moving the dragonfly to the end of the motion guide path

Animate an instance of a movie clip and resize an object

1. Click **Frame 1** on the dragonfly layer, then click the **Add Motion Guide icon** on the bottom of the timeline.
2. Verify that **Frame 1** of the dragonfly layer is selected, click **Insert** on the menu bar, point to **Timeline**, then click **Create Motion Tween**. The motion tween appears on the dragonfly layer.
3. Click **Frame 1** on the Guide: dragonfly layer, click the **Pencil tool** on the Tools panel, click the **Smooth option** in the Options section of the Tools panel.
4. Point to the middle of the dragonfly, then draw a path between the trees, as shown in Figure 18.
5. Click the **Selection tool** on the Tools panel, click the **dragonfly** on the stage, then drag the **dragonfly** to the start of the path, if necessary.
6. Click **Frame 30** on the dragonfly layer, then drag the dragonfly to the end of the path, as shown in Figure 19.
7. Verify that the **dragonfly** is selected, then use the Property inspector to resize the dragonfly to width **22** and height **16**.
8. Reposition the dragonfly on the end of the path.
9. Click **Frame 1** of the dragonfly layer, then click **Orient to path** in the Property inspector.
10. Click **Control** on the menu bar, then click **Test Movie** to preview the movie. The dragonfly moves between the trees along the path, its wings fluttering at the same time.
11. Click **File** on the menu bar, click **Close** to close the preview window, then save your work.

You used a motion guide to animate an instance of a movie clip and resized the animated object.

ANIMATE BUTTONS WITH
MOVIE CLIP SYMBOLS

What You'll Do

In this lesson, you will create an animated button and put together a short interactive movie using ActionScript.

Understanding Animated Buttons

As you learned in a previous lesson, a button symbol does not have the standard timeline, but instead has four states associated with it. You can animate a button by nesting a movie clip symbol inside any one of the three visible states of the button: Up, Over, or Down. Although Up and Over are most common.

Depending on the state in which you nest the symbol, you will have different results. If you nest the animation inside the Up state, the movie/button will continue to animate as long as the button is visible on the stage in the main timeline. If you nest the movie inside the Over state, the animation will be visible only when the user's mouse is over the button. If the animation is nested inside the Down state, the user will see only a brief flicker of animation as they click the mouse. The first two are the most common and both have obvious interface benefits as well—if your users

see something animated, they are more inclined to interact with it and discover it is actually a button.

Building an Animated Button Symbol

To build an animated button symbol, you need at least two symbols in the Library panel. First, you need to create a movie clip symbol with the animation. In building this animation, make sure you design it to repeat cleanly, especially if you plan to use it in the Up state of a button. Once you have built the movie clip symbol, you need to create a button symbol in which to nest the animation. Remember, because movie clips have independent timelines, the clip will run continually while the button symbol is on the stage, even if the main movie pauses or stops. Figure 20 shows the Information bar for a movie clip symbol nested inside of a button.

As with a movie clip, you must export the movie in order to see the animation of a button. The Enable Simple Buttons option will not play the movie clip—you will see only a static view of the first frame of the clip.

Creating an Interactive Movie

Adding interactivity to a movie simply means you are asking your user to be involved in the movie in some way other than watching it. It can be as simple as adding a button for a user to click or giving them a choice to make. Interactivity can also be complex, in the case of a game where a user must assemble a puzzle, as shown in Figure 21. Because adding interactivity means you are forcing the user to become involved in your movie, you are more likely to hold your users' interest.

You can also create complex interactions by using ActionScript in combination with movie clip symbols. With ActionScript, you can set up movie clips to play, pause, or perform other actions based on user input such as clicking the mouse or pressing a key on the keyboard, similar to the interactions you can create with a button. You can also use ActionScript to instruct movie clips to perform actions without waiting for user input and to jump to specific frames on the timeline of a movie clip symbol.

FIGURE 20
Movie clip symbol nested inside a button

FIGURE 21
Interactive game created with symbols, buttons, and ActionScript

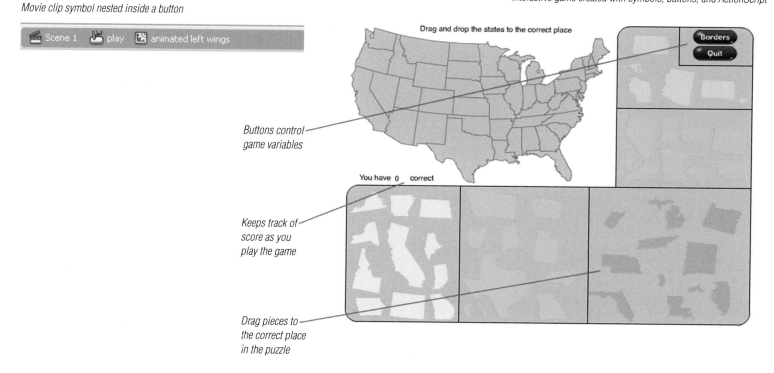

Create an animated button

1. Verify that the dragonfly document is open, then click **Insert** on the menu bar, then click **New Symbol**.

2. Type **play** in the Name text box, click the **Button option button**, then click **OK**.

3. Click the **Up frame** on Layer 1, click the **Text tool A** on the Tools panel, then open the Property inspector, if necessary.

4. Click the **Text tool pointer** ┼A in the center of the stage.

5. Click the **Font list arrow**, click **Verdana**, click the **Font Size list arrow**, then drag the slider to **24**.

6. Click the **Text (fill) color button** ■▾, click the **black color swatch** in the top row, then click the **Bold button B**.

7. Type **PLAY**.

8. Click the **Selection tool ▸** on the Tools panel, drag the **animated left wings movie clip symbol** from the Library panel to the left of the word "PLAY," then drag the **animated right wings movie clip symbol** from the Library panel to the right side of the word, as shown in Figure 22.

(continued)

FIGURE 22
Adding the animated wings to the text

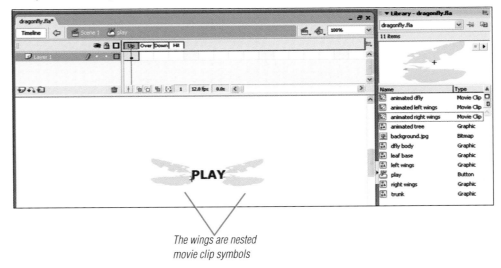

The wings are nested movie clip symbols

FIGURE 23

Setting the Hit area

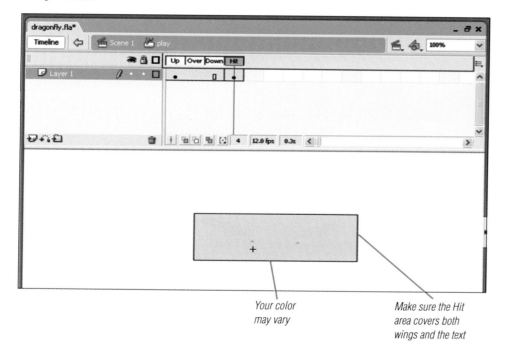

Your color
may vary

Make sure the Hit
area covers both
wings and the text

9. Verify that the **Selection tool** ▶ on the Tools panel is selected, click the word **PLAY** on the stage, click the **Text (fill) color button** 🔲▼ on the Property inspector, then click the **left wing** on the stage with the eyedropper pointer 🖋.

   The text and the wings are now the same color.

10. Insert a keyframe in the Hit frame of the button, click the **Rectangle tool** 🔲▼ on the Tools panel, then draw a box around both sets of wings and the text, as shown in Figure 23.

    TIP Remember that the Hit state is invisible on the stage, but defines the clickable area of a button.

11. Click **Scene 1** on the timeline to return to the main timeline.

12. Collapse the Property inspector panel.

You created a button symbol and placed an animation inside the symbol.

Place the animated button on the stage

1. Insert a new layer above the Guide: dragonfly layer, name it **button**, then click **Frame 1** of the button layer.

2. Drag the **play button symbol** from the Library panel underneath the right tree, as shown in Figure 24.

3. Insert a new layer above the button layer, then name it **actions**.

4. Open the Actions panel, then click **Frame 1** of the actions layer.

5. Verify that the **Script Assist button** is selected and that actions :1 is displayed at the lower left of the Actions panel.

6. Click **Add a new item to the script button** ⊕ in the Script Assist window, point to **Global Functions**, point to **Timeline Control**, then click **stop**. Your Actions panel should resemble Figure 25.

7. Click **Control** on the menu bar, then click **Test Movie**.

   The wings flutter on the animated button. Notice that while the dragonfly's wings also move, the dragonfly does not fly on the motion guide, nor do the leaves on the trees animate. This is because both the dragonfly's motion and the leaves are dependent on the main timeline, which is stopped on Frame 1.

8. Close the test movie window.

You placed an animated button on the stage and added a stop action.

FIGURE 24
Placing the button on the stage

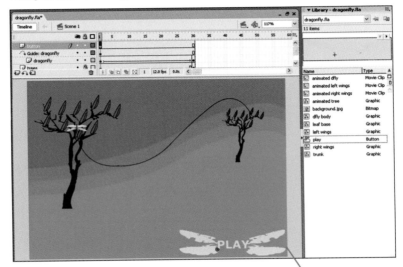

The animated button is made up of text and two movie clip symbols

FIGURE 25
Adding a stop action

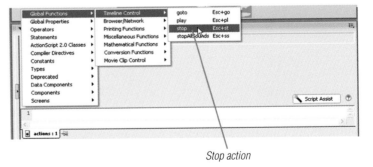

Stop action

Building Complex Animations

FIGURE 26

Adding the button action in the Actions panel

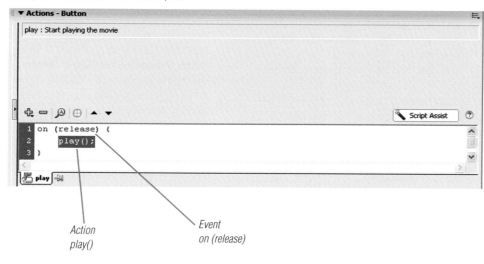

Action
play()

Event
on (release)

Add a button action

1. Close the Actions panel, click the **Selection tool** on the Tools panel, then click the **Play button** on the stage to select it.

2. Open the Actions panel, verify that the play button symbol is displayed in the lower left of the Actions panel.

3. Click **Add a new item to the script button** in the Script Assist window, point to **Global Functions**, point to **Timeline Control**, then click **play**. Your Actions panel should resemble Figure 26.

4. Click **Frame 30** on the actions layer, click **Insert** on the menu bar, point to **Timeline**, then click **Blank Keyframe**.

5. Click **Add a new item to the script button** in the Script Assist window, point to **Global Functions**, point to **Timeline Control**, then click **stop**.

6. Click **Control** on the menu bar, then click **Test Movie**.

7. Click the **Play button**.

    Notice that the movie plays to the end—the leaves on the trees animate, the wings on the play button animate, and the dragonfly flies on the motion guide.

8. Close the test movie window.

9. Save your work, then close the movie.

10. Exit Flash.

You added actions to the movie, creating interactivity.

Plan for complex movies and animations, and create an animated graphic symbol.

1. Start Flash, open fl8_4.fla from the drive and folder where your Data Files are stored, then save it as **skillsdemo8**.
2. Play the animation in the main timeline.
3. Add a background color and a border with the same dimensions as the stage.
4. Cut all the frames from the two layers on the main timeline. (*Hint*: Click Edit on the menu bar, point to Timeline, then click Cut Frames.)
5. Create a new graphic symbol named **TV**.
6. Paste the frames you cut into the new graphic symbol. (*Hint*: Click Edit on the menu bar, point to Timeline, then click Paste Frames.)
7. Return to Scene 1 and delete the TV screen layer.
8. Click Frame 1 on the TV set layer, then drag the TV animated graphic symbol from the Library panel to the top center of the stage.
9. Play the animation, then save your work.

Create a movie clip symbol.

1. Create a new movie clip symbol named **clock**.
2. Name Layer 1 on the timeline of the new movie clip **clock face**.

3. Drag the clock face graphic symbol from the Library panel to the exact center of the stage. (*Hint*: Use the arrow keys to move the clock face symbol so the cross hairs in the center of the face line up with the cross hairs on the stage.)
4. Insert a new layer above the clock face layer, then name it **clock hands**.
5. Drag the clock hands graphic symbol from the Library panel to the exact center of the stage, again using the cross hairs to line up elements.
6. Verify that the clock hands graphic is selected, click the Free Transform tool on the Tools panel, then drag the Transformation point (empty circle in the middle of the graphic) to the lower left corner of the graphic.
7. Insert keyframes in Frame 10 and Frame 20 of the clock hands layer, and in Frame 20 of the clock face layer.
8. Click Frame 10 of the clock hands layer, and then use the Free Transform tool to move the hands about halfway around the clock, so that the time reads 9:30.
9. Create two motion tweens in the clock hands layer, first from Frame 1 to Frame 10, then from Frame 10 to Frame 20. Use the Property inspector to set the Rotate option to CW (clockwise) for both tweens.

10. Test the animation using the Play button in the preview area at the top of the Library panel, then return to Scene 1. (*Hint*: Select the clock movie clip symbol in the Library panel.)

Animate buttons with movie clip symbols.

1. Create a new button symbol named **change channels**.
2. Insert the clock movie clip symbol in the Up state of the button.
3. Insert a keyframe in the Over state of the button, then add the text **Time to change channels** to the right of the clock movie clip symbol with the following properties: Font: Verdana, Font Size: 12 pt, Color: black. (*Hint*: Insert new lines after "to" and "Change".)
4. Insert a keyframe in the Hit state of the button, then create a hit area that encompasses the clock and text. (*Hint*: Use the Rectangle tool on the Tools panel to create the hit area.)

5. Return to Scene 1, insert a new layer above the TV set layer, then name it **button**.

6. In Frame 1 on the button layer, drag the change channels button symbol from the Library panel to the stage, directly beneath the TV.

7. Insert a new layer above the button layer, name it **actions**, then insert a stop action in Frame 1.

8. Add a goto action to the button on the stage, and specify **2** as the frame to go to.

9. Test your movie, compare your screen to Figure 27, then click the button to see the animation.

10. Save your work.

11. Exit Flash.

FIGURE 27
Completed Skills Review

Ultimate Tours has decided they want to add animation to the opening page of their "summer in December" Web site, which is promoting a series of tours to Florida, Bermuda, and the Caribbean. They would like the animation to draw attention to the company name and to the navigation buttons, so visitors will click to find out more information about specific tours. Though the site is still at an early stage, they would like to see some prototypes of potential animations.

1. Open ultimatetours7.fla (the file you created in Chapter 7 Project Builder 1) and save it as **ultimatetours8**.
2. On paper, plan how you might add animations to this page that will fulfill the criteria Ultimate Tours has established.
3. Build the animation you have planned for emphasizing the company name. For example, you might convert the text of the company name ("Ultimate Tours") to a graphic symbol, then create a movie clip symbol in which the text dissolves and reappears (using a text tween), changes color, rotates, or moves across the screen.

4. Build the animation you have planned for encouraging visitors to click the navigation buttons. For example, you might create an animation of an orange ball representing the sun rolling across the sand image already in the button. Then create one sample button, inserting the animation into the Up state.
5. Save your work, then compare your image to the example shown in Figure 28.

FIGURE 28
Sample completed Project Builder 1

You have been asked to create a short interactive movie on ocean life for the local elementary school, which is planning a visit to an oceanographic institute. This project should be colorful, interactive, and full of images, in order to appeal to 7–12-year-old children.

The opening page of the site should show some images of sea creatures which, when clicked, lead to more information. You must include at least three clickable objects on this opening page.

1. Obtain some images of fish, coral, and other ocean creatures from your computer, the Internet, or from scanned media.
2. Create a new Flash document, then save it as **ocean_life8**.
3. Set the document properties including the size and background color, if desired.
4. Create animated movie clips for at least three life forms. Try to use as many different types of animation as you can think of for these movie clips. For example, you might use motion tweening to move, resize, or rotate objects, or fade them in or out.
5. Create buttons for the life forms, using your animated movies in the Up state and also designating a Hit state. (*Hint*: Be creative about the appearance of the buttons—use different shapes and sizes, or try cropping and making the images themselves clickable.)
6. Place the three buttons in the scene.
7. Add some explanatory text.
8. Save your work and compare your image to the example shown in Figure 29.

FIGURE 29
Sample completed Project Builder 2

Click an image to learn about these ocean creatures...

Figure 30 shows a birthday card created in Flash. Study the figure and complete the following. For each question, indicate how you determined your answer.

1. Connect to the Internet, go to *www.course. com*, navigate to the page for this book, click the Online Companion link, then click the link for this chapter.

2. Open a document in a word processor or create a new Macromedia Flash document, save the file as **dpc8**, then answer the following questions. (*Hint*: Use the Text tool in Macromedia Flash.)

■ Without seeing the source file in this movie, make a list of objects you believe to be in the Library panel and why you think they should be stored there.

■ Do you think all the images in this work were drawn in Macromedia Flash? Explain.

■ What in this scene could be animated?

■ Would you use animated graphic symbols or movie clip symbols to create the animations? Explain.

■ Are there any animated graphic symbols or movie clip symbols you could create once and use in multiple places?

■ What other buttons would you add and why?

■ Suppose you want to create an animation sequence where one jester strums his lute, some text appears and then dissolves, the other jester bangs his tambourine, more text appears and dissolves, then both jesters play simultaneously while the words "Happy Birthday" float across the screen. Plan a strategy for creating this animation that will streamline the timeline, reuse symbols to conserve file size, and allow you to easily set up the timing of the sequence so the text appears at the appropriate time.

FIGURE 30
Design Project

To add some pizzazz to your existing portfolio, you want to change the navigation on your homepage. Your goal is to have visitors mouse over the navigation buttons and see an animation that, hopefully, will better entice employers and potential clients with your skills. The animation should be fairly subtle and elegant, and showcase your animation skill.

1. Open portfolio7.fla (the file you created in Chapter 7 Portfolio Project) and save it as **portfolio8**.
2. Insert a new movie clip symbol named **animated button**.
3. Inside the movie clip symbol create an animation that would be appropriate for the mouse-over of your primary navigation buttons in the portfolio.

4. Open each of your button symbols and place the animation in the Over state. (*Hint*: Your new animation should integrate with existing work, or you should update all button states to reflect the new style.)
5. If necessary, add appropriate goto actions from the buttons to the areas of your portfolio that you have built, such as the samples section.
6. Save your work, then compare your movie to the example shown in Figure 31.

FIGURE 31
Sample completed Portfolio Project

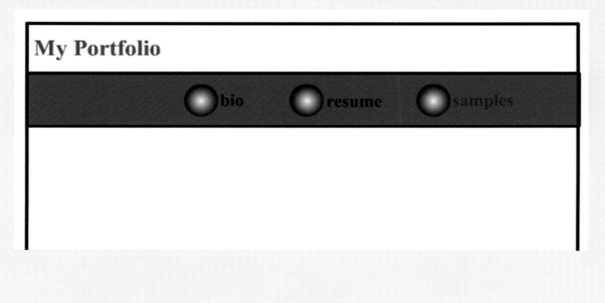

9

USING
ACTIONSCRIPT

1. Work with the Actions panel.

2. Work with targets and movie clip symbols.

3. Create interactive movie clip symbols.

4. Define variables.

9 USING
ACTIONSCRIPT

Introduction

In the previous chapters, you began working with ActionScript, the built-in scripting language for Macromedia Flash. In this chapter, you will explore more of the ways in which ActionScript can take your movies to the next level of interactivity and sophistication. For example, you can create ActionScript that changes the appearance of objects in a movie based on the actions a user takes. Or, you can create a form that captures user data and displays it elsewhere in your site.

You can add actions to a frame, any object such as a button, or a movie clip symbol.

Since ActionScript is a type of programming language, using exact syntax—spelling action names correctly and including the necessary parameters—is essential. The Actions panel, in which you add ActionScript to frames and objects, helps ensure that your ActionScript follows the required syntax and runs efficiently. The Script Assist feature was used in earlier chapters, so the focus in this chapter will be to learn how to use the Actions panel to create ActionScript code without using Script Assist.

Tools You'll Use

ActionScript target paths

```
// navigation for button
on(release) {
    gotoAndStop("one_on_one");
}
```

Input text field

WORH WITH THE
ACTIONS PANEL

What You'll Do

In this lesson, you will use ActionScript and frame labels to create navigation to specific frames on the timeline.

Using the Actions Panel

The Actions panel is used to build the ActionScript code that enhances a movie by adding complex interaction, playback control, and data manipulation.

The Actions panel has three panes, as shown in Figure 1:

- **Actions Toolbox pane**—provides the categories of actions that can be selected to build ActionsScript code. For example, the Global Functions category contains Timeline controls such as stop and goto.
- **Script Navigator pane**—provides a list of elements (objects, movie clips, frames) that contain scripts. It can be used to quickly locate an object, such as a button, and display its code.
- **Script pane**—displays the code and a toolbar for editing the code. Also, displays the Script Assist dialog box.

There are two ways to work with the Actions panel, with the Script Assist turned on or turned off.

Script Assist is good for basic actions such as stop, play, and goto. You merely use the Script Assist menus and dialog box to select the desired actions and the code is written for you. Script Assist is useful if you have limited knowledge of ActionScript. However, when using Script Assist you are limited in the actions you can work with and you cannot edit code directly in the Script pane. With Script Assist turned off you build the ActionScript code by selecting actions listed in folder categories in the Toolbox pane. As with Script Assist, the code is generated as you make your selections.

However, unlike Script Assist, you can type directly into the Script pane to create and edit code. This allows greater flexibility, more control, and for those with some programming experience, the ability to write code that creates more sophisticated interactions and animations.

Figure 2 shows two views of the Actions panel. One with the Script Assist feature turned on and another with it turned off. Both modes show the result of creating a goto action. With Script Assist turned on, you start by clicking the Add a new item to the script button and then use the menus

FIGURE 1
Actions panel panes

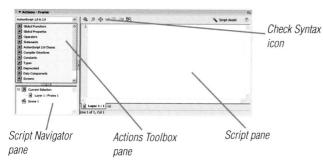

Script Navigator pane

Actions Toolbox pane

Script pane

Check Syntax icon

FIGURE 2
The Actions panel with Script Assist on and off

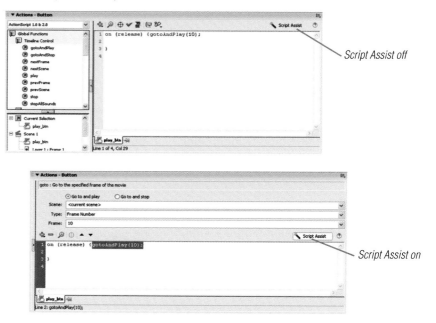

Script Assist off

Script Assist on

to choose the desired action (goto). Next you use a dialog box to specify the desired frame to go to (10). Without Script Assist you can type the code directly into the script window. Or you can click the categories in the Toolbox pane to choose the desired action, then type in the frame number to go to. You click the Script Assist button to toggle this feature on and off.

Configuring the Actions panel

There are two windows, left and right, in the Actions panel. The left window displays the Actions Toolbox pane and the Script Navigator pane. The right window displays the Script pane where the ActionScript code is displayed and edited. You will need to display the right window at all times. You can collapse and expand the left window by clicking the Expand/Collapse arrow between the windows. You can resize the left window by dragging the border between the two windows. In addition, you can drag the top border of the Actions panel up to view more of the Script pane. Before writing any code be sure to check the element (button, frame, movie clip, object) that is displayed in the lower left of the Script pane to verify it is the element you want to apply the code to.

Writing ActionScript Code

There are certain syntax rules you must follow when writing ActionScript. You must use exact case for action names; for example, when typing the gotoAndPlay action, be sure to capitalize the "A" and "P."

A semicolon (;) terminates an ActionScript statement. Functions or parameters for an action are enclosed in parentheses. Text strings appear between quotation marks. To group actions, you enclose them in curly brackets—{}. After you are done entering actions, you should click the Check Syntax icon above the Script pane to check the code and display errors in an output window.

If you need help, you can display code hints. Code hints give the syntax or possible parameters for an action in a pop-up window as you are entering the action. To see a code hint, type the action statement, then type an opening parenthesis. To dismiss the code hint, type a closing parenthesis or press [Esc]. To disable the code hints, click Edit on the menu bar, click Preferences, then click to deselect the Code Hints check box in the ActionScript category.

Referencing the Timeline in Actions

One of the most common uses of ActionScript is to create navigation buttons that jump between frames on a user action, such as a click of the mouse. Referencing a specific frame allows you to break your movies out of the sequential movement of the timeline. You can use either a frame number or frame label to reference the timeline in actions. A **frame label** is simply a text name for a keyframe.

Frame labels have an advantage over frame numbers, in that adding or deleting frames won't disrupt any navigation or frame references you have already included in actions, since the label remains attached to the frame even if the frame moves.

FIGURE 3

Creating a frame label

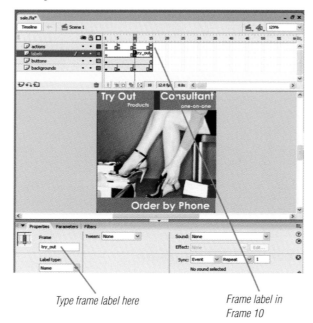

Type frame label here

Frame label in
Frame 10

1. Open fl9_1.fla from the drive and folder where your Data Files are stored, then save it as **sale**.

2. Drag the **playhead** through the timeline to see the scenes in the movie.

   There are four different screens, in Frames 1, 5, 10, and 15. There are also four stop actions in the corresponding frames in the actions layer, which stop the movie after each screen displays.

3. Insert a layer above the buttons layer, then name it **labels**.

4. Insert a keyframe in Frame 10 on the labels layer.

5. Open the Property inspector, click **Frame 10** on the labels layer, click the **Frame Label text box** on the left side of the Property inspector, type **try_out** for the frame label, press **[Enter]** (Win) or **[return]** (Mac), then compare your Property inspector to Figure 3.

(continued)

6. Insert a keyframe in Frame 15 on the labels layer, click the **Frame Label text box**, then name the frame **one_on_one**.

7. Close the Property inspector panel.

   You added a new layer and used the Property inspector to create frame labels.

Adding comments to a frame

You can add a comment to a frame, instead of a label, by prefacing the text you enter with two slashes: //. Space permitting, comments appear on the timeline with two green slashes to the right of the frame. You cannot reference comments in actions, however, because Macromedia Flash does not export comments with the final movie. Comments can be of any length.

FIGURE 4

Adding a `goto` *action that references a frame label*

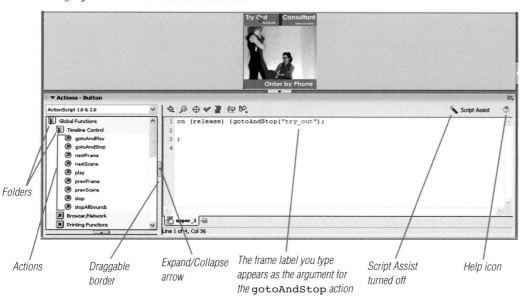

Folders

Actions

Draggable
border

Expand/Collapse
arrow

The frame label you type
appears as the argument for
the `gotoAndStop` action

Script Assist
turned off

Help icon

Getting help on ActionScript

If you're not sure what an action does, or need some guidance on which parameters to use, the Help panel can provide more information. To display the Help panel, highlight an action in the Actions Tools panel, then click the Help icon. An explanation of the action, along with details about its usage and parameters, appears in a separate panel. You can navigate through this panel to show information about other actions in the same way you navigate the Actions panel.

Use frame labels with actions

1. Open the Actions panel, set the view to **Fit in Window**, then click the **Try Out button** on the stage to select it.

   TIP You can also press [F9] to open the Actions panel.

2. Click the **Expand/Collapse arrow** and drag the border between the panes to view the Toolbox pane (if necessary) to approximate Figure 4.

3. Verify that Script Assist is turned off.

4. Verify **upper_1** is displayed at the bottom left of the Script pane.

   The button is named upper_1.

5. Click **Global Functions** to expand the folder (if necessary), then click **Movie Clip Control** to display a list of controls.

6. Double-click **on**, double-click **release**, then click after the opening curly bracket on the first line to set the insertion point.

7. Click **Timeline Control** in the Actions list, double-click **gotoAndStop**, then type **"try_out"**, as shown in Figure 4.

8. Click **Control** on the menu bar, then click **Test Movie** to test the movie, then click the **Try Out button**.

   The movie jumps to the shoes product frame.

   TIP You can also press [Ctrl][Enter] (Win) or ⌘[option][return] (Mac) to test the movie.

9. Close the test movie window.

You created navigation by referencing an action to a frame label.

Work in the Actions panel

1. Click the **View Options icon** ☰ on the Actions panel.

2. Verify that **Line Numbers** has a check mark next to it.

   TIP You can press [Ctrl][Shift][L] (Win) or ⌘[Shift][L] (Mac) to toggle the display of line numbers.

3. Click the **Consultant button** on the stage, then verify the upper_2 button symbol is displayed in the lower left of the Script pane.

4. Click next to 1 in the Script pane, then type **// navigation for button**.

   This comment will be ignored when the ActionScript runs. Comments that explain the intent of your ActionScript can help when troubleshooting, and are especially important if you are working collaboratively on a movie.

5. Press **[Enter]** (Win) or **[return]** (Mac) to insert a new line, then type **on (**.

   The code hint list appears, displaying the options for the action.

   TIP You can also click the Show Code Hint button ⌨ to display the code hint list.

6. Double-click **release** to select it, type **)** to end the function, press **[Spacebar]**, then type **{**, as shown in Figure 5.

   (continued)

FIGURE 5
Adding an `on (release)` action

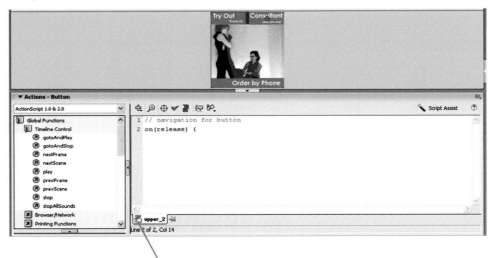

Identifies the Consultant button

Commenting the code

You can add a comment to your ActionScript by placing a slash and asterisk (/*) at the beginning and an asterisk and slash (*/) at the end of one or more lines of text. Any text between the set of symbols will be ignored when the ActionScript runs. If your comment is only a single line, you can alternatively place two slashes (//) at the beginning of the line, and that line will be ignored when the ActionScript runs. Comments are helpful reminders as to your intentions as you write the code.

FIGURE 6

Adding a `gotoAndStop` *action*

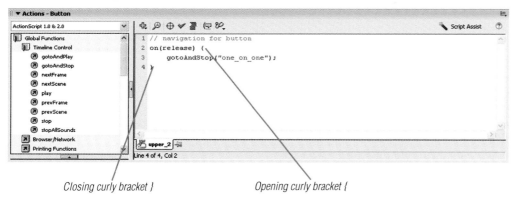

Closing curly bracket }   Opening curly bracket {

7. Press **[Enter]** (Win) or **[return]** (Mac) to move to line 3, then type **gotoAndStop (**.

   A code hint appears, displaying the syntax for the action.

   > TIP   Be sure to use exact case when typing actions.

8. Immediately after the opening parenthesis, type **"one_on_one");**.

   The quotation marks indicate that one_on_one is a frame label to which you want the button to jump to when clicked. The semicolon indicates the end of a line of code.

9. Press **[Enter]** (Win) or **[return]** (Mac) to move to Line 4, type **}** then compare your Script pane to Figure 6.

10. Test the movie then click the **Consultant button**.

   The movie jumps to the consultation frame. NOTE: If the Consultant button does not work, check your code carefully. It needs to be precise. Make sure that the curly brackets are used as specified.

11. Close the test movie window, save your work, then close the file.

You created navigation by writing code using a frame label in the Actions panel.

WORK WITH TARGETS AND
MOVIE CLIP SYMBOLS

What You'll Do

In this lesson, you will use ActionScript to control movie clip timelines.

Working with Movie Clips

Most large Macromedia Flash documents include many movie clip symbols. Using movie clips helps you better manage your document by breaking down complex tasks into smaller components, and also lets you reuse content and reduce file size. Another advantage to movie clips is you can use actions with them, allowing you greater control over the objects on the stage.

You can set up the actions you associate with movie clips to run when a user performs an action, to run automatically when the movie plays, or to run when a condition is met, such as if the movie clip has been dropped on top of another movie clip. Some common uses of ActionScript with movie clip symbols include creating actions that run a specific frame within the movie clip symbol's timeline, and making a movie clip draggable, so users can move it in games, shopping carts, or simulations.

QUICKTIP

The ActionScript that you associate with movie clips will run only when you test, export, or publish your movie.

Referencing Movie Clip Symbols as ActionScript Targets

To control movie clip symbols and their timelines with ActionScript, you must **target** the movie clips, or refer to them by path and name. Since actions are associated with specific instances of objects, you cannot just use the movie clip symbol name that appears in the Library panel. Instead, you must use the Property inspector to create an instance name for the movie clip to which you want to refer. You can target movie clip symbols at any level, even movie clips nested inside other movie clips.

QUICKTIP

To ensure that your ActionScript will run correctly, do not include spaces in movie clip symbol instance names.

The "with" action lets you target a movie clip on which to perform other actions. You can specify the movie clip symbol either by typing a path and name directly using dot syntax, which is explained below, or by clicking the Insert a Target Path icon. The Insert Target Path dialog box, shown in Figure 7, displays movie clip symbol names hierarchically. You can click the plus sign next to a name to see nested movie clips.

In addition, Macromedia Flash allows you to use **dot syntax** to create targets. A dot (.) identifies the hierarchical nature of the path to a movie clip symbol, similar to the way slashes are used to create a path name to a file in some operating systems. For example, "myShirt.myPattern", as shown in the ActionScript statement in Figure 8, refers to a movie clip symbol named myPattern nested within the symbol myShirt. You can also use dot syntax in an ActionScript statement to set actions and variables for a movie clip. For example, "square._x = 150" sets the X-axis position of a movie clip symbol named square to 150.

There are also three special terms: _root, _parent, and this, which you can use when creating target paths with dot syntax. _root refers to the main timeline. You can use it to create an absolute path, or a path that works downward from the top level of a movie. _parent refers to the movie clip in which the current clip is nested. You can use it to create a relative path, or a path that works backward through the hierarchy. (_parent essentially means "go up one level from where I currently am.") Relative paths are helpful when writing ActionScript you intend to reuse for multiple objects. The term this in a dot syntax statement refers to the current timeline.

QUICKTIP

You also use dot syntax when creating ActionScript target paths to variables, functions, and other objects.

FIGURE 7

Insert Target Path dialog box

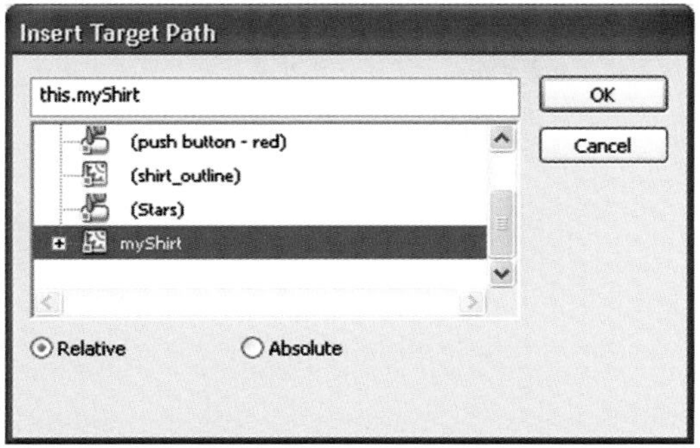

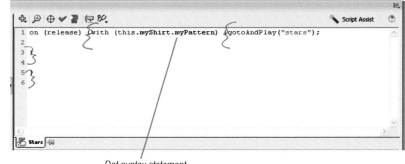

FIGURE 8

ActionScript statement using dot syntax

Dot syntax statement referring to a nested movie clip symbol

Assign an instance name to a movie clip symbol

1. Open fl9_2.fla, then save it as **shirt**.

2. Click the **Selection tool** ↖ on the Tools panel (if necessary), then double-click the **yellow shirt** on the stage to open the shirt_color movie clip symbol.

   This movie clip symbol has a layer (shirt) that changes the color of the shirt, a layer that includes actions to stop the clip after each frame, and a layer that includes a nested movie clip to change the pattern of the shirt.

3. Drag the **playhead** along the movie clip timeline to see how the shirt changes color, then click **Scene 1** on the Information bar to return to the main timeline.

4. Click the **shirt** on the stage to select it.

5. Open the Property inspector, then verify shirt_color is displayed for the Instance of.

6. Click the **Instance Name text box**, type **myShirt** for the instance name, press **[Enter]** (Win) or **[return]** (Mac), as shown in Figure 9.

7. Close the Property inspector.

You viewed a movie clip in the edit window and then assigned an instance name to the movie clip.

FIGURE 9
Naming a movie clip symbol instance

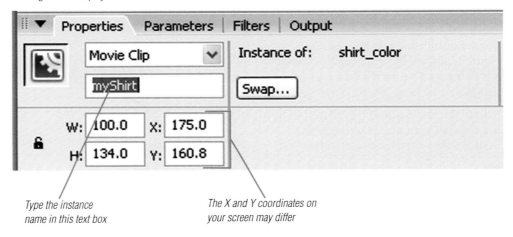

Type the instance name in this text box

The X and Y coordinates on your screen may differ

FIGURE 10

Movie clip symbol instance name in Insert Target Path dialog box

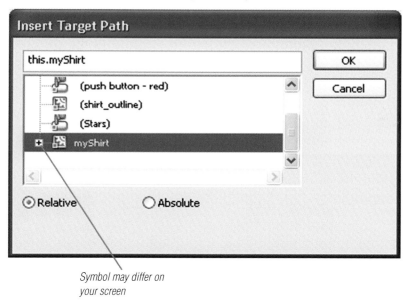

Symbol may differ on
your screen

FIGURE 11

ActionScript to change the color of the shirt on button release

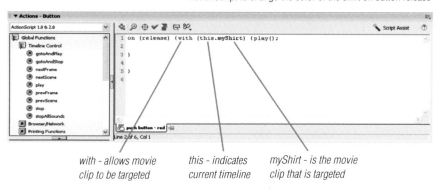

with - allows movie
clip to be targeted

this - indicates
current timeline

myShirt - is the movie
clip that is targeted

Use ActionScript to control the timeline of a movie clip symbol

1. Click the **red button** on the stage (under the words "Click to Pick a Color"), open the Actions panel (if necessary), then verify the push button - red button symbol is displayed in the lower left of the Script pane.

2. Display the **Movie Clip Control** actions in the Global Functions folder.

3. Double-click **on**, double-click **release**, then click to the right of the opening curly bracket in line 1.

4. Click **Movie Clip Control** in the Toolbox pane to collapse the folder.

5. Click **Statements** in the Actions Toolbox pane, click **Variables**, then double-click **with**.

6. Click the **Insert a Target Path icon** ⊕ to open the Insert Target Path dialog box, click the **myShirt movie clip symbol**, as shown in Figure 10, then click **OK**.

7. Click after the opening curly bracket in line 1 to set the insertion point, click **Global Functions**, then click **Timeline Control**.

8. Double-click **play**, then compare your image to Figure 11.

9. Test the movie, then click the **red button** repeatedly.

   Each time you click the button, the shirt color changes.

10. Close the test movie window, then collapse the Actions panel.

You used ActionScript to control the timeline of a movie clip symbol.

Use ActionScript to control the timeline of a nested movie clip symbol

1. Verify that the **Selection tool** is selected, double-click the **shirt** on the stage, double-click the **shirt** again to open the pattern_shirt nested movie clip symbol, then compare your image to Figure 12.

   The pattern_shirt movie clip symbol is a nested movie clip symbol that changes the pattern of the shirt. It includes two frame labels, "circles" and "stars".

2. Drag the **playhead** along the movie clip symbol timeline to see how the shirt pattern changes.

3. Click the **shirt_color movie clip** on the Information bar to return to the shirt_color edit window.

4. Click the **shirt** on the stage, open the Property inspector, click the **Instance Name text box**, type **myPattern** for the instance name, press **[Enter]** (Win) or **[return]** (Mac), then close the Property inspector.

   TIP The Property inspector changes the settings for the currently selected object. To select a nested movie clip, the parent movie clip must be open.

5. Click **Scene 1** on the Information bar to return to the main timeline.

6. Click the **Stars button** on the stage (under the word "Patterns") to select the Stars button.

7. Open the Actions panel (if necessary), then verify that the **Stars button symbol** is displayed in the lower left of the Script pane.

(continued)

FIGURE 12

Timeline of a nested movie clip symbol

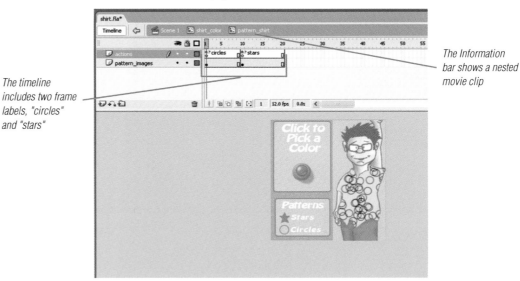

The timeline includes two frame labels, "circles" and "stars"

The Information bar shows a nested movie clip

Using ActionScript

FIGURE 13
Nested movie clip symbol in the Insert Target Path dialog box

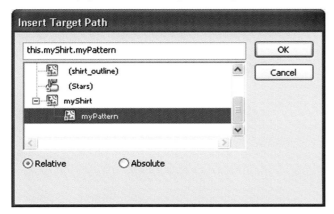

8. Click **Movie Clip Control** under the Global Functions folder, double-click **on**, double-click **release**, then click after the opening curly bracket to set the insertion point.

9. Click **Statements** in the Toolbox pane click **Variables**, then double-click **with**.

10. Click the **Insert a Target Path icon** ⊕ , click ⊞ (Win) or **triangle** (Mac) to expand the myShirt path, click the **myPattern movie clip symbol**, as shown in Figure 13, then click **OK**.

   A path is inserted into the nested movie clip symbol in dot syntax format.

11. Click after the opening curly bracket to set the insertion point, click **Global Functions** in the Toolbox pane, click **Timeline Control**, then double-click **gotoAndPlay**.

12. Type **"stars"**, then compare your Actions panel to Figure 14.

13. Test the movie, then click the **Stars button**.

   The shirt pattern changes to stars.

14. Close the test movie window, then save your work.

You used ActionScript to control the timeline of a nested movie clip symbol.

FIGURE 14
Referencing a frame label in the nested movie clip symbol in the `gotoAndPlay` *action*

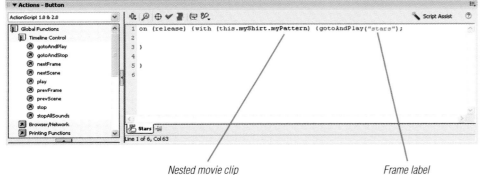

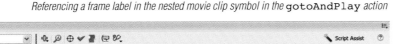

Nested movie clip   Frame label

Copy ActionScript between objects

1. Right-click (Win) or [control] click (Mac) in the **Script pane**, then click **Select All** to select the ActionScript, as shown in Figure 15.

2. Right-click (Win) or [control] click (Mac) the selection, then click **Copy**.

3. Click the **Circles button** on the stage to select it.

4. Click in the **Script pane**, right-click (Win) or [control] click (Mac), then click **Paste**.

(continued)

FIGURE 15

Selecting the ActionScript to copy

5. Double-click the word **stars** in the Script pane to select it, then type **circles**, as shown in Figure 16.

6. Test the movie then click the **Stars button** and **Circles button**.

The shirt pattern changes to circles when you click the Circles button. The shirt pattern changes to stars when you click the Stars button.

7. Close the test movie window, save your work, then close the document.

You copied and edited ActionScript.

FIGURE 16

Editing the copied ActionScript

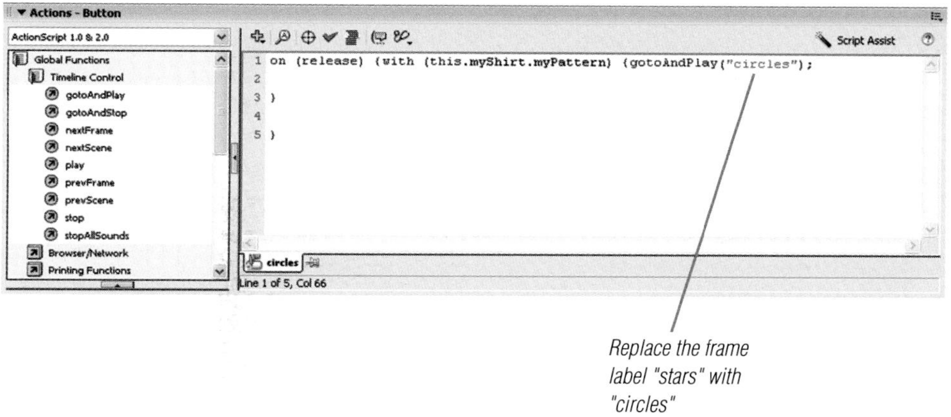

Replace the frame label "stars" with "circles"

CREATE INTERACTIVE
MOVIE CLIP SYMBOLS

What You'll Do

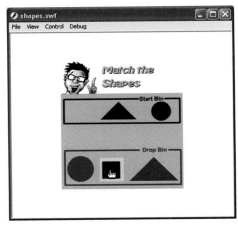

In this lesson, you will use ActionScript to make a movie clip draggable and change the properties of a movie clip based on user actions.

Understanding Interactive Movie Clips

Using ActionScript with movie clip symbols offers many opportunities for creating a richer user experience. With the startDrag and stopDrag actions, you can make a movie clip draggable while a movie is playing; that is, you can allow a user to click the movie clip and then move it to another location on the screen. You have probably seen draggable movie clips in games created with Macromedia Flash, as shown in Figure 17, or in user interface features such as scroll bars and sliders in Web applications created with Macromedia Flash.

Another action, _droptarget, extends the draggable movie clip feature by allowing Macromedia Flash to determine if a movie clip has collided with (been placed on top of) another movie clip or a specified area on the stage. Macromedia Flash can then take another set of actions based on where the user has dragged the clip.

ActionScript statements can also change the properties of movie clip symbols as a movie is playing. You can control such properties as position, rotation, color, size, and whether the movie clip is visible or hidden. Actions that change movie clip properties are often used in combination with actions that test for user input or interactions. For example, you can create ActionScript that makes a movie clip disappear when it is dragged onto another movie clip.

Creating Conditional Actions

If-then statements are familiar to anyone who has had minimal programming exposure. ActionScript includes an if action that can test whether certain conditions have been met and, if so, can perform other actions. Such conditional statements offer many possibilities for building more interactive and involving movies. You should enclose all the actions you want Macromedia Flash to carry out in brackets following the if action. If the conditions are not met, the actions in the brackets are ignored, and Macromedia Flash jumps to the next action.

When creating conditions in ActionScript, you must use two equals signs (==). A single equals sign (=) sets a variable to a specific value. For example, $x=9$ in ActionScript sets a variable named x to the value 9, where $x==9$ is a conditional statement that checks if the variable x has a value of 9, and if so, performs another action. Figure 18 shows an example of a conditional statement.

QUICKTIP

ActionScript includes many other actions for creating conditional statements and loops, such as **else,** which lets you specify actions to run when an if statement is false, and **do while,** which lets you specify a set of actions to run continuously until a certain condition is met. See the Help feature for more information.

FIGURE 17
Draggable movie clips in a Macromedia Flash game

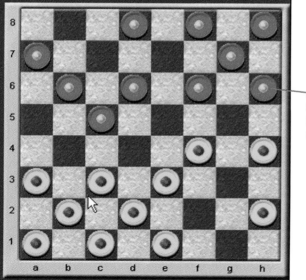

—*Each checker is a movie clip symbol, which you can drag to a square*

FIGURE 18
Example of a conditional ActionScript statement

```
1 on (release) {
2     if (x==9) {
3         gotoAndPlay(1);
4     }
5 }
6
```

Use ActionScript to make a movie clip symbol draggable

1. Open fl9_3.fla, then save it as **shapes**.

2. Drag the **playhead** through the timeline.

   This movie contains two frame labels, "start" and "play", which are associated with two separate screens. The actions layer contains stop actions that correspond to each screen. All the shapes on the "play" screen are movie clip symbols.

3. Click **Frame 7** on the timeline to display the play screen, click the black square in the Start Bin, then open the Actions panel (if necessary).

4. Double-click **on** in the Movie Clip Control folder in the Actions Toolbox pane, double-click **press**, then compare your image to Figure 19.

5. Click after the opening curly bracket to set the insertion point, then double-click **startDrag** in the Movie Clip Control folder on the Actions Toolbox pane.

6. Type "".

7. Click after the closing curly bracket, double-click **on** in the Movie Clip Control folder in the Actions panel, then double-click **release**.

   The on (release) action is inserted after the closing curly bracket, indicating the start of a new action.

   (continued)

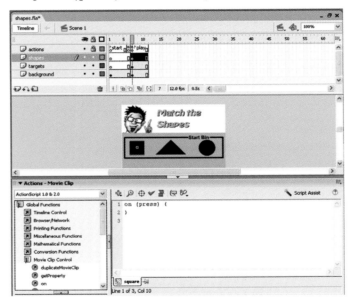

FIGURE 19

Adding an on (press) *action in the Actions panel*

FIGURE 20

ActionScript to make the movie clip draggable

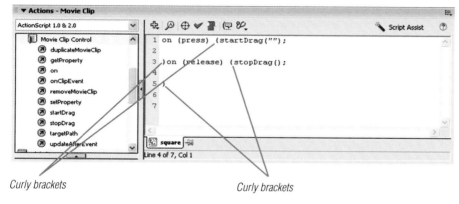

Curly brackets   Curly brackets

8. Click after the opening curly bracket in line 3 to set the insertion point, double-click **stopDrag** in the Movie Clip Control folder on the Actions Toolbox pane, then compare your image to Figure 20.

9. Test the movie, click the **Start button**, then drag and drop the square around the screen.

10. Close the test movie window.

> TIP To make the other two movie clip symbols draggable, you could cut and paste between Script panes. The same ActionScript will work for all three symbols.

You made a movie clip symbol draggable.

Create a conditional action

1. Double-click the **yellow square** in the Drop Bin on the stage to open the square movie clip, then drag the playhead along the movie clip timeline.

   This movie clip symbol has two states: one with the square filled in, and one with just an outline. In the steps below, you'll create a conditional statement that moves the movie clip to Frame 2 when a user drops the square from the Start Bin onto the square in the Drop Bin.

2. Click **Scene 1** on the Information bar to return to the main timeline.

3. Click the **yellow square** to select it, open the Property inspector, then click the **Instance Name text box**.

4. Type **targetSquare** for the instance name, press **[Enter]** (Win) or **[return]** (Mac), then close the Property inspector. You must name the square so it can be referenced in the ActionScript code.

(continued)

5. Click the **black square** to select it, then open the Actions panel (if necessary).

6. Click the end of the **StopDrag Line** in the Script pane (after the semicolon), press **[Enter]** (Win) or **[return]** (Mac) to create a new line, then type the following ActionScript, as shown in Figure 21: **if (_droptarget=="/targetSquare")**.

   This line of ActionScript creates a condition. If the square from the Start Bin is placed on top of the square in the Drop Bin, then perform the next set of actions enclosed in curly brackets.

7. Press **[Enter]** (Win) or **[return]** (Mac) to create a new line, then type the following ActionScript, as shown in Figure 22: **{_root.targetSquare.gotoAndPlay (2)}**.

   This line of ActionScript plays Frame 2 of the targetSquare movie clip.

8. Test the movie, click the **Start button**, then drag and drop the **black square** from the Start Bin onto the yellow square in the Drop Bin.

   Macromedia Flash plays the second frame of the targetSquare movie clip, which changes the square in the Drop Bin to just an outline.

9. Close the test movie window.

You created a conditional ActionScript statement that plays a specified frame in a movie clip symbol when two movie clips collide.

FIGURE 21
ActionScript to create a conditional statement

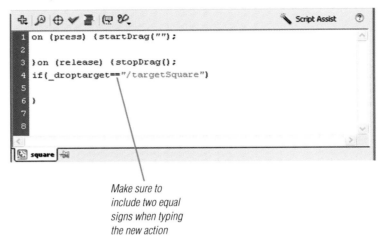

Make sure to include two equal signs when typing the new action

FIGURE 22
Actions to execute if the conditional statement is true

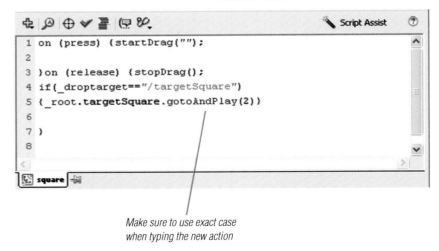

Make sure to use exact case when typing the new action

FIGURE 23

ActionScript to hide the square

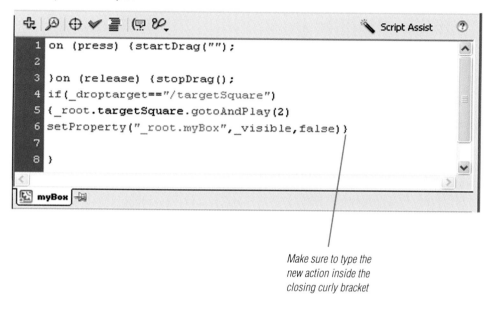

```
1 on (press) {startDrag("");
2
3 }on (release) {stopDrag();
4 if(_droptarget=="/targetSquare")
5 {_root.targetSquare.gotoAndPlay(2)
6 setProperty("_root.myBox",_visible,false)}
7
8 }
```

*Make sure to type the
new action inside the
closing curly bracket*

Understanding the / (slash) in the _droptarget action

_droptarget was first introduced in Macromedia Flash Version 4.0, before dot syntax
was available, and when only slash syntax was supported. The slash in
"/targetSquare" is the equivalent of _root in dot syntax: it tells Macromedia Flash
where the movie clip is relative to the main timeline. Other actions may also require
paths that use slash syntax; be sure to check the Help panel when using a new action.
Macromedia Flash includes an eval action with which you can convert dot syntax
paths to slash syntax in an ActionScript statement.

Use ActionScript to change the properties of a movie clip symbol

1. Click the **black square** in the Start Bin, open
   the Property inspector, name the movie clip
   symbol **myBox**, then close the Property
   inspector.

   You must name the square so you can reference it in ActionScript.

2. Verify that the **black square** is still selected,
   and **myBox** is displayed in the lower left of
   the Script pane.

3. Click the **Script pane** between the closing
   parenthesis and closing bracket at the end of
   the gotoAndPlay Line, then press **[Enter]**
   (Win) or **[return]** (Mac) to create a new line.

   The closing curly bracket should move down
   one line.

4. Before the closing curly bracket, type the following ActionScript, as shown in Figure 23:

   setProperty ("_root.myBox", _visible, false)

5. Test the movie, click the **Start button**, then
   drag and drop the square from the Start Bin
   onto the square in the Drop Bin.

   The square becomes invisible.

6. Close the test movie window, save your
   work, then close shapes.fla.

*You created an ActionScript statement that hides a
movie clip symbol when a condition is met.*

DEFINE
VARIABLES

What You'll Do

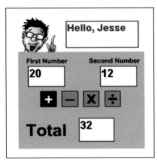

 In this lesson, you will use ActionScript with interactive text and number variables.

Understanding Variables

A **variable** is a container that holds information. Variables are dynamic; that is, the information they contain changes depending on an action a user takes or another aspect of how the movie plays. A Macromedia Flash game that keeps track of scores is an example of using variables, as is a form in which a user enters credit card information while making an online purchase.

You create variables in ActionScript with the setvar action or by using an equals sign (=). You do not have to specify a data type for the variable when you create it, but it is good practice to give the variable an initial value so you can keep track of how it changes as you use it in expressions. To create a **string variable**, which is a sequence of characters including letters, numbers, and punctuation, place quotation marks around the string. For example, the ActionScript statement myExam = "Pop Quiz" sets the variable myExam to the string Pop Quiz. To create a **number variable**, just write the num-

ber. For example, myScore = 93 sets a variable named myScore to the number 93.

Macromedia Flash includes the following data types for variables: String, Number, Boolean, Object, Movieclip, Null, and Undefined. See the Macromedia Flash Help system for a full explanation of each type.

QUICKTIP

To ensure your ActionScript will run correctly, do not include spaces in variable names.

Using Text Fields to Collect User Information

One of the most powerful uses of variables is to collect and work with information from users. To do this, you create input and dynamic text fields.

An **input text field** takes information entered by a user and stores it as a variable. To create an input box, first create a text box with the Text tool on the Tools panel, then open the Property inspector. You then change the field type and assign a variable name, as shown in Figure 24. You can also set other properties, such as whether the input box appears with a border, or the maximum number of characters allotted for user input.

A **dynamic text field** displays information derived from variables. You use the Text tool and Property inspector to create a dynamic text field. If you want exactly what a user has typed to appear in the dynamic text field (for example, a name to appear on a series of pages), assign the dynamic text field the same name as the input text field. If you want to manipulate variables using

ActionScript before populating the dynamic text field, assign the field a unique name.

Understanding Expressions

Expressions are formulas for manipulating or evaluating the information in variables. This can range from string expressions that concatenate (join together) user and system-derived text (as in a paragraph that inserts a user's name right in the text) to numeric expressions that perform mathematical calculations like addition, subtraction, or incrementing a value. Macromedia Flash also lets you enter logical expressions that perform true/false comparisons on numbers

and strings, with which you can create conditional statements and branching.

Note that some expressions have different results depending on whether they are performed on string or number variables. For example, the comparison operators $>$, $>=$, $<$, and $<=$ determine alphabetical order when used with string variables, and the mathematical operator $+$ concatenates strings.

The Operators and Functions folders on the Actions Tools panel contain operators and functions you can use to build expressions in ActionScript, as shown in Figure 25.

FIGURE 24
Using the Property inspector to create an input text field

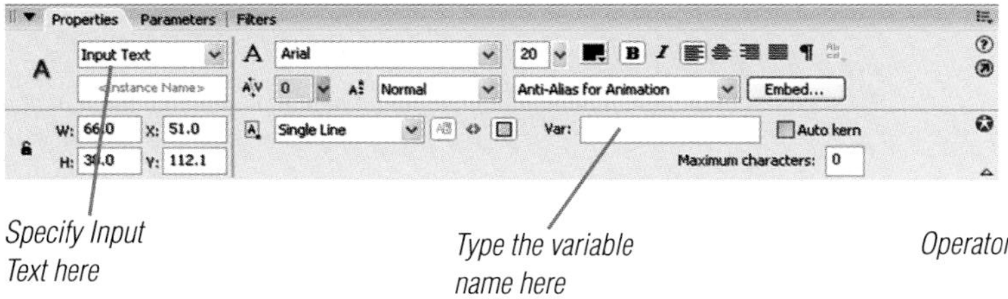

Specify Input Text here

Type the variable name here

FIGURE 25
Folders with actions to create expressions

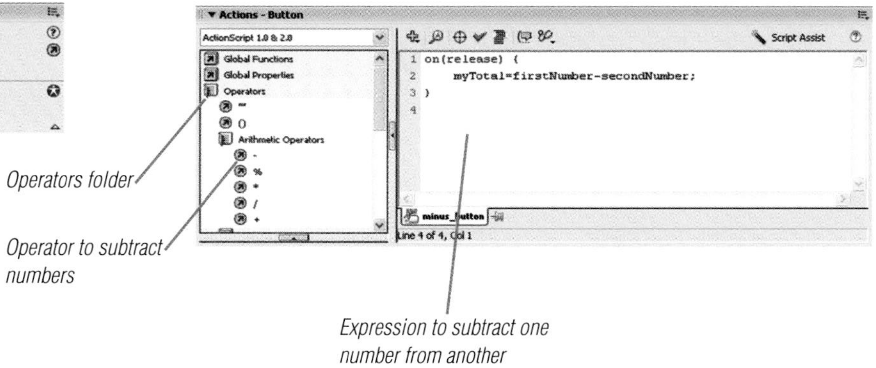

Operators folder

Operator to subtract numbers

Expression to subtract one number from another

Create an input text box

1. Open fl9_4.fla, then save it as **math**.

2. Drag the **playhead** through the timeline.

   This movie has two screens, an introduction that allows you to type in a name, and a screen to enter numbers and perform calculations.

3. Click **Frame 1** on the background layer, then click the **Text tool** **A** on the Tools panel.

4. Open the Property inspector, then draw a text box, as shown in Figure 26.

   > TIP   Start drawing a few lines below the words "and hit Enter". Use [Enter](Win) or [return](Mac) to add a blank line. Use the pointer to move the box. Use the handles to resize the text box.

5. Make the following changes to the Property inspector panel: Font: **Arial**; Font size: **18**; Text (fill) color: **#990000**; Emphasis: **bold**.

6. Click the **Text type list arrow** in the Property inspector, click **Input Text**, then click the **Show border around text icon** ▢ .

7. Click the **Variable text box** in the Property inspector, type **myname**, then press **[Enter]** (Win) or **[return]** (Mac). Compare your screen to Figure 27.

   > TIP   Close the Property inspector or the Actions panel, if necessary.

8. Test the movie.

   A white input text box appears.

9. Close the test movie window.

You created an input text box in which users can type their name. You also specified the formatting for the input text.

FIGURE 26
Drawing the text box for the input text field

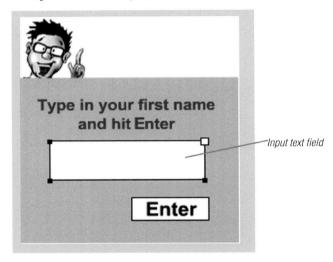

Input text field

FIGURE 27
Creating the input text field

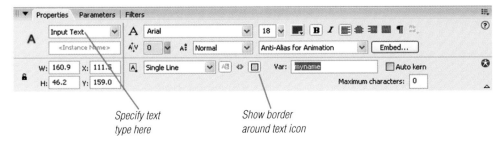

Specify text type here

Show border around text icon

FIGURE 28
Drawing the text box for the dynamic text field

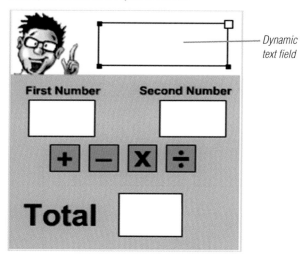

*Dynamic
text field*

1. Click **Frame 5** on the background layer.

2. Verify that the **Text tool A** on the Tools panel is selected, click the white area next to the character, draw a text box in the white area of the stage to the right of the cartoon character, as shown in Figure 28.

3. Click the **Selection tool** ⟍ on the Tools panel, then click the text box to select it.

4. Open the Property inspector.

5. Click the **Text type list arrow**, click **Dynamic Text**, click the **Variable text box**, type **mywelcome**, then press **[Enter]** (Win) or **[return]** (Mac), as shown in Figure 29.

6. Close the Property inspector.

You created a dynamic text box to hold the name the user enters.

FIGURE 29
Creating the dynamic text field

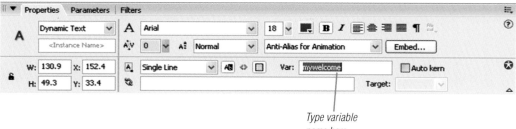

*Type variable
name here*

Use ActionScript to collect and modify string variables

1. Click **Frame 1** on the buttons layer, click the **Selection tool** ↖ on the Tools panel, then click the **Enter button** on the stage.

2. Open the Actions panel, then verify that the enter button symbol is displayed in the lower left of the Script pane.

3. In the Script pane, click at the end of Line 2, press **[Enter]** (Win) or **[return]** (Mac) to create a new blank line after Line 2 but before the closing curly bracket, then type the following line of ActionScript, as shown in Figure 30: **mywelcome = " Hello, " + myname;**.

   When the user clicks the Enter button, this ActionScript takes the name the user has entered in the myname input field, prefaces it with the word "Hello", then places the text string in the mywelcome dynamic text box.

4. Test the movie, click the name input field, type **Jesse**, then click **Enter**.

   The name "Jesse" appears in the dynamic text field, prefaced by "Hello".

5. Close the test movie window.

You used ActionScript to modify a text variable and place it in a dynamic text box.

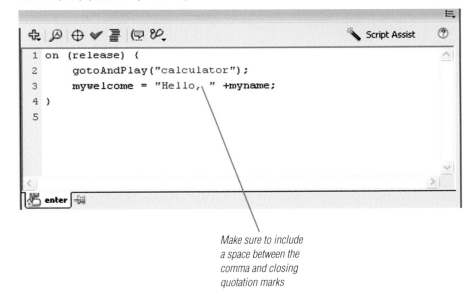

FIGURE 30
ActionScript to populate the mywelcome dynamic text box

```
1  on (release) {
2      gotoAndPlay("calculator");
3      mywelcome = "Hello, " +myname;
4  }
5
```

Make sure to include a space between the comma and closing quotation marks

FIGURE 31
ActionScript for subtraction operation

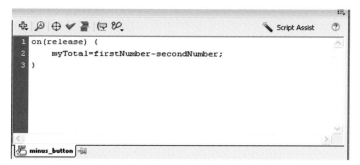

```
1  on(release) {
2      myTotal=firstNumber-secondNumber;
3  }
```

minus_button

FIGURE 32
The working formula

Hello, Jesse

First Number   **Second Number**
20   10

+ — X ÷

Total 10

Use ActionScript to collect and perform a mathematical operation on a numeric variable

1. Click **Frame 5** on the timeline to display the second screen.

   This screen already contains two input text boxes (First Number and Second Number) and a dynamic text box (Total).

2. Click the **Selection tool** ⬉ on the Tools panel (if necessary), click the **subtraction button**, then open the Actions panel, if necessary.

3. Verify that the **minus_button** symbol is displayed in the lower left of the Script pane, then type the three lines of ActionScript in the Script pane, as shown in Figure 31.

   When the user clicks the subtraction button, this ActionScript subtracts the number the user has typed in the secondNumber input field from the number in the firstNumber field, then places the result in the myTotal dynamic text field.

4. Test the movie, type **Jesse**, click the **Enter button**, type **20** in the First Number box, type **10** in the Second Number Box, click the **subtraction button**, then compare your screen to Figure 32.

5. Close the test movie window.

You used ActionScript to create a mathematical operation that works with variables.

Copying ActionScript code

1. Right-click (Win) or [control] Click (Mac) the **ActionScript code** in the Script pane, then click **Select All**.

2. Right-click (Win) or [control] Click (Mac) the **ActionScript code** in the Script pane, then click **Copy**.

3. Click the **multiplication button** on the stage, right-click (Win) or [control] click (Mac) in the Script pane, then click **Paste**.

4. Double-click the **minus sign**, type * (an asterisk), then compare your Script pane to Figure 33.

5. Click the **division button** on the stage, click in the Script pane, right-click (Win) or [control] click (Mac), then click **Paste**.

6. Double-click the **minus sign**, then type / (forward slash).

   The forward slash is the division operator.

7. Test the movie, click the **Enter button**, then experiment with entering numbers in the input boxes and clicking the subtraction, multiplication, and division buttons.

8. Close the test movie window.

You copied ActionScript code from one object to another and made a change in the code.

FIGURE 33
ActionScript for multiplication operation

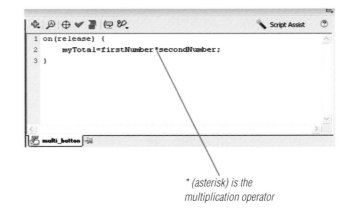

* (asterisk) is the multiplication operator

FIGURE 34

ActionScript utilizing the Number function

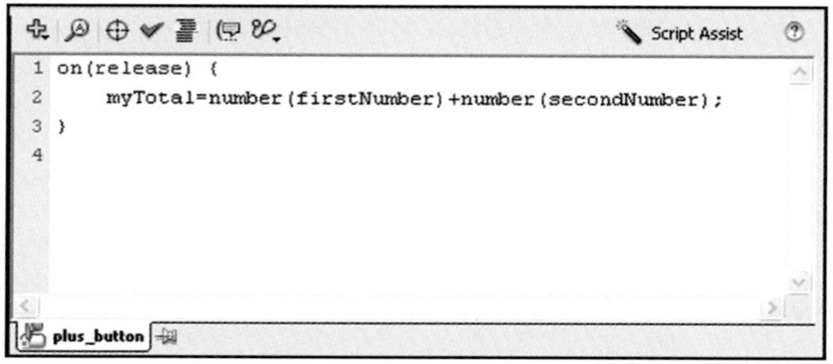

```
1 on(release) {
2     myTotal=number(firstNumber)+number(secondNumber);
3 }
4
```
plus_button

Use the Number function to create an addition operation for numeric variables

1. Click the **addition button** on the stage, then open the Actions panel, if necessary.

2. Verify the **plus_button button** symbol is displayed in the lower left of the Script pane.

3. Click in the **Script pane,** right-click (Win) or [control] click (Mac), then click **Paste**.

4. Edit the second line of the ActionScript to the following, as shown in Figure 34:
   myTotal=number (firstNumber)+number (secondNumber);.

   The number function indicates the variable in parentheses is a number, which ensures an addition operation, rather than a concatenation.

5. Test the movie by clicking the **Enter button**, then experiment with typing numbers in the input boxes and clicking the plus sign.

6. Close the test movie window, save your work, then close math.fla.

7. Exit Flash.

You used the Number function to create an addition operation in ActionScript.

Work with actions.

1. Start Flash, open fl9_5.fla, then save it as **skillsdemo9**.
2. Use the playhead to look at all the frames in the movie.
   (*Hint*: This movie includes three different screens, starting in Frames 1, 5, and 10. There are stop actions in Frames 4, 9, and 15.)
3. Use the Property inspector to label Frame 5 **seasonChange** on the title_screens layer. (*Hint*: You can create the frame label in any layer, but you must add the label to a keyframe.)
4. Click Frame 1 on the timeline, unlock the Buttons layer, select the Start button, then use the Actions panel to create a link to the seasonChange frame when a user clicks the button. (*Hint*: Use the goto action to create the link.)
5. Test the scene, then save your work.

Work with targets and movie clip symbols.

1. Unlock all layers, then click Frame 5 on the timeline.
2. Double-click the tree on the stage, then move the playhead through the timeline of the movie clip symbol.

The movie clip symbol animates the changing seasons.

3. Return to Scene 1, then use the Property inspector to name this instance of the movie clip **change**.
4. Select the green button to the right of the word "Seasons", then use the Actions panel to add actions that will play the movie clip when a user clicks the button. (*Hint*: You can use three actions: on, with, and play.)
5. Test the movie, click the Start button to move to the second screen, then click the green button repeatedly.
   (*Hint*: Each time you click the button, the season changes.)
6. Close the test window, then save your work.

Create interactive movie clip symbols.

1. Click Frame 10 on the timeline.
2. Select the scarf movie clip symbol, then use the Property inspector to name the instance **scarf**.
3. Select the winter movie clip symbol in the upper-right corner of the screen, then use the Property inspector to name the instance **winter_mc**.

4. Select the scarf movie clip symbol, then use the Actions panel to add startDrag and stopDrag actions that allow users to drag the scarf. (*Hint*: Be sure to include an on (press) action with the startDrag action, and an on (release) action with the stopDrag action.)
5. Use the Actions panel to add an if action to the scarf movie clip symbol that uses _droptarget to test whether the scarf has been placed on top of the movie clip instance named winter_mc.
6. Use the Actions panel to add a setProperty action to the scarf movie clip symbol that turns the scarf invisible if it is dropped onto the winter_mc movie clip. (*Hint*: Remember to enclose the action in its own set of curly brackets, within the closing curly bracket of the on (release) action.)
7. Test the scene, then save your work.

Define variables.

1. Click Frame 1 on the title_screens layer.
2. Below the "All About Seasons" title, insert the text **What is your favorite season?** using these settings: font color: black, font: Arial, font size: 12, Bold style.

3. Directly beneath the text, create an input text field with the variable name **mySeason**. Click the Show border around text icon for the field. (*Hint*: Be sure to type the variable name in the "Var" field in the Property inspector, not the Instance Name field.)

4. Click Frame 5 on the title_screens layer.

5. Below the "All About Seasons" title, create a dynamic text field with the variable name **mySeasonText**. (*Hint*: You might want to select the Multiline option in the Property inspector and change the font size as needed to ensure that all the dynamic text displays.)

6. Click Frame 1 on the timeline, select the Start button, then use the Actions panel to create ActionScript which, upon a click of the button, populates the mySeasonText dynamic text field with the season the user has typed in the mySeason input field, prefaced with the words **My favorite season is**. (*Hint*: Be sure to insert the new action before the closing curly bracket of the on (release) action, and to include a space at the end of the "My favorite season is" text.)

7. Test the scene, then save your work.

8. Exit Flash.

FIGURE 35
Completed Skills Review

Ultimate Tours wants to add a page to their Web site that will provide price information for various tour packages so visitors can sample packages and find one within their budget. Ultimate Tours would like the page to provide information on airfare, hotel, and estimated food costs, based on a destination chosen by the visitor. They would also like the page to have some visual interest beyond just a series of text and numbers so that it is engaging to the visitor.

1. Open ultimatetours8.fla (the file you created in Chapter 8 Project Builder 1) and save it as **ultimatetours9**.

2. Create a new screen or scene with a title of **Package Rates** and a subheading of **Click a button below to see price estimates on selected packages**.

3. Insert two buttons on the page that include the text **Cozumel** and **St. Lucia**.

4. Insert a movie clip symbol on the page that includes three frames with a different image in each frame. You can use the images supplied with Project Builder 1 at the end of Chapter 7, or find your own images.

5. Label Frame 2 of the movie clip symbol **cozumel_graphic** and Frame 3 **stlucia_graphic**.

6. Add stop actions to each frame of the movie clip symbol.

7. Name the movie clip symbol instance **rates**.

8. Create three dynamic text fields on the Package Rates page with the variable names **myHotel**, **myAirfare**, and **myFood**. Format the text fields in any way you wish.

9. Use the Text tool on the Tools panel to label the dynamic text fields **Hotel**, **Airfare**, and **Estimated Food Cost**.

10. Attach ActionScript to the two buttons you created which, upon a click of each button, sets the dynamic text field variables to different figures for each location (for example, **100** for hotel in Cozumel, **50** for hotel in St. Lucia, **200** for airfare to Cozumel, etc.) and also displays the appropriate image for the location in the rates movie clip symbol (that

is, either the frame labeled cozumel_graphic or the frame labeled stlucia_graphic). (*Hint*: To set a variable to a specific value, just type the variable name, an equals sign, and the value. Separate multiple variables with a semicolon.

11. Create a button that links the Ultimate Tours introductory page to the Package Rates page, then a button that links the Package Rates page back to the introductory page. Use ActionScript and frame labels to create this navigation.

12. Save your work, then compare your image to the example shown in Figure 36.

FIGURE 36
Sample completed Project Builder 1

Using ActionScript

You work in the multimedia department of a university. A professor asks you to build an interactive study guide in Macromedia Flash that includes a series of test questions. The professor would like to see a prototype of a multiple choice style test question with two choices, similar to the following:

What is the periodic symbol of oxygen?

1. Ox
2. O

The professor would like you to build in feedback telling students whether the answer they supply is correct or incorrect. (In this case, the correct answer is choice 2, "O".)

1. Create a new Flash document, then save it as **test_question9**.
2. Set the movie properties including the size and background color, if desired.
3. Use the Text tool on the Tools panel to create a multiple choice style question of your own, or use the example given in this Project Builder. The question should have two choices.
4. Create an input text field in which a student can type an answer.
5. Create a text label for the field that reads **Your answer:**
6. Create a Submit button near the input field.
7. Create two feedback screens. One screen should indicate an answer is correct, and the other that an answer is incorrect.
8. Attach ActionScript to the Submit button which, upon a click of the button, uses if actions to compare the number the student has typed in the input text field with the correct answer, then sends the student to the appropriate "correct" or "incorrect" screen.
9. Create a Start Again button that uses ActionScript to return the student to the original question, and also sets the input text field to blank. Add the Start Again button to each of the feedback screens.
10. Save your work, then compare your image to the example shown in Figure 37.

FIGURE 37
Sample completed Project Builder 2

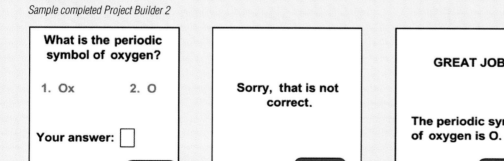

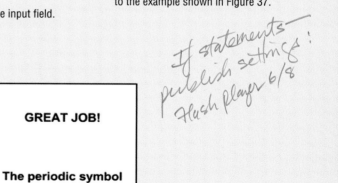

Figure 38 shows a page from a Web site created using Macromedia Flash. Study the figure and complete the following. For each question, indicate how you determined your answer.

1. Connect to the Internet, go to *www.course.com*, navigate to the page for this book, click the Online Companion link, click the link for this chapter, then click instrument Frenzy.

2. Open a document in a word processor or create a new Macromedia Flash document, save the file as **dpc9**, then answer the following questions. (*Hint*: Use the Text tool in Macromedia Flash.)

   ■ In this game, the visitor uses the arrow keys on the keyboard to move the maestro back and forth. The maestro has to catch the instrument as it drops. The visitor then moves the maestro to the correct bin for the captured instrument and presses the down arrow to drop it in the bin by category (woodwind, brass, percussion, strings). If the instrument is dropped into the correct bin, the visitor is awarded points. Missed catches are also tabulated. What are some of the actions that might be used to enable the user to drag and drop an instrument to the correct bin rather than using the arrow keys?

   ■ Which elements of the movie must be movie clip symbols? Would all the movie clips need instance names?

   ■ What actions might be used to allow the visitor to enter a name at the beginning of the game and have the name displayed at the end of the game?

   ■ When the question mark (?) button near the lower-right of the screen is clicked, instructions for playing the game appear. How would you create this navigation?

   ■ Suppose you wanted the text "Good job" to appear for one second each time a visitor successfully dragged an instrument into the correct bin. How might you go about creating this effect?

FIGURE 38
Design Project

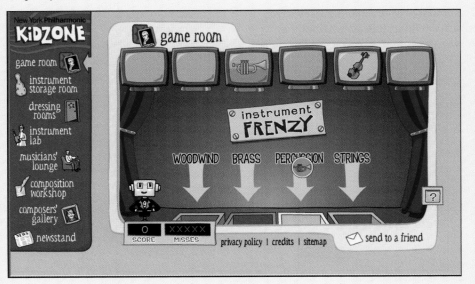

In a previous chapter, you created a page for your portfolio Web site that contained thumbnail pictures of work samples. Another way to highlight your work might be to create a slide show, which would display a different sample each time the visitor clicks a button. Such a strategy could motivate the visitor to look at more samples, and would allow you to display a larger area of the sample without forcing the visitor to follow a link.

1. Open portfolio8.fla, then save it as **portfolio9.fla**.

2. Create a series of screen shots with at least four samples of your work, or use the screen shots you created for the Portfolio Project at the end of Chapter 7.

3. Create a new page or scene with the title **Portfolio Slide Show**.

4. Create a new movie clip symbol that includes a series of screens with a sample of your work and some explanatory text. Each sample and associated text should appear in a separate frame.

5. Add stop actions to each frame in the movie clip symbol.

6. Return to the scene and add the movie clip symbol in the center of the Portfolio Slide Show page. Use the Property inspector to name the instance of the movie clip symbol **samples**.

7. Add a button with the text **Click to view next slide** on the Portfolio Slide Show page. Program the Over and Down states for the button in any way you'd like.

8. Attach ActionScript to the button which, upon a click, will advance the samples movie clip one frame.

9. If desired, create navigation from your current samples page to the Portfolio page, then back to the samples page from the Portfolio page. Use ActionScript and frame labels to create the navigation.

10. Save your work, then compare your movie to the example shown in Figure 39.

FIGURE 39
Sample completed Portfolio Project

10

ADDING
SOUND AND VIDEO

1. Work with sound.

2. Specify synchronization options.

3. Use ActionScript with sound.

4. Work with video.

10 ADDING
SOUND AND VIDEO

Introduction

Like animation and interactivity, sound is an important tool you can use to express a message and make your site appealing to visitors. In an earlier chapter, you added sound to the timeline and to a button. In this chapter, you will see that there is much more you can do with sound in Macromedia Flash. For example, you can set a short sound clip to play continuously, creating a musical backdrop for your movie. Or, you can synchronize sound with an animation or movie clip, perhaps providing a voice-over that explains what's happening on the screen.

Sound can add significantly to the size of published movies, so you should plan ahead and try to use sound strategically. Apply sound only where it will have the most impact. Macromedia Flash includes a number of compression options that can help you achieve a balance between sound quality and file size in your movies. Effective and judicious use of sound is a key ingredient in making a Macromedia Flash site a truly multimedia experience.

Tools You'll Use

```
1 on (release) {
2 this.colorBars.gotoAndPlay ("startBars");
3 music=new Sound();
4 music.attachSound("song1");
5 music.start();
6
7
8 }
```

Script Assist

start_music

WORK WITH
SOUND

What You'll Do

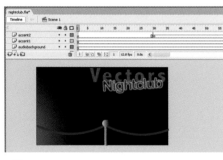

▶ *In this lesson, you will add background music to a movie and work with layering and repeating sounds.*

Importing Sound Files

Before you can add a sound to an object or the timeline in Macromedia Flash, you must import the file that contains the sound. Macromedia Flash stores sounds in the Library panel. Table 1 shows the types of sound files you can import.

Adding a Sound to the Timeline

When you want a sound to play in the background, rather than tie it to a specific object on stage like a button, you can add an instance of the sound to a frame in the timeline. You can drag a sound from the Library panel to the stage to add the sound to the current keyframe, or you can add a sound through the Property inspector to the keyframe. Using the Property inspector is the recommended method, because it ensures that the sound appears in the keyframe you intend.

TABLE 1: Sound Files that Macromedia Flash Imports

sound type	Windows	Mac
Waveform Audio File (.wav)	Yes	Yes, requires QuickTime
Audio Interchange File (.aif)	Yes, requires QuickTime	Yes
MPEG-1 Audio level 3 (.mp3)	Yes	Yes
Sound only QuickTime movies (.mov)	Yes, requires QuickTime	Yes, requires QuickTime
System 7 sounds (.snd)	No	Yes, requires QuickTime
Sound Designer II (.sd2)	No	Yes, requires QuickTime
SunAU (.au)	Yes, requires QuickTime	Yes, requires QuickTime

Sounds are represented on the timeline by either a straight or waveform line, as shown in Figure 1. The approximate duration of the sound is indicated by the number of frames the line occupies. Although the line extends no further than the last frame, the duration of the sound may be longer than the duration of the movie.

You can play multiple sounds at once by placing the sounds on different layers. For example, you might have background music that plays continuously, but then play accent sounds at various points to act as a supplement or counterpoint to the background. You can stagger where each sound begins by creating a keyframe at a later point in the timeline, and then adding the sound to this keyframe. You can also add multiple instances of the same sound to different layers.

Understanding Event Sounds

By default, sounds you add in Macromedia Flash are considered event sounds. Event sounds are like movie clip symbols in that they play independently of the timeline. The sound starts in the keyframe to which you add it, but can continue playing even after a movie ends. In addition, event sounds may play at a faster or slower rate than indicated by the frames on the time-line, depending on the speed of the computer on which the movie is played.

Event sounds have an advantage in that you can use them as many times as you like in a movie, with no increase in the file size of your published movie. However, when a movie is played over the Web, event sounds do not begin until the entire sound file is downloaded; this may cause a disconnection between sound and images for some visitors.

There is another type of sound in Macromedia Flash, called **streaming sound**. Streaming sounds are similar to animated graphic symbols because they are closely tied to the main timeline; whatever its length, a streaming sound stops at the end of the movie. Streaming sounds can also start playing as your computer downloads them. You will work with streaming sounds in the next lesson.

Repeating Sounds

Repeating lets you replay a sound a specified number of times. This is useful in certain situations, such as creating background music for a movie. If you want your audio to loop continuously, you can select the Repeat Sound Loop option in the Property inspector.

The default repeat setting is 1, indicating that the sound will play one time.

FIGURE 1
A sound on the timeline

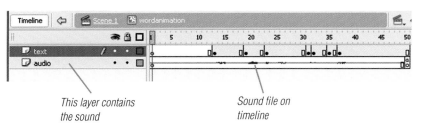

This layer contains the sound

Sound file on timeline

Add sound to a timeline

1. Open fl10_1.fla from the drive and folder where your Data Files are stored, then save it as **nightclub**.

2. Open the Library panel, click the **Audio folder** to open it (if necessary), click **accent1** then click the **Play button** ▶ in the preview area at the top of the Library panel to preview the sound.

3. Preview the **accent2** and **background** sounds.

4. Close the Library panel.

5. Insert a new layer above the actions layer, then name it **audiobackground**.

6. Click **Frame 1** on the audiobackground layer, open the Property inspector (if necessary), click the **Sound name list arrow** ∨ , click **background**, then verify that Event appears in the Sync sound text box, as shown in Figure 2.

   Macromedia Flash adds the sound file to the layer, as indicated by the horizontal line through the frames on the audiobackground layer.

   TIP   When you click the Sound name list arrow, a list appears of all sound files you have imported into the Library panel. The Library panel already contains several sounds.

7. Test the movie.

   The background music sound clip plays, ending after about 13 seconds.

8. Close the test movie window.

You added a sound to the timeline and verified it was an event sound.

FIGURE 2
Selecting a sound file in the Property inspector

If necessary, click list arrow to select Event

Click list arrow to see a list of sounds in the Library panel

FIGURE 3

A timeline with layered sounds

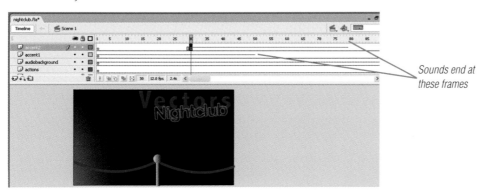

Sounds end at these frames

Layer sounds

1. Insert a new layer above the audiobackground layer, then name it **accent1**.

2. Click **Frame 1** on the accent1 layer, click the **Sound name list arrow** ∨ in the Property inspector, click **accent1**, then verify that Event appears in the Sync sound text box.

3. Insert a new layer above the accent1 layer, then name it **accent2**.

4. Insert a keyframe in Frame 30 on the accent2 layer.

5. Click the **Sound name list arrow** ∨ in the Property inspector, click **accent2**, then compare your image to Figure 3.

6. Test the movie.

   All three sound files play simultaneously for a short time. However, since the sound clips are of different durations, they do not all play to the end of the movie.

   TIP   When you look at the timeline, sound lines are blue and layer border lines are black.

7. Close the test movie window.

You layered sounds of different durations.

Create a sound loop

1. Click **Frame 1** on the audiobackground layer, verify that **Repeat** is displayed in the Sound Loop text box in the Property inspector, double-click the **Number of times to loop text box**, type **3**, press **[Enter]** (Win) or **[return]** (Mac), then compare your image to Figure 4.

   The sound line in the audiobackground layer now stretches to the end of the movie, Frame 200.

2. Click **Frame 1** on the accent1 layer, double-click the **Number of times to loop text box** in the Property inspector, type **5**, then press **[Enter]** (Win) or **[return]** (Mac).

3. Click **Frame 30** on the accent2 layer, double-click the **Number of times to loop text box** in the Property inspector, type **4**, then press **[Enter]** (Win) or **[return]** (Mac).

   Since the accent2 sound starts in a later keyframe than the accent1 sound, you do not have to repeat it as many times to have it play until the end of the movie.

   (continued)

FIGURE 4
Specifying a number of repetitions for a sound

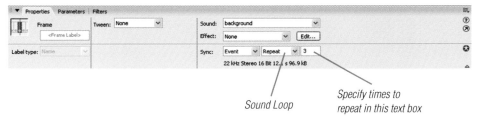

Sound Loop

Specify times to
repeat in this text box

FIGURE 5

Sounds in timeline extend to end of movie

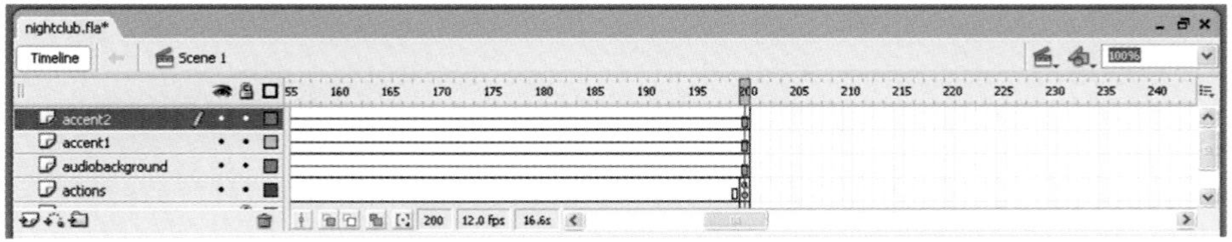

4. Drag the **playhead** to Frame 200 in the timeline, as shown in Figure 5.

   All the sounds now extend at least through the end of the movie.

5. Test the movie until the sound stops playing.

   The sound files play simultaneously until the end of the movie. (You can tell the movie has ended when the words "Vectors Nightclub" stop flashing.) Because the sounds are event sounds, they continue to play even after the movie ends, each stopping only when it reaches the number of loops you specified.

6. Close the test movie window, then save your work.

You repeated three sounds so they play until the end of a movie.

SPECIFY SYNCHRONIZATION
OPTIONS

What You'll Do

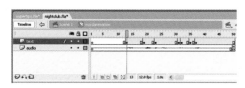

 In this lesson, you will synchronize a streaming sound with an animation, and you will set a button to play a sound in the Over state and stop playing the sound in the Up state.

Understanding Synchronization Options

As you've seen, Event is the default synchronization sound option in the Property inspector. You can also choose from one of three other synchronization options: Start, Stop, and Stream, as shown in Figure 6.

Understanding Streaming Sounds

Unlike event sounds, streaming sounds are tied to the timeline and the number of frames in the timeline. When you add a sound and set it to be streaming, Macromedia Flash breaks up the sound into individual sound clips and then associates each clip with a specific frame on the timeline. The frame rate of your movie determines the number of clips that Macromedia Flash creates. If the sound is longer than the number of frames on the timeline, it still stops at the end of the movie.

On the Web, streaming sounds will start to play as soon as a computer has downloaded

a part of the sound file; this provides a usability advantage over event sounds. However, unlike event sounds, streaming sounds increase the file size of your movie each time they are looped or reused, which means you should use them only when necessary. It is especially recommended that you do not loop streaming sounds.

One important use of streaming sounds is to synchronize animation and audio, since the sounds can be better coordinated with the timeline during both development and playback. If the computer playing a movie is slow, Macromedia Flash will skip frames of an animation in order to maintain synchronization with a streaming sound. To avoid a jumbled or jerky playback, you should try to keep your animation simple when using streaming sound.

QUICKTIP

Once you set a sound to be streaming, you can preview the sound by dragging the playhead through the timeline.

Understanding the Start and Stop Synchronization Options

Start sounds act just like event sounds, but will not begin again if an instance of the sound is already playing. The Start option is often used with sounds associated with buttons or with movies that loop back to the beginning, in order to avoid overlapping sounds.

The Stop option lets you end an event sound at a specific keyframe. For example, you can start a sound in Frame 1 and then stop it playing in Frame 40, even if the sound is of a much longer duration. You must specify the name of the sound you want to stop in the Property inspector for the keyframe when using this option. If you want to stop multiple sounds, you must insert separate Stop options in keyframes

on each sound layer. Macromedia Flash indicates a Stop option with a small square in the keyframe, as shown in Figure 7.

QUICKTIP

You can stop a streaming sound at a specific frame by adding a keyframe in the sound's layer. Event sounds will continue to play through a keyframe unless it includes a Stop option.

FIGURE 6

The Sync sound options in the Property inspector

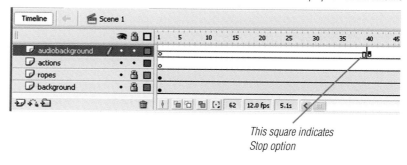

Click the Sync list arrow to display the options

FIGURE 7

A Stop option on the timeline

This square indicates Stop option

Set synchronization to the Stream option

1. Verify that the nightclub.fla movie is open, click **Insert** on the menu bar, then click **New Symbol**.

2. Type **wordanimation** in the Name text box, click the **Movie clip option button** (if necessary), then click **OK**.

3. Rename Layer 1 **audio**.

4. Insert a keyframe in Frame 50 on the audio layer.

5. Open the Actions panel, then verify that Script Assist is turned off and the Actions Toolbox pane is displayed.

6. Click to open **Global Functions**, click to open **Timeline Control**, double-click **stop**, as shown in Figure 8, then collapse the Actions panel.

   Inserting a keyframe creates a movie clip of sufficient length for the sound to play, and adding a stop action to the keyframe stops the movie clip timeline from repeating.

7. Click **Frame 1** on the audio layer, click the **Sound name list arrow** ✓ in the Property inspector, then click **bitmaps_free_vo**.

8. Click the **Sync sound list arrow** ✓ , click **Stream**, then compare your image to Figure 9.

9. Drag the **playhead** through the timeline, starting at Frame 1.

   As you drag, the sound file plays, "Tonight all bitmaps get in for free."

You created a movie clip, specified a stop action, added a sound, and set the synchronization of a sound to streaming.

FIGURE 8
Adding a stop *action*

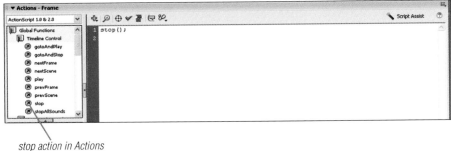

stop action in Actions Toolbox pane

FIGURE 9
The streaming sound in the timeline and Property inspector

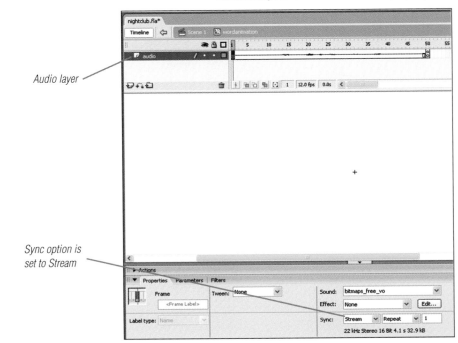

Audio layer

Sync option is set to Stream

Adding Sound and Video

FIGURE 10

Property inspector for instance of the tonight graphic symbol

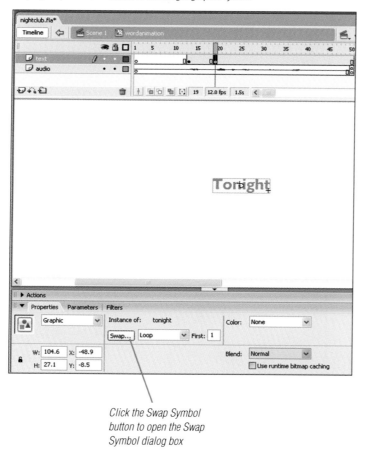

Click the Swap Symbol
button to open the Swap
Symbol dialog box

1. Insert a new layer above the audio layer in the wordanimation movie clip, then name it **text**.

   You will add text that synchronizes text with spoken voice-over.

2. Insert a keyframe in Frame 13 on the text layer, open the Library panel, double-click the **Text folder** in the Library panel to open it, then drag the **tonight graphic** symbol approximately to the middle of the stage.

   | TIP Scroll down the Library panel as necessary to view the Text folder symbols.

3. In the Property inspector, double-click the value in the X text box, type **-48.9**, double-click the value in the Y text box, type **-8.5**, then press **[Enter]** (Win) or **[return]** (Mac).

   The word Tonight appears centered on the stage.

4. Insert a keyframe in Frame 19 on the text layer, click the word **Tonight** on the stage to select it, then click the **Swap Symbol button** Swap... in the Property inspector, as shown in Figure 10, to open the Swap Symbol dialog box.

   | TIP The Swap Symbol dialog box lets you replace an object on the stage with a different object, keeping all other properties the same, including any actions you have assigned to the original object.

(continued)

5. Click the **all graphic symbol** in the Text folder, as shown in Figure 11, then click **OK**. Macromedia Flash replaces the instance of the tonight graphic symbol with an instance of the all graphic symbol. The X and Y coordinates change slightly in order to keep the word centered on the stage.

6. Insert a keyframe in Frame 23 on the text layer, click the word **all** on the stage to select it, click the **Swap Symbol button** Swap... , click the **bitmaps graphic symbol** in the Text folder, then click **OK**.

7. Insert a keyframe in Frame 31 on the text layer, click the word **Bitmaps** on the stage to select it, click the **Swap Symbol button** Swap... , click the **get graphic symbol** in the Text folder, then click **OK**.

8. Insert a keyframe in Frame 32 on the text layer, click the word **Get** on the stage to select it, click the **Swap Symbol button** Swap... , click the **in graphic symbol** in the Text folder, then click **OK**.

9. Insert a keyframe in Frame 35 on the text layer, click the word **in** on the stage to select it, click the **Swap Symbol button** Swap... , click the **for graphic symbol** in the Text folder, then click **OK**.

10. Insert a keyframe in Frame 37 on the text layer, click the word **for** on the stage to select it, click the **Swap Symbol button** Swap... , click the **free graphic symbol** in the Text folder, compare your timeline to Figure 12, then click OK.

11. Drag the **playhead** through the timeline starting at Frame 1.

12. Click **Scene 1** on the Information bar to return to the main timeline.

You created a text animation, then synchronized the appearance of each word in the animation with a voice-over saying the word.

FIGURE 11
The Swap Symbol dialog box

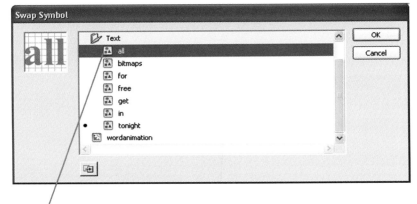

This list includes all symbols in the Library panel

FIGURE 12
The wordanimation movie clip symbol timeline

The keyframes containing graphic symbols in the text layer synchronize with the spoken words in the audio layer

FIGURE 13
Movie clip symbol on the stage

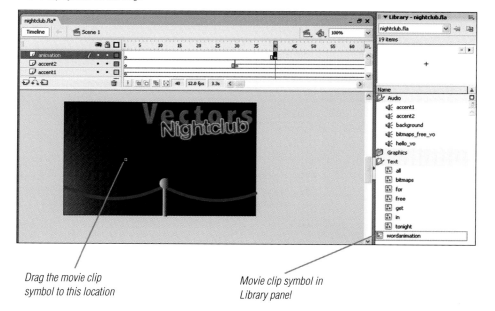

Drag the movie clip
symbol to this location

Movie clip symbol in
Library panel

Add the synchronized animation to the stage

1. Insert a new layer above the accent2 layer, then name it **animation**.

2. Insert a keyframe in Frame 40 on the animation layer, then drag the **wordanimation movie clip symbol** from the Library panel to the left side of the stage, as shown in Figure 13.

3. Click **Control** on the menu bar, then click **Test Movie** to test the movie.

   The words and streaming sounds appear synchronized.

4. Close the test movie window, save your work, then close nightclub.fla.

You added an animation synchronized with sound to the stage.

Set synchronization to the Start option

1. Open fl10_2.fla, then save it as **supertips**.

2. Click the **Selection tool** ⬦ on the Tools panel (if necessary), then double-click the green **Views button** on the stage to open it in the edit window.

3. Drag the **playhead** through the timeline.

   The gel Right button symbol currently has four layers, which create the visual effects of the button.

4. Insert a new layer above Layer 4, then name it **audio**.

5. Insert a keyframe in the Over frame on the audio layer.

6. Click the **Sound name list arrow** in the Property inspector, then click **accent2**.

   Macromedia Flash adds the sound file, as indicated by the straight line in the audio layer, which will start to play once you move the mouse pointer over the button, and continues even after you move off the button.

7. Click the **Sync sound list arrow**, click **Start**, then compare your image to Figure 14.

8. Click **Scene 1** on the Information bar to return to the main timeline.

9. Click **Control** on the menu bar, then click **Test Movie** to test the movie, position the mouse pointer over a button, then move the mouse pointer off the button.

   The music starts playing when you hover over a button, and continues even if you move the mouse pointer away from the button.

10. Close the test movie window.

You added sound to the Over state of a button.

FIGURE 14

Inserting a start sound in the Over state of a button

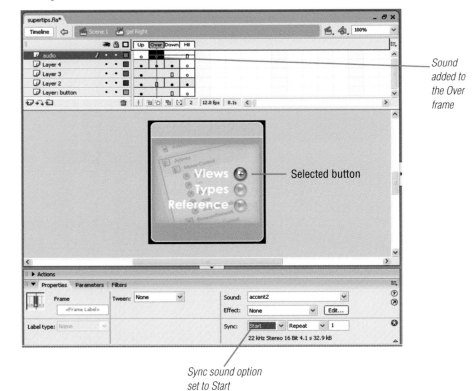

Sound added to the Over frame

Selected button

Sync sound option set to Start

FIGURE 15

Inserting a Stop option in the Up state of a button

Square
indicates
Stop option
in Up frame

Views button

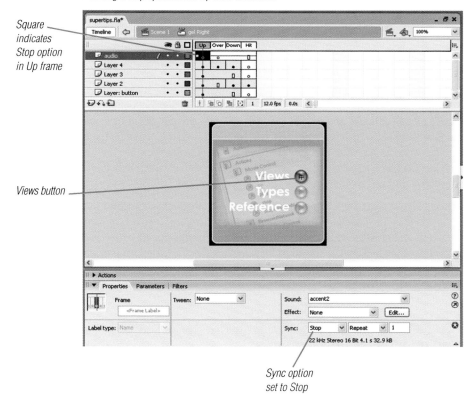

Sync option
set to Stop

1. Click **Frame 1** on the timeline, then double-click the **Views button** on the stage to open it in the edit window.

2. Click the **Up frame** on the audio layer.

3. Click the **Sound name list arrow** ⌄ in the Property inspector, then click **accent2**.

4. Click the **Sync sound list arrow**, click **Stop**, then compare your image to Figure 15.

5. Click **Scene 1** on the Information bar to return to the main timeline.

6. Click **Control** on the menu bar, then click **Test Movie** to test the movie, position the mouse pointer over a button, then move the mouse pointer off the button.

   The music stops playing when you move the mouse pointer away from the button.

7. Close the test movie window, save your work, then close the file.

You directed a sound to stop when a button is in the Up state.

USE ACTIONSCRIPT WITH
SOUND

What You'll Do

▶ *In this lesson, you will use ActionScript to play and stop sounds.*

Understanding ActionScript and Sound

ActionScript and sound are a powerful combination. You can use actions to set how and when sounds play in a movie, and to start or stop sounds in response to user interactions. You can also use actions to trigger an event such as navigating to a frame or scene based on when a sound ends.

To reference a sound from the Library panel in ActionScript, you must assign a **linkage identifier string** and create a **sound object**. Sounds you reference in ActionScript may never appear on the stage or be associated with a specific frame, which means they will not be exported with the movie. You use the Linkage Properties dialog box, shown in Figure 16, to make sure a sound in the Library panel will be exported for ActionScript, and also to assign a linkage identifier string, which is the name you will use to identify the sound in ActionScript. The identifier string may be the same as the sound name.

A sound object is a way for ActionScript to recognize and control a sound. Creating a sound object is similar to creating an instance of a sound on the stage, except it happens entirely in ActionScript. First, you create the object using the new Sound

Sound and Movie Clip Symbols

Another way to control sound through ActionScript is to embed the sound in a movie clip symbol. You must still create a sound object in ActionScript, but you specify the movie clip symbol instance name as part of the new Sound action, rather than using attachSound. For example, the following line of ActionScript creates a sound object called "music" and attaches a movie clip symbol named "Verdi" to it:

```
music = new Sound (verdi)
```

action, and then you attach a sound to the object using the Sound.attachSound action. You reference the sound using the linkage identifier string, as shown in Figure 17.

> **QUICKTIP**
>
> If you do not associate a sound or movie clip symbol with a sound object, actions that reference the object will affect all sounds in the movie.

Starting and Stopping Sounds with ActionScript

Once you have created a sound object and attached a sound to it, you can begin controlling the sound using ActionScript.

The Sound.start action starts a sound playing. When using this action, you substitute the name of a sound object for "Sound." For example, if you have a sound object named "BackgroundMusic," you would include the action BackgroundMusic.start to play the sound. Sound.start includes optional parameters that let you specify a sound offset (for example, if you want to start playing a sound that is 15 seconds long at the 10-second mark) and also the number of times to repeat the sound.

The stopAllSounds action stops all sounds currently playing, regardless of whether the sound is event or streaming. It's a good idea to include a stopAllSounds action at the end of a movie, especially if the movie uses event sounds. If your movie uses sound jumps between scenes, you may also want to include a stopAllSounds action in the first frame of each scene to ensure that any sounds still playing from the previous scene will not overlap sounds in the new scene.

> **QUICKTIP**
>
> There is also a Sound.stop action you can use to stop the playing of a specific sound object. If you do not want the sound to start over from the beginning, you can use the Sound.setVolume action to temporarily mute a sound without stopping it, then increase the volume again at a later point in the movie.

FIGURE 16
The Linkage Properties dialog box

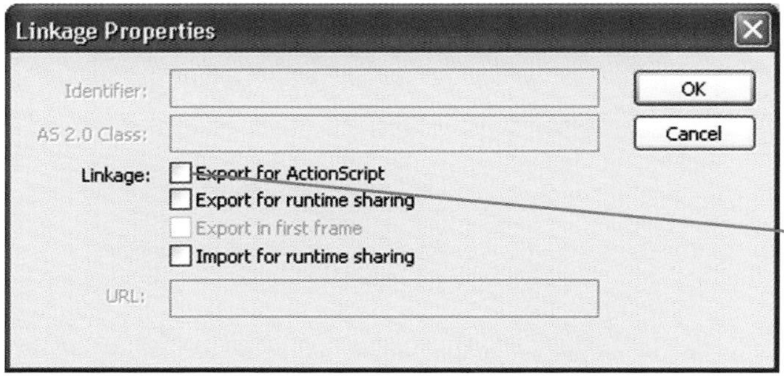

Click check box to export a sound that does not appear on the timeline

FIGURE 17
Example of ActionScript to create a sound object

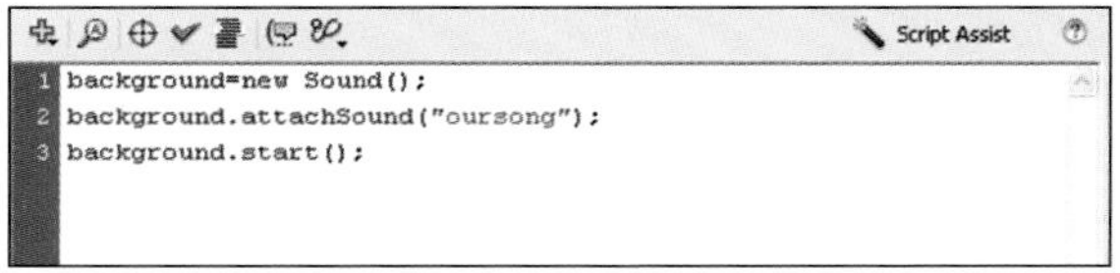

Link a sound file with a movie

1. Open fl10_3.fla, then save it as **levels**.

2. Open the Library panel (if necessary), click the **song1 audio file**, click the **Options menu icon** 🗐 at the top of the Library panel, then click **Linkage** to open the Linkage Properties dialog box.

3. Click the **Export for ActionScript check box** to select it, as shown in Figure 18.

   NOTE: If Flash Player 8 is not your default player, a warning box may open indicating that it is required. If so, click the Publish Settings button in the warning box, click the Flash tab in the Publish Settings dialog box, click the list arrow for the version, click Flash Player 8, then click OK.

   When you click the check box, Macromedia Flash adds the sound name to the Identifier field and automatically selects the Export in first frame check box.

   | TIP   The identifier is the name you will use to reference this sound clip in ActionScript.

4. Click **OK**.

You used the Linkage Properties dialog box to link a sound with a movie without adding the sound to the timeline.

FIGURE 18
Using the Linkage Properties dialog box to export a sound and create an identifier string

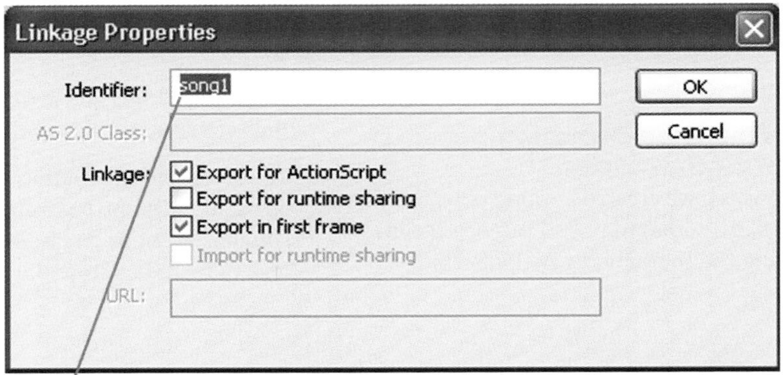

ActionScript indentifier
string for sound

Adding Sound and Video

FIGURE 19
ActionScript to create a new sound object

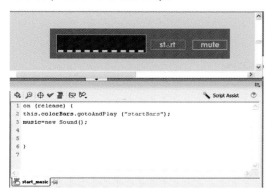

FIGURE 20

ActionScript to play a sound object

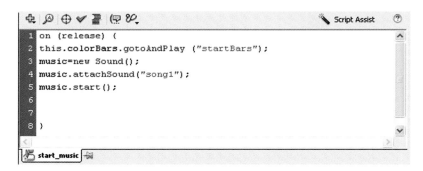

1. Click the **Selection tool** ▶ on the Tools panel (if necessary), click the **start button** to select it, then open the Actions panel.

2. Verify that Script Assist is turned off and that the start_music button symbol appears in the lower left of the Script pane.

3. Open the Actions Panel, click **View Options icon** ≣▾, then click **Line Numbers** if it does not already have a check mark next to it.

4. Click the end of Line 2 in the Script pane (after the semicolon), press **[Enter]** (Win) or **[return]** (Mac) to create a new Line 3, then type **music = new Sound ();**

   Your screen should look like Figure 19.

   This ActionScript statement creates a new sound object named "music."

5. Press **[Enter]** (Win) or **[return]** (Mac) to create a new Line 4, then type **music.attachSound ("song1");**.

   This ActionScript statement attaches the sound with the linkage identifier song1 to the sound object.

6. Press **[Enter]** (Win) or **[return]** (Mac) to create a new Line 5, then type **music.start ();** as you refer to Figure 20.

   This ActionScript statement plays the sound object.

   (continued)

7. Click **Control** on the menu bar, then click **Test Movie** to test the movie, click the **start button**, then click the **mute button**.

   The sound file plays when you click start; when you click mute, the color bars stop playing, but the sound file does not.

8. Close the test movie window.

You wrote an ActionScript for a button that creates a sound object, attaches a sound to the object, and plays the sound.

Stop sounds using ActionScript

1. Click the **mute button** on the stage to select it.

2. Verify that the mute button symbol appears in the lower left of the Script pane.

3. Click **Line 4** in the Script pane of the Actions panel.

4. Double-click **stopAllSounds**, in the Timeline Control folder within the Global Functions folder of the Actions Toolbox pane, as shown in Figure 21.

5. Click the **start button** on the stage to select it, then verify that the start_music button symbol appears in the lower left of the Script pane.

   (continued)

FIGURE 21
ActionScript to stop all sounds when Mute button is clicked

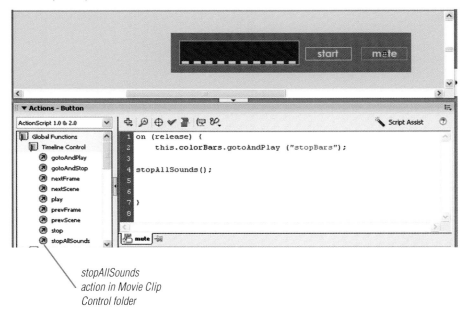

stopAllSounds action in Movie Clip Control folder

Adding Sound and Video

FIGURE 22

ActionScript to stop currently playing sounds before starting sound

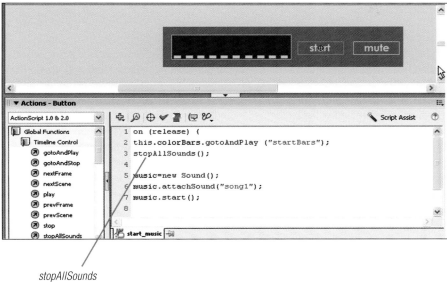

stopAllSounds
action added on Line 3

6. Click the end of Line 2 in the Script pane of the Actions panel, press **[Enter]** (Win) or **[return]** (Mac) to create a blank Line 3, then double-click **stopAllSounds**, in the Timeline Control folder, as shown in Figure 22.

   Inserting stopAllSounds ensures that the sound starts at the beginning each time the visitor clicks the button and that multiple copies of the sound file do not play at the same time.

7. Test the movie, click the **start button**, click the **mute button**, then click the **start button** again.

   The music plays when you click start, then stops when you click mute.

8. Close the test movie window, save your work, then close levels.fla.

You added actions to stop sounds from playing.

WORK WITH
VIDEO

What You'll Do

In this lesson, you will import a video, add actions to video control buttons, and then synchronize sound to a video clip.

Incorporating Video

Macromedia Flash allows you to import several video file formats, as shown in Table 2. Also, you can load external FLV (Macromedia Flash video) files. Flash provides several ways to add video to a movie, depending on the application and, especially, file size. Video content can be embedded directly into a Flash document, progressively downloaded or streamed.

Embedded video becomes part of a SWF file similar to other objects, such as sound and graphics. A placeholder appears on the stage and is used to display the video during playback. The placeholder can be edited by rotating, resizing, and even animating. Embedded video becomes part of the SWF file and, therefore, is best used for small video clips in order to keep the file size down. The process for embedding video is to

TABLE 2: File Formats that Macromedia Flash Imports as Embedded Video		
Video type	with QuickTime 4 installed	with DirectX 7 or later installed
Audio Video Interleaved (.avi)	X	Windows only
Motion Picture Experts Group (.mpg, .mpeg)	X	Windows only
Digital video (.dv)	X	
QuickTime video (.mov)	X	
Windows Media file (.wmf,.asf)		Windows only

Adding Sound and Video

import a video file using the Import Wizard and make changes to the settings including the encoding which specifies the compression. Then, you place the video on the stage and add controls as desired. Figure 23 shows a video placeholder for an embedded video. The video file (fireworks.mov) is in the Library panel and the video layer in the timeline contains the video object.

Progressive downloading allows you to use ActionScript to load an external FLV file into a SWF file, and play it back at runtime. An FLV file is a Flash video file that is created by importing a video file into a Flash document and then exporting it as a FLV file. The FLV file resides outside of the SWF file. Therefore, the SWF file size can be kept lower. The video begins playing soon after the first part has been downloaded.

Streaming video provides a constant connection between the user and the video delivery. Streaming has several advantages over the other methods of delivering video, including starting the video quicker and allowing for live video delivery. However, streaming video requires the Flash Communication Server.

Using the Import Video Wizard
The Import Video Wizard is used to import video files into Flash documents. The Wizard, in a step-by-step process, leads you through a series of windows that allow you to select the file to be imported. The deployment method (embed, progressive, streaming), specifies the encoding (including the compression settings), and even edits the clip. Figure 24 shows the Split Video window with a video clip that is being clipped.

FIGURE 23
An embedded video

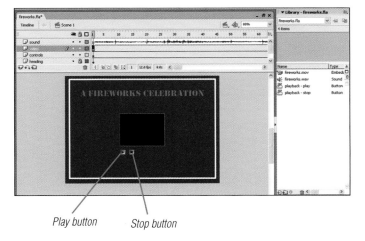

Play button   *Stop button*

FIGURE 24
Using the Import Video Wizard to edit a video clip

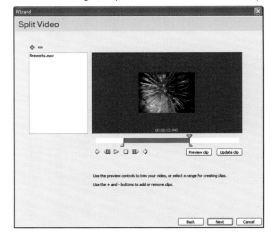

Import a video

1. Open fl10-4, then save it as **fireworks**.

   Note: If the Missing Font Warning message appears indicating that you are missing a font, click **Use Default** to use the default font.

2. Hide all panels, display the Tools, Property inspector, and Library panels, then set the view to **Fit in Window**.

   The movie has three layers, 85 frames, and a blue background. The actions layer has a stop action in Frame 1. The heading layer contains the text and white border objects. The controls layer contains start and stop buttons that will be used to control the video. The Library panel contains the two button symbols and a sound file.

3. Insert a new layer above the controls layer, name it **video**, then click **Frame 1** of the video layer.

4. Click **File** on the menu bar, point to **Import**, then click **Import Video**.

   The Import Video Wizard begins by asking for the path to the video file, as shown in Figure 25.

5. Click **Browse** (Win) or **Choose** (Mac), navigate to the drive and folder where your Data Files are stored, click **fireworks.mov**, then click **Open**.

   (continued)

FIGURE 25
The Import Video Wizard

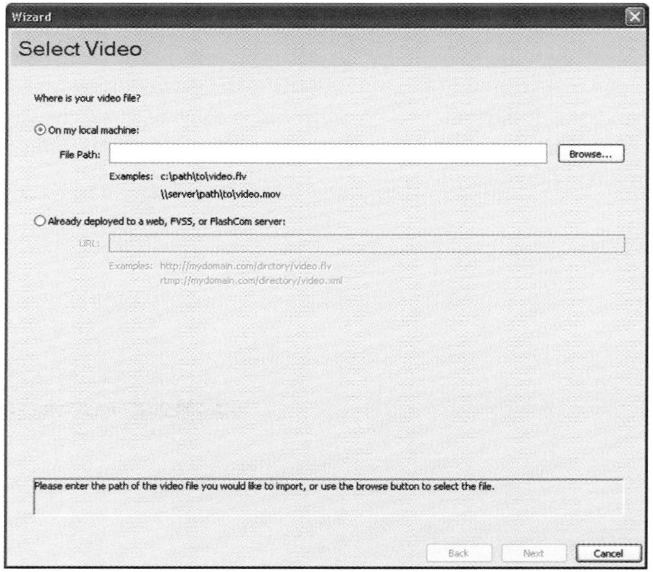

FIGURE 26

The embed video options

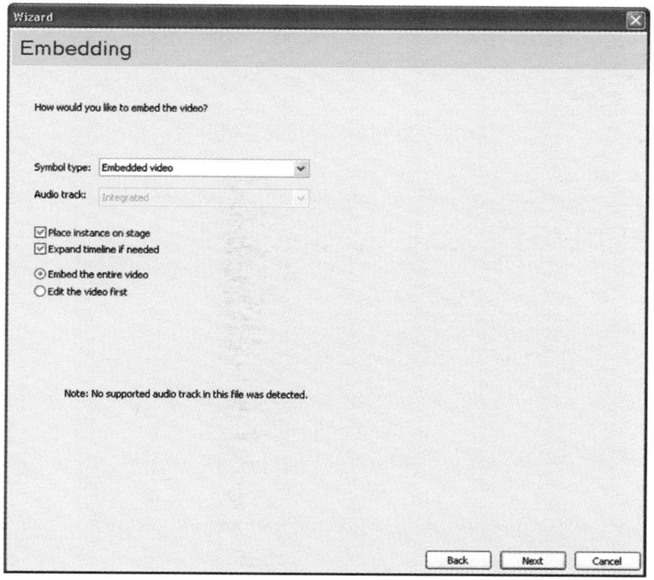

6. Click **Next** (Win) or **Continue** (Mac) in the Wizard, then click each **option button** and read the description for the Deployment options.

7. Click **Embed video in SWF and play in Timeline**.

8. Click **Next** (Win) or **Continue** (Mac).

9. Click the **Symbol type list arrow** ∨ to view the choices for embedding the video, click **Embedded video**.

Your screen should resemble Figure 26.

10. Verify **Embed the entire video** is selected, then click **Next** (Win) or **Continue** (Mac).

11. Verify **Flash 8 Medium Quality (400kbps)** is displayed for the encoding option, then click **Next** (Win) or **Continue** (Mac).

12. Read the Finish Video Import screen, then click **Finish**.

The video is encoded and placed on the stage and in the Library panel.

You imported a video, specified the embed and encoding type, and edited the video.

Attach actions to video control buttons

1. Test the movie, then click the **control buttons**.

   Nothing happens because there is a stop action in Frame 1 and no actions have been assigned to the buttons.

2. Close the test movie window.

3. Open the Actions panel.

4. Click the **play button** on the stage, then verify the playback–play button symbol appears at the lower left of the Script pane.

5. Double-click **on** in the Movie Clip Control folder within the Global Functions folder of the Actions Toolbox pane.

6. Double-click **release**, click after the opening curly bracket, then double-click **play** in the Timeline Control folder within the Global Functions folder, as shown in Figure 27.

7. Repeat steps 5 through 7 for the stop button, changing the action from play to **stop**.

8. Test the movie, then click each button.

9. Close the test movie window.

You assigned play and stop actions to video control buttons.

FIGURE 27

The completed Script pane

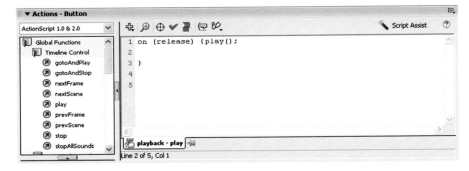

FIGURE 28

The completed Property inspector panel

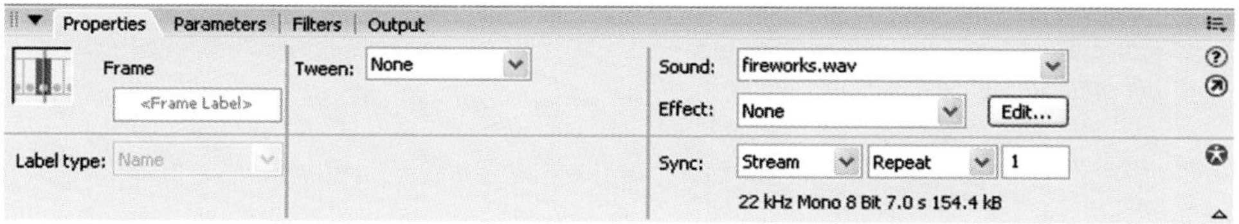

▼ Properties	Parameters	Filters	Output				≣
	Frame	Tween: None ▼		Sound:	fireworks.wav ▼		?
	<Frame Label>			Effect:	None ▼	Edit...	▣
Label type: Name ▼				Sync:	Stream ▼ Repeat ▼ 1		✪
					22 kHz Mono 8 Bit 7.0 s 154.4 kB		▲

Synchronize sound to a video clip

1. Insert a new layer above the video layer, then name it **sound**.

2. Click **Frame 1** of the sound layer.

3. Click the **Sound name list arrow** ✔ in the Property inspector, then click **fireworks.wav**.

4. Click the **Sync sound list arrow** ✔ , click **Stream**, then compare your image to Figure 28.

5. Test the movie, click the **play button**, then click the **stop button**.

6. Save your work, close the file, then exit Flash.

You inserted a layer, then you synchronized a sound to the video clip.

Work with sounds.

1. Start Flash, open fl10-5.fla, then save it as **skillsdemo10**.
2. Move the playhead through the timeline of the movie. Notice there are two pages that are partially completed. The callouts in Figure 29 indicate the types of changes you will make to the movie.
3. Insert a new layer above the buttons layer, then name it **ambient1**.
4. Select the background_loop1 sound from the Sound list in the Property inspector and add it to Frame 1 of the new layer.

5. Set the synchronization for the sound on the ambient1 layer to Event, then set the number of times to repeat to **10**.
6. Insert a new layer above the ambient1 layer, then name it **ambient2**.
7. Select the background_loop2 sound from the Sound list in the Property inspector and add it to Frame 1 of the new layer.
8. Set the synchronization for the sound on the ambient2 layer to Event, then set the number of times to repeat to **10**.

9. Insert a new layer above the ambient2 layer, name it **song**, then add an instance of the song1 sound to Frame 15 of the new layer. (*Hint*: Insert a keyframe in Frame 15 before you add the sound.)
10. Set the synchronization for the sound on the song layer to Event, then set the number of times to loop to **10**.
11. Save your work.

FIGURE 29
Completed Skills Review

Voice-over and background music begin when page is displayed; voice-over is synchronized with words

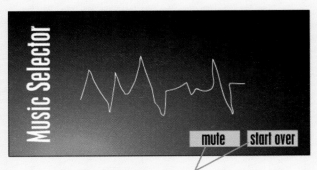

Click the mute button to stop all sounds; click the start over button to stop currently playing sounds and restart song from the beginning

Specify synchronization options.

1. Create a new movie clip symbol named **animated_text**.
2. Name Layer 1 of the animated_text movie clip symbol **audio**, select the music_selector_audio sound from the Sound list in the Property inspector, add it to Frame 1 of the new layer, then set the synchronization to Stream.
3. Insert a keyframe in Frame 75 on the audio layer, then add a stop action to the keyframe. (*Hint*: Adding a keyframe lets you see the full streaming sound. Adding the stop action keeps the movie clip from repeating.)
4. Insert a new layer above the audio layer, name it **text**, insert a keyframe in Frame 13 of the layer, then drag the Welcome graphic symbol from the Text folder in the Library panel to the stage.
5. Open the Property inspector (if necessary), double-click the value in the X text box, type **–58.5**, double-click the value in the Y text box, type **–16.7**, then press [Enter] (Win) or [return] (Mac).

6. Insert a keyframe in Frame 17 on the text layer, select the word "Welcome" on the stage, click the Swap button in the Property inspector, click the "to" graphic symbol, then click OK.
7. Insert a keyframe in Frame 20 on the text layer, select the word "to" on the stage, click the Swap button in the Property inspector, click the "the" graphic symbol, then click OK.
8. Insert a keyframe in Frame 23 on the text layer, select the word "the" on the stage, click the Swap button in the Property inspector, click the "music" graphic symbol, then click OK.
9. Insert a keyframe in Frame 27 on the text layer, select the word "Music" on the stage, click the Swap button in the Property inspector, click the "selector" graphic symbol, then click OK.
10. Insert a blank keyframe in Frame 32 of the text layer.
11. Play the movie clip symbol, then click Scene 1 to return to the main timeline. (*Hint*: there is an extra word, "online", in the voice-over.)

12. Create a new layer above the song layer, name it **animation**, click Frame 1 on the new layer, then add an instance of the animated_text movie clip symbol to anywhere on the stage from the Library panel.
13. Open the Property inspector for the movie clip symbol instance, double-click the value in the X text box, type **60**, double-click the value in the Y text box, type **40**, then press [Enter] (Win) or [return] (Mac).
14. Click Frame 1 on the buttons layer, double-click the right arrow button on the stage to open it, click the Over frame, add an instance of the Plastic Click sound to the frame, then set the synchronization to Start.
15. Click the Up frame, then set the Sync sound to Stop for the Plastic Click sound.
16. Return to Scene 1, then save your work.

Use ActionScript with sounds.

1. Click the right arrow button on the stage to select it, open the Actions panel, then click the beginning of Line 2 in the Script pane.

2. Add a stopAllSounds action to the beginning of Line 2, before the gotoAndPlay action.

3. Move the playhead to Frame 15 on the timeline to display the second page.

4. Select the song1 sound in the Sounds folder in the Library panel, then display the Linkage for the sound symbol.

5. Select the Export for ActionScript check box, then close the Linkage Properties dialog box and the Library panel.

6. Click the mute button on the stage to select it, then in the Actions panel add an on (release) action to the button. As the statements for the on (release) action, add a stopAllSounds action, then a gotoAndPlay action that plays the frame named mute in the waveform movie clip symbol.

7. Click the start over button on the stage to select it, then in the Actions panel add an on (release) action to the button. As a statement for the on (release) action, add a gotoAndPlay action that plays the frame start in the movie clip symbol named waveform.

8. In the Actions panel for the start over button, add the following additional statements for the on (release) action: a stopAllSounds action after the gotoAndPlay action to stop all currently playing sounds and actions to start playing the sound with the linkage identifier song1. (*Hint*: You will have to create a sound object, use attachSound to attach the song1 sound to the sound object, then use the start action to start the sound.)

9. Test the movie, compare your screen to Figure 29, then save your work.

10. Close the file, but do not exit Flash.

Work with video.

1. Open fl10-6.fla, then save it as **skillsdemo10-video**.
2. Add a new layer above the headings layer, then name it **video**.
3. Import tour-video.mov to the Library as an embedded video. Specify Flash 8 Medium Quality (400kbps) as the encoding option.
4. Verify that the video is in the Library panel and on the center of the stage, then note the number of frames needed to display the entire video.
5. Add a new layer, then name it **controls**.
6. Use the Text tool to create a text box with the word Play beneath and to the left side of the video.
7. Convert the text to a button symbol with the name **play_btn**.
8. Edit the button symbol so that the color of the letters changes when the mouse pointer is over the word Play.
9. Use the Actions panel to assign a play action to the button.
10. Use the Text tool to create a text box with the word **Pause** beneath and to the right side of the video.
11. Convert the text to a button symbol with the name **pause_btn**.
12. Edit the button symbol so that the color of the letters changes when the mouse pointer is over the word Pause.
13. Use the Actions panel to assign a stop action to the button.
14. Add a new layer, then name it **stopMovie**.
15. Add a stop action to Frame 1 of the stopMovie layer.
16. Add a keyframe at the end of the movie to the headings layer.
17. Test the movie, compare your screen to Figure 30, then save your work.
18. Exit Flash.

FIGURE 30
Completed Skills Review

Ultimate Tours would like you to create a banner promoting its "Japan on a Budget" tours. The graphics for the banner are complete; now you need to add music and voice-over. Ultimate Tours would like a musical background to play continuously while the banner is displayed, and they have also provided a voice-over they would like to be synchronized with text on the screen. Finally, Ultimate Tours would like an accent sound to play when a visitor clicks the navigation button on the banner.

1. Open fl10_7.fla, then save the file as **ultimatetours10**.
2. Test the movie and notice the text banner that appears across the screen against a series of background images.
3. Insert a new layer above the text animation layer, name it **audio**, add the sound named ultimate_background to Frame 1 of the layer, then set synchronization to Event.
4. Set repetition for the sound to **15** to ensure the music plays the entire time the banner is displayed.
5. Open the Library panel, then open the words movie clip symbol in the movie clips folder.

6. Insert a new layer above the buttons layer, name it **audio**, add the ultimate_voiceover sound to the layer, then set synchronization to Stream, if necessary.
7. Move the keyframes that control when each word of text appears on the stage to synchronize with when the word is spoken in the voice-over. (*Hint*: Use the playhead to hear the streaming sound, then drag the keyframes on the text layer to create the synchronization effect.)

8. Return to Scene 1, unlock the button layer, then set the arrow button to play the Switch Small Plastic sound when a visitor clicks the button and stops playing the sound when a visitor moves the mouse off the button. (*Hint*: Be sure to use the Start synchronization option for the Down state and the Stop option for the Up state of the button.)
9. Test the movie.
10. Save your work, then compare your image to the example shown in Figure 31.

FIGURE 31
Sample completed Project Builder 1

Voice-over is synchronized with appearance of words

Sound plays when visitor clicks button

You work for a software game company. Your newest game, "Match the Shapes," will be developed in Macromedia Flash and marketed to preschoolers. You are working on a prototype of the game to show upper management. You have already completed the visual aspects of the prototype; now you must add sound.

1. Open fl10_8.fla, then save it as **game_prototype10**.
2. Test the movie to see how the matching game works, then close the test window.
3. Add the ambient_audio sound from the Library panel to the movie as an event sound. Repeat the sound 10 times to ensure it plays the entire time the visitor is viewing the page. Set the Effect in the Property inspector to Fade in.
4. Add a stopAllSounds action that stops the sound from playing when a visitor navigates to the second page of the site. (*Hint*: You can add the action to the Start button or to a frame in the actions layer.)
5. Create a movie clip symbol that synchronizes the welcome_voiceover sound from the Library panel with the words "Welcome to Match the Shapes." Alternatively, create another sort of animation, such as a motion tween from off the stage for the words, and

synchronize this animation with the streaming sound. (*Hint*: Be sure to include a stop action in the last frame of the movie clip symbol, so the movie clip doesn't play continuously.)
6. Add an instance of the movie clip symbol to the first screen of the movie.
7. Add Switch Small Plastic sound from the Library panel to the Down state of the Start button on the first page of the site.

8. On the second screen of the movie, attach ActionScript to the square, triangle, and circle in the Start Bin that, when a visitor correctly places the shape on its corresponding shape in the Drop Bin, stops any currently playing sounds, then plays the match sound in the Library panel. (*Hint*: Remember to first create a linkage identifier for the match sound, then create a sound object in the ActionScript for each instance where you want to play the sound.)
9. Test the movie.
10. Save your work and compare your image to Figure 32.

FIGURE 32
Sample completed Project Builder 2

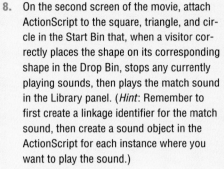

Background music plays low in volume during voice-over/text synchronized animation; button sound plays when the button is clicked

Voice-over plays when visitor successfully drops a shape into the correct position in the drop bin

Figure 33 shows a page from a Web site created using Macromedia Flash. Study the figure and complete the following. For each question, indicate how you determined your answer.

1. Connect to the Internet go to *www.course.com*, navigate to the page for this book, click the Online Companion link, then click the link for this chapter.

2. Open a document in a word processor or open a new Macromedia Flash document, save the file as **dpc10**, then answer the following questions. (*Hint*: Use the Text tool in Macromedia Flash.)

   ■ This site uses a video clip of the San Francisco earthquake. Do you think that the video is embedded in a Flash SWF file? Why or Why not?

   ■ If Flash was used to deliver the video content, what would be the most effective process and why?

   ■ Currently, this site does not have any sounds. How might sound be used to enhance this site?

   ■ If this site were created in Flash, how might you incorporate sounds?

   ■ What user controls might be appropriate when including video and sound in a Flash movie and why?

FIGURE 33
Sample Design Project

In the previous chapter, you created a slide show for your work samples, which displayed a different sample each time the visitor clicked a button. Now add sound to the slide show. If you have access to sound-recording software, you can record your own voice-overs that describe the sample being shown. Alternatively, use the sample files to provide a musical background.

1. Open portfolio9.fla, then save it as **portfolio10**.

2. Import to the Library panel the voice-overs describing your work, or import the following sound files:
   accent1.mp3
   accent2.mp3
   background.mp3
   portfolio_voiceover.wav

3. Open the samples movie clip symbol, add a new layer named **audio**, and then add a different sound to each frame of the movie clip. You can use either voice-over clips that describe the sample, or the voice introduction and musical backgrounds provided in the sample files.

4. If you used the sample files, set repetition for each musical background sound to **50**, to ensure the music plays continuously for the entire time the visitor views the page.

5. If you are using the musical backgrounds, experiment with adding effects to the sounds, such as fades or shifts between channels.

6. Add a stopAllSounds action to keep the different sounds from overlapping as the visitor presses the "Click to view next slide" button. (*Hint*: You should add the action to the button, not the movie clip symbol.)

7. Test the scene.

8. Save your work, then compare your movie to Figure 34.

FIGURE 34
Sample completed Portfolio Project

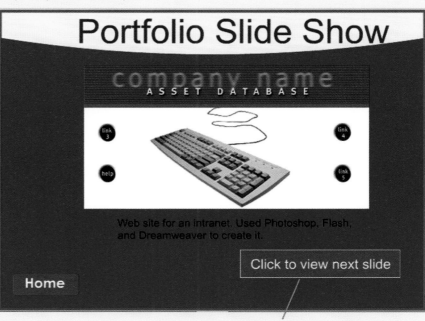

Voice-over or background music begins when page is displayed; new voice-over or music begins when visitor clicks button to view next slide

11

USING ADVANCED
ACTIONSCRIPT

1. Create complex interactivity.

2. Use ActionScript to create external links.

3. Load new movies.

4. Work with conditional actions.

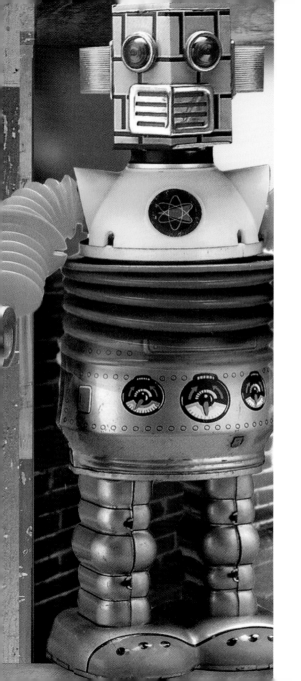

Introduction

In this chapter, you will continue to build on your knowledge of ActionScript, with an emphasis on adding actions that encourage user interaction and enhance the user experience. For example, you can replace the mouse cursor with a custom cursor; track user interactions, and offer feedback based on the data you gather; and send information you collect from users to another Web site or program for processing. Breaking down your movies into multiple, smaller movies, then using ActionScript to load these movies when appropriate, can help you better organize a large Web site and provide users relief

from lengthy downloads. Conditional actions let you implement complex branching in your movies; looping actions help streamline your ActionScript and provide a way to repeat a set of actions based on a value provided by the user or a task you want the user to perform.

With all the new actions and cool techniques you will see in this chapter, remember that you're still just scratching the surface of ActionScript. The more you research and experiment, the more surprised you will be by all you can accomplish with ActionScript, and the more your users will appreciate your efforts.

Tools You'll Use

```
1  onClipEvent (enterFrame){
2       _root.myCursor._x=_root._xmouse;
3       _root.myCursor._y=_root._ymouse;
4  }
```

Script Assist

```
1  on (release) {
2       loadMovie("frog.swf",2);
3  }
```

```
1  on (release) {
2       getURL("http://search.yahoo.com/bin/search","_self","GET");
3
4  }
5
```

Script Assist

```
1  on(release){
2       n=0;
3       while(n<amount){
4            duplicateMovieClip("_root.face","face_"+n,n);
5            setProperty("face_"+n,_x,random(250));
6            setProptery("face_"+n,_y,random(200));
7            n++
8       }
9  }
```

Script Assist

duplicate_bt

CREATE COMPLEX
INTERACTIVITY

What You'll Do

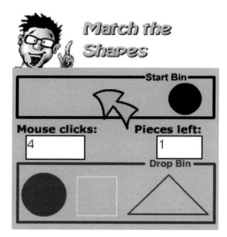

In this lesson, you will use ActionScript to create a custom cursor and count user interactions.

Creating a Custom Cursor

Creating a custom cursor is a fun way to make a Macromedia Flash site distinctive. You might create a cursor with your face on it for a personal site; or you can tie in the cursor with the theme of the site, such as a picture of a yo-yo for an e-business site selling toys. You can also integrate a custom cursor with the purpose of the site: for example, in a game site, the custom cursor might be a cartoon figure the user has to lead through a maze with the mouse. The custom cursor can be a graphic, photograph, or even an animation. The only requirement is that it be a movie clip symbol.

The first step toward implementing a custom cursor is to hide the regular cursor.

You do this with the mouse.hide action. There is a corresponding mouse.show action you can use to redisplay the cursor at any point.

There are two ways to add your own cursor to a movie. In both methods, the custom cursor is an instance of a movie clip symbol. The first method uses the startDrag action. As you add this action to an instance of the movie clip symbol, you should select the Lock mouse to center option. This option centers the hidden mouse pointer beneath the custom cursor, so both the mouse pointer and the custom cursor move when the user drags the mouse. Figure 1 shows the ActionScript for this method.

Using mouse coordinate information

There are many other ways to use the mouse coordinate information returned by the _xmouse and _ymouse actions to enhance interaction. For example, you might create ActionScript that changes the color of an object or screen area whenever the user passes the mouse over it, or ActionScript that creates a panoramic view of an automobile or other product as the user moves the mouse.

Because only one movie clip symbol at a time can be draggable in a movie, if there are other elements in the movie you want users to be able to drag, startDrag might not be the best method for implementing your custom cursor. A second method uses actions that determine the X and Y coordinates of the hidden mouse pointer, then sets the coordinates of your custom cursor to the same position. As the user moves the mouse, the values constantly update, so the custom cursor tracks where the mouse would be on the screen if it wasn't hidden. The _xmouse and _ymouse actions return the coordinates of the mouse pointer; the _x and _y actions control the coordinates of an instance of a movie clip symbol. Figure 2 shows the ActionScript for a custom cursor implemented using this method.

Tracking User Interactions

One aspect of interactivity involves responding to user actions, such as jumping to a different point in a movie when a user clicks a button. Another aspect involves providing users with individual feedback based on the actions they take or information they supply. This can be as simple as creating a dynamic text box to display the user's name in a greeting, as you did in Chapter 9. You can also use ActionScript to gather and display more complex information, such as the number of times a user clicks the mouse or a user's progress in a game or quiz. Collecting such information presents many opportunities to offer users custom feedback. Tracking interactions can also provide you with insight on the way people work with your site.

The increment and decrement actions are useful when tracking user interactions. The **increment action**, ++ (two plus signs), adds 1 to a variable or expression; the **decrement action**, – – (two minus signs), subtracts 1 unit. For example, the ActionScript statement x++ is the equivalent of the expression $x=x+1$. Both add 1 to the variable. You might use the increment operator to keep track of and display the number of correct answers a user has given during an online test.

QUICKTIP

The increment and decrement operators are also useful when setting up the number of times to run a conditional loop. For example, you might want to allow a user to attempt to answer a question a specified number of times before providing the correct answer.

FIGURE 1

ActionScript to create a custom cursor using `startDrag`

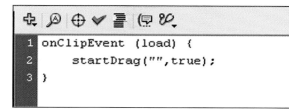

```
1  onClipEvent (load) {
2      startDrag("",true);
3  }
```

FIGURE 2

ActionScript to create a custom cursor by setting X and Y coordinates

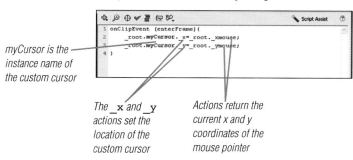

```
1  onClipEvent (enterFrame){
2      _root.myCursor._x=_root._xmouse;
3      _root.myCursor._y=_root._ymouse;
4  }
```

myCursor is the instance name of the custom cursor

The _x and _y actions set the location of the custom cursor

Actions return the current x and y coordinates of the mouse pointer

Hide the cursor

1. Open fl11_1.fla from the drive and folder where your Data Files are stored, then save it as **interactive**.

2. Drag the **playhead** to view the contents of the frames.

3. Click **Frame 1** on the actions layer, then open the Actions panel.

4. Verify that Script Assist is turned off, click the **View Options icon** ⯆ in the Actions panel, then verify that **Line Numbers** is selected.

5. Click the **ActionScript 2.0 Classes folder** in the Actions panel, click the **Movie folder**, click the **Mouse folder**, then click the **Methods folder**.

6. Double-click **hide** in the Methods folder, as shown in Figure 3.

7. Test the movie.

   The mouse no longer appears in the scene.

8. Close the test movie window.

You used ActionScript to hide the mouse cursor.

FIGURE 3
ActionScript to hide the mouse

FIGURE 3
ActionScript to hide the mouse

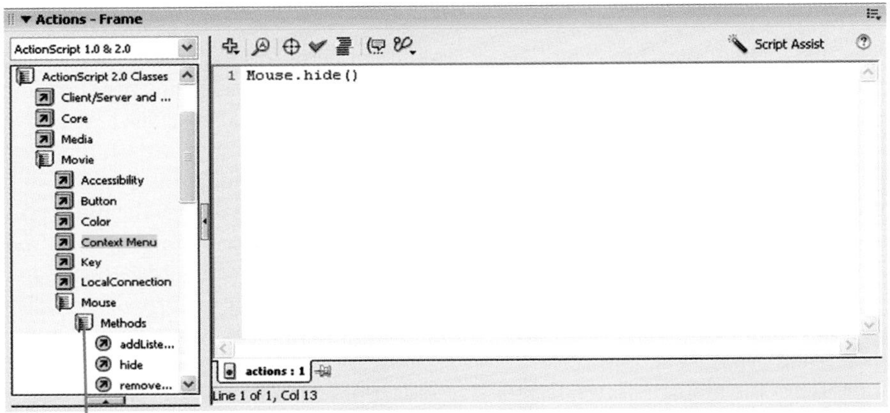

The action to hide the mouse is located in the Methods folder

---

Using onClipEvent

onClipEvent determines when to run actions associated with an instance of a movie clip. Options include running the actions when the movie clip instance is first loaded onto the timeline, upon a mouse event, upon a key press, or upon receiving data. You can associate different options with the same movie clip instance.

FIGURE 4

Instance of custom cursor movie clip symbol on the stage

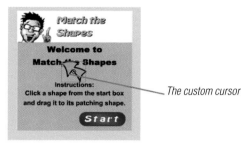

The custom cursor

FIGURE 5

Naming the movie clip instance

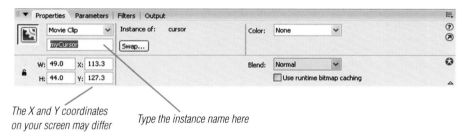

The X and Y coordinates on your screen may differ

Type the instance name here

FIGURE 6

ActionScript to create the custom cursor using X and Y coordinates

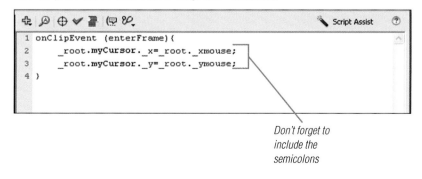

```
1  onClipEvent (enterFrame){
2      _root.myCursor._x=_root._xmouse;
3      _root.myCursor._y=_root._ymouse;
4  }
```

Don't forget to include the semicolons

Create a custom cursor using X and Y coordinates

1. Insert a new layer above the shapes layer, name it **cursor**, then click **Frame 1** of the cursor layer.

2. Open the Library panel, drag the **cursor movie clip symbol** to the center of the stage, as shown in Figure 4, then close the Library panel.

3. Click the **cursor movie clip symbol** to select it, open the Property inspector, click the **Instance Name text box**, type **myCursor**, press **[Enter]** (Win) or **[return]** (Mac), compare your image to Figure 5, then close the Property inspector.

4. Click **line 1** of the Script pane, type **onClipEvent (enterFrame) {**, then press **[Enter]** (Win) or **[return]** (Mac).

5. Type **_root.myCursor._x = _root._xmouse**; then press **[Enter]** (Win) or **[return]** (Mac) to use the current X coordinate.

6. Type **_root.myCursor._y = _root._ymouse**; then press **[Enter]** (Win) or **[return]** (Mac) to use the current Y coordinate.

7. Type **}**, then compare your Script pane to Figure 6.

8. Click **Control** on the menu bar, click **Test Movie** to test the movie. Use the custom cursor to click the button on the first screen and to drag and drop the shapes on the second screen.

   TIP The cursor reverts back to the shape for your operating system when you position the mouse pointer on the title bar, menu, or taskbar of the test movie window.

9. Close the test movie window.

You used ActionScript to designate an instance of a movie clip symbol to act as the mouse cursor using X and Y coordinates.

Track user interactions with the increment operator

1. Click **Frame 7** on the background layer, click a gray area on the stage to deselect all objects, click the **Text tool A** on the Tools panel, collapse the Actions panel, then open the Property inspector.

2. Set the text properties to: Font: **Arial**; Font size: **14**; Text fill color: **#990000**, then verify that bold is turned off.

3. Click the **Text type list arrow** ∨, click **Dynamic Text**, click the **Show border around text icon** ▣, then, using Figure 7 as a guide, draw a text box below the words Mouse clicks.

   TIP If the text box overlaps other elements on the screen, click the Selection tool on the Tools panel after drawing the text box, then use the mouse or arrow keys to move the box.

4. Click the **text box** to select it (if necessary), click the **Variable text box** in the Property inspector, type **myClicks**, press **[Enter]** (Win) or **[return]** (Mac), then collapse the Property inspector.

5. Click **Frame 7** on the actions layer, then open the Actions panel.

6. Type **myClicks = 0**; on Line 1 in the Script pane, as shown in Figure 8.

   This ActionScript resets the value of the myClicks variable to 0 each time a user navigates to the page.

   (continued)

FIGURE 7
Drawing the dynamic text box

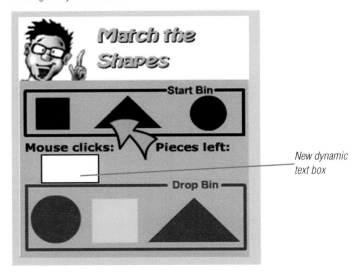

New dynamic text box

FIGURE 8
ActionScript to set the initial value of the variable to 0

Using Advanced ActionScript

FIGURE 9
ActionScript to count mouse clicks

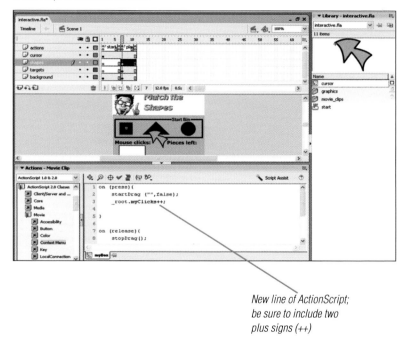

New line of ActionScript; be sure to include two plus signs (++)

7. Click the **Selection tool** on the Tools panel, click the black square in the Start Bin to select it, click at the end of Line 2 in the Script pane, then press **[Enter]** (Win) or **[return]** (Mac) to create a blank line.

8. Verify that the **myBox movie clip symbol** is displayed in the lower left of the Script pane.

9. Type **_root.myClicks++;** on Line 3 in the Script pane, as shown in Figure 9.

   This ActionScript increases the value of the myClicks variable by one each time the mouse is clicked. Including _root in the target path ensures that Macromedia Flash looks for the variable at the main timeline level.

10. Test the movie, click the **Start button**, then click the **black square** in the Start Bin repeatedly.

    The value in the Mouse clicks dynamic text box updates each time you click the square.

11. Close the test movie window, then repeat Steps 7, 8 and 9 to add the ActionScript that increases the value of the myClicks variable by one each time the mouse is clicked for the black triangle and black circle in the Start Bin.

12. Test the movie, click the **Start button**, click each shape, close the test movie window.

You used the increment operator action to maintain a count of the number of times a user clicks a set of objects.

Track user interactions with the decrement operator

1. Click **Frame 7** on the background layer.

2. Click the **Text tool A** on the Tools panel, click a gray area on the stage to deselect all other objects, then draw a text box below the words Pieces left:, as shown in Figure 10.

   The new text box will be a dynamic text box with the same settings you specified for the Mouse clicks: dynamic text box.

3. Open the Property inspector, verify that the **text box** is selected, click the **Variable text box** in the Property inspector, type **myPieces**, press **[Enter]** (Win) or **[return]** (Mac), then close the Property inspector.

4. Click **Frame 7** on the actions layer, click at the end of Line 1 in the Script pane, then press **[Enter]** (Win) or **[return]** (Mac) to create a blank line.

5. Type **myPieces = 3;** on Line 2 in the Script pane, as shown in Figure 11.

   This ActionScript resets the value of the myPieces variable to 3 each time a user navigates to the page.

6. Click the **Selection tool** on the Tools panel, double-click the yellow square in the Drop Bin to open the movie clip symbol, then click **Frame 2** on the movie clip symbol timeline.

   In this movie clip, Frame 2 appears when a shape from the Start Bin is successfully dropped on a shape in the Drop Bin.

   (continued)

FIGURE 10
Drawing the dynamic text box

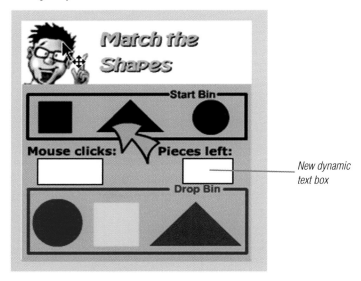

New dynamic
text box

FIGURE 11
ActionScript to change the color of the shirt on button release

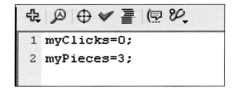

```
1 myClicks=0;
2 myPieces=3;
```

FIGURE 12

ActionScript to decrement a variable as pieces are successfully matched

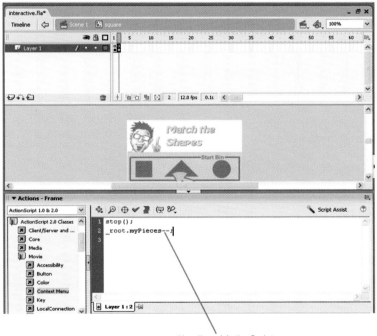

New line of ActionScript;
be sure to include two
minus signs (--)

7. Click at the end of Line 1 in the Script pane, press **[Enter]** (Win) or **[return]** (Mac) to create a blank line, then type **_root.myPieces– –;** on Line 2 in the Script pane, as shown in Figure 12.

   This ActionScript decreases the value of the myPieces variable by one each time Frame 2 displays, which will count down the number of pieces still left to match.

   TIP You can press the hyphen key on the keyboard to type – (minus sign).

8. Click **Scene 1** Scene 1 on the Information bar to return to the main timeline.

9. Test the movie, click the **Start button**, then drag the **black square** to the yellow square.

   The value in the Pieces left: dynamic text box changes to 2 when you match the square, but does not update for the other shapes.

10. Close the test movie window, then repeat Steps 6 and 7 for the red circle and blue triangle in the Drop Bin.

11. Test the movie, close the test movie window, save your work, then close interactive.fla.

You used the decrement action to maintain a count of the user's score in the game.

USE ACTIONSCRIPT TO
CREATE EXTERNAL LINKS

What You'll Do

 In this lesson, you will create e-mail and Web page links.

Creating a Link to a Web Site

Many Web sites contain links to other sites. You might want to lead the user to a site related to your own, or just another site you want to share. The getURL action lets you jump from a button or movie clip symbol to another Web site or open another file, as shown in Figure 13. The new site or file can appear in the same browser window as your site, or in a new window. Table 1 displays the target options for a Web site and external file links.

When you use getURL to lead to another Web site, you must supply the URL for the file. Make sure to include the entire URL, including the protocol prefix, for example, *http://www.yahoo.com*, which is known as

TABLE 1: Target Options for Web Site Links	
option	opens site or link in:
_self	The current frame in the current window
_blank	A new window
_parent	The parent of the current frame
_top	The top-level frame in the current window

an absolute path. If you are creating a link to a file, you can include an **absolute path**, which specifies the exact location of the file, or a **relative path**, which indicates location based on the current location of your movie file. For example, to jump to a file you will be including in the same server location to which you will be publishing, you can include just the file name, without any path.

QUICKTIP
You can link static text to a Web site or external file using the Property inspector. You can choose from the same target options for the link.

Creating a Mailto: Link
You can also use getURL to create a mail link from a button or movie clip symbol. When a user clicks an e-mail link, a new e-mail message window opens, with an address field you have specified already filled in. If you want to create an e-mail link from text, not a button or movie clip symbol, you can use the Property inspector.

To create an e-mail link, include mailto: and then the e-mail address in the URL field of the getURL action. To test an e-mail link, you must display your movie in a browser by clicking File on the main menu, then clicking Publish Preview. The e-mail link is not active in the test window.

Posting Information to a Web Site
The best kind of communication is two-way, and along with displaying a Web site, getURL can send variables to another application or a Common Gateway Interface (CGI) script located on a Web server. The application or script can perform actions using, storing, or responding to the variables—creating instant feedback that can be displayed on a user's site. Forms with user surveys and shopping carts are examples of posting information. Figure 14 shows a form to send an e-mail message.

There are two options when sending variables: GET and POST. Both methods collect all the variables defined at the main timeline level of a movie and send them to the URL you specify in the getURL action for processing. GET is best for small amounts of information, as it can send a string of up to 1,024 characters. Information sent using GET is also less secure, as the variables are appended to the URL string, and so appear in the Address field of the browser. POST can accommodate more variables, and is also more secure, because the variables are collected and sent in a file. POST is the recommended way to send data to a script.

FIGURE 14
A form that posts information to a CGI script

FIGURE 13
Using `getURL` *to link to a Web site*

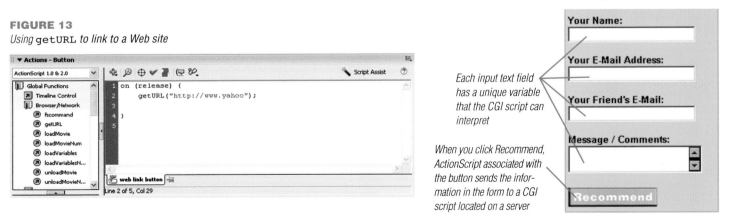

Each input text field has a unique variable that the CGI script can interpret

When you click Recommend, ActionScript associated with the button sends the information in the form to a CGI script located on a server

Create a Web site link

1. Open fl11_2.fla, then save it as **links**.

2. Click the **Selection tool**  on the Tools panel (if necessary), click the **Visit our Web site button** to select it, then open the Actions panel.

3. Click the **Global Functions folder**, click the **Movie Clip Control folder**, double-click **on**, then double-click **release**.

4. Click after the opening curly bracket to set the insertion point, then press **[Enter]** (Win) or **[return]** (Mac) to add a blank line.

5. Click the **Browser/Network folder**, then double-click **getURL**.

6. Type **"http://www.macromedia.com"**, **"_self"**, then compare your Script pane to Figure 15.

7. Test the movie, then click the **Visit our Web site button**.

   The Macromedia Web site opens in a browser window.

   Hint: If you are not connected to the Internet, you will not be able to view the site.

8. Close the browser window, then close the test movie window.

You created a button that links to a Web site.

FIGURE 15
ActionScript to link to a Web site

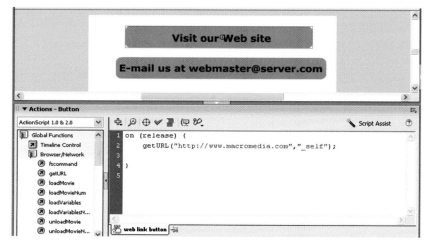

FIGURE 16
ActionScript to create an e-mail link

1. Click the **E-mail us at webmaster@server.com button** to select it.

   TIP It's good practice to include the e-mail address as part of a link, just in case your user doesn't have access to an e-mail program.

2. Double-click **on** in the **Movie Clip Control folder**, then double-click **release**.

3. Click after the opening curly bracket, then press **[Enter]** (Win) or **[return]** (Mac).

4. Double-click **getURL** in the Browser/Network folder in the Actions panel.

5. Type **"mailto:webmaster@server.com"**, **"_self"** for the e-mail address, then compare your Script pane to Figure 16.

6. Click **File** on the menu bar, point to **Publish Preview**, then click **Default – (HTML)**.

   The movie opens in a browser window.

7. Click the **E-mail us at webmaster@server.com button**.

   A new e-mail message window opens in your default e-mail program, with the To: field already filled in.

   TIP If an e-mail message does not appear, your current computer may not have access to an e-mail program.

8. Close the mail message window, do not save changes if prompted to do so, then close the browser window.

9. Save your work, then close links.fla.

You created a button with a link to an e-mail address.

Sending an e-mail through the Web

To send an e-mail completely through the Web, you can collect the recipient and message information for the e-mail in variable fields, then send the variables to a CGI (Common Gateway Interface) script for processing. Common mail scripts include mailform.pl and tellafriend.cgi. See your Webmaster or network administrator for information about scripts available on your server.

Post information to a Web site

1. Open fl11_3.fla, then save it as **search**.

2. Click **Frame 1** on Layer 1, then click off the stage to deselect any selected objects.

3. Click the **Text tool**  on the Tools panel, open the Property inspector, then set the properties to: Font: **Arial;** Font size: **18;** Text fill color: **#000000**.

4. Click the **Text type list arrow** ∨ , click **Input Text**, click the **Show border around text icon** 🔲 (if necessary), then draw a text box below the Yahoo! graphic, as shown in Figure 17.

5. Click the **Variable text box** in the Property inspector, type **p**, press **[Enter]** (Win) or **[return]** (Mac), then close the Property inspector.

   p is a variable used in the CGI script to which you will be sending information. The script conducts a search using the information in the p variable.

6. Click the **Selection tool** ▶ on the Tools panel, click the **search button** to select it, then open the Actions panel.

7. Click the **Movie Clip Control folder**, double-click **on**, then double-click **release**.

8. Click after the opening curly bracket, press **[Enter]** (Win) or **[return]** (Mac), then double-click **getURL** in the Browser/Network folder.

(continued)

FIGURE 17

Drawing the text box to collect the variable information

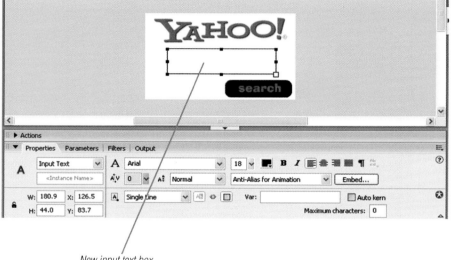

New input text box

FIGURE 18

ActionScript to send variable information to a CGI script

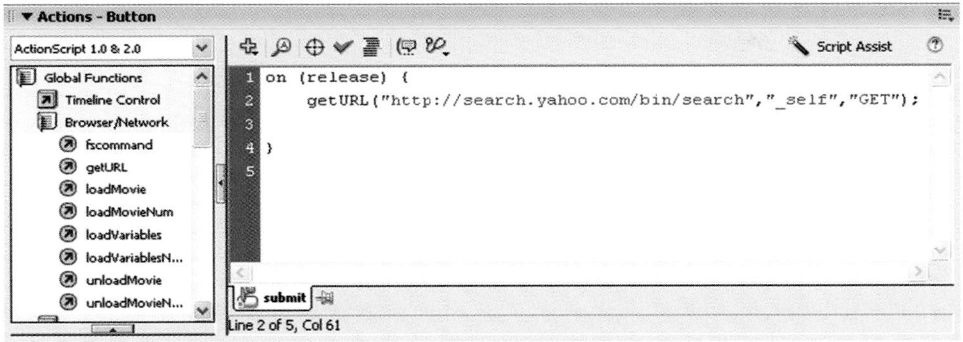

9. Type **"http://search.yahoo.com/bin/search"**, **"_self"**, **"GET"** to enter the CGI script location and name, then compare your Script pane to Figure 18.

   "search" is the name of the CGI script to which you will be sending a variable.

10. Test the movie, type **ActionScript** in the input text box, then click the **search button**.

   The Yahoo! Search Web site opens, with the Search field already filled in and search results displayed. You can see the format in which the GET option sent the variable by looking in the Address field of the browser. The URL includes the search term.

11. Close the browser window, close the test movie window, save your work, then close search.fla.

You sent information to a CGI script.

LOAD NEW
MOVIES

What You'll Do

 In this lesson, you will load new movies into and unload movies from the Flash Player.

Understanding Multiple Movies

In previous chapters, you have seen how you can use scenes and movie clip symbols to break large movies up into smaller, more manageable components. Another strategy is to split a single movie into a number of different movies, and then use ActionScript to load the movies as needed. For example, you might have a site with a number of discrete areas, not all of which are of interest to every user. By splitting each area into its own movie you can save download time for the user, since instead of having to download a large movie for the entire site, the movie for each area will be downloaded only when the user visits it. Multiple movies can create smoother transitions between pages, since the new movies load into the current HTML page. Using multiple movies can also help you keep organized during development of a movie, especially if different people are working on different parts of the movie. Figure 19 shows an example of a way to use multiple movies.

Loading Movies

You use the loadMovie action to load a movie. You must know the name of the Flash Player movie file you want to load (Flash Player files have a .SWF extension) and also its location. As with the getURL action, you can specify an absolute or relative path for the location.

You can load a new movie either in place of, or on top of, the current movie, or into a movie clip symbol. If you load a new movie into the current movie, the new movie will inherit the frame rate, dimensions, and background color of the current movie. The new movie will appear starting in the upper-left corner of the current movie, which may cause design issues if your movies are not the same size; make sure to test how the additional movies will load before publishing a site. Loading a new movie into a movie clip gives you more control over the size and placement of the movie. One useful technique is to create a blank movie clip symbol, position it on the stage where you want the new movie to appear, and then load the movie into the blank movie clip symbol. Figure 20 shows the Action Script for loading movies.

Understanding Levels

The concept of levels becomes important when you add new movies to the current movie. Levels are similar to layers on the timeline; they establish a hierarchy that determines what's displayed on the screen. The current movie, also called the base movie, is considered to be at Level 0. You can add the new movie at Level 0, in which case it replaces the current movie; or at Level 1, in which case it appears on top of the current movie. The movie originally at Level 0 continues to control the frame rate, dimensions, and background color of all other movies, even if you replace it.

For example, a new movie could appear on top of the current movie if loaded at Level 1. Parts of the current movie, such as the links or areas of a background image, could remain in view and active. Alternatively, you could load the new movie at Level 0, in which case none of the original movie would remain in view.

As you load additional movies, you can continue to add them in place of an existing movie, or at a higher level. Movies at higher levels appear on top of movies at lower levels. Each level can contain only one movie.

> **QUICK**TIP
>
> The loadMovie action becomes loadMovieNum when you specify a level at which to load a movie.

Unloading Movies

Macromedia Flash also includes unloadMovie (for movies loaded into movie clips) and unloadMovieNum (for movies loaded at a level) actions to remove a movie from the Flash Player. Including this action when you no longer need a movie loaded can create smoother transitions between movies, ensure there's no visual residue between movies of different sizes, and reduce the memory required by the Flash Player.

> **QUICK**TIP
>
> Loading a new movie into the same level as an existing movie automatically unloads the existing movie from the Flash Player.

FIGURE 19
A Macromedia Flash site that takes advantage of using multiple movies

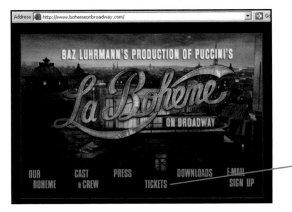

Each of the links on this page could open a separate .SWF file, saving the user download time

FIGURE 20
Action Script for loading a movie

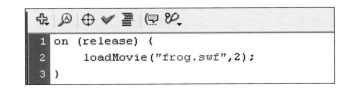

```
1  on (release) {
2      loadMovie("frog.swf",2);
3  }
```

Load a movie

1. Open fl11_4, then save it as **letterf**.

   TIP The steps use relative paths to load new movies. Make sure to copy the two movies you will load, fish.swf and frog.swf, to the same drive and folder where you save the Data File, letterf.fla.

2. Click the **Selection tool** on the Tools panel (if necessary), click the **fish button** to select it, then open the Actions panel.

3. Click the **Global Functions folder**, click the **Movie Clip Control folder**, double-click **on**, then double-click **release**.

4. Click after the opening curly bracket to set the insertion point, then press **[Enter]** (Win) or **[return]** (Mac) to add a blank line.

5. Double-click **loadMovie** in the Browser/Network folder in the Global Functions folder of the Actions panel.

6. Type **"fish.swf",0**, then compare your image to Figure 21.

   The 0 indicates the level.

7. Test the movie, click the **fish button**, then compare your image to Figure 22.

   The fish movie replaces the original movie.

   TIP If an error occurs, make sure that fish.swf is in the same location as letterf.fla.

8. Close the test movie window.

You specified that a new movie replace the currently playing movie in the Flash Player when the user clicks a button.

FIGURE 21
ActionScript to replace a movie with a new movie

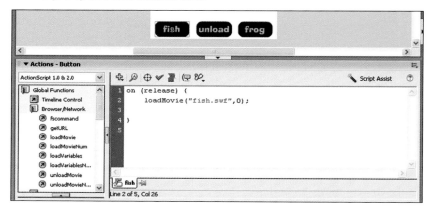

FIGURE 22
The fish movie loaded in place of the original movie

FIGURE 23

Setting the movie to load at Level 1

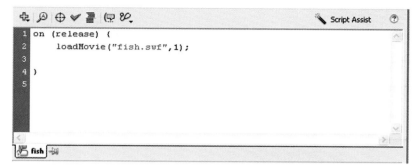

```
on (release) {
    loadMovie("fish.swf",1);

}
```

Set a level for a movie

1. Verify the **fish button** is still selected, double-click the **0** in line 2 of the script, then type **1**, as shown in Figure 23.

2. Test the movie, click the **fish button**, then compare your image to Figure 24.

   The 1 causes the fish movie to appear on top of the original movie.

3. Close the test movie window.

You set a level for a movie.

FIGURE 24

The fish movie loaded on top of the original movie

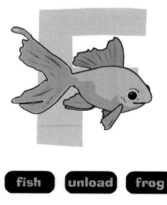

Stack movies

1. Click the **frog button** to select it.

2. Double-click **on** in the Movie Clip Control folder, then double-click **release**.

3. Click after the opening curly bracket to set the insertion point, then press **[Enter]** (Win) or **[return]** (Mac) to add a blank line.

4. Double-click **loadMovie** in the Browser/Network folder, then type **"frog.swf",2**.

5. Test the movie, click the **fish button**, click the **frog button**, then compare your image to Figure 25.

   Each movie appears on top of the original movie. No matter the order in which you click the buttons, the frog movie will always appear on top.

6. Close the test movie window.

You loaded two movies at different levels.

FIGURE 25
The fish movie loaded at Level 1 and the frog movie at Level 2

Referencing loaded movies in ActionScript

You can create a reference to the timeline of a loaded movie by including the level number of the movie. For example, to add a goto action that goes to Frame 10 of the movie loaded at Level 1, type _level1.gotoAndStop(10);

FIGURE 26

ActionScript to unload movies at Levels 1 and 2

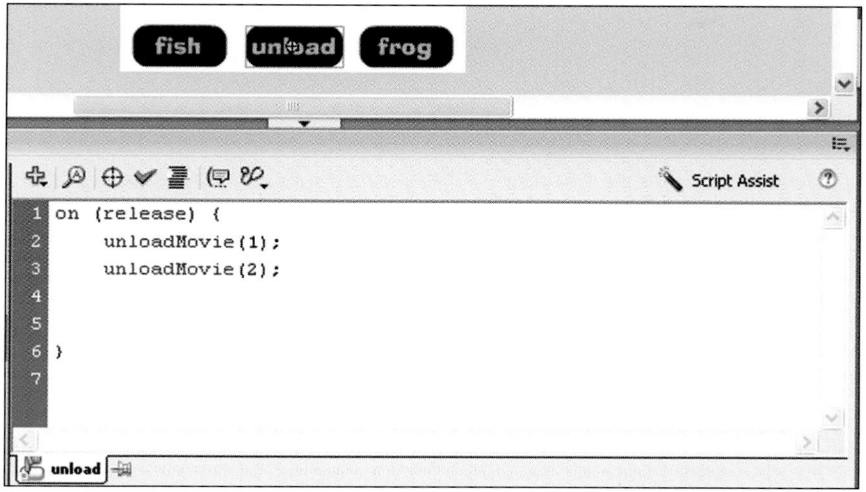

1. Click the **unload button** to select it.

2. Double-click **on** in the Movie Clip Control folder, then double-click **release**.

3. Click after the opening curly bracket to set the insertion point, then press **[Enter]** (Win) or **[return]** (Mac) to add a blank line.

4. Double-click **unloadMovie** in the Browser/ Network folder, then type **1**.

   This line of ActionScript removes the movie loaded at Level 1, which is fish.swf.

5. Click after the semi-colon in line 2, then press **[Enter]** (Win) or **[return]** (Mac) to add a blank line.

6. Double-click **unloadMovie** in the Browser/ Network folder, type **2**, then compare your Script pane to Figure 26.

   This line of ActionScript removes the movie loaded at Level 2, which is frog.swf.

7. Test the movie, clicking the **fish**, **frog**, and **unload buttons** in different sequences.

   The fish and frog movies both unload when you click the unload button.

8. Close the test movie window, save your work, then close the file.

You added actions to unload movies.

WORK WITH
CONDITIONAL ACTIONS

What You'll Do

 In this lesson, you will work with conditional actions and use ActionScript to duplicate movie clip symbols.

Using the else and else if actions

In Chapter 9, you used the *if* action to test for a condition. If the condition was true, the *if* action ran a series of actions enclosed in curly brackets. Otherwise, it skipped the actions in brackets and ran the next set of actions in the Script pane.

ActionScript also includes an *else* action you can use to create more sophisticated branching. An *else* action lets you specify one set of actions to run if a condition is true, and an alternate set to run if the condition is false. If a condition has more than two possible states, you can use *else if* to set up a series of possible branches. For example, if you are creating an online test, there might be four possible answers a student could provide, and you might want to create a different branch for each answer. Figure 27 shows ActionScript that uses *else if* to create multiple branches.

Creating conditional loops

A **loop** is an action or set of actions that repeat as long as a condition exists. Creating a loop can be as simple as taking a variable, assigning a value to it, executing a statement, and if the statement is false adding one to the variable and trying again. You can often just use an *if* action to create loops.

ActionScript includes other actions with which you can create more sophisticated conditional loops. The *for*, *while*, and *do while* loops all let you set up conditions for a loop and actions to run repeatedly. The *for* loop takes a series of arguments with which you set up a condition, a series of actions to take if the condition is true, and a counter that keeps track of the number of loops; this counter is often used in conjunction with the condition, for instance, to run the loop a user-specified number of times. The *while* and *do while* loops let you enter a series of actions to run while a condition is true. The difference is that *do while* runs the actions at least one time, then evaluates if the condition is true, where *while* evaluates the condition and then runs the actions. Figure 28 shows some examples of using ActionScript to create loops.

Duplicating movie clip symbol instances

An action frequently used with conditional loops is *duplicateMovieClip*. This action displays one of the more powerful abilities of ActionScript, which is to add and remove movie clip symbols as a movie is playing. The *duplicateMovieClip* creates a copy of a movie clip symbol instance; it includes arguments that let you specify a new instance name and a depth level at which to insert the new movie clip symbol (either in place of or on top of existing instances). You can then use the *setProperty* action or specific Properties actions (such as _x and _y) to change the location and appearance of the new instance of the movie clip symbol.

The *duplicateMovieClip* is often used in games to create multiple copies of an object based on a variable or user interaction—for example, a juggling game could ask a user how many balls they want to try to keep up in the air. Based on the answer, a looping action determines the number of times to run the duplicateMovieClip action.

QUICKTIP

There must already be an instance of the movie clip symbol on the stage for you to create duplicate instances. The new instance of the movie clip symbol always begins playing at the first frame.

FIGURE 27
ActionScript to create multiple branches

```
1  on (release) {
2      if (answer == A) {
3          gotoAndStop(2);
4      } else if (answer == B) {
5          gotoAndStop(3);
6      } else if (answer == C) {
7          gotoAndPlay(4);
8      }
9  }
```

If the user types the answer A in an input text box, the movie jumps to Frame 2; other answers jump to other frames

FIGURE 28
ActionScript to create loops

This for *loop increments the variable n a number of times specified by a separate variable named counter*

```
1  on (press) {
2      for (counter=0; counter<100; counter++) {
3          n++;
4      }
5  }
```

```
1  on (release) {
2      n = 0;
3      do {
4          (n++);
5      } while (n<100);
6  }
```

This do while *loop also increments a variable n, but repeats based on the value of n*

Create conditional branching using if and else actions

1. Open fl11_5.fla, save it as **branching**, then drag the **playhead** to view the three screens.

2. Click the **Selection tool** on the Tools panel (if necessary), click the **login button** on the stage to select it, then open the Actions panel.

3. Double-click **on** in the Movie Clip Control folder, then double-click **release**.

4. Click after the opening curly bracket to set the insertion point, then press **[Enter]** (Win) or **[return]** (Mac) to add a blank line.

5. Click the **Statements folder**, click the **Conditions/Loops folder**, then double-click **if**.

   The action appears in the Script pane without a condition set.

6. Type **pass == "letmein"**.

   "pass" is the variable for the input text field on the Super Secure Login page.

7. Click after the opening curly bracket to set the insertion point, then press **[Enter]** (Win) or **[return]** (Mac) to add a blank line.

8. Double-click **gotoAndStop** in the Timeline Control folder within the Global Functions folder, type **2**, then compare your screen to Figure 29.

9. Click following the semi-colon to set the insertion point, then press **[Enter]** (Win) or **[return]** (Mac) to add a blank line.

10. Double-click **else** in the Conditions/Loops folder within the Statements folder.

(continued)

FIGURE 29
Adding an if *action*

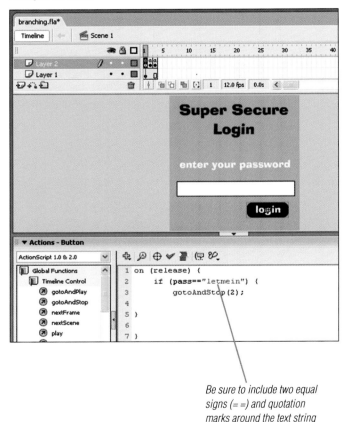

Be sure to include two equal signs (= =) and quotation marks around the text string

FIGURE 30
Adding an else action

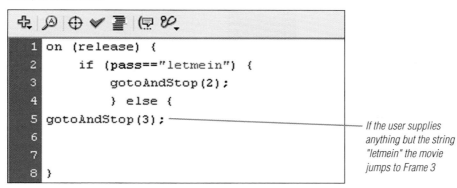

```
1  on (release) {
2      if (pass=="letmein") {
3          gotoAndStop(2);
4          } else {
5  gotoAndStop(3);
6
7
8  }
```

*If the user supplies
anything but the string
"letmein" the movie
jumps to Frame 3*

FIGURE 31
Entering the password to log in

11. Double-click **gotoAndStop** in the Timeline Control folder within the Global Functions folder, type **3**, then compare your Script pane to Figure 30.

12. Test the movie, type **xyz** for the password, then click the **login button**.

    The movie jumps to the "Access Denied" screen.

13. Close the test movie window, test the movie again, type **letmein** for the password, as shown in Figure 31, then click the **login button**.

    The movie jumps to the "Access Granted" screen.

14. Close the test movie window.

You used if and else actions to create a conditional branch that takes different actions based on user behavior (correct input of password).

Create a loop using if

1. Click **Frame 1** on Layer 2, click the beginning of Line 1 in the Script pane, then press **[Enter]** (Win) or **[return]** (Mac) to move the **stop()**; action to Line 2 and create a blank Line 1.

2. Click **Line 1** in the Script pane, then type **n = 0**; on the line, as shown in Figure 32.

   This line of ActionScript creates a variable named "n" and sets the value of the variable to 0.

3. Click a gray area on the stage to deselect all objects, click the **login button** to select it, click at the end of Line 4 in the Script pane of the Actions panel, then press **[Enter]** (Win) or **[return]** (Mac) to create a blank Line 5.

4. Type **n++**; on Line 5 in the Script pane, then press **[Enter]** (Win) or **[return]** (Mac).

   This line of ActionScript increments the variable n by one each time the else statement is processed—that is, each time the user provides the wrong password.

   (continued)

FIGURE 32
Creating a variable and setting the value to 0

FIGURE 33

Using an `if` *action to create a loop*

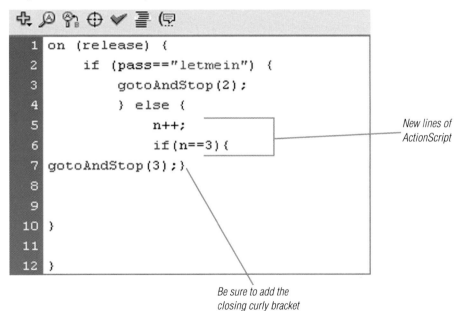

```
1  on (release) {
2      if (pass=="letmein") {
3          gotoAndStop(2);
4          } else {
5              n++;
6              if(n==3){
7  gotoAndStop(3);}}
8
9
10 }
11
12 }
```

New lines of
ActionScript

Be sure to add the
closing curly bracket

5. Type **if (n == 3) {** on Line 6 in the Script pane.

   This line of ActionScript creates a condition: the statements that follow the **if** action will only be processed when the variable n is equal to 3.

6. Click at the end of Line 7 in the Script pane, type **}**, then compare your Script pane to Figure 33.

   The closing curly bracket is necessary to complete the new if action.

7. Test the movie, type **xyz** for the password, then click the **login button**.

8. Type **abc**, then click the **login button**.

9. Type **123**, then click the **login button**.

   The movie jumps to the Access Denied screen only after the third attempt to log in.

10. Close the test movie window.

You used the if action to create a loop that, based on user behavior, repeats three times and then takes another action.

Add user feedback to the loop

1. Click the **Text tool A** on the Tools panel, then open the Property inspector.

2. Use the Property inspector to set the Font to **Arial**, the Font size to **14**, and the emphasis to **bold**.

3. Click the **Text type list arrow** ∨ , click **Dynamic Text**, click the **Show border around text icon** ▤ to deselect it, then draw a text box below the words "Super Secure Login," as shown in Figure 34.

4. Click the **Variable text box** in the Property inspector, type **feedback**, press **[Enter]** (Win) or **[return]** (Mac), then close the Property inspector.

5. Open the Actions panel, click the **Selection tool** ▸ on the Tools panel, click the **login button** to select it, click at the end of Line 5 in the Script pane, then press **[Enter]** (Win) or **[return]** (Mac) to create a blank Line 6.

6. Type **feedback = "Sorry. Tries left: "** + **(3-n);**, then press **[Enter]** (Win) or **[return]** (Mac).

   This line of ActionScript populates the dynamic text field named feedback with a text string and number. The number is calculated by subtracting 3 (the maximum number of tries) from the variable n, which is incrementally counting the number of attempts the user makes.

   | TIP Be sure to include a blank space after the colon and before the closing quotation mark.

   (continued)

Using Advanced ActionScript

FIGURE 34
Drawing the dynamic text box

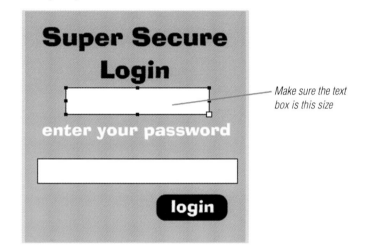

Make sure the text box is this size

FIGURE 35
ActionScript to provide user feedback

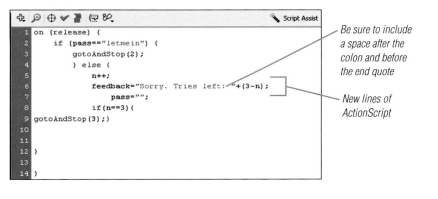

Be sure to include
a space after the
colon and before
the end quote

New lines of
ActionScript

FIGURE 36
Logging in with an incorrect password with user feedback

The **feedback = "Sorry. Tries
left: " + (3-n);** *ActionScript
statement populates the dynamic
text box*

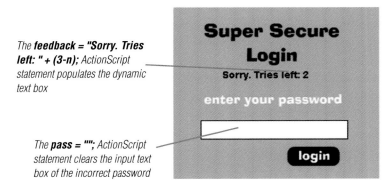

The **pass = "";** *ActionScript
statement clears the input text
box of the incorrect password*

7. Type **pass = ""**; on Line 7 in the Script pane,
   then compare your Script pane to Figure 35.

   This line of ActionScript clears the incorrect
   password the user has entered.

8. Test the movie, type **xyz** for the password,
   click the **login button**, as shown in Figure
   36, then repeat twice more using different
   passwords.

   The password screen provides feedback, and
   the movie jumps to the "Access Denied"
   screen only after the third attempt to enter
   the password.

9. Close the test movie window, then test the
   scene again by typing **letmein** and clicking
   the login button.

10. Save and close branching.fla.

*You added actions to provide user feedback as
part of a conditional loop.*

Using the Password line type in an input field

You may not want passwords to be visible onscreen as users enter them. For security,
you can set an input text field to display asterisks rather than the actual keystrokes
being typed by a user. To do this, display the Property inspector for the text field,
click the Line type list arrow, then click Password.

Create a while loop to duplicate movie clip symbols

1. Open fl11_6.fla, then save it as **duplicator**.

   This file contains an input text field with the variable name "amount" and the face movie clip symbol.

2. Click the **Selection tool** ![cursor] on the Tools panel (if necessary), then click the **duplicate button** to select it.

3. Click **Line 1** on the Script pane in the Actions panel, type **on (release) {** then press **[Enter]** (Win) or **[return]** (Mac).

   Figure 37 shows the ActionScript code you will be creating in the following steps. An explanation of the code follows each step.

4. Type **n = 0;** on Line 2, then press **[Enter]** (Win) or **[return]** (Mac).

   This line of ActionScript creates a variable, n, and sets its value to 0.

5. Type **while (n < amount) {** on Line 3, then press **[Enter]** (Win) or **[return]** (Mac).

   This line of ActionScript creates a `while` loop that takes the n variable and checks to see if it is less than the amount variable.

6. Type **duplicateMovieClip ("_root.face", "face_" + n, n);** on Line 4, then press **[Enter]** (Win) or **[return]** (Mac).

   This line of ActionScript runs as long as the while condition is true. It duplicates the face movie clip symbol instance, assigning it a name of the text string "face_" concatenated with the current value of the variable n, and putting it on a level determined by the current value of the variable n.

(continued)

FIGURE 37

ActionScript to create a loop to duplicate a movie clip symbol

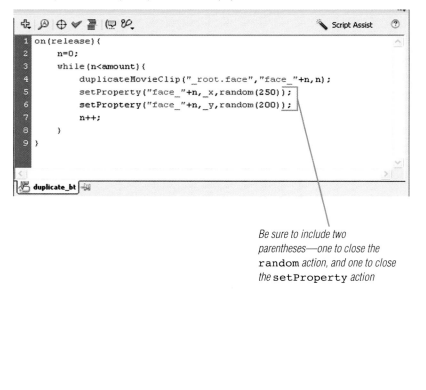

Be sure to include two parentheses—one to close the random *action, and one to close the* setProperty *action*

FIGURE 38

Ten duplicate instances of the movie clip symbol appear on the stage

Using the random action

The random action returns a random integer between 0 and one less than the value specified as an argument for the action. You can use random with setProperty to create unpredictable behavior for movie clip symbols or to generate random numbers for variables. When using random to position movie clip symbols, consider adding an offset value to keep the movie clip symbols from overlapping other objects on the screen. For example, setProperty("instance_" + n, _y, random(200)+130); adds 130 units to the random number generated for the Y coordinate of the new movie clip symbols.

7. Type **setProperty ("face_" + n, _x, random(250));** on Line 5, then press **[Enter]** (Win) or **[return]** (Mac).

   This line of ActionScript sets the x coordinate of the new instance to a random number between 0 and 249 (1 less than 250, which is the argument value for the random action).

8. Type **setProperty ("face_" + n, _y, random(200));** on Line 6, then press **[Enter]** (Win) or **[return]** (Mac).

   This line of ActionScript sets the y coordinate of the new instance to a random number between 0 and 199.

9. Type **n++;** on Line 7, then press **[Enter]** (Win) or **[return]** (Mac).

   This line of ActionScript increments the value of the n variable by 1.

10. Type **}** on Line 8, then press **[Enter]** (Win) or **[return]** (Mac).

11. Type **}** on Line 9, then compare your Script pane to Figure 37.

12. Test the movie, type **10** in the box next to the words "enter a number," click the **duplicate button**, then compare your image to Figure 38.

   The ActionScript loops 10 times, creating 10 instances of the movie clip symbol on the screen.

13. Close the test movie window, then save and close duplicator.fla.

14. Exit Flash.

You used a while action to create a loop that duplicates a movie clip symbol a number of times specified by a user.

Create complex interactivity.

1. Start Flash, open fl11_7.fla, then save it as **skillsdemo11**.
2. Click Frame 1 on the actions layer, open the Actions panel, then add a mouse.hide (); action on Line 1 in the Script pane to hide the mouse cursor. (*Hint*: Don't forget to include a semicolon at the end of the action and move the other actions down one line.)
3. Select the cross-hairs symbol on the stage, then open the Property inspector.
4. Assign the movie clip an instance name of **aim**, then close the Property inspector.
5. Open the Actions panel, then type **onClipEvent (enterFrame) {** on Line 1 in the Script pane to indicate the next set of actions should happen as soon as the movie clip instance displays, then add a new line.
6. Type **_root.aim._x = _root. _xmouse;** on Line 2 in the Script pane to set the x coordinate of the aim movie clip instance equal to the x coordinate of the hidden mouse pointer, then add a new line. (*Hint*: If a code hint menu appears, continue typing to dismiss the menu.)
7. Type **_root.aim._y = _root. _ymouse;** on Line 3 in the Script pane to set the y coordinate of the aim movie clip instance equal to the y coordinate of the hidden mouse pointer, then add a new line.

8. Type **}** (a closing curly bracket) on Line 4 in the Script pane.
9. Test the scene. (*Hint*: The game ends when the value in the "shots" box falls below 0.)
10. Save your work.

Use ActionScript to create external links.

1. Click Frame 51 on the actions layer, then select the More Games button.
2. Open the Movie Clip Control folder in the Actions Toolbox pane, double-click on, double-click release, click to set an insertion point after the opening curly bracket, then double-click getURL in the Browser/ Network folder in the Actions Toolbox pane.
3. Type **"http://www.macromedia.com"**, **"_self"** for the URL address and the Window.
4. Select the Comments? button on the stage, double-click on, double-click release, click to set an insertion point after the opening curly bracket, then double-click getURL in the Browser/ Network folder in the Actions Toolbox pane.
5. Type **"mailto:webmaster@server.com"**, **"_self"** as the URL link and the Window.
6. Save your work.

Load new movies.

1. Click Frame 1 on the actions layer, then select the Easy button on the stage.

2. Click at the end of Line 3 in the Script pane, press [Enter] (Win) or [return] (Mac), then double-click loadMovie from the Browser/ Network folder in the Actions Toolbox pane.
3. Type **"easy_level.swf",1** for the URL address for the movie to load and the Level. (*Hint*: The two movies you will load, easy_level.swf and hard_level.swf, must be in the same file location where you saved skillsdemo11.fla.)
4. Click the Hard button to select it.
5. Click at the end of Line 3 in the Script pane, press [Enter] (Win) or [return] (Mac), then double-click loadMovie from the Browser/ Network folder in the Actions Toolbox pane.
6. Type **"hard_level.swf",1** as the URL address for the movie to load and the level.
7. Click Frame 50 on the actions layer, click at the beginning of Line 1 in the Script pane, double-click unloadMovieNum from the Browser/ Network folder in the Actions Toolbox pane, then type **1**.
8. Preview the movie in your default browser from the File menu.
9. Close the browser window, then save your work.

Work with conditional actions.

1. Click Frame 51 on the actions layer, then switch to the Actions panel.

2. Click Line 1 in the Script pane, add a new line to move the stop (); action to Line 2, then click Line 1 again to begin adding actions.

3. Type **if (hits > 8) {** on Line 1 in the Script pane to set a condition, then press [Enter] (Win) or [return] (Mac).

4. Type **feedback = "You're a winner";}** on Line 2 in the Script pane to specify the actions to perform if the condition is true, then press [Enter] (Win) or [return] (Mac). (*Hint*: "feedback" is the variable name of a dynamic text box on this screen.)

5. Type **else {** on Line 3 in the Script pane to perform different actions when the if condition is not true, then press [Enter] (Win) or [return] (Mac).

6. Type **feedback = "Better luck next time";}** on Line 4 in the Script pane to specify the alternate actions.

7. Test the scene.

8. Compare your image to Figure 39, save your work, then close skillsdemo11.fla.

9. Exit Flash.

FIGURE 39
Completed Skills Review

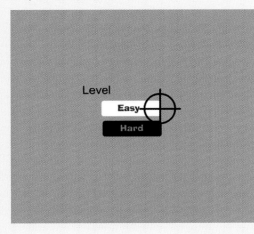

Ultimate Tours would like you to build a banner for their Web site which, when a button on the banner is clicked, will load a new movie containing their latest travel specials. By creating the banner in one SWF file and the specials in another, Ultimate Tours can update the specials at any time, just by replacing one file. As a way to encourage users to look at and interact with the banner, they would also like you to create an input text field in the banner which, when the user types in the name of a city and clicks a button, displays a page from *www.weather.com* with the current weather for that location.

1. Open fl11_8, then rename the file **ultimatetours11**.

2. Select the see specials button, then open the Actions panel.
3. Add actions which, upon a click of the button, load a new movie called **specials.swf** at Level 1. (*Hint*: Use the on (release) and loadMovieNum action to create this effect. The specials.swf movie must be in the same file location where you saved ultimate-tours11.fla.)
4. Click Frame 1 on the content layer, click the Text Tool on the Tools panel, then draw an input text box beneath the text that reads, "Traveling? Type a city name to check the weather:" Use these settings: color of black, font of Times New Roman, font size of 14, Bold, with a border displayed around text. Assign the new input text box a variable name of **where**.

5. Select the get weather button, then in the Script pane of the Actions panel add a getURL action which, upon a click of the button, uses the GET method to send variables to a CGI script with a URL of **"http://www.weather.com/search/search"**. The new Web site should open in the current browser window.
6. Test the movie, click the see specials button to load the new movie, then type a city name and click the get weather button.
7. Save your work, then compare your image to Figure 40.

FIGURE 40

Sample completed Project Builder 1

You have volunteered to use Macromedia Flash to create an interactive, educational counting game that will get first-graders comfortable with computers. The game will display a random number of cookies spilled from a cookie jar, ask students to count the cookies and type the number, and then give feedback on whether or not the answer is correct.

1. Open fl11_9.fla, then save it as **counting_game11**.
2. Click Frame 1 on the content layer, then create an input text box with a variable named **check** above the go button that is big enough to accommodate a two-digit number. Settings: Arial, 16 pt, black, with a border displayed around the text.
3. Click Frame 2 on the content layer, then create a dynamic text box with a variable named **score** that fills the area above the cookie jar image. Use these settings: Arial, 24 pt, black, Multiline line type.
4. Copy the dynamic text box named score from Frame 2 of the content layer to the same location in Frame 3 of the content layer.
5. Select the cookie movie clip symbol in Frame 1 on the content layer, open the Property inspector, then assign it an instance name of **cookies**.
6. Select the start button in Frame 1 on the content layer, then add ActionScript which, upon a click of the button, does the following:
   - Creates a variable named value and sets it to a random number between 1 and 5

- Creates a variable named n, and sets its value to 0
- Creates a loop using the while action, which says that while the variable named n is less than the variable named value, duplicate the cookie movie clip symbol, name the new instance with the word "cookie," an underscore, and the value of the variable n, and set the new instance at a depth of the value of the variable n. The while loop should also use two SetProperty actions to set the location of the new movie clip instance: the x coordinate should be set to a random number between 1 and 200, with an offset of 10, and the Y coordinate should be set to a random number between 1 and 100, with an offset of 250.
- Increments the value of the variable n by 1

7. Select the go button in Frame 1 of the content layer, then add ActionScript that, upon a click of the button, does the following:
   - Uses the if action to check if the number in the variable named check is equal to the number in the variable named value and, if so, jumps to Frame 2 and populates the dynamic text box named score with the words "**Good job, the number of cookies that spilled is**" and then the variable named value.

- Uses the else action to perform the following actions when the condition is not true: jump to Frame 3 and populate the dynamic text box named score with the words "**No, that's not right. The number of cookies that spilled is** " and then the variable named value.

8. Test the movie, compare your image to Figure 41, then save your work.

FIGURE 41
Sample completed Project Builder 2

Figure 42 shows a page from a Web site created using Macromedia Flash. Study the figure and complete the following. For each question, indicate how you determined your answer.

1. Connect to the Internet, go to *www.course.com*, navigate to the page for this book, click the Online Companion link, then click the link for this chapter.

2. Open a document in a word processor or open a new Macromedia Flash document, save the file as **dpc11**, then answer the following questions. (*Hint*: Use the Text tool in Macromedia Flash.)

   ■ What is the purpose of this site? Does the design of the site contribute to its purpose?

   ■ Move the mouse pointer around the screen and note the different effects as you pass over links and buttons. Do you think these effects were achieved with ActionScript, or some other way?

   ■ Click the links in the main navigation bar. What changes occur on the screen? Do you think the links are jumping to a different frame in this movie, or loading a new movie? What specific actions could be used to achieve this effect?

   ■ List some of the advantages of loading a new movie for links, in the context of this site.

■ Click the Portfolio link, then click the Launch button for the featured Web site. What happens? What specific actions might be associated with the Launch button to achieve this effect?

■ Click the Contact button near the top of the screen, then click the Sales button to display a form. There is a field to enter your contact information including an e-mail address. Also, there is a Send button. What do you think happens when you press the Send button? What specific actions might be involved in the processing of the e-mail information?

FIGURE 42
Design Project

You have decided to create a portfolio with five screens, each in a separate frame and on a separate layer. One screen contains examples of the Macromedia Flash work you have done throughout this book, and one creates a password-protected clients-only area. You will create the links to your Macromedia Flash movies by loading new SWF files. You can use your favorites from the files you have developed throughout this book, or any other SWF files you have created on your own.

1. Open a new Flash document, then save it as **portfolio11**.

2. Create a screen with a title of **home** in Frame 1 of a layer called Home Page. Add another layer named **Navigation-buttons** and create 3 buttons named home, flash examples, and clients only.

3. Create a screen in Frame 2 of a layer called **Flash Samples**, using a format that fits in visually with the rest of your site. On this screen include a title and at least three buttons, each of which, when clicked, loads a new Flash movie at Level 1. (*Hint*: New movies appear starting in the upper-left corner of the current movie. You may need to reduce the size of your SWF files or change the location of your navigation buttons to achieve the effect you want.)

4. Create a screen in Frame 3 of a layer called **Clients Only**. On this screen, create text that reads "Enter password," and then create an input text box with the variable name **password**.

5. Create another screen that says, **Welcome to the client's area.**

6. Create another screen that says, **Sorry, that is not correct. Please contact me to receive or verify your password.** Then add a button to the page which, when clicked, opens the user's default e-mail program to a new mail message with your e-mail address filled in.

7. On the Clients Only screen that prompts for a password, create a button with the text **Submit**. Open the Actions panel, then set up a conditional action which, if the user types the word "password" in the input text box, jumps to the "welcome" screen, or, if the user types anything else, jumps to the "sorry" screen.

8. Add actions to the buttons on the home screen which, when clicked, jumps to the new Flash Samples and Clients Only screens.

9. Add an unloadMovieNum(1) action to each navigation button on the "Flash Samples screen" that jumps to a new screen. (*Hint*: If you don't add this action, the movies you load on the Flash Samples screen will remain loaded, even when you navigate away from the Flash Samples screen.)

10. Test the movie, then compare your movie to Figure 43.

11. Save your work.

FIGURE 43
Sample completed Portfolio Project

chapter

WORKING WITH BEHAVIORS
AND COMPONENTS

1. Work with Behaviors.

2. Work with Components.

12 WORKING WITH BEHAVIORS
AND COMPONENTS

Introduction

Completion of an effective Macromedia Flash application depends on several factors, including the nature of the application (straightforward versus complex), the allotted development time, and the developer's expertise. Macromedia Flash provides two features, Behaviors and Components, that enable developers to speed up the development process and create effective applications without writing ActionScript code.

Behaviors

In previous chapters, you learned how to use ActionScript to add control, interactivity, and multimedia to an application. Using Behaviors, you can quickly and easily incorporate these features into your application. **Behaviors** are blocks of prewritten ActionScript code that you can apply by using pop-up menus and dialog boxes without having to write the ActionScript code yourself. For example, you can create a button and then use a Behavior to apply a gotoAndPlay action to the button.

Tools You'll Use

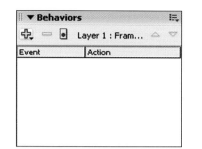

Load Sound from Library

Type the linkage ID of the sound in the library to play:

Type a name for this sound instance for later reference:

☑ Play this sound when loaded

[OK]   [Cancel]

Properties	Parameters	Filters

Component
<Instance Name>

W: 100.0   X: 223.3
H: 100.0   Y: 187.3

autoLoad	true
contentPath	
scaleContent	true

Goto and Play at frame or label

Choose the movie clip that you want to begin playing:

this

🎬 _root

⦿ Relative   ○ Absolute

Enter the frame number or frame label at which the movie clip should start
playing. To start from the beginning, type '1':

1

[OK]   [Cancel]

Macromedia Flash has several built-in Behaviors that you can use as you develop an application. These built-in Behaviors are for the most common types of functions, such as jumping to a frame, playing a sound, or linking to a Web site. Other Behaviors are available from third-party companies and independent developers; some are free and others must be purchased. The Macromedia Web site is one source for obtaining third-party Behaviors. While many of the more common functions can be incorporated using built-in Behaviors, more complex interactions require a knowledge of ActionScript.

Components

Components are another time saving feature of Macromedia Flash. There are three categories of components:

- **User interface (UI)**—components (such as buttons and menus) that are used to create the visual interface for a Flash application
- **Media**—components used to add streaming video to a Flash application
- **Data**—components used to connect to a data source, download data to a Flash application, and update the data remotely

Components are commonly used for creating check boxes, drop-down menus, and forms with boxes for entering user data such as name and address. You can quickly add functionality to a movie by dragging and dropping Components (predeveloped movie clips) from the Components panel to the stage.

As with Behaviors, you are not required to enter ActionScript code when using Components. When you select a Component to use, it is placed in the Library panel for reuse in another part of the movie.

In addition to the Components provided in Flash, you can obtain other Components from third-party companies and individuals. Often these are mini-applications, such as calendars, photo galleries, and pre-loaders that add functionality to a Flash movie.

Behaviors and Components can work together. For example, you can add a button Component to the stage and then apply a Behavior to the button that creates a link to an external Web site. Figure 1 shows several pages of a Web site. Each page has one or more Components and/or Behaviors.

FIGURE 1

Web pages with Components and Behaviors

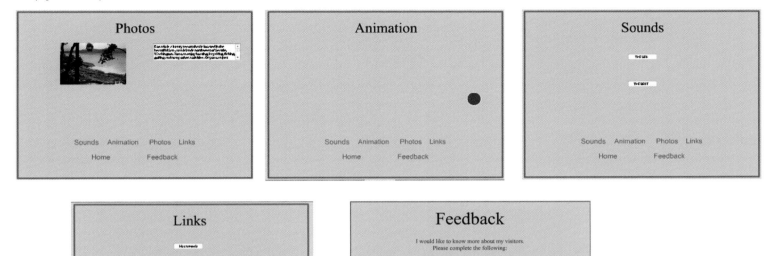

WORK WITH
BEHAVIORS

What You'll Do

 In this lesson, you will learn how to use Behaviors to create a button link.

Using Behaviors

A Behavior, like any ActionScript, can be linked to an instance of an object, such as a button (which is a movie clip), or placed on a frame. If the Behavior is placed on a frame, the ActionScript is run when the playhead gets to the frame. If the Behavior is linked to an object, the ActionScript is run when a particular event occurs that triggers the Behavior. For example, a Behavior assigned to a button could be triggered by a button click (event). Therefore, when working with Behaviors assigned to an object, you must specify the event.

To use Behaviors, first you must select the frame or object instance that the Behavior will be applied to. Then you select the desired Behavior from the Behaviors panel and complete any dialog boxes that appear. For example, if you want to use the Behaviors feature to assign a gotoAndPlay script to a button, you would first select the button on the stage and then open the Behaviors panel. Figure 2 shows the Behaviors panel with the drop-down menu listing the categories of Behaviors. The Movieclip category is selected and the "Goto and Play at frame or label" behavior is selected from the submenu. After making a choice from the submenu, a dialog box appears allowing you to specify the movie clip and frame to begin playing when the event (click) occurs. The ActionScript, as shown in Figure 3, is automatically assigned to the button. In this case, when the user clicks the button ("release"), the playhead goes to frame 1 of the current timeline ("this" indicates the current timeline).

The default event that triggers the script is click, however you can specify a different event such as pressing a key. Behaviors can be edited or deleted using the Behaviors panel, and the ActionScript they create can be edited using the Actions panel.

The Behaviors panel with the category list and submenu displayed

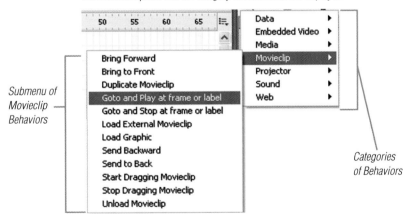

Submenu of
Movieclip
Behaviors

Categories
of Behaviors

The ActionScript developed using Behaviors

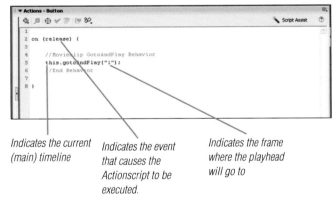

Indicates the current (main) timeline

Indicates the event that causes the Actionscript to be executed.

Indicates the frame where the playhead will go to

Set up the workspace

1. Start Macromedia Flash.

2. Open **fl12_1.fla** from the drive and folder where your Data Files are stored, then save it as **portfolio**.

3. Click **Control** on the menu bar, then click **Test Movie**.

4. Click each of the **navigation text buttons** at the bottom of the screen.

   This is a basic Web site with simple screen headings. There is no content except for the Feedback form, which has several text boxes. The Home button has not been completed.

5. Click **File** on the menu bar, then click **Close** to close the Flash Player window.

6. Click **Window** on the menu bar, then click **Hide Panels**.

7. Drag the **timeline border** down to reveal the navigation layer, as shown in Figure 4.

8. Using the Windows menu, open the following panels: **Tools, Properties, Library, Actions, Behaviors**, and **Components**.

9. Click the ▼ arrow in the title bar of each panel to collapse all panels except the Tools panel.

(continued)

FIGURE 4
Dragging the timeline border to display the layers

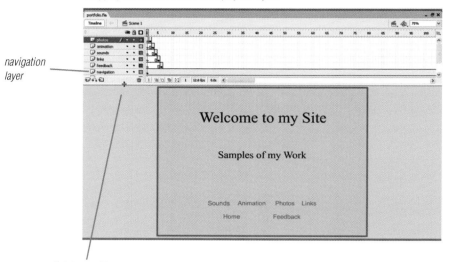

navigation layer

Pointer used to drag the border

FIGURE 5
The configured workspace

Layer for
each screen

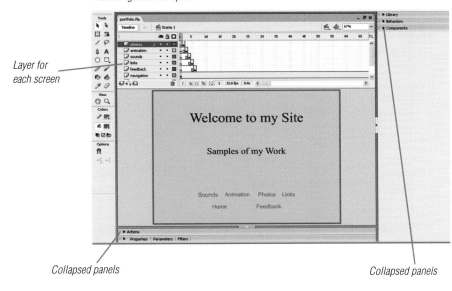

Welcome to my Site

Samples of my Work

Sounds   Animation   Photos   Links
Home   Feedback

Collapsed panels

Collapsed panels

You may need to move the panels by dragging the panel move icon ⫶ located in the title bar of each panel. You can dock (attach) panels to each other by dragging one on top of the other.

10. Click **View** on the menu bar, point to **Magnification**, then click **Fit in Window**.

Your screen should resemble Figure 5.

11. Look at the timeline and notice there is a layer for each of the screens.

12. Drag the **playhead** to view each frame from Frame 1 to 6 and notice how the objects on the stage change.

13. Save the file to save the changes to your workspace.

You configured the workspace by displaying and arranging panels and setting the magnification. You then viewed each frame of the movie.

Use Behaviors to create a button link

1. Click **Home** to select this text button.

2. Expand the **Behaviors panel**, then click the **Add Behavior button** ✣ to display the options.

3. Point to **Movieclip**, then click **Goto and Play at frame or label**.

   A dialog box appears, as shown in Figure 6, allowing you to specify the movie clip to begin playing when the event (click) occurs and to specify the frame number for the movie clip. In this case, the movie clip to be played is main (_root) timeline. Frame 1 is the default; this is the frame you want displayed when the user clicks the Home button.

4. Click **OK**.

5. Click **Control** on the menu bar, then click **Test Movie**.

6. Click **Photos**, then click **Home**.

(continued)

FIGURE 6
Specifying the movie clip and frame to play

Goto and Play at frame or label

Choose the movie clip that you want to begin playing:

`this`

📷 _root

◉ Relative   ○ Absolute

Enter the frame number or frame label at which the movie clip should start playing. To start from the beginning, type '1':

`1`

[OK] [Cancel]

Default frame

Working with Behaviors and Components

7. When you are done, close the Flash Player window.

8. Verify **Home** is selected, then expand the Actions panel.

9. If necessary, click the **Hide/Display arrow** to display the Actionscript code.

10. Study the ActionScript code that was automatically created using the Movieclip Behavior.

11. Collapse the Actions panel.

12. Save your work.

You used Behaviors to create a link for the Home button.

WORK WITH COMPONENTS

What You'll Do

Sounds

THE SEA

THE BEAT

Sounds   Animation   Photos   Links

Home   Feedback

In this lesson, you will learn how to use Components and Behaviors to load external graphics and animations, play sounds, link to external Web sites, and create forms.

Using Components

Figure 7 shows the Component panel expanded and the list of available User Interface Components displayed. Each Component name and icon provides a clue to its type, such as Button, CheckBox, and ScrollPane. Many of the User Interface Components are used to create forms that can gather data from a user. Some, such as the Loader Component, are used to display content. The Loader Component can load external jpg graphic files and swf movie files. The files do not have to be in the Library panel or on the stage in the original movie. They are loaded when the movie is running. This can reduce the size of the movie and allow for easy update of Web site content by simply changing the jpg or swf files on the external site.

Depending on the type of Component used, you will need to specify one or more of the following parameters:

- contentPath—This parameter is used to specify the location (server, directory, folder, etc.) for the content that is to be displayed using the Component. For example, when using the Loader component, if the jpg file is not located in the same folder as the movie file, a path to the jpg file needs to be specified.
- scaleContent—This parameter can be set to true or false. If it is set to true,

the content will automatically resize (reduced or enlarged but not cropped) to the size of the component. For example, a Loader Component has a default size of 100px by 100px. If a graphic with dimensions of 50px by 50px is loaded, the graphic will expand to the larger size. If it is set to false, the component will be scaled to the size of the graphic.

- autoLoad—This parameter can be set to true or false. If it is set to true, the Component will automatically display the specified contents. If it is set to false, the contents will not be displayed until some other action, such as a button click, occurs.

- label—This parameter allows you to type a text label. For example, you could label a button Component Contact us. The text appears on the button graphic.

To use a Component, you first select the frame and layer where the Component will be placed, then drag the Component from the Component panel to the desired location on the stage. To complete the process, you use the Parameters option within the Property inspector panel to set the Component parameters.

FIGURE 7

The Component panel with the User Interface Component displayed

Use Behaviors and Components to create links to Web sites

1. Verify that the portfolio.fla file is open in Flash, then click **Frame 5** of the links layer.

2. Expand the **Components panel**, then click the **User Interface expand icon** ⊞ (Win) to display the UI components, if necessary.

3. Drag a **Button component** to the stage and position it below the Links heading.

4. Click **Parameters** in the Property inspector, click **Button**, then type **Macromedia**, as shown in Figure 8.

5. Expand the **Behaviors panel** if (necessary), click the **Add Behavior button** ⊹ , point to **Web**, then click **Go to Web Page**.

   Verify http://www.macromedia.com is specified for the url, and "**_self**" is specified for the Open in option, as shown in Figure 9.

6. Click **OK**.

7. Drag a second **Button component** to the stage and position it below the first button.

8. Repeat steps 4 through 7 changing the label to **FAVORITE SITE**, the URL to a site of your choice, and the Open in option to "**_blank**".

(continued)

FIGURE 8
Setting the parameters for the button

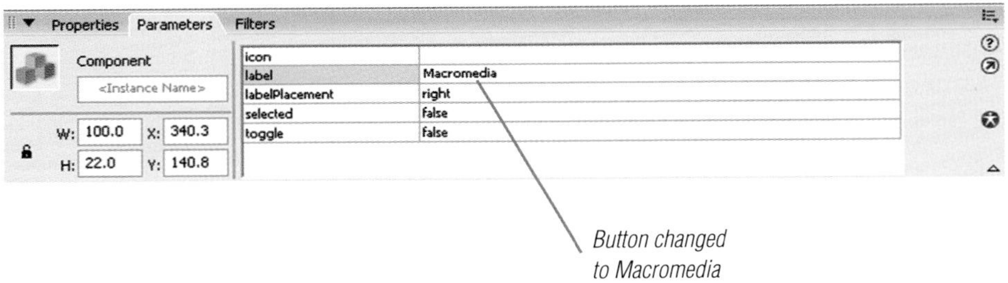

Button changed
to Macromedia

FIGURE 9

The completed dialog box for the Behavior settings to link to a Web page

The Open in option allows you to specify the browser window where the Web page will be displayed. The "_self" option will display the Web page in the current browser window, replacing the Flash swf movie. The "_blank" option will display the Web page in a new browser window, separate from the one displaying the Flash swf movie.

9. Click **File** on the menu bar, point to **Publish Preview**, then click **Default – (HTML)**.

   The Web page appears in a browser window.

10. Click **Links**.

11. Click the **Macromedia button**.

   Note: A security message may appear requiring you to specify the connection to the URL (*http://www.macromedia.com*) as a safe operation. Read the message, then follow the instructions. When done, close your browser and redo the Publish Preview feature from Flash.

12. Click the **Back button** on your browser to return to the Portfolio site.

13. Click **FAVORITE SITE**.

14. View the Web site, then close the browser window to return to the Portfolio site.

15. Close the browser window for the Portfolio site.

16. Save your work.

You used Components and Behaviors to create buttons that link to external Web pages.

Use Components to load graphics

1. Click **Frame 2** on the photos layer.

2. Drag a **Loader Component** from the Components panel to the left side of the stage, as shown in Figure 10.

3. Click the **contentPath text box** on the Parameters tab of the Property Inspector panel, then type **rosario.jpg**.

    The rosario.jpg file should be in the same folder as the portfolio.fla file. If it is not, the complete path to the rosario.jpg file needs to be specified.

4. Verify that autoLoad is set to **true**.

5. Click the **scaleContent text box**, which is set to true, click the **scale content list arrow**, then click **false**.

    The Parameters tab on the Property inspector panel should resemble Figure 11.

You placed a Loader Component on the stage and changed the parameters to have it scale to the size of the graphic. You also specified the graphic to be loaded.

FIGURE 10
Positioning the Loader Component on the stage

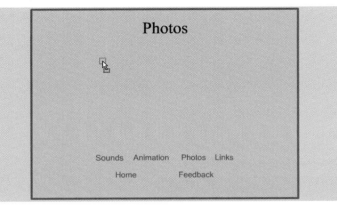

FIGURE 11
The completed parameters settings for the Loader Component

The X and Y coordinates on your screen may differ

FIGURE 12
The rosario.txt in a text editor

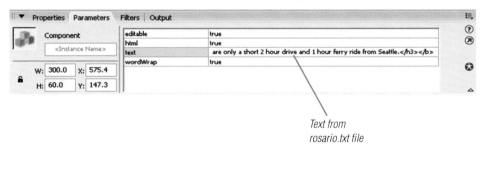

FIGURE 13
The text pasted into the text line in the Parameters tab

Text from
rosario.txt file

Use Components to load text

1. Drag a **TextArea** component from the Components panel to the stage and position it to the right of the loader.

2. Using the Parameters tab in the Property inspector panel, set editable, html, and wordWrap to **true**.

3. Double-click the **width (W:) text box**, type **300**, press **[Tab]** to select the **height (H:) text box**, type **60**, then press **[Enter]**.

4. Navigate to the drive and folder where your Data Files are stored, then double-click **rosario.txt** to open the file in a text editor, as shown in Figure 12.

   TIP If the text appears on one long line in Notepad, click Format on the menu bar, then click WordWrap.

   Notice there is some html coding <h3> and <b>, which is used to format the text.

5. Use the text editor menu commands to copy all the text.

6. Return to the Flash document, click in the **text text box** on the Parameters tab of the Property inspector panel, press and hold **[Ctrl]**, then press **[v]** (Win) **[or]** **[command] [v]** (Mac) to paste the text into the text line, as shown in Figure 13.

7. Click **Control** on the menu bar, then click **Test Movie**.

8. Click **Photos**, then drag the scroll buttons to read all the text in the text box.

   Note: If the text box overlaps the photo, you can adjust the position of either object.

   (continued)

9. When you are done, close the test movie window, then save your work.

You used the TextArea component to display text by copying the text to the Parameters tab of the Property inspector panel.

Use Components to load an animation (.swf file)

1. Click **Frame 3** of the animation layer.

2. Drag a **Loader component** from the Components panel to the stage and position it below the heading Animation.

3. On the Parameters tab of the Property inspector panel, verify that **autoLoad** is set to **true**.

4. Click in the **contentPath text box**, then type **animation.swf**.

   The animation.swf file should be in the same folder as the portfolio.fla file. If it is not, the complete path to the animation.swf file needs to be specified.

5. Set **scaleContent** to **false**, as shown in Figure 14.

6. Click **Control** on the menu bar, then click **Test Movie**.

7. Click **Animation**.

8. When you are done, close the test movie window, then save your work.

You used a Loader Component to display a .swf file by specifying the autoLoad, contentPath, and scaleContent parameters.

FIGURE 14

The Parameters tab of the Property inspector panel with the completed parameter settings

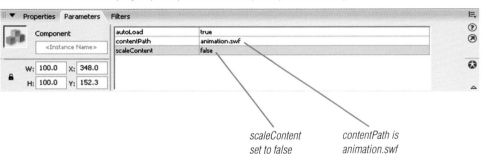

scaleContent set to false

contentPath is animation.swf

FIGURE 15
The completed Linkage Properties dialog box

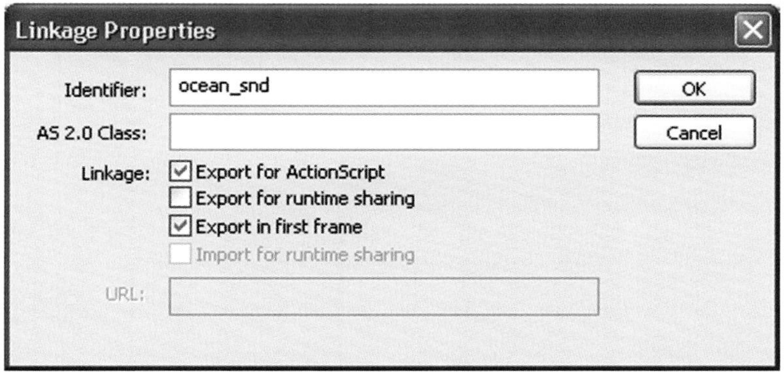

Linkage Properties

Identifier:	ocean_snd
AS 2.0 Class:	
Linkage:	☑ Export for ActionScript
	☐ Export for runtime sharing
	☑ Export in first frame
	☐ Import for runtime sharing
URL:	

OK
Cancel

FIGURE 16
The completed dialog box for playing a sound from the Library panel

Load Sound from Library

Type the linkage ID of the sound in the library to play:

ocean_snd

Type a name for this sound instance for later reference:

ocean_snd

☑ Play this sound when loaded

OK   Cancel

Use Components and Behaviors to load a sound from the Library panel

1. Click **Frame 4** on the sounds layer.

2. Drag a **Button** component from the Components panel to the stage and position it below the heading.

3. On the Parameters tab of the Property inspector panel, change the label to **THE SEA**.

4. Expand the **Library panel**, then click the **sounds folder** to expand it, if necessary.

5. Right-click (Win) or [ctrl] click (Mac) **ocean.wav**, then click **Linkage**.

6. Click the **Export for ActionScript check box**, then type **ocean_snd** as the identifier, as shown in Figure 15.

   For a sound to be loaded from the Library panel, it needs to be made available through a process called linkage. The sound is selected in the Library panel and, using the Linkage dialog box, an identifier is specified. The identifier is used in the ActionScript (which is created using the Load Sound from Library Behavior) to cause the sound to play when the button is clicked.

7. Click **OK**.

8. Expand the **Behaviors panel** (if necessary), click the **Add Behavior button** ⊕ , point to **Sound**, then click **Load Sound from Library**.

9. Type **ocean_snd**, press **[Tab]**, type **ocean_snd**, as shown in Figure 16, then click **OK**.

You used a Button Component and a Behavior to set up a sound to be loaded from the Library panel.

Use Components and Behaviors to add a streaming sound

1. Drag a second **Button component** to the stage and position it below the first button.

2. In the Parameters tab of the Property inspector panel, change the label to **THE BEAT**.

3. Click the **Add Behavior button** ⊕ on the Behaviors panel, point to **Sound**, then click **Load streaming MP3 file**.

4. Type **thebeat.mp3** as the URL, press **[Tab]**, then type **thebeat_snd** for the instance name, as shown in Figure 17.

   MP3 sound files can be loaded dynamically into a Flash movie as it is running—a process called streaming. The MP3 file does not have to be in the Library panel or on the stage. The process is to select the object (such as a button) that will cause the sound to stream, then use the Load streaming MP3 file Behavior to identify the file name (and path, if necessary), as well as specifying an instance name. The instance name is used in the ActionScript that causes the sound to stream.

5. Click **OK**.

6. Click **Control** on the menu bar, click **Test Movie**, then click **Sounds**.

7. Click **THE SEA button** and listen to the sounds.

8. When you are done, click **THE BEAT** button and listen to the sounds.

9. When you are done, close the test movie window, then save your work.

You used a Button Component and a Behavior to add a streaming sound.

FIGURE 17
The completed dialog box for specifying a MP3 file to stream

FIGURE 18

Changing a label in the Parameters tab of the Property inspector panel

▼ Properties	Parameters	Filters	
Component	data		
	groupName	radioGroup	
<Instance Name>	label	F	
	labelPlacement	right	
W: 100.0 X: 263.8	selected	false	
H: 22.0 Y: 218.3			

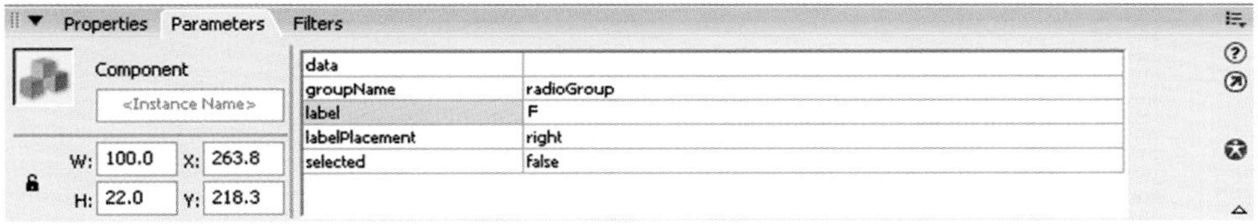

Use Components to create a form

1. Click **Frame 6** of the feedback layer.

2. Drag a **RadioButton** from the Component panel and position it next to **Sex**.

3. Change the label in the Parameters tab of the Property inspector panel to **F**, as shown in Figure 18.

4. Repeat steps 2 and 3 to add a second RadioButton with the label set to **M**.

5. Drag a **ComboBox** from the Component panel and position it next to **Age**.

6. In the Parameters tab of the Property inspector panel, double-click **[]** on the labels line.

    The **Values dialog box** opens.

7. Click the **Add value button** ➕, click **defaultValue**, then type **under 20**.

8. Click the **Add value button** ➕, click **defaultValue**, then type **21 – 40**.

9. Click the **Add value button** ➕, click **defaultValue**, then type **41 – 60**.

(continued)

10. Click the **Add value button** ✚, click **defaultValue**, then type **over 60**.

Your screen should resemble Figure 19.

11. Click **OK**.

12. Drag a **CheckBox** from the Component panel and position it below **How did you hear about my site?**

13. Change the label in the Parameters tab of the Property inspector panel to **Search**.

14. Repeat steps 12 and 13 to add three more check boxes for **Surfing, Friend,** and **Other,** as shown in Figure 20.

15. Drag a **TextInput** component from the Component panel to the stage and position it next to Comments.

(continued)

FIGURE 19
The completed Combobox Values settings

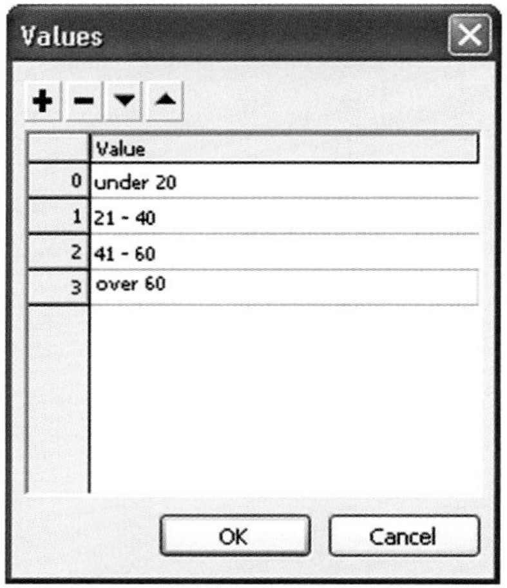

FIGURE 20
The completed Checkboxes

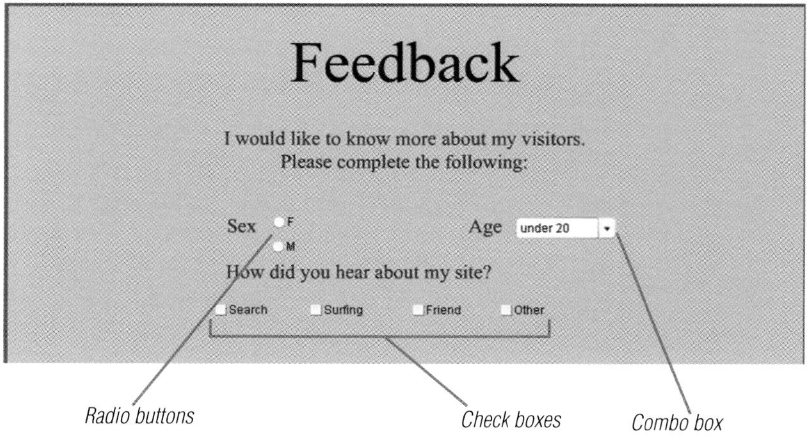

Radio buttons   Check boxes   Combo box

Working with Behaviors and Components

FIGURE 21
The completed form

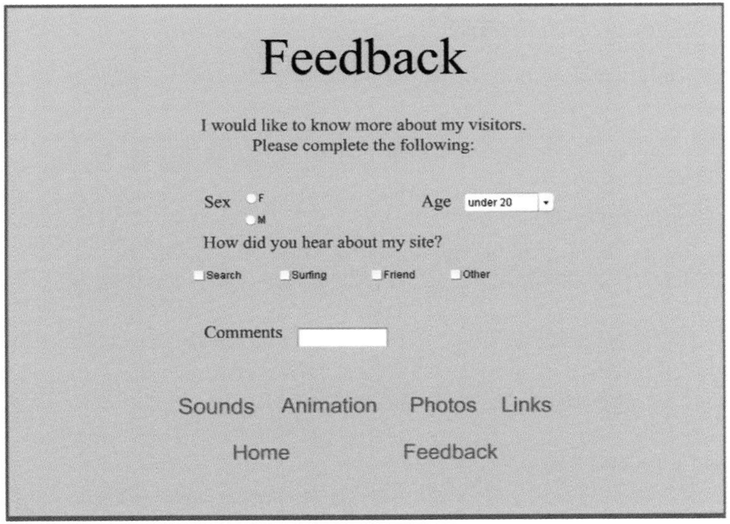

16. Verify that **editable** is set to **true** in the Parameters tab of the Property inspector.

    Your screen should resemble Figure 21.

17. Click **Control** on the menu bar, then click **Test Movie**.

18. Click **Feedback**, then fill in the form.

    Notice that you can only select one radio button, and you can only select one option from the list in the combo box. You can select as many check boxes as you want, and you can type freely in the comments text input box.

19. When you are done, close the test movie window.

20. Save your work, then exit Flash.

You used Components to create a form.

Use Behaviors to create a button link.

1. Start Flash, open fl12_2.fla, then save it as **skillsdemo12**.
2. Click Home to select this text button.
3. Display the Behaviors panel.
4. Click the Add Behavior Button, point to Movieclip, then click Goto and Play at frame or label.
5. Verify that the main (_root) timeline is specified in the dialog box and **1** is specified for the frame number, then click OK.
6. Save your work.

Use Behaviors and Components to create a Web link.

1. Select Frame 2 of the Web links layer.
2. Display the Components panel, expand the User Interface folder, then drag a Button component to the middle of the stage.
3. Display the Parameters tab in the Property inspector panel, then change the label to **My School**.
4. Click the Add Behavior button in the Behaviors panel, point to Web, then click Go to Web Page.
5. Type in the URL for your school, change the Open in option to _blank, then click OK to close the dialog box.
6. Click File on the menu bar, point to Publish Preview, then click Default–(HTML).
7. Click the button for the links to Web sites option, then click the My School button.

8. Close your browser and display the Flash document.
9. Save your work.

Use Components to load graphics.

1. Select Frame 3 of the loading graphics and text layer.
2. Drag a Loader component to the left side of the stage.
3. Set the width to **200** and the height to **200**.
4. Click the contentPath text box on the Parameters tab of the Property inspector panel, then type **kayaking.jpg**.
5. Verify that autoLoad and scaleContent are set to true.
6. Verify that the kayaking.jpg file is in the same folder as the skillsdemo12.fla file.
7. Save your work.

Use Components to load text.

1. Drag a TextArea component to the stage and position it to the right of the loader.
2. Using the Parameters tab in the Property inspector panel, set editable, html, and wordWrap to true.
3. Change the width to **250** and the height to **100**.
4. Navigate to the drive and folder where your Data Files are stored, then open the file kayaking.txt in a text editor.
5. Copy the text in the kayaking.txt file, then paste the text into the text parameter of the Property inspector.

6. Test the movie, then click the arrow button for Loading graphics and text.
7. Use the scroll bar to read the text, as needed.
8. When done, close the test movie window, then save your work.

Use Components to load an animation.

1. Select Frame 4 of the loading animations layer.
2. Drag a Loader component to the left edge of the stage beneath the heading.
3. Use the Parameters tab to verify that autoLoad is set to true, then set the scaleContent to false.
4. Type **kayaker.swf** for the contentPath.
5. Test the movie and click the Loading animations arrow button to view the animation.
6. When done, close the test movie window.
7. Save your work.

Use Components and Behaviors to load a sound from the Library panel.

1. Select Frame 5 of the loading sound layer.
2. Drag a Button component to the stage below the heading.
3. Change the label parameter to **Background-1**.
4. Display the Library panel, right-click (Win) or [Ctrl]-click (Mac) accent1.mp3, then click Linkage to open the Linkage Properties dialog box.
5. Select the Export for ActionScript check box, then type **accent1_snd** as the identifier.
6. Click OK to close the dialog box.

7. Verify that the Background-1 button is selected on the stage.
8. Click the Add Behaviors button in the Behaviors panel, point to Sound, then click Load Sound from Library.
9. Type **accent1_snd** for the linkage ID and the sound instance, then click OK to close the dialog box.
10. Test the movie, click the Loading sounds button, then click the Background-1 button.
11. Close the test movie window, then save your work.

Use Components and Behaviors to add a streaming sound.

1. Drag a button component to the stage beneath the first button.
2. Change the label to **Background-2**.
3. Click the Add Behavior button in the Behaviors panel, point to Sound, then click Load streaming MP3 file.
4. Type **accent2.mp3** as the URL and **accent2_snd** for the instance name, then click OK.
5. Verify that the accent2.mp3 file is located in the same folder as the skillsdemo12.fla file.
6. Test the movie, click the Loading sounds button, then click the Background-2 button.
7. Close the test movie window, then save your work.

Use Components to create a form.

1. Select Frame 6 of a form layer.
2. Drag two radio button components to the right of the financial aid question and label them **yes** and **no**.
3. Drag four check box components to the right of the Areas of Interest question and label them: **Arts/Hum**; **Business**; **Science**; and **Soc Science**.
4. Drag a check box component to below the Art/Hum check box and label it: **other (specify)**.
5. Drag a TextInput component to the right of the other (specify) check box.

FIGURE 22
Completed Skills Review

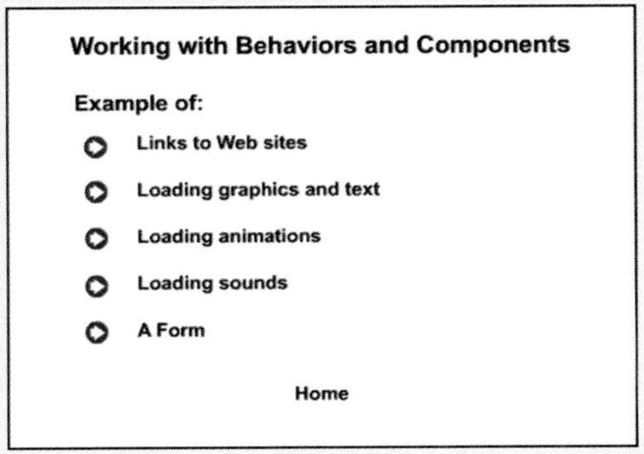

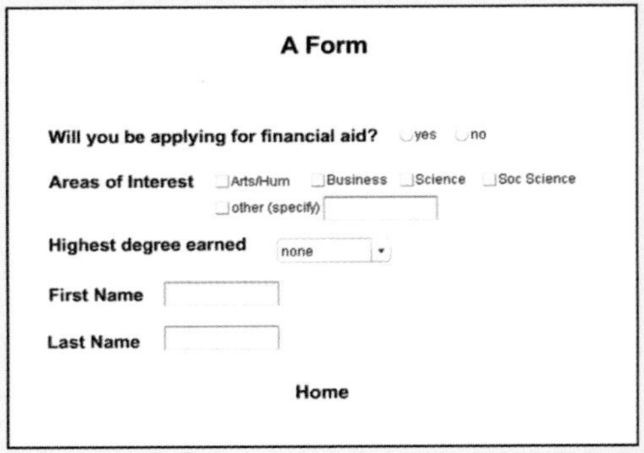

6. Drag a ComboBox to the right of Highest degree earned and add the following labels: **none**; **High School**; **2-Year**; **4-Year**; **Masters**; **Doctorate**.
7. Drag TextInput components to the right of First Name and Last Name.
8. Test the movie, test each component, and compare your images to Figure 22.
9. Close the test movie window.
10. Save your work.
11. Exit Flash.

The Ultimate Tours travel company wants to promote a special destination that changes periodically. They have asked you to design a page that will be called "Destination Revealed." The page will contain an animated heading, photo of the site, short description, and sound, as appropriate. The page will link to the home page. You have decided to create the page using components so that the company can easily update the photos, description, and sound. Figure 23 shows the link on the home page created using a Button component; the destination page created using Loader components for the animated heading and photo; TextArea component for the description; and a play sound button using a button component.

1. Open fl12_3.fla, then save it as **ultimatetours12**.
2. Click Control on the menu bar, then click Enable Simple Buttons to remove the check mark from the command if it is active.
3. Select the button with the question mark (?) and use the Behaviors panel to add an action to go to and stop at Frame 2 when the button is clicked.
4. Insert a new layer, name it **Destination page**, then add a keyframe to Frame 2 of the layer.

5. Add a Loader component to the top left corner of the destination page and have it load the destination.swf file when the viewer enters the page.
6. Add a Loader component to the top middle of the destination page and change the height and width to **200** pixels.
7. Have the Loader component load the kapalua.jpg file.
8. Add a TextArea component below the graphic Loader component and change the width to **200** pixels and height to **60** pixels.

FIGURE 23
Sample completed Project Builder 1

9. Open kapalua.txt in a text editor and copy the text to the text parameter text box for the TextArea component.
10. Drag a Button component to the right of the graphics loader, label the button **Sounds**, then have the seashore.wav sound play from the Library panel when the button is clicked.
11. Test the movie, then compare it to the sample images shown in Figure 23.
12. Close the test movie window, then save your work.

The International Student Association (ISA) is interested in obtaining information that could be used to determine the effectiveness of their Web site and improve the site contents. They would like to add a page with a survey form to their Web site. They have asked you to help them by developing three sample forms. After reviewing the forms, they will select one to be linked to their home page. The intent is to keep the survey short so that site visitors are encouraged to complete and submit it. Figure 24 shows a sample form. Using this as a guide, you will create three similar forms.

1. Create a new Macromedia Flash document, then save it as **isa_survey1**.
2. Add a background color.
3. Place the following on separate layers:
   - a border
   - the ISA heading
   - the text for the form
   - radio buttons for the ratings with appropriate labels
   - comboBox for the times visited with appropriate labels
   - check boxes for the sections visited with appropriate labels
   - TextInput box for the comments

   Make sure the parameters of the components have the appropriate settings, such as editable for the TextInput component.

4. Test the movie, then close the test movie window.
5. Publish the movie and display it in a browser.
6. Close your browser, then save your work.
7. Create and test two more forms of your choice.

FIGURE 24
Sample completed Project Builder 2

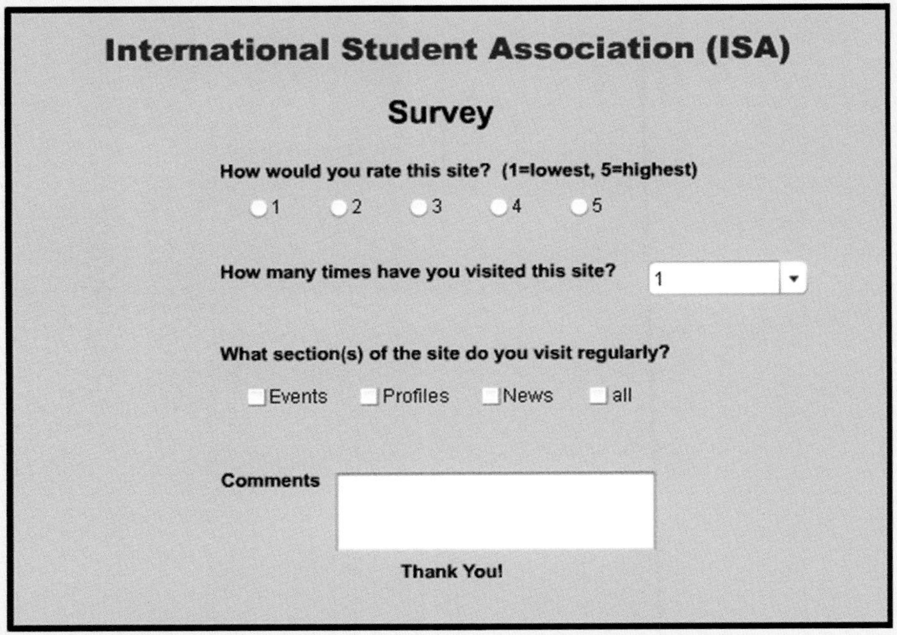

Working With Behaviors and Components

DESIGN PROJECT

Figure 25 shows the home page of a Web site. Study the figure and complete the following questions. For each question, indicate how you determined your answer.

1. Connect to the Internet, go to *www.course.com*, navigate to the page for this book, click the Online Companion, then click the link for this chapter.

2. Open a document in a word processor or create a new document in Flash, save the file as **dpc12**, then answer the following questions.
   - Whose Web site is this?
   - What is the goal of the site?
   - Who is the target audience?
   - How might components and behaviors be used in this site?
   - What types of forms might the site developers create?

FIGURE 25
Design Project

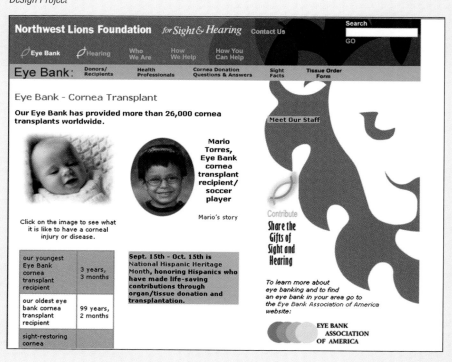

You have been asked by a local artist to help design the gallery page for her Web site. The page will include samples of her artwork and will be linked to her home page. The gallery page could be used to showcase her work as an online portfolio. Figure 26 shows the home page and a sample gallery page.

1. Open fl12_4.fla, then save it as **gallery**. (*Hint*: The Edwardian Script ITC font is used in this file. If this font is not available on your computer, you can choose to use a default font or substitute another font.)

2. Select the Gallery button and use the Behaviors panel to add an action that displays Frame 2 when the button is clicked.

3. The following steps will create the Gallery page. Add layers as indicated and name them appropriately. Frame 2 will be used for the Gallery page.
   - Add the Gallery heading in Frame 2 on its own layer.
   - Insert a new layer, name it **paintings**, then use Loader components to have the six paintings appear on the Gallery page. Set the scaleContent parameter so that the Loader scales to the size of the jpg file.
   - Insert a new layer, name it **captions**, then use TextArea components to have the six painting captions appear on the Gallery page. Set the width of each TextArea component to **150**.

   - Insert a new layer, name it **home**, then create a Home button in Frame 2.
   - Use the Behaviors panel to add an action that displays Frame 1 when the Home text button is clicked.

4. Verify that all of the .jpg files are in the same folder as the gallery.fla file.

5. Test the movie and test the Gallery and Home buttons.
6. Close the test movie window.
7. Publish the movie and display it in a browser.
8. Close the browser window, then save your work.

FIGURE 26
Sample completed Portfolio Project

Read the following information carefully!

Find out from your instructor the location where you will store your files.

- To complete many of the chapters in this book, you need to use the Data Files provided on the CD at the back of the book.
- Your instructor will tell you whether you will be working from the CD or copying the files to a drive on your computer or on a server. Your instructor will also tell you where you will store the files you create and modify.

Copy and organize your Data Files.

- Use the Data Files List to organize your files to a USB storage device, network folder, hard drive, or other storage device if you won't be working from the CD.
- Create a subfolder for each chapter in the location where you are storing your files, and name it according to the chapter title (e.g., Chapter 1).
- For each chapter you are assigned, copy the files listed in the **Data File Supplied** column into that chapter's folder. If you are working from the CD, you should still store the files you modify or create in each chapter in the chapter folder.

Find and keep track of your Data Files and completed files.

- Use the **Data File Supplied** column to make sure you have the files you need before starting the chapter or exercise indicated in the **Chapter** column.
- Use the **Student Creates File** column to find out the filename you use when saving your new file for the exercise.
- The **Used in** column tells you the lesson or end of chapter exercise where you will use the file.

DATA FILES LIST

Files Used in this Book

Macromedia Flash 8

Chapter	Data File Supplied	Student Creates File	Used In
1		workspace.fla	Lesson 1
	fl1_1.fla		Lesson 2
		tween.fla	Lesson 3
		layers.fla	Lesson 4
	*layers.fla		Lesson 6
	fl1_2.fla		Skills Review
		demonstration.fla	Project Builder 1
	fl1_3.fla		Project Builder 2
		dpc1.fla	Design Project
			Portfolio Project
2		tools.fla	Lessons 1-4
	fl2-1.fla		Lesson 5
		skillsdemo2.fla	Skills Review
		ultimatetours2.fla	Project Builder 1
		thejazzclub2.fla	Project Builder 2
		dpc2.fla	Design Project
		portfolio2.fla	Portfolio Project
3	fl3-1.fla		Lesson 1
	fl3-2.fla		Lessons 2-4
	fl3_3.fla		Skills Review
	**ultimatetours2.fla		Project Builder 1
		isa3.fla	Project Builder 2
		dpc3.fla	Design Project
	**portfolio2.fla		Portfolio Project

*Created in a previous Lesson or Skills Review in current chapter

**Created in a previous chapter

Chapter	Data File Supplied	Student Creates File	Used In
4	fl4-1.fla		Lesson 1
	fl4-2.fla		Lesson 2
	fl4-3.fla		Lesson 3
	fl4-4.fla fl4-5.fla		Lesson 4
	*frameAn.fla		Lesson 5
	fl4-6.fla		Skills Review
	**ultimatetours3.fla ship.giv		Project Builder 1
		summerBB4.fla	Project Builder 2
		dpc4.fla	Design Project
	**portfolio3.fla		Portfolio Project
5	fl5-1.fla fl5-2.fla fl5-3.fla		Lesson 1
	fl5-4.fla		Lesson 2
	fl5-5.fla CarSnd.wav beep.wav		Lesson 3
	fl5-6.fla *rallySnd.fla		Lesson 4
	fl5-7.fla		Lesson 5
	fl5-8.fla		Skills Review
	**ultimatetours4.fla foghorn.wav		Project Builder 1
		zodiac5.fla	Project Builder 2
		dpc5.fla	Design Project
	**portfolio4.fla		Portfolio Project

*Created in a previous Lesson or Skills Review in current chapter

**Created in a previous chapter

Chapter	Data File Supplied	Student Creates File	Used In
6	fl6-1.fla	planeLoop.gif planeLoop.jpg	Lesson 1
	fl6-2.fla	planeFun.html	Lesson 2
	fl6_3.fla		Lesson 3
	*planeFun.fla		Lesson 4
	fl6_4.fla	*skillsdemo6.html	Skills Review
	**ultimatetours5.fla		Project Builder 1
	**summerBB4.fla		Project Builder 2
		dpc6.fla	Design Project
	**portfolio5.fla		Portfolio Project
7	dragonfly.png tree.ai background.jpg	gsamples.fla	Lesson 1
	dayMoon.jpg hedge.jpg		Lessons 2-4
	logo.FH10 nightsky.jpg roses.jpg mountain.jpg	skillsdemo7.fla	Skills Review
	gtravel1.jpg gtravel2.jpg gtravel3.jpg gtravel4.jpg gtravel5.jpg gtravel6.jpg	ultimatetours7.fla	Project Builder 1
	gantho1.jpg gantho2.jpg gantho3.jpg gantho4.jpg gantho5.jpg	anthoart7.fla	Project Builder 2
		dpc7.fla	Design Project
		portfolio7.fla	Portfolio Project

*Created in a previous Lesson or Skills Review in current chapter

**Created in a previous chapter

Chapter	Data File Supplied	Student Creates File	Used In
8	fl8-1.fla		Lesson 1
	fl8-2.fla		Lesson 2
	fl8-3.fla		Lessons 3-4
	fl8-4.fla		Skills Review
	**ultimatetours7.fla		Project Builder 1
		ocean_life.fla	Project Builder 2
		dpc8.fla	Design Project
	**portfolio7.fla		Portfolio Project
9	fl9-1.fla		Lesson 1
	fl9-2.fla		Lesson 2
	fl9-3.fla		Lesson 3
	fl9-4.fla		Lesson 4
	fl9-5.fla		Skills Review
	**ultimatetours8.fla		Project Builder 1
		test_question9.fla	Project Builder 2
		dpc9.fla	Design Project
	**portfolio8.fla		Portfolio Project

**Created in a previous chapter

Chapter	Data File Supplied	Student Creates File	Used In
10	fl10-1.fla accent1.mp3 accent2.mp3 background.mp3		Lessons 1-2
	fl10-2.fla		Lesson 2
	fl10-3.fla		Lesson 3
	fl10_4.fla fireworks.mov		Lesson 4
	fl10_5.fla fl10-6.fla tour-video.mov		Skills Review
	fl10-7.fla		Project Builder 1
	fl10-8.fla		Project Builder 2
		dpc10.fla	Design Project
	**portfolio9.fla accent1.mp3 accent2.mp3 background.mp3 portfolio_voiceover.wav		Portfolio Project

**Created in a previous chapter

Chapter	Data File Supplied	Student Creates File	Used In
11	fl11-1.fla		Lesson 1
	fl11-2.fla fl11-3.fla		Lesson 2
	fl11-4.fla frog.swf fish.swf		Lesson 3
	fl11-5.fla fl11-6.fla		Lesson 4
	fl11-7.fla easy_level.swf hard_level.swf		Skills Review
	fl11-8.fla specials.swf		Project Builder 1
	fl11-9.fla		Project Builder 2
		dpc11.fla	Design Project
	shirt.swf shirt2.swf sounds.swf	portfolio11.fla	Portfolio Project

Chapter	Data File Supplied	Student Creates File	Used In
12	fl12-1.fla		Lesson 1
	rosario.jpg rosario.txt animation.swf thebeat.mp3		Lesson 2
	fl12_2.fla kayaking.jpg kayaking.txt kayaker.swf accent1.mp3 accent2.mp3		Skills Review
	fl12_3.fla destination.swf kapalua.jpg kapalua.txt		Project Builder 1
		isa_survey1.fla	Project Builder 2
		dpc12.fla	Design Project
	fl12_4.fla AutumnVineyrds.jpg DistantVineyards.jpg Mustangs.jpg Novlight.jpg Rendezvous.jpg ValleyRespite.jpg yakimariver.jpg		Portfolio Project

Absolute path

A path that specifies the exact location of a file.

ActionScript

The Macromedia Flash scripting language used by developers to add interactivity to movies, control objects, exchange data, and create complex animations.

Actions panel

The panel where you create and edit actions for an object or frame.

ADPCM (Adaptive Differential Pulse-Code Modulation)

A sound compression option best used for short sounds, such as those used for buttons or accents.

Animated graphic symbol

An animation stored as a single, reusable symbol in the Library panel.

Animation

The perception of motion caused by the rapid display of a series of still images.

Balance

In screen design, the distribution of optical weight in the layout. Optical weight is the ability of an object to attract the viewer's eye, as determined by the object's size, shape, color, and other factors.

Bandwidth Profiler

A feature used when testing a Flash movie that allows you to view a graphical representation of the size of each frame and the frame-by-frame download process.

Behaviors

Blocks of prewritten ActionScript code that you can apply by using pop-up menus and dialog boxes without having to write the ActionScript code.

Bitmap image

An image based on pixels, rather than mathematical formulas. Also referred to as a raster image.

Break apart

The process of making each area of color in a bitmap image into a discrete element you can manipulate separately from the rest of the image. Also, the process of breaking apart text to place each character in a separate text block.

Broadband

A type of data transmission in which a wide band of frequencies is available to transmit more information at the same time.

Button symbol

Object on the stage that is used to provide interactivity, such as jumping to another frame on the timeline.

Code hints

Hints appearing in a pop-up window that give the syntax or possible parameters for an action.

Components

Predeveloped movie clips that can quickly add functionality to a movie by dragging and dropping them from the Components panel to the stage. Commonly used for creating forms with boxes for entering user data (name, address, and so on), check boxes, and drop-down menus.

Conditional action

ActionScript that tests whether or not certain conditions have been met and, if so, can perform other actions.

Controller

A window that provides the playback controls for a movie.

Decrement action

An ActionScript operator, indicated by -- (two minus signs), that subtracts 1 unit from a variable or expression.

Design notes

A file (.mno) that contains the original source file (.png or .fla) when a Fireworks document or Flash file is exported to Dreamweaver.

Document

A Flash file which, by default, is given the .fla file extension.

Dot syntax

A way to refer to the hierarchical nature of the path to a movie clip symbol, variable, function, or other object, similar to the way slashes are used to create a path name to a file in some operating systems.

DSL
A broadband Internet connection speed that is available through phone lines.

Dynamic text field
A field created on the stage with the Text tool that takes information entered by a user and stores it as a variable.

Embedded video
A video file that has been imported into a Flash document and becomes part of the SWF file.

Event sound
A sound that plays independently of the timeline. The sound starts in the keyframe to which it is added, but can continue playing even after a movie ends. An event sound must download completely before it begins playing.

Expressions
Formulas for manipulating or evaluating the information in variables.

External links
Links from a Flash file or movie to another Web site, another file, or an e-mail program.

File Transfer Protocol (FTP)
A standard method for transferring files from a development site to a Web server.

Flash player
A free program from Macromedia that allows Flash movies (.swf and .exe formats) to be viewed on a computer.

Frame-by-frame animation
An animation created by specifying the object that is to appear in each frame of a sequence of frames (also called a frame animation).

Frame label
A text name for a keyframe, which can be referenced within ActionScript code.

Frames
Individual cells that make up the timeline in Flash.

GET
An option for sending variables from a Flash movie to another URL or file for processing. GET is best for small amounts of information, as it can only send a string of up to 1,024 characters.

Graphic Symbols
Objects, such as drawings, that are converted to symbols and stored in the Library panel. A graphic symbol is the original object. Instance (copies) of a symbol can be made by dragging the symbol from the Library to the stage.

Graphics Interchange Format (GIF)
A graphics file format that creates compressed bitmap images. GIF graphics are viewable on the Web.

Guide layers
Layers used to align objects on the stage.

Increment action
An ActionScript operator, indicated by ++ (two plus signs), that adds 1 unit to a variable or expression.

Input text field
A field created on the stage with the Text tool that displays information derived from variables.

Instances
Editable copies of symbols that are placed on the stage.

Joint Photographic Experts Group (JPEG)
A graphics file format that is especially useful for photographic images. JPEG graphics are viewable on the Web.

Keyframe
A frame that signifies a change in a movie, such as the end of an animation.

Layers
Rows on the timeline that are used to organize objects and that allow the stacking of objects on the stage.

Level

A hierarchical designation used when loading new movies into the current movie; similar to layers on the timeline.

Library panel

The panel that contains the objects (graphics, buttons, sounds, movie clips, etc.) that are used in a Flash movie.

Linkage identifier string

The name used to identify a sound from the Library panel in an ActionScript statement. You assign a linkage identifier in the Linkage Properties dialog box.

Loader Component

A Component that can load external jpg graphic files and swf movie files.

Macromedia Flash 8

A development tool that allows you to create compelling interactive experiences, often by using animation.

Main Timeline

The primary timeline for a Flash movie that is displayed when you start a new Flash document.

Mask layer

A layer used to cover up the objects on another layer(s) and, at the same time, create a window through which you can view various objects on the other layer.

Merge Drawing Model

A drawing mode that causes overlapping drawings (objects) to merge, so that a change in the top object, such as moving it, may affect the object beneath it.

Morphing

The animation process of changing one object into another, sometimes unrelated, object.

Motion guide

Feature that allows you to draw a path and attach motion-tweened animations to the path. A motion guide has its own layer.

Motion tweening

The process used in Flash to automatically fill in the frames between keyframes in an animation that changes the properties of an object such as the position, size, or color. Motion tweening works on groups and symbols.

Movement

In screen design, the way the viewer's eye moves through the objects on the screen.

Movie clip symbol

An animation stored as a single, reusable symbol in the Library panel. It has its own timeline, independent of the main timeline.

MP3 (MPEG-1 Audio Layer 3)

A sound compression option primarily used for music and longer streaming sounds, but which can also be applied to speech.

Nesting

Including another symbol within a symbol, such as nesting a graphic symbol, button, or another movie clip symbol within a movie clip symbol.

Number variable

In ActionScript, a double-precision floating-point number with which you can use arithmetic operators, such as addition and subtraction.

Object Drawing Model

A drawing mode that allows you to overlap objects which are then kept separate, so that changes in one object do not affect another object. You must break apart these objects before being able to select their stroke and fills.

Objects

Items, such as drawings and text, that are placed on the stage and can be edited and manipulated.

Onion Skin

Feature that displays the outlines of an animated object so that the positions of the object in a series of frames can be viewed all at once.

Panels

Components in Flash used to view, organize, and modify objects and features in a movie.

Parameters
Properties of Components, such as autoload, that can be changed using the Property inspector panel or the Component Inspector.

_parent
In creating target paths with dot syntax, the movie clip in which the current clip is nested.

Parent-child relationship
A description of the hierarchical relationship that develops between nested symbols, especially nested movie clip symbols. When you insert a movie clip inside another movie clip, the inserted clip is considered the child and the original clip is the parent.

Persistence of vision
The phenomenon of the eye capturing and holding an image for one-tenth of a second before processing another image.

Playhead
An indicator specifying which frame is playing in the timeline of a Flash movie.

Portable Network Graphics (PNG)
A graphics file format developed specifically for images that are to be used on the Web.

POST
An option for sending variables from a Flash movie to another URL or file for processing. POST collects variables and sends them in a file. POST can accommodate more variable information and is more secure than the alternate method of sending variables, GET.

Preloader
An animation and ActionScript code (which could be a movie clip) that is played at the beginning of a movie to provide feedback to the viewer on the progress of downloading the movie frames.

Progressive download
The process of delivering an external Flash FLV video file at runtime.

Projector
A standalone executable movie such as a Windows .exe file.

Property inspector
A panel that allows you to display and edit the properties of a selected object.

Publish
The process used to generate the files necessary for delivering Flash movies on the Web, such as swf and HTML files.

QuickTime
A file format used for movies and animations that requires a QuickTime Player.

Raster image
An image based on pixels, rather than mathematical formulas. Also referred to as a bitmap image.

Raw
A sound compression option that exports a sound with no compression. You can set stereo to mono conversion and a sampling rate.

Registration point
The point on an object that is used to position the object on the stage using ActionScript code.

Relative path
A path for an external link or to an object that is based on the location of the file in which the path is entered.

_root
Refers to the main timeline when creating target paths with dot syntax.

Scene
A timeline designated for a specific part of the movie. Scenes are a way to organize long movies by dividing the movie into sections.

Script Assist
A feature found in the Actions panel which can be used to generate ActionScript without having to write programming code.

Shape hints
Indicators used to control the shape of a complex object as it changes appearance during an animation.

Shape tweening
The process of animating an object so that its shape changes. Shape tweening requires editable graphics.

Sound object
A built-in object that allows ActionScript to recognize and control a sound. To associate a specific sound with a sound object, use the new Sound action.

Speech compression
A sound compression option best used for voice-overs and other speech. You can set a sampling rate when you choose this option.

Stage
The area of the Flash workspace that contains the objects that are part of the movie and that will be seen by the viewers.

Stage-level object
A vector object that you draw directly on the stage, unlike a symbol, which you place on the stage from the Library panel.

Start synchronization option
A synchronization option that can be applied to sounds and that acts just like event sounds, but will not begin again if an instance of the sound is already playing.

Stop synchronization option
A synchronization option that can be applied to sounds and lets you end an event sound at a specific keyframe.

Streaming sound
A sound that is tied to the timeline. No matter its length, a streaming sound stops at the end of the movie. Streaming sounds can start playing as they download.

Streaming video
The process of delivering video content using a constant connection established with a Flash Communication Server.

String variable
In ActionScript, a sequence of characters including letters, numbers, and punctuation. To indicate a string variable, enclose it in single or double quotation marks.

Symbols
The basic building blocks of a Flash application. There are three types: graphic, button, and movie clip.

T

T1
An extremely fast Internet connection that is widely used by businesses.

Target
A reference in an action to a movie clip symbol or other object that includes a path and name.

Time In control, Time Out control
Controls in the Edit Envelope dialog box that let you trim the length of a sound file.

Timeline
The component of Flash used to organize and control the movie's contents over time by specifying when each object appears on the stage.

Timeline effects
Pre-built animation effects (such as rotating, fading, and wiping) that can be applied to objects using a dialog box.

Tools panel
The component of Flash that contains a set of tools used to draw, select, and edit graphics and text. It is divided into four sections.

Trace
The process of turning a bitmap image into vector paths for animation and other purposes.

Transformation point
The point used to orient an object as it is being animated and the point of an object that snaps to a motion guide.

Tweening
The process of filling the in-between frames in an animation.

U

Unity
How the various screen objects relate in screen design. Inter-screen unity refers to the design that viewers encounter as they navigate from one screen to another.

Upload

The process of transferring files from a local drive to a Web server.

Variables

A container that holds information and is used in ActionScript code.

Vector image

An image calculated and stored according to mathematical formulas rather than pixels, resulting in smaller file size and the ability to resize the images without a loss in quality.

Web server

A computer dedicated to hosting Web sites that is connected to the Internet and configured with software to handle requests from browsers.